ELEMENTS
OF
ECONOMICS

ELEMENTS
OF
ECONOMICS

Second Edition

James A. Phillips

Carl Pearl

Cypress College

MACMILLAN PUBLISHING CO., INC.
New York
COLLIER MACMILLAN PUBLISHERS
London

Macmillan Publishing Co., Inc.
866 Third Avenue, New York, New York 10022

Collier Macmillan Canada, Ltd.

Library of Congress Cataloging in Publication Data

Phillips, James, (date)
    Elements of economics.

    Includes bibliographies and index.
    1. Economics. I. Pearl, Carl, joint author.
II. Title.
HB171.5.P53   1977   330   76–9630
ISBN 0–02–395350–0

Printing: 1 2 3 4 5 6 7 8   Year: 7 8 9 0 1 2 3

For:

Those who love life
and dare to be real,
and those who reach out,
and be, and feel.

PREFACE

We believe that a knowledge of economics is a most important requirement for the citizen who would achieve an intelligent grasp of public affairs. Indeed, such knowledge is as important for society as it is for the individual citizen. Most college students are now voters. They have the right to help, and the responsibility of helping, elect the people who design and implement public economic policies.

In this second edition we are even more convinced of the necessity of economic understanding for effective citizenship. The ever-faster-expanding economic events since 1973 require the citizen to understand, to evaluate, and to act in complex economic issues. Thus, we have thoroughly revised, expanded, and clarified the first edition and have attempted to speak even more directly to the student's daily economic life. The student will evaluate the extent to which these promises are fulfilled, and economic reality will demand his attention to our challenge.

This text aims to help the student achieve a basic understanding of contemporary economics. *Elements of Economics* is intended for those enrolled in a course of study usually dubbed a "survey" and typically occupying a period of one term of the school calendar. We have kept in mind the needs of the general student and have not directed our book at economics or business majors, although we hope that these students will also find it of value. Our approach places the individual at the center of economic issues. Economic theory is presented to analyze economic issues; illustrations and other graphic material are used to amplify textual explanations.

We wish to thank our former teachers, Professor Flanders and Professor Wagner of the University of Illinois and Professor Calderwood of the University of Southern California, as well as our many students at Cypress College. We also extend to Abel Soto, of the Cypress College audiovisual department, our great appreciation for his contributions to the art work.

J. A. P.
C. P.

Cypress, California

[Consider] the concept of man as a heroic being, with his own happiness as the moral purpose of his life, with productive achievement as his noblest activity, and reason as his only absolute.

AYN RAND

CONTENTS

WHAT IS ECONOMICS?

SHORT ANSWER. Economics is the study of making decisions about how to use scarce resources. The decision-making process used in economics can also be helpful in other everyday activities.

WELCOME, STUDENT

Would you like to know more about what is happening in society? Are you ready to be intellectually challenged? Do you want to have a few myths removed? Do you enjoy analyzing your own life and the society around you? If your answers are yes to any of these questions, perhaps you are ready to learn about economics. For the study of economics encompasses all the preceding and much more. Your study of economics should make you a more aware citizen, and it should be fun!

Is the beginning of this book interesting and challenging? What do the authors wish to say? How will their ideas affect the ideas I presently have?

FIG. 1–1. Economics studies choice making.

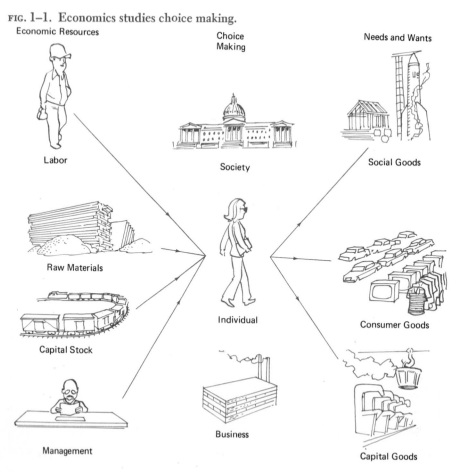

Economic Resources

Choice Making

Needs and Wants

Labor

Society

Social Goods

Raw Materials

Individual

Consumer Goods

Capital Stock

Management

Business

Capital Goods

Do the authors' proposals reflect ivory-tower concepts, or will they "tell it like it is" and describe real-world activities with which I am already familiar? Why is it really necessary for me, as a student and citizen, to be concerned with the rational allocation of scarce resources? Let's begin to find some answers to all these questions by acquainting you with economics and economists. First, economics is surely not ivory-tower. The list (very incomplete) of economic issues in Figure 1-2 should convince you that economics is indeed relevant and useful to you as an individual and to society as a whole. Economics deals with very real choices that individuals and societies must make daily for their economic survival.

The study of economics is a blend of scientific observation, precision, measurement, and a great deal of guesswork (not always accurate, as recent years have witnessed). As a social scientist, the economist observes and examines the sometimes erratic behavior of his fellow citizens and choice makers. Economists also employ the "scientific method" in studying the choice-making process. By using these methods economists are in step with chemists, mathematicians, biologists, and the other physical scientists. However, because economists are social scientists and deal with human beings in terms of individual and collective activities rather than the precise world familiar to the physical scientist, we cannot be consistently accurate in our predictions or conclusions. Thus, the deep concern of economists with human relationships and activities injects an unpredictable and often frustrating element into our studies. We are, however, compensated by the knowledge that we normally do not need the infinite accuracy required for a rocket launching to be effective. Besides, the unpredictability of social relationships is what makes our subject matter interesting.

What do economists do, and what are they like? Some are college pro-

FIG. 1–2. Economic issues.

Wage Levels	Profit Levels
Government Spending	Balance of Payments
Taxes	Economic Growth Rates
Unemployment	Automation
Inflation	Labor Strikes
Prices	Welfare Reform
Pollution	National Debt
Mass Transit	Foreign Aid
Saving Levels	Foreign Exchange Rates
Investment Growth	Costs of Production

Type of Employer	Per Cent of Economists Employed
Educational Institutions	44.7
Federal Government	11.3
Other Government	2.5
Military Services	0.7
Nonprofit Organizations	4.1
Industry and Business	35.0
Self-employed	1.7
	100.0

Type of Work Activity	Per Cent of Economists Employed
Management or Administration	34.8
Teaching	34.2
Research and Development	19.0
Production and Inspection	12.0
	100.0

Source: "The Structure of Economists' Employment and Salaries, 1964," Supplement to the *American Economic Review* (Vol. LV, No. 4, Part 2, December, 1965), pp. 21-22.

FIG. 1-3. What economists do.

fessors, teaching classes, composing journal articles, lecturing audiences, consulting with private companies or government agencies, and even writing textbooks. (Do the names Samuelson, Friedman, Galbraith, Heller, Schultz, or Boulding ring any bells?) Other economists work in private industry, preparing sales projections, calculating the costs, revenues, and profits that result from various business decisions, running statistical research, searching out alternative products, and tabulating consumer sentiment. Or the economist may perform any number of statistical gathering and processing duties in a wide assortment of government (federal, state, local) agencies, often evaluating cost and benefits of alternative government policies.

Has this introduction stirred your interest for economics and economists? The answer, we hope, is yes, for we now must proceed to a more formal definition of *economics*. Let us become a bit more technical and define *economics* as the *study of the rational allocation of scarce resources among competing goals*. Dictionaries aside, we know that *rational* means "logical" or "orderly." We can say that economics is the study of the logical or orderly allocation of scarce resources. *Allocation* refers to distribution (or who gets what). Our definition now becomes "the logical distribution" of scarce resources. *Scarce*, of course, means "not plentiful" or "rare." We will see later how the relative scarcity or abundance of goods is the major factor in determining the prices at which these goods sell. *Resources* are the elements (natural resources, labor, capital stock, managment) used in producing and distributing the items we buy or sell. Finally, the term *competing goals* is used to denote the many different uses to which resources might be put.

Our formal definition complete, we can now change our initial phrase to state that economics is the study of the logical or orderly distribution of goods and services to those uses most desired by individuals and societies.

ECONOMICS: THE STUDY OF CHOICES

If you picked up the rather heavy hint thus far that economics studies how individuals and societies make choices, you're on the right track. Both individuals and societies are continually faced with the necessity of deciding what they want most and which goods or what actions they cannot undertake.

Despite the apparent belief of many legislators, the goose that lays the golden eggs really exists only in fairy tales. You should realize that choice

FIG. 1–4. Economics studies choice making.

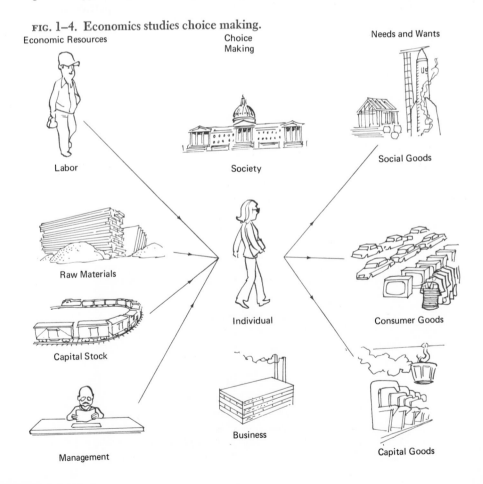

Economic Resources

Choice Making

Needs and Wants

Labor

Society

Social Goods

Raw Materials

Individual

Consumer Goods

Capital Stock

Management

Business

Capital Goods

making arises because scarcity forces limitations on the individual or the society making the choice. If there were no limits (no personal budget amount, an infinite amount of economic resources), there would be no need to choose; one would simply consume what one wanted. But there are limits (you only have so much time and income, and every society has a finite amount of resources); therefore, we must choose items or actions of greatest importance. It is this very necessary process of choice making, comparing alternatives, setting priorities, and evaluating impacts of choices that defines the arena of economics. The economist analyzes why a businessman produces ten trucks rather than eight, why consumers don't enjoy the fourth six-pack as much as the first, and what occurs when the federal government runs a deficit budget.

We keep stating that in studying economics we must constantly ask, "How shall we make proper choices in using the resources available to us?" A person might, for instance, make a choice in the marketplace. This usually means that he or she has limited funds with which to choose from an almost unlimited selection of goods. When people decide which items they will buy, they are also deciding which items they won't buy. The choice made at this particular time reflects the buyer's personal wants, preferences, and way of life. Another person, with a different outlook, may choose different items from the same selection even if he or she has the same amount of money as the first buyer. Each of these buyers uses his or her experience to allocate spending rationally.

Notice we are emphasizing the individual here—you—and his or her daily economic choices. Does Figure 1-5 seem familiar to you?

If we total all individuals making all their own choices, we have one view of *social choice making*. A *society* is really nothing more than *all the citizens combined*. When the economist studies social choice making in a form such as that shown in Figure 1-6 (doesn't a "social budget" reflect collective choices as your personal budget reflects individual choices?), you may begin to see some differences between social and individual choice making.

FIG. 1–5. Individual economic choices.

How many of the following are similar to your own daily choices?

1. What school or class to attend?
2. What to purchase for breakfast, lunch, or dinner?
3. How much gas and what brand to buy?
4. What size and model (make) of automobile to drive?
5. What type of job to train for?
6. How to spend (or save) your paycheck?
7. How much and in what manner should you save?
8. Should I buy insurance (type, amount, company)?
9. Should I buy a home (size, location, age) or rent (price, location)?
10. Should I do my own taxes or call an accountant for aid?

Receipts by Source	Dollar Estimate (in billions)	Per Cent
Individual Income Taxes	106.3	35.7
Corporation Income Taxes	47.7	16.0
Social Insurance Taxes and Contributions	91.6	30.8
Excise Taxes	32.1	10.8
Estate and Gift Taxes	4.6	1.5
Customs Duties	4.3	1.4
Miscellaneous Receipts	10.9	3.8
Total Receipts	297.5	100.0
Outlays by Function		
National Defense	94.0	26.9
International Affairs	6.3	1.8
General Science, Space, and Technology	4.6	1.3
Natural Resources, Environment, and Energy	10.0	2.9
Agriculture	1.8	.5
Commerce and Transportation	13.7	3.9
Community and Regional Development	5.9	1.7
Education, Manpower, and Social Services	14.6	4.2
Health	28.0	8.0
Income Security	118.7	34.0
Veterans Benefits and Services	15.6	4.5
Law Enforcement and Justice	3.3	.9
General Government	3.2	.9
Revenue Sharing and General Purpose Fiscal Aid	7.2	2.1
Interest	34.4	9.9
Allowances	8.0	2.3
Undistributed Offsetting Receipts	−20.2	−5.8
Total Outlays	394.4	100.0

Source: *The United States Budget in Brief, Fiscal Year 1976* (Washington, D.C.: U.S. Government Printing Office, 1976), pp. 49–50.

FIG. 1–6. Proposed budget, fiscal 1976.

What we're getting at here is that choices may be viewed from an individual viewpoint and from the perspective of society as a whole and that there are some differences in perspective. Although the economist is surely interested in you, the individual, the focus of economics study is often on the entire society and economic process. In fact, when the economist concentrates on individual family or business choice making, he is termed as dealing in *microeconomics*. (This approach is roughly covered by Chapters 1–10 of this text.) When the economist analyzes choice making for the economy as a whole, he or she is in the realm of *macroeconomics* (Chapters 11–20 of this text).

CHOICE OF ECONOMIC RESOURCES

When we turn from individual choice making to the larger economic world around us, we are emphasizing that choice making also occurs in a collective sense. Such collective, or social, choice making basically involves use by entire societies of the economic resources available to achieve social priorities. In our society, as well as in countries with different economic and political systems, there are four basic types of economic resource groups that are used in producing the goods and services required in everyday life. It is from these limited quantities and qualities of economic resources that the particular societal output is generated. Because these limited amounts of resources cannot provide unlimited amounts of goods and services, every society must have some mechanism (its economic system) for choice making to allocate these resources. In later chapters we learn how the United States and other nations use their four basic resource groups.

Professional (and amateur) economists label these four resource groups as *labor, capital stock, natural resources,* and *management.* In varying intensity and with continually changing proportions, we, as Americans, have used our country's labor, capital stock, natural resources, and management to produce for our fellow citizens the highest level of living in the world. But even our vast array of resources is limited and is being rapidly depleted, and too many Americans do not receive a fair share of our wealth. Figure 1-7 presents some background to these issues, and is more deeply analyzed in Chapter 12.

What do economists mean by the preceding labels? The following definitions will give both teachers and students a common basis for discussion:

Labor. The most human of our four research groups, *labor* is a broad

FIG. 1–7. Family distribution of personal income.

Families	Per Cent of Total Income Received		
	1950	1960	1972
Lowest 20%	4.5	4.8	5.4
Second 20%	11.9	12.2	11.9
Third 20%	17.4	17.8	17.5
Fourth 20%	23.6	24.0	23.9
Highest 20%	42.7	41.3	41.4
Top 5%	17.3	15.9	15.9

Source: Department of Commerce, Bureau of the Census.

term the economist uses in referring to all of humankind's physical and mental talents used in producing goods and services. We include in this group the sewer cleaner and secret agent, the baseball player and ballet dancer, the ditch digger and diamond polisher, the factory worker and college teacher. Included, in fact, is every type of gainful, legal employment conceivably performed in our society, with one general exception: the work performed by a businessman, or *entrepreneur*, in starting and running his own business. The reason for this exception is the separate resource category of management.

Capital stock. Capital stock is a property resource; it includes machines, tools, buildings, and other equipment used in making goods. The most common example is, of course, a factory (building) in which machines and tools are used by workers (labor) to create the wide variety of devices that make our everyday life pleasant. Unlike consumer goods, which give us great satisfaction but do not produce anything other than pleasure or leisure, capital stock (or goods) is used to produce or reproduce additional goods. A male and female rabbit are, by our definition, capital stock, whereas their numerous offspring usually become consumer goods.

Natural resources. Natural resources, sometimes termed *land* by the economist, constitute another property resource. These are the "free gifts of nature" that are usable in the productive process. Natural resources involve everything that comes from the land, sea, and air, including the land, sea, and air themselves. All animal, vegetable, and mineral products are included. Although most of us realize that coal, wood, and seafood cost money to obtain, many people consider air and water to be "free" (that is, attainable without cost). Yet for some of us living in large metropolitan areas, clean air is certainly not free. Industry and government spend billions of dollars yearly to keep air pollution levels down. These costs are passed on to us as consumers in the form of higher prices and taxes. Those of us living in rural areas must, like our city brothers and sisters, pay for the convenience of having the water we use brought from distant mountains and rivers.

Management. Management is another human resource. It could as well be termed *specialized labor*, but it is important enough to be separately classified. In order to produce any item, the other resource groups—labor, capital stock, and natural resources—must be combined in proper proportions in order for goods and services to materialize. Labor must be hired, services ordered, and equipment arranged. These and many other similar decision-making functions are the special role of management. Our managers, or entrepreneurs, are the dynamic force in combining other resources in production to gain a profit.

PRIORITIES AND CHOICE

Let us return to individual choice making and try to see how we can get the most efficient use of the resource groups mentioned. Economic problems in general arise because the means society has for satisfying the material wants

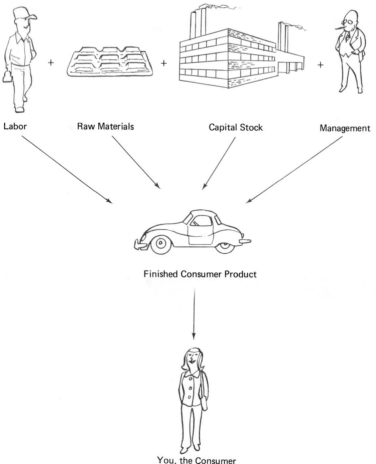

Labor   Raw Materials   Capital Stock   Management

Finished Consumer Product

You, the Consumer

FIG. 1–8. The productive process: resources to products.

of its citizens are limited relative to those wants. Human desires for material goods—for services, for luxury, or for show—generally exceed the volume of goods that can be made available for satisfying these desires.

Because all needs cannot be met, the individual and the society must have some basis to select those needs considered most important. Such choice making requires that priorities be set up or a ranking of what is considered most vital for choice making. Once these priorities are set, choices are made so as to satisfy those needs of highest priority. Put more simply, we as individuals and members of a society have limited means to satisfy unlimited wants. Therefore, we must make choices of resource use and must have priorities for effective choices.

How, then, does one go about setting a list of priorities (for we must establish priorities to determine production of the goods and services needed for our present life-style and future growth). One scale of priorities might be the following:

1. Food.

2. Shelter and clothing.

3. Movies and records.

4. Education.

5. Guns and bombs.

The preceding example is, of course, just one person's opinion. Some of us might share part of the opinion or substitute other priorities based on our own particular background and interests. In modern American society the decisions to purchase and not to purchase are made by individuals with virtually no central command from government. We usually vote with our dollar bills for the list of priorities that best suits us. We can say that our economic system is *market oriented* in that most decisions to buy and sell are made in the marketplace.

In fact, choices in our market economy are largely the result of "adding up" individual choices, with some element of social choice; that is, what American society "chooses" depends upon the priorities and choices made by

1. Individual consumers (you)—as you buy or avoid products, businesses respond to your desires. Notice how compact car production continued increasing as consumers avoided large cars.

2. Private businessmen—profits serve as a guide to determine which goods and services are produced. Notice how businesses are actively seeking alternative energy sources as oil supplies dwindle.

3. Government (federal, state, local)—as representatives of the public, government bodies spend, tax, and regulate to satisfy social priorities. Notice the increased pollution control programs resulting from public outcry in the 1970s.

Viewing the list of priority makers, the student may feel that the study of choice making, especially in the U.S. market economy, is quite confusing. Well, you are correct. And such study, in fact, constitutes the aim and efforts of this entire textbook.

Other societies, such as that of the Soviet Union, have *command-type* economic systems, and the decisions to produce in those societies are mostly made by the central government. Consumers do not, with some exceptions, "vote" with their rubles in the Soviet Union. The priorities are determined by a small group within the ruling body (the Supreme Soviet in the U.S.S.R.), and choices must then conform to these priorities. In the Soviet Union, such pri-

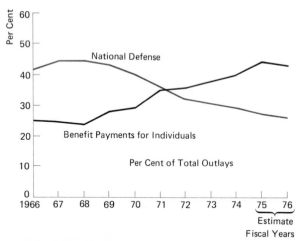

FIG. 1–9. Changing priorities in the federal budget.

orities take the form of five-year plans, with most economic choices then made to achieve these output quotas. Consumers and business managers do choose within narrow limits, but they generally do not contribute significantly to the establishment of overall priorities.

One further point to ponder about priorities is that they often change through time. Individuals and societies want different priorities at different times, and economic choices must change accordingly. An illustration of this changing priority is shown in Figure 1-9: As social values have changed in the United States over time, an increasing percentage of resources has been devoted to income security programs, whereas a decreasing percentage has gone to defense. Whether you agree with such priorities or not, the point is that all societies wishing to perpetuate themselves must have some mechanism to respond to changing priorities. Czarist Russia is a glaring example in this century of a country whose leaders refused to accommodate changing societal priorities.

Three Fundamental Economic Questions

We've emphasized thus far the importance of choosing among economic resources, as well as the priorities determining this choice-making process. We will now detail the components of this choice process. Remember, we're talking of choices for entire societies and are thus concerned with individual choice, but not necessarily in terms of each individual. You decide whether to buy a new car, but society as a whole (through a government program) chooses a welfare plan to provide basic living standards.

Whether you live in the United States, the Soviet Union, or any other nation, there are three fundamental economic questions that must be answered. Although all these questions are not universally applicable, they do constitute significant issues in our modern U.S. economy.

1. What goods and services should be produced?
    a. What mixture of consumer goods, social goods, capital goods seems best?
    b. What quality or production and safety standards should be required?
    c. Are any products to be prohibited?
    d. What are the ecological impacts of the chosen output?

2. How should we produce these items?
    a. What mixture of labor and machinery shall we adopt? (Hand labor or automation?)
    b. What production standards should we enforce?
    c. What limits should be set, if any, on excessive profits or non-competitive practices?
    d. How can we secure both economic growth and protection of the environment?

3. How should these products be distributed?
    a. What ratio of welfare and competition is desired?
    b. Why do wages differ, and what's a "fair" difference?
    c. What level and structure of taxes is tolerable and what is desirable?
    d. To what degree should society provide for those unable (unwilling?) to attain basic living standards?

1. *What goods and services should be produced?* Choices must be made daily in answer to this question. Shall we produce more television sets? Should they be color or black and white, consoles or portables? Should they be 15-, 17-, 19-, 21-, or 23-inch models? If we decide to produce more automobiles at the sacrifice of television production (as we will soon see, production of any good usually involves sacrificing the production of other goods), in which style and model will these automobiles be produced, and with what options? If we decide to produce both television sets and automobiles, then we will, of necessity, reduce output of other items as well as limit the output of each. The resources used for retooling the new automobile models could have been used to produce new schools, clear slums, and build more hospitals. Should our priorities in making these decisions be guided by our personal self-interest or by the welfare of society in general?

In making these types of choices, the economist often speaks of an *oppor-*

tunity cost: the output foregone or given up because of choices made, for society, by using resources to produce television sets, cannot at the same time use those resources to produce other items. When we decide to produce TVs, we also decide not to produce some autos. Thus the "decision cost" (opportunity cost) of more TVs is fewer autos.

The importance of opportunity cost is that it forces choice makers to consider alternative actions, to weigh benefits and costs against priorities and then choose. (Do you think this same way daily? Do you see social decisions made this way?) This view of choice making also emphasizes that the dollar expense of any output is really only a matter of convenience in exchange. The real importance of an output or action is the alternative output or action foregone, its opportunity cost. Milton Friedman, a former president of the American Economic Association, puts it another way: TANSTAAFL ("There Ain't No Such Thing As A Free Lunch"!). Do you see the connection with opportunity cost?

Another decision in this area that must be made is the choice between consumer and social or capital (or producer) goods. *Consumer goods* are those goods and services you obtain by your private purchase for your use only. Such consumer goods include food, clothes, autos, entertainment, and television sets. *Social goods*, however, are for use by all citizens and are usually paid for by all (taxes). Typical social goods are your college and classroom, police and fire services, defense armaments, and public highways. *Capital goods* are usually the output of private business, but are used to produce other goods and services. Capital goods thus include trucks, tractors, drill presses, factory buildings, and computers.

The more consumer goods a nation produces, the higher the standard of living its citizens may enjoy. But unless a nation sacrifices some current consumption so that it may use the nonconsumed resources to replenish its capital stock, its consumer-oriented society eventually will have a lower level of living. Moreover, some amount of social goods is usually required to meet societal justice needs, improve quality of life, remedy deficiencies of market operation, and guarantee national security. Every nation's present selection of goods and services will affect the daily and future comfort level of the nation's citizenry.

Figure 1-10 presents a perhaps abstract, but concise, view of this social choice of output. The society's ability to produce either consumer goods or social and capital goods is limited at any time by the quantity and quality of economic resources the society possesses. The limit is shown by the *production possibilities curve*: the society could choose all consumer goods, all social and capital goods, or (more usual) some combination of the two. As social choice emphasizes one output type, less can be produced of the other type, the difference representing opportunity cost. (In moving from A to B in Figure 1-10, the opportunity cost of more social and capital goods is fewer consumer goods.)

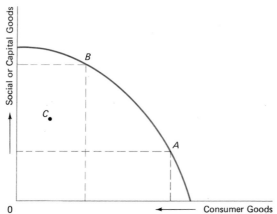

FIG. 1–10. Production possibilities curve (more capital goods means fewer consumer goods, from A to B).

Of course, society could choose (or develop difficulties that dictate a choice) not to use all its resources, thus falling below its production possibilities curve (point *C*). If, on the other hand, more economic resources or more productive ones become available, the production possibilities curve would expand outward. In either case, the society must choose both the type and quantity of goods and services to produce.

2. *How shall we produce these goods?* Not only must society decide *what* to produce, but it must also decide *how* to produce. Should these items decided upon be produced by small or large business firms? If we want siding for a house, should we use asbestos, wood, steel, brick, aluminum, or tin? In some parts of the world mud, reeds, or grass is used for siding. Should we heat the house with natural gas, oil, electricity, coal, or wood? Will we dry our clothes in a gas or electric dryer or hang them out on a line? Will we cook our meals with natural gas, electricity, wood, or coal? Will the clothes we wear be made of cotton, wool, silk, Orlon, Dacron, paper, or aluminum? The decisions made in this area will depend upon many factors we have not yet discussed. We can say, in general, that the best choices will be the ones that allocate scarce resources most efficiently.

Conflict of social priorities often arises in choosing how to produce. For example, the current "energy crisis" requires choices between increased use of fossil fuel and increased deterioration of the environment (oil wells off coastlines, pipelines in Alaska, shale processing in Colorado, coal strip mining in New Mexico). This conflict becomes even more pronounced when unemployment rates, family incomes, oil imports, and societies' health standards are all affected by the choices made.

What is the proper use of labor resources in a sophisticated society such as that of the United States? Most of our working force is composed of edu-

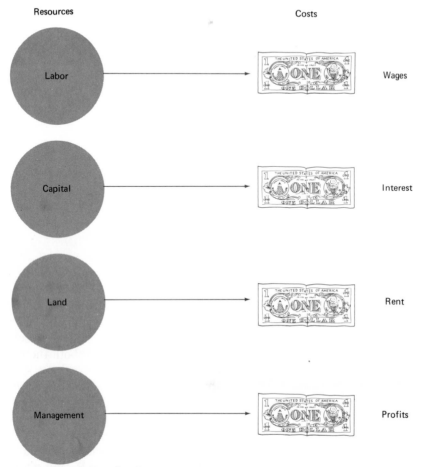

FIG. 1–11. The production process.

cated and skilled workers, a preponderance that reflects the higher degree of training necessary to produce the many complex goods and services we use daily. Most American workers have a high school education, and a rapidly rising segment has college degrees. Most people without high school degrees have technical or industrial skills. In other nations, such as India, the vast majority of people does not have either much formal education or industrial skills. Consequently, the production choices of India for solving problems of scarcity are much more limited than those of the United States. In many societies the working conditions of the average person have improved drastically as modern technology replaces the old drudgery of physical labor with mechanical and electronic assistance. Automated society is, however, not an unmixed blessing. The problems of boredom and the lack of interest in the job may cause many problems.

3. *To whom shall these products go?* In America the decision regarding *who* should get the goods and services produced is assumed to be made mainly by "dollar-voting," or consumer sovereignty. It is made in the market-place and is based to a great degree on the level of the consumer's income. We believe that people should be able to receive in monetary rewards as much as their talents and drive allow them. There should be no upper limitations set arbitrarily by government. Some societies feel that although every person should not get the exact amount of income as his or her neighbor, the wide income differences found in American society should not be allowed. (Review Figure 1-7?) Even in countries such as the United States limitations are occasionally imposed, such as rationing in wartime to allot how much citizens can buy. We must also decide which products we will consume. Will we be allowed freely to smoke all the cigarettes or drink all the alcohol we wish, or should there be some limitations imposed? What about those members of our society who, by virtue of skin color, lack of training, or even plain bad luck, do not partake of the prevailing well-being? Should we ask some of the more affluent members of our society to forego some things so that some of the less affluent members can obtain the bare necessities of life?

Perhaps an even larger issue in this area of choice is the responsibility of government (representing society as a whole) to provide basic living standards. Should our society guarantee a basic minimum living standard, and at what level ($5,400 for an urban family of four in 1976), and by what method (negative income tax, food stamps, unemployment compensation, public employment)? This issue is by no means settled at present, though it appears that U.S. society is becoming increasingly inclined to provide some form of income maintenance for its citizens.

The answers to the three fundamental economic questions comprise the essential decision-making processes through which all societies must go. The process by which the four basic resource groups are used to answer the three fundamental economic questions constitutes an economic system. All economic systems strive for the most efficient use of the four basic resource groups, but market-oriented and command-type economic systems emphasize different items in answering these fundamental economic questions. We concentrate throughout this text on how a market-oriented society answers these questions.

We will also learn that for all the economic, political, social, and philosophical differences between market-oriented and command-type systems, there are surprisingly many common areas of agreement in answering the fundamental economic questions. We will see how the Soviets are letting more market-oriented forces affect their central decision-making processes. We will also learn how in our country the search for economic justice is a significant factor that is drastically changing the role of our traditional free enterprise orientation. Is there, as the Nobel Prize winner Jan Tinbergen notes, a "convergence thesis" in operation?

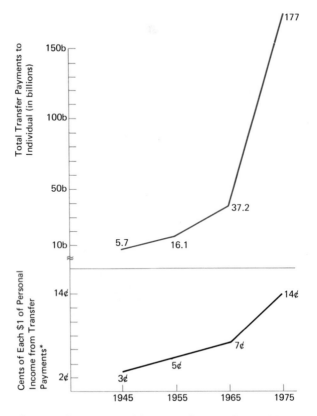

Source: U.S. Department of Commerce, *Economic Report of the President*, 1976.

*Transfer payments include government payments to individuals, such as social security, welfare, unemployment benefits, medical benefits, and other income assistance programs.

FIG. 1–12. Transfer payments.

PATTERN OF THIS BOOK

What this text seeks to impart is an *understanding of the choice-making process* so that any economic issue can be broken down to these essential questions: How do we go about making rational choices? What are alternative choices? What are the comparative benefits and costs of different choices? To what extent is choice regulated or modified by government? How free, really, is the consumer in making daily economic choices?

We analyze the role of prices in our economy as it affects us as consumer choice makers. We examine the framework of federal, state, and local government activity within the scope of a market-oriented society. Business structure and competition are also investigated, as is the economic role of labor unions. Throughout these chapters the student should attempt to relate

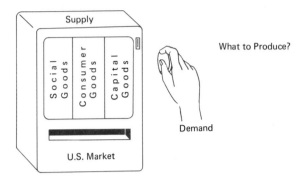

What to Produce?

How to Produce?

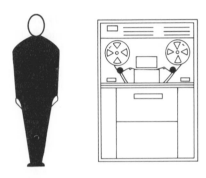

For Whom to Produce?

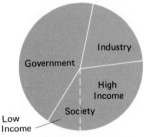

FIG. 1–13. Economic choice making: answers to the three fundamental economic questions.

each topic to the overall study of society making choices. We probably raise more questions than we answer.

TERMS

Fundamental (basic) questions. Those questions that all societies must, through their economic system, answer. They must decide how resources will be used and therefore decide what and how much to produce, how to produce, and for whom to produce.

Opportunity cost. The item or activity sacrificed in order to secure another item or activity.

Production possibility curve. An economic theory of societal ability to produce consumer and social and capital goods and a representation of choice alternatives to that society.

Resources. Necessary (and limited) elements of any productive process, comprising labor, raw materials, capital stock, and management.

QUESTIONS FOR STUDY

1. Why is choice necessary in all societies?
2. Identify the four types of economic resources.
3. What is the difference between microeconomics and macroeconomics?
4. Compare choice making in a market economy and in a command economy.
5. How do government regulations affect your daily choice?
6. What noneconomic aspects of choice making do you think are important?
7. What effect does increased social goods output have on the level of consumer goods output?
8. Is too much or too little of our resources devoted to social goods production?

REFERENCES

Economic Education in the Schools. Report of the National Task Force on Economic Education, Second Edition. New York: Committee for Economic Development, 1960.

Fels, Rendigs, and Robert G. Uhler. *Casebook of Economic Problems and Policies.* New York: West Publishing Co., 1975.

Gill, Richard T. *Economics and the Public Interest,* Second Edition. Pacific Palisades, Calif.: Goodyear Publishing Co., 1975.

Heyne, Paul T. *The Economic Way of Thinking.* Chicago: Science Research Associates, Inc., 1973.

Lee, Dwight R., and Robert F. McNown. *Economics in Our Time.* Chicago: Science Research Associates, Inc., 1975.

McKenzie, Richard B., and Gordon Tullock. *The New World of Economics.* Homewood, Ill.: Richard D. Irwin, Inc., 1975.

2

WHAT IS AN ECONOMIC SYSTEM?

SHORT ANSWER. An economic system is an accepted pattern of behavior adopted by a society to answer the three fundamental economic questions.

YOU AND THE ECONOMIC SYSTEM

"But I know about the American market system; I grew up in it! Why should I study economics to learn what I do every day?" Not a bad question, if the student is challenging this text. (You should be. Remember the opportunity cost you are paying in study time.) After all, the students are in the

FIG. 2–1. Economic systems make choices.

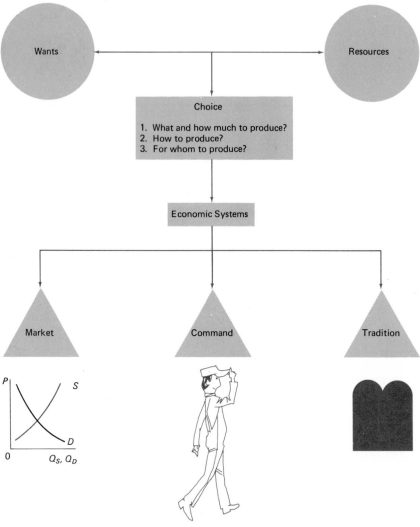

U.S. economy daily (purchases, work, school, savings, taxes, and so forth) and, one hopes, observe the world activity around them.

Let us respond directly to this question. You should be aware that there is a big difference between activity and knowledge. You may well engage in economic activity without ever knowing what causes the "goings on" behind that activity. In fact, it is usually the activities we take for granted that we really know the least about. An example would be the purchase of gasoline for your car. What could be simpler or more commonplace? Do you know, however, why the price is what it is and why it has been rising rapidly in recent years? Do you know which government policies have affected these prices? Are you aware that the average American family spent over $450 on foreign oil imports in 1975? What are oil companies doing with their profits? How is the entire economy affected by your buying less gas or a compact car? These are the "goings on" we attempt to explain.

The concept we're driving at is that studying choice making in economics involves answers to all these questions. You are an important part of the total economic system, true, but there is also a great deal more to economic choice making beyond your own personal choices. It is this overall economic choice-making process that this text proposes to help you examine and understand. By understanding how our economy as a whole answers the basic economic questions (recall Chapter 1?), you should gain a more complete knowledge and appreciation of economic problems and issues. This understanding should aid you in daily consumer activity, expand your awareness of economic issues, and assist you in becoming a more effective citizen and voter. (Economic understanding should even help your pocketbook!)

Our goal, then, is to examine throughout this text the process by which the American economic system arrives at the answers to the basic economic questions of *what, how,* and *for whom* to produce. Chapter 2 examines what we really mean when we say "the American economy." (Does Figure 2-1 give you any overview ideas?) Remember that we are analyzing a process when we look at an economy, so let's begin with your own daily activities.

We realize that as an individual you are mainly concerned with your own particular wants and may not see the overall system or even be interested in it. Naturally, you do know quite a bit about your own activities and would probably feel this book is more relevant if you could see how that system affected you. In fact, this approach is the one we will use throughout the text: We will go from the individual to our total economic structure.

First of all, you obtain income either from working, your parents, a savings account, or from a variety of other sources. And let's also say you want some new clothes, a John Denver album, a motorcycle, or a multitude of what-evers.

Right away, you have a basic problem: *choice.* (See Chapter 1.) Your "wants" now may cost more than your income. You may have $50 to spend but want clothes that cost $75 to begin school in the fall. (By the way, did

Consumer Decisions

FIG. 2–2. Consumer choice making.

you forget about the $75 for textbooks or your automobile insurance of $150?) Put simply, yours is the problem of unlimited wants. You're "short" and must choose the item you will do without. If you should feel alone in this choice-making problem, remember that all of us face the same decisions. Just ask any of your friends or classmates.

There is another element to your purchasing decisions that plays a large role, both in your own personal choices and in our economy as a whole; that element is *competition*. Your choice of a particular item or brand may depend greatly on a wide variety of advertising appeals. You may buy bell-bottomed pants because of the styling appeals in ads or because your own group of friends favors them. Or you may buy "Hip-Hugger"pants over the "Sloppy Joes" brand because of lower prices or better quality. Additionally, you may buy these pants at a discount store rather than at a prestigious department store because of advertising, lower prices, ease of parking, friendliness of employees, and a whole host of other reasons.

To summarize, you make choices in your daily purchase decisions by involving such factors as income, price, style, brand, and store. These choices are important to you, as you want to get the most for your money. As you and more than 215 million other Americans make these kinds of choices, you comprise a major part of what is referred to as our economic system. In fact, you and those other 215 million Americans constitute the *consumer sector* of our economy, the largest source of spending and job generation in the American economy (see Figure 2-3). When you spend or save you affect business decisions on output and price, employment and unemployment levels, government tax receipts, and countless interdependent mechanisms throughout our economy. (Makes you feel pretty important? You are!)

There is one other item we should note in your daily purchasing ventures, the aspect of *money and credit*. You may pay for your purchases with cash (currency and coins), with a check, or by credit (credit card or charge account). Although you've probably not given it a great deal of thought,

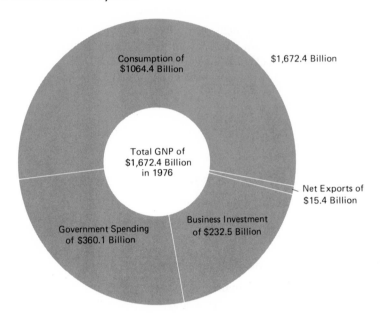

Consumption of
$1064.4 Billion

$1,672.4 Billion

Total GNP of
$1,672.4 Billion
in 1976

Net Exports of
$15.4 Billion

Government Spending
of $360.1 Billion

Business Investment
of $232.5 Billion

Source: Department of Commerce estimate, 1976.

FIG. 2–3. Gross national product composition, 1976.

consider the importance of the sellers' accepting your money. Suppose they won't accept your cash or wouldn't honor your check or wouldn't extend credit to you. This is not as farfetched as it may initially seem. Rural western merchants often refused to accept paper "greenbacks" well into the early years of the twentieth century. Most of us have had personal experiences, or know someone who has, with stores refusing to accept our checks or credit being denied. How many of you or your parents would own a house if you had to pay cash instead of using the common credit instrument called a *mortgage?*

Do you see how these reactions could limit greatly the amount of goods and services you receive or the significant effect on the total economy? Although we will examine our money system in Chapter 15, you might consider now how you probably take this mechanism for granted, yet really know little about its origin or control.

The point being made here is that your own purchase decisions are an integral part of the way our economy operates. In addition, in order for your choices to be made, a monetary system (currency, banks, savings and loan companies, stock and commodity markets, and so on) is required. Further, these choices and mechanisms are affected daily by government policies, regulations, and controls. You've probably experienced some of these, such as marijuana laws, veteran's benefits, income taxes, lending rate, public education, and fair trade laws. Although the interrelationships just described appear to be far removed from your everyday activities, they do shape the form of these various activities. Let's see if we can develop this relationship a bit in the next section and relate your individual activity to that of the entire economy.

QUESTIONS

1. List what is involved in your purchase of any item.

2. Develop a budget (your own or one for your family).

3. How is your purchasing decision affected by government?

Overall Economic Relationships

We should now tie some major components of our economic system together, again emphasizing *you* as a starting point from which to work. Figure 2-4 depicts such relationships. At first glance, this figure may not appear like anything you've ever experienced (or want to), much less our U.S. economy. Remember, however, that we are depicting an abstract view of the entire economy so that you can understand its parts and working mechanisms. We can pull apart Figure 2-4 to understand it; as we do, try to see yourself going through these routine interrelationships.

While we're talking of the economic system in the United States—"market-oriented" (or "capitalistic" or "mixed free enterprise")—remember that the same basic parts exist in all forms of economic systems. It is the way in which the relationships (who tells whom what to do) of these parts differ that gives us the various types of economic systems that presently exist in our country and other nations.

First of all, we have you, the individual or family unit. On the one hand, you buy goods and services, paying for them with currency, checks, or credit. So we now have you the household and the businesses from whom you buy. The Business Sector circle represents some 14 million private business firms, all of different sizes and outputs and all after your patronage. Between these sectors circulates money—the currency, checks, and credit. The Product Market rectangle represents the commonplace exchanges you make of money for goods and services and could be the grocery store, gas pumps, or a Ticketron line for John Denver tickets. Can you see now how the basic parts of our economic system are tied together and depend upon each other? Business needs your purchases; you need business products, and money is necessary to both.

There is another large component of our economic system (also shown in Figure 2-4) that directly or indirectly affects you daily, and that is the role

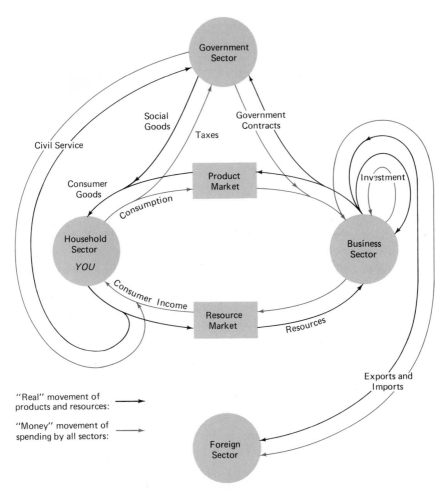

FIG. 2–4. Circular-flow model of market economy.

of various levels of government. Government regulations affect work and safety standards, sometimes fix minimum and maximum prices for many regulated business firms, set pollution control standards, prohibit some goods and services from production, and ensure competition and nonfraudulent consumer practices. In fact, you also can buy goods and services from various government levels (federal, state, local) through the indirect payment of taxes. You pay state, federal, and occasionally city income tax; state and sometimes local sales taxes; and local property tax. These taxes pay for (see the Government Contracts flow in Figure 2-4?) the services of national defense, highways, school systems, welfare, recreation, and an almost unending amount of other services. These goods and services are then supplied to you, the taxpayer and citizen, as social goods (the public college you attend, the roads you drive on, the police who ticket you, and the public beach you sun at). (We discuss this further in Chapter 11.)

You may also buy foreign-made products (termed *imports* in flow; *exports* are what foreign customers buy from us) from local retailers. On the one hand, this provides you, the consumer, a greater variety and competitive market; on the other, it may drive American firms out of business. (We discuss this further in Chapter 20.)

One further and most important spending aspect of Figure 2-4 is that of business *investment*. Although you do not directly make these investments, your savings may be borrowed by businessmen for investment spending. By the way, you may be saying, "But I do invest when I buy stocks or land for speculation or put my money in a certificate of deposit." From the economist's point of view, this is not investment: You are saving, not spending on final goods or services. *Investment* means "the production of new capital stock," such as trucks, tractors, machinery, or factory buildings; this spending is usually made only by a business firm. This distinction of saving versus investment is important, because

1. Excess saving may cause reduced output, unemployment, and decreased consumer and business income. Note that Figure 2-4 is based on spending flows, and saving does not represent spending.

2. Investment creates increased productive capacity, new jobs, greater output, and economic growth. (See Chapter 18.) It is a spending component flow of Figure 2-4.

3. Investment requires saving but the two activities cannot be far out of balance, or economic problems of inflation or recession may arise. (We discuss this further in Chapter 12.)

So much for now for the buying aspect of our total system, whereby you, the consumer, purchase goods and services from private business and from foreign and governmental sources. Now we will direct our attention to the resource side, for, as you well know, in order to buy, you must have an income. For a business to produce, it must hire resources.

The lower portion of Figure 2-4 illustrates this *income aspect* of our economy. Again, starting with you, the individual or family, the consumer is also a worker (labor resource) for a particular business. Not only do you need the income to buy what you wish, but businesses need your talents and abilities to produce those goods and services.

The Resource Market rectangle represents the exchange of your labor resources for the business firm's paycheck. In addition, the other resources of raw materials and management (capital stock is "hired" through the investment flow, if you recall the previous discussion) are also hired in the *resource market*. This resource exchange process may involve your college placement center, your job at the gas station, a labor union contract, or even the unemployment office.

Note this essential point here about our economy of interdependence: You need income from employment by a business, and you need products produced by business. The business needs your labor to produce products, and it also must have sales to consumers to remain profitable. Therefore, your income provides consumer spending, which purchases business output, generates jobs and resources for hire, and provides income for further spending. (Run this cause-effect-cause mechanism around Figure 2-4 a few times, and try to see your own activity in this new perspective.)

You may see from this "interdependence" why Figure 2-4 is often called the *circular-flow economy* model of our economic system. There is "circular causation," in that everything depends on everything else. An event in one part of our economy will likely lead to reactions throughout the economy. It is also the reason why the economist often gives evasive answers such as, "It depends." As an example, consider the energy crisis and its impact upon auto purchasing patterns in recent years:

1. Oil embargo and price increases help cause higher gasoline prices.

2. Consumers reduce auto purchases in general, especially of cars that are not economical with fuel.

3. Auto manufacturers experience large inventory buildup, lay off employees, and begin producing more compact autos.

4. Unemployed auto workers buy fewer homes and less furniture and reduce spending in general.

5. Other workers (you?) in other industries are now unemployed. A recession deepens.

Perhaps we should also add in the resource flow description that the individual may work for various levels of government, as well as for a private enterprise. The authors, for example, are teachers at a public community college, a local government agency. A government employee receives an income originating from tax payments, and his or her labor produces social goods received by you, the citizen consumer. Thus, we see that consumers work for both private and public employers and buy goods from both private business and government agencies.

In addition, consumer income may arise from *transfer payments* of government agencies. These are government payments designed to maintain income (Social Security, veteran's benefits, unemployment compensation, food stamps, and so on) and are also paid for through taxes. We discuss this further in Chapters 11 and 14.

Well, have we described in overall fashion what our economy really *is*?

FIG. 2–5. Total spending equals total income.

Look at your daily life, and compare it to Figure 2-4 and the preceding explanation. Figure 2-5 may also summarize this discussion, as it totals both the spending and income flows of our economy. Note that the totals are equal, for someone's spending is always someone else's income. We can now summarize briefly the components of our economic system.

1. *Consumer.* The individual or family earns income by working for private or public employer. He or she could also receive income from interest, rent, or profit payments and even from government transfer payments. These individuals use the income received to buy goods and services of their own choice supplied by private or foreign businesses or indirectly, by taxation, from government. Individuals act to better themselves in both employment and purchases and choose their employment and purchases accordingly.

2. *Businesses.* The business owner must employ various resources— labor, natural materials, capital stock, managerial skills—in order to produce goods and services to sell to consumers (domestic sales, foreign export, or government contract for social goods) to make a profit. Production and selling must be in accordance with certain laws and regulations.

3. *Government.* We speak here of federal, state, or local agencies. These groups resemble private businesses in some aspects of their providing social goods and services (defense, roads, police and fire protection, education) to the consumer and of their hiring resources with payment received from consumers via taxation or special fees. But, in addition, government bodies serve as regulatory agencies in passing laws to govern such activity as type of product to produce (no impure foods), the manner of production (no ten-year-olds working), the quality of product (no worms in diet pills, no faulty automobiles, no tricky wording in contracts), the amount of competition (no agreement among firms to fix prices), and many other economic activities.

4. *Foreign Spending.* American consumers purchase foreign imports, whereas U.S. businessmen export products for sale in the foreign

trade markets. In addition, the U.S. government may send foreign aid to other nations, while U.S. businessmen may invest abroad and foreign businessmen may invest here. Although foreign spending may appear small in Figure 2-5, recall the large impacts resulting from the oil embargo of 1973 and higher crude oil prices.

QUESTIONS

1. "The consumer needs business, and business needs the consumer." Explain this statement.
2. What would happen to your own job if everyone stopped buying products?
3. How does investment differ from saving?

PURPOSE OF AN ECONOMIC SYSTEM

What have we done thus far? We have looked at your own daily economic activity of earning income and purchasing products. Your personal activity has been put into the perspective of our entire economic system in tying your own actions to those of the other sectors in our economy.

Do you see what our American (or any other) economic system really does and why its operation is important to you? Perhaps we should be more precise here and really lay out our economic system's functions.

We emphasized earlier that you have to make individual choices every day. You must make the choice of what career to pursue and the choices of what to buy, how much, and where. All other individuals in our society must make the same choices daily.

But if each and every person must make choices, the entire economy must too. Now, our "economic system" is not a person or even a place, so the choice process is not the same. In fact, the economic system's choices are really a result of "adding together" all individuals' choices; that is, this society has certain amounts of labor, natural resources, capital stock, and managerial skills, and if these resources are "put together," we get products. It's not quite that simple, of course. There must be decisions made as to *what and how much to produce, how to produce,* and *who gets* these products. (Recall Chapter 1?) Note that these questions must be answered by all societies, though the way these questions are answered may differ. (This is where we get into systems of *market* orientation, *command*, and *tradition* —or capitalism, communism, and so on, as they're often termed.) Let's detail each of these questions and briefly explain how our own market economic system works. Then we'll follow up with a brief survey of other types of economic systems.

What and How Much to Produce

The first question, that of what and how much to produce, must be answered by all societies because no society can have all the goods it desires. If you use resources to produce a tank, you can't at the same time use the same resources to produce a car (opportunity cost). A choice must be made. Just as you, as an individual, must choose what to buy, our society as a whole must decide how many of each item to produce.

At this point, you might ask just how such a system makes choices. Well, in our system, we get overall economic choices as a result of all individuals making individual choices. For example, the question of how many cars to produce is answered by the number of people willing to pay prices that are profitable to auto manufacturers. If a lot is spent, automobile manufacturers will produce a great deal. When people save their money, car sales will drop, and auto production will be shut down. Should people vote for higher taxes, more schools and roads will be built (although the individual may then have less income to buy textbooks to use in the schools and cars to drive on the roads).

Note here that you make a choice of what to buy depending on your income, your needs and wants, and your goals. The business firm produces and sells these products only if it can make a profit in doing so. Thus, when we say our "market-oriented economic system" (capitalism) makes the choice, what we really mean is that the choice results from many people making many separate decisions. Businesses respond to consumer desires because they want a profit, and consumers respond to production changes to "get the most for their money." What may appear as a simple choice really involves a complex process of decision making in our economy.

Remember that we're describing how our *market* economic system works, because in other systems the process varies. For example, under a command economic system (socialism or communism), a single leader or group of people could draw up a list of goods to be produced for the entire society and then order workers to produce these products. This may be the clearest way to distinguish *consumer sovereignty* (consumer maker decisions in market-oriented system) from *economic planning* (rulers determine output in a command system).

How to Produce

There's another question that must be answered, that of how to produce. By this we mean that products do not just materialize by someone wishing for them or merely decreeing they will be produced. You must get resources together, coordinate their activities in some type of manufacturing process, and get the resulting product to a retailer.

Again, in a market economic system no one usually tells a business firm what to produce or how many resources to hire or how to organize an assembly line or where to locate or even what price to charge (except for regulated products, such as utilities—gas, water, electricity, and telephone—and price controls did limit rates of increase on many prices from 1971–1974). The business owner basically desires a profit and must make decisions on these matters in terms of his or her customers. Think about the many decisions involved the next time you walk into a supermarket or discount store. Then consider that we have some 14 million business firms in the United States making these decisions. Of course, the businessman's decisions must also consider government regulations, labor union pressures, and consumerism lobbies to force fair business practices. On the other hand, business can try to persuade the consumer by advertising and may also lobby in Congress and state legislatures for favorable legislative treatment. Our circular-flow diagram of Figure 2-4 becomes quite messy when real world politics are considered!

The alternative to our economic process of decision making based on the incentive of profit may be seen from the viewpoint of a command economic system. Some leaders or groups would have to set quotas of items to produce for certain factories and would have to coordinate the entire operation. Without the decision making by separate but interdependent business owners, there would have to be some central decision making to determine product output and resource hire. Perhaps at this point you may appreciate what all those prices are really accomplishing.

For Whom to Produce

Now comes the really important question, the one that has always caused most problems in any society: "Who gets what? For whom do we produce?" Bluntly put, any society must have some system of dividing among its members that which is available for consumption. Of course, all members of a society generally want as many of the goods produced as possible. Down through history, this *for whom* question has always aroused the greatest domestic hassle and still does. Consider current economic issues, all involving the for whom question, of welfare levels, discriminatory working and housing practices, labor union negotiation and strikes, tax reform proposals, and political reform campaign platforms in general.

Now, of course, there are many methods of dealing with this for whom question—supreme ruler, fighting, and so on—and every option has been used by one society or another in the past. In our own market system, we use perhaps the most complex and indirect method of dividing our total output. In our society, as you well know, you consume what you're able to pay for! If you have enough income, you can live in a mansion, drive a luxury auto, own a yacht, and be a jet setter. On the other hand, you might only be able to afford a tar-paper shack, a used auto, and beans. The majority, perhaps, lives in a three- or four-bedroom home in an urban or suburban community, drives a two-year-old car, has a color TV and many appliances, eats well, and complains about high taxes.

Again, the method of dividing output in our society depends on income available, and this income depends on your type of work and rate of pay. Additional factors would include education level, unionization, and racial background. Moreover, income levels are affected and modified by government legislation, including minimum wage laws, transfer payments, anti-discrimination laws, public education, and progressive income tax structures. Although such an economic system sometimes does result in great inequities, it also promotes a maximum of free choice in types of career choices and uses of income.

YOU AND OTHER ECONOMIC SYSTEMS

Doubtless you've often heard of economic political "isms," such as capitalism, communism, socialism, fascism, and so on (if not, see the Ebenstein reference at end of chapter). You probably also realize that the existence of these competing economic, political, and social systems does to some degree pose a "threat" to our own market-oriented system. In addition, you may have studied these varying systems and perhaps see that the differences in the "isms" comprise facets of economic organization, political process, and social values and heritage.

You may well ask if such "isms" really affect you as an individual or if such differences are really important. The answer is that such differences are indeed important to you in understanding the world about you, as well as the impact on your own pocketbook. Understanding and pocketbooks are important enough, we hope, for you to read a bit further.

To get at the "understanding the world better" aspect, perhaps the vital point is to realize all peoples and governments of the world do not view that world or react to it alike. To comprehend the significance of international events and issues, you need some understanding of how these foreign nations solve their economic, political, and social problems. All nations do not function exactly as the United States does (even if they're also basically market systems), and you really can't project our American daily behavior as a measure of the activities and attitudes of a citizen of a foreign state. Note here that the authors are not judging any system as "good" or "bad" (they have preferences, of course), but, rather are emphasizing that differences must be appreciated to understand the reactions of others. The authors would view such world understanding as quite important, especially in view of a rapidly shrinking (technology of transportation and communication) and *interdependent* (power blocks of nations, alliances, foreign trade, oil embargoes) world.

If we go a step further along the "pocketbook effect" aspect, perhaps this entire cold war (a battle of isms?) issue might be illustrated by U.S. defense expenditures required in answer to possible foreign threats to U.S. security. Although experts' estimates of just how much of a threat is posed by the existence of other economic systems differ greatly, the fact that over $100 billion annually (of a total U.S. budget in fiscal 1977 of approximately $400 billion) is spent for defense has its effect, however accurately its causes are assessed. Such defense costs support preparedness not only in a cold war, but also for the hot wars (Korea, Vietnam, the Middle East). Another "pocketbook effect" of the cold war is the $197 billion (1946–1974) spent by the United States to aid other nations and, in so doing, to spur their emulation of the U.S. economic system.

The preceding paragraphs, we hope, convince you of the value of studying comparative economic systems. What we aim for in the following is a very brief survey of the more basic differences among economic systems and the issues arising from such differences. This survey is limited here by time, space, and the authors' ability to "get it all together" in a bite-sized chunk. Such a topic is a large study order (see the Loucks reference if you want a 600-page study on this topic), and we intend only to outline the issues here but hope to "turn you on" to further study by such description.

Basic Questions for All Systems

Let's return for a minute to a review of our discussion thus far in Chapter 2. Recall that the science of economics proceeds from the basic problems of scarcity: limited economic resources vs. unlimited wants for goods and services. Bluntly put, all societies must make choices as to how such resources are to be used because all wants cannot be satisfied. More specifically, these choices include (1) what goods and services to produce and in what quantities, (2) how to produce these goods and services, and (3) for whom to produce the goods and services. To repeat, *all* societies (United States, U.S.S.R., India, Brazil, all nations) must make these choices.

The point of any society's economic system is that this system is the process responding to these fundamental questions; that is, an economic system is the society's own choice maker, and must come up with answers to these questions. The authors hope that the following eighteen chapters of this text will give you some fair idea of how our own market type of economic system answers such questions.

We should also go a step further. Although all societies necessarily have an economic system to provide answers to these fundamental questions, the economic systems do not have to be identical. Not only may the structure and mechanism of the economic systems differ, but the answers given to the fundamental questions may differ as well. Any analytical examination of other nations' economic activities will, in fact, show you that these differences do occur in greater or lesser degree, with some quite similar to the United States and others fundamentally dissimilar.

Such differences in structure and answers of economic systems should, however, not be so unexpected or surprising to you; for, recall, we have already noted (and you can observe this in your own behavior) that the way an economy works and the answers provided depend on the political values of that society, its cultural norms, its history, and a host of factors produced over time. Economic choices depend on cultural values held by the society, and economic processes follow accepted social norms of the society. Put another way, the economic system of any society is a result of that society's values, and the values change over time!

Therefore, to reiterate, it is not a big surprise to find that economic systems vary in structure and performance because societies vary in values and heritage. As an example, striving for a private profit may be accepted and condoned in one society and economic system, but the same behavior may be socially unacceptable and illegal in another society. To go one step further, it should also be no surprise that, as societal values change, there occur changes in the structure and performance of an economic system. There is little reason why such changes should be identical between two societies.

If we have made good on this logic about economic systems differing, you may well conclude that all economic systems are unique and that no valid comparisons are possible. Well, you're right that all systems are unique; thus, any comparison is one of generalities at best. However, even though no two economic systems are exactly alike, there are some basic similarities that make possible a meager level of classifying economic systems. Note that the idea of setting up categories of economic systems is not to pigeonhole such systems or force rigid classifications. Rather, the idea is to point out that many nations share fundamental characteristics in their economic systems, even though the exact form of that similarity will differ. Thus, we can distinguish those groups that "somewhat resemble" from those that "radically differ," and such classification does go a step further in providing additional economic understanding.

Types of Systems

Even though the authors would accept each economic system as unique, let's examine one classification scheme used by Heilbroner. (See reference at the end of this chapter.) The types of economic systems specified are those of *market, command,* and *tradition.* Notice that none of these types has an "ism" in it (such as capitalism, communism, and so on) but is assigned for the specific purpose of looking at the functioning of each economic system. By this we mean that such a term as capitalism or communism really includes reference not only to an economic system, but also to political processes, social values, and cultural heritage. Therefore, such "ism" terms only confuse the issue when the question is exactly how an economic system works. Such terms are also emotion-laden and produce more heat than analysis. (A "dirty Communist" or a "running dog of capitalist imperialism," depending on societal reference, is indeed an emotional classification; but a "dirty market" or a "dirty command" doesn't get into the same problems!)

Given these three categories of economic system—market, command, and tradition—let's try to summarize the differences and similarities. Perhaps the best way to do this, as details of comparison abound, is by presenting the rather lengthy outlines of Figures 2-6, 2-7, and 2-8. Note that in each category an example is given of nations generally sharing (similar, but not identical) that type of economic system. Also provided are some overall descriptive points about the system, overall answers given by that type of economic system to the fundamental questions, and a summary of general structural characteristics. Compare the three types of economic systems on each of these points, especially as to the answers given to the fundamental questions.

Again, the comparison in Figures 2-6 through 2-8 is in very general terms, as there are many differences between the United States, England, Japan, and Canada, even though they all have basically a market type of economic system. Another point is that there are few examples of a "pure" type of economic system in any category. The United States is indeed basically a market system, but we don't operate only on market process and answers. Government policies affect many aspects of the American economy. (Is the school you're in perhaps a social good provided by local government through taxes?)

FIG. 2–6. Market economic system.

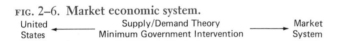

United States	← Supply/Demand Theory Minimum Government Intervention →	Market System

Market

a. United States, England, Canada, Japan.

b. Basically business for profit and goverment regulation in some areas.

c. Heritage plus values = competition and profit.

d. Overall answers:

   (1) What and how much to produce? (GNP figures by class.) Business produces for profit, depending on demand for goods. The government also buys on contracts.

   (2) How to produce? Business combines resources in most profitable (least cost) proportions. The government also regulates production conditions (health, pollution, safety, minimum wage).

   (3) For whom? Income earned enables purchases wanted by consumer. Government influences by civil services, minimum wage, welfare spending.

e. In general, societal choices made via individual choices "added up" result in little central decision or the "invisible hand" concept (Smith).

   (1) High consumer living standards.

   (2) Some instability and cyclical fluctuation.

   (3) High degree of personal freedom and choice.

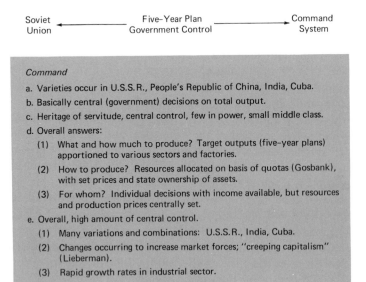

FIG. 2–7. Command economic system.

The same lack of "purity" holds for other types of economic systems. For example, the U.S.S.R. has certain aspects of market operation with a basically command system in that market incentives are now used to ensure efficient production and meet consumer needs (Liberman reforms). Japan and France use a high degree of economic planning in their market economics.

Current Trends and Directions

As we come to the end of the discussion of comparative economic systems, two questions might pop into your mind. (You are thinking over all this, aren't you?) You might ask, (1) "Which system is best?" and (2) "How are systems changing?" Well, those are difficult questions, but let's have a go at them.

First, to term a system good or bad is logically quite difficult if you recall the earlier discussion on why economic systems differ. If one is going to evaluate the operation of an economic system, one must logically do so in terms of what values that society holds. You must judge an economic system's performance on the basis of what its own society has set as goals and priorities and not in terms of your own goals and priorities. An example might be that the authors enjoy hiking because it provides them with satisfaction. Suppose you don't like hiking. Is your judging their behavior as bad a valid judgment? A similar example for economic systems would be to say that an economic system was bad because it had low consumer goods output when that system had capital goods output as a top priority.

> **Tradition**
>
> a. Much of South America, Africa.
>
> b. Basically custom, little change; individual action based on tribal codes.
>
> c. Traditions very strong; little central decision yet strong "control."
>
> d. Overall Answers:
>
>   (1) What and how much to produce? Goods customarily consumed in available amounts: low output, little variety.
>
>   (2) How to produce? Do tasks accorded by family position and history, in socially customary ways.
>
>   (3) For whom? Generally share output among group, with shares first to honored groups.
>
> e. Generally describes smaller nations or tribal groups in underdeveloped status.
>
>   (1) Low living standards and little economic growth.
>
>   (2) Much social tension as growth desire escalates.
>
>   (3) Foreign aid often provided by developed economies.

FIG. 2–8. Tradition economic system.

By the way, the authors realize that such a philosophy is open to criticism from those who feel their way is the only right one. The authors also have preferences about what type of economic system they wish to live under, but the point is that judgment of the performance of a social institution (an economic system) must proceed on the basis of what goals the particular society sets for that system. The authors may prefer other goals, but a "good-bad" judgment about other societies on this basis says little about performance standards. If one really wants to look at performance comparisons of comparative economic systems, one should have a list of societal goals (what are they for the United States?) and then compare economic system achievement against these goals. Without such comparisons, one has a sort of "second best" comparison.

Having thus admitted that they really can't say too much about judging comparative economic systems, the authors will now compound their obvious lack of insight by saying they aren't too sure of future changes in economic systems! Actually, this uncertainty is mostly caution because there are some clear trends, but projection of present trends into the future is always risky.

Perhaps the first trend is that command and market systems appear to move closer, with more changes on the market side toward a command position. By this we mean that market systems appear to develop progressively greater degrees of governmental intervention, particularly as higher levels of economic development are reached (welfare, regulation of dissent, social goods provision). On the other hand, it also appears that command systems develop increasing amounts of market-incentive operation as economic development· proceeds. Such a trend somewhat doubtfully points toward a "compromise" position between the two "pure" types of command and market. The Swedish Nobel Prize-winning economist Jan Tinbergen has made a somewhat similar analysis and projection in his "convergence thesis" of economic systems, stating that differing systems are becoming more similar over time. But caution should be exercised in such projections.

The other trend appears to be that traditional economies tend to remain just as they are, unless awakened by some outside influence to desire economic development. (The "Revolution of Rising Expectations" perhaps?) In this quest for economic development, some form of command economic system is often adopted to force investment and capital stock development. Whether nations now adopting these command systems, such as those in Asia, Africa, and Latin America, will subsequently become more market-oriented remains to be seen. If the target output goals emphasize capital stock production, the economy will grow rapidly (recall the production possibilities curve of Figure 1-10?) but have low consumer goods living standards. At some point, such "live for the future" directives may require revision.

Given such a fantastic predictive ability of future trends, it's probably well that the authors reach the end of this chapter. The objective of this chapter is to survey economic systems. We hope we got across some basic economic concepts to achieve this objective. We'll now treat these mechanisms in detail throughout the remainder of this text. At the end of Chapter 20 perhaps you will understand "the whole thing."

FIG. 2–9. "Convergence Thesis" of economic systems.

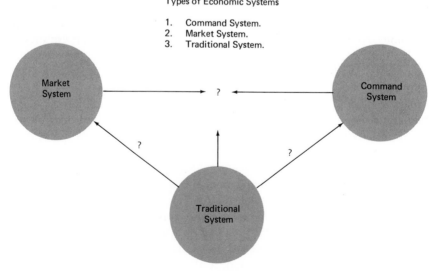

Types of Economic Systems

1.   Command System.
2.   Market System.
3.   Traditional System.

TERMS

Basic questions. Those questions that all economic systems must answer of what and how much to produce, how to produce, and for whom to produce.

Circular-flow economy model. Pictorial representation (Figure 2-4) of the United States market economy, including consumer, business, government, and foreign sectors.

Command economy. An economic system in which the basic questions are answered by some central ruling group.

Consumer sovereignty. The economic mechanism whereby business output decisions depend on consumer spending preference.

Convergence thesis. The Tinbergen hypothesis that economies become more similar over time.

Economic planning. Intervention by the government into output decisions of business firms to achieve or encourage some social goal.

Investment. Spending (usually by the business sector) that results in new productive capacity.

Market economy. An economic system in which the basic questions are answered by supply and demand decisions of businesses and consumers in response to market prices.

Saving. The act of nonspending on final goods and services (often by the consumer), possibly providing future investment.

Social goods. Output supplied to citizens by government and often purchased from private business with tax monies (examples of colleges, highways, defense, police, and so forth).

Traditional economy. An economic system in which the basic questions are answered by custom and acceptance of established activities.

Transfer payments. Government payments to certain groups to maintain income levels (examples of Social Security, veterans' benefits, unemployment compensation, food stamps, and so on).

QUESTIONS FOR STUDY

1. "Economics is the study of the principles governing the allocation of scarce means among competing ends." Explain this statement.
2. "Goods and services are scarce because resources are scarce." Explain this statement.

3. State and discuss the three fundamental questions that all economies face.

4. What is the basic function of any economic system?

5. What are the three basic types of economic systems? What type does the United States have?

6. How do economic systems differ in their mechanism and answers to the basic economic questions?

7. Which economic system is "best"?

8. How has the U.S. economic system changed since 1930? What changes do you predict in the future? (Are you pleased by such changes?)

REFERENCES

"The American System." *Fortune*, April 1975. Special Bicentennial Issue.

Dalton, George. *Economic Systems and Society*. Baltimore: Penguin Education, 1974.

Ebenstein, William. *Today's Isms*, Third Edition. Englewood Cliffs, N.J.: Prentice-Hall, Inc., 1961.

Galbraith, John K. *American Capitalism*, Revised Edition. Boston: Houghton Mifflin Company, 1956, Chapter 2.

Grossman, Gregory. *Economic Systems*. Englewood Cliffs, N.J.: Prentice-Hall, Inc., 1967.

Heilbroner, Robert. *The Making of Economic Society*, Fourth Edition. Englewood Cliffs, N.J.: Prentice-Hall, Inc., 1975.

Jackstadt, Steve, and Yukio Hamada. *The Adventures of Primo Dinero*. Honolulu: University of Hawaii, 1970.

Loucks, William N. *Comparative Economic Systems*, Sixth Edition. New York: Harper & Row, Publishers, Incorporated, 1961, Chapters 22–28.

Wilcox, Clair; Willis D. Weatherford, Jr.; and Holland Hunter. *Economies of the World Today*. New York: Harcourt Brace Jovanovich, Inc., 1961.

3

WHAT ARE PRICES?

SHORT ANSWER. Prices are a reflection, usually expressed in terms of money, of the rate at which buyers and sellers are willing to make an exchange.

"So what is a 'rate of exchange'?" you might ask. "And why an entire chapter on something I know about?" The student who asks these questions should go back to Chapter 2, and also look at Figure 3-1. Recall that in Chapter 2 we said that (1) all societies had to make choices (answer basic questions) because of limited resources and unlimited wants, and (2) a society's economic system made such choices. Now, the importance of prices in a market system, such as we have in the United States, is that prices are the central mechanism in making these choices. We exchange money for goods and services daily, always at some price (see the "rate of exchange" idea), and in doing so are giving our answers to the basic questions.

There are all kinds of prices in the U.S. economy, as Figure 3-1 points out. You're most familiar with *product prices*, but your wage is a *resource price*, as is the rent you pay, interest you receive or pay, or profits you earn. Taxes actually represent a price for social goods provided to you, as the state sales or income tax you pay may provide your college's revenue. Furthermore, every time you buy a foreign-made product, the wheels of foreign trade turn in response to the current foreign exchange rates.

All these prices and exchanges should be familiar from your daily economic activity, and perhaps you should reflect on their importance. In fact, a good exercise to appreciate the important role of prices is to try to imagine what your daily activity would be without any prices: Have you ever tried direct barter for every exchange you make? To analyze the daily mechanism of prices in our society's choice-making process, let's now turn to your daily economic activity and see you and prices battle it out.

FIG. 3–1. Prices in the U.S. economy.

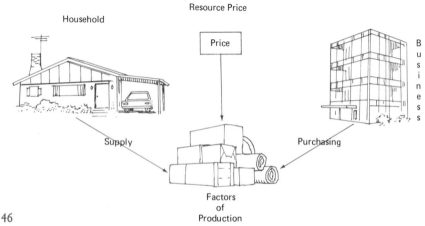

Taxes as a Price

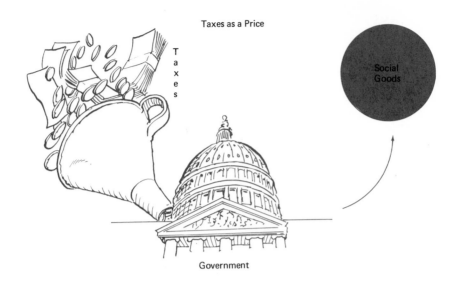

Government

Foreign Exchange Rates as a Price of Foreign Currency

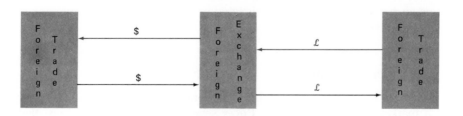

Transferring Purchasing Power. . .

FIG. 3–1. Continued.

47

YOU AND PRICES

Ads blast at you daily from newspapers, radio, TV, billboards, and mail-boxes. Note the repeated emphasis on price. The ads bluntly state, "Buy mine: I'm cheaper!" That appeal may interest you, the buyer and choice maker. Note also the ads relating to job pay (a resource price). Would you personally like to receive a higher price? And how about the taxes and interest rates you pay?

How important are these prices to you? That is, what do they do to influence you? How do you react? How are your daily economic choices affected, and how do your choices affect the entire U.S. economy? At this point we want to direct your attention to exactly what a real-life price does for or to you and to reinforce the concept that the mechanism is at the heart of our market economy.

Take a small, perhaps common, example—dinner. What did you have to-day—beans or steak? Did the price of each item have anything to do with your choice? How about where you had that dinner? Was it in a three-bed-room tract house or a Park Avenue luxury apartment? Did price play a role in determining where you live? What about the car in which you went off to school? Is it a Ford or Ferrari? Did price influence your choice? And, finally, how about price at your job? Would you rather be a part-time store clerk at $2 per hour or a $200,000-a-year business executive? Do prices influence all your previous consumption choices?

With respect to your savings choices, do you prefer a time deposit at a commercial bank at 5 per cent, a savings and loan certificate of deposit at 7½ per cent, or perhaps a risky 20 per cent return on a stock market tip? And how might you vote in the upcoming college bond issue election or on the congressmen who recently voted in favor of an income tax rebate?

The preceding list of questions is indeed very long. Such questions are typical of decisions we make daily on what and how much we will consume. The decisions depend a great deal on the prices of the items we are considering. As Figure 3-3 illustrates, you are a decision maker, daily balancing, on the one hand, your available income (the result of the price of your labor resource) and, on the other, all the goods and services you'd like to have. Price bears on this decision process by showing just how far (type and amount of purchases) your income will go.

Price Functions

The purpose of this long example is to point out a basic function of price in a market economy, *rationing*. Prices serve to ration, or divide up, that which is available among those who want it. More simply put, if you want an item and can pay for it, it's yours. If you can't afford the price, you settle for a cheaper item. Remember the basic question of "Who gets what?" in Chap-

FIG. 3–2. Advertising affects consumer choice.

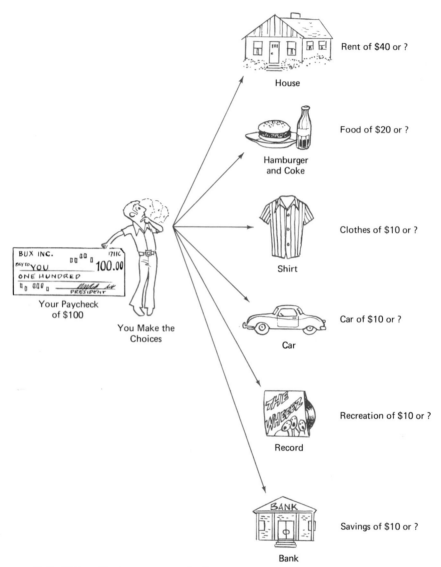

FIG. 3–3. Price affects consumer choice.

ter 2? Do you now understand how a market economy basically answers that question? (Do you drive a Rolls-Royce? Why? Why not?)

By the way, you may reply, "But that's not fair! Some people get more than others!" OK, it may not be fair, but economics never promised you a rose garden or anything else! The point is that every society must have a rationing mechanism of some type; and if prices didn't do it, then some other mechanism would have to be found. You could, for instance, try drawing lots, government edicts, a fast-draw shoot-out, or a common pot for all. But there *must* be some rationing mechanism to divide up the limited output among unlimited wants, and prices appear a bit more practical and civilized than some of these other methods. These other methods, in fact, may not give perfect equality either.

A thought point: Who says there has to be equality? How about provision for incentive, competition, and that "rugged American spirit"? These are big issues we pass over here, but we shall take them up in detail later. Suffice it to say that our U.S. economy basically uses the price mechanism to ration goods and services but modifies this choice process with mechanisms designed to provide a greater degree of equality than expected under a free enterprise result (progressive income tax, minimum wages, welfare payments, public education, and so forth).

You probably understand the rationing function of price pretty well by now. Price also serves another function, that of *guiding*. The guiding function of price is perhaps a bit more subtle to you, the consumer. Consider, for example, your choice of a career: Does the possible income, the price of your labor, play a role in your choice? Of course, interest, ability, family background, education, and a host of other factors also play significant roles, but higher starting salaries do tend to attract people. (Would you switch jobs instead of fighting if offered more money?) Thus prices guide resources to where they are most wanted. When salaries differ, job choices are influenced by such differences.

Interest rates also play a resource guiding function in that your choice of savings outlet may be directed to those institutions willing to pay the most interest. Land or rent prices certainly dictate that only those who can profitably use a particular space will try to operate in it. As an example, consider why orange groves have been uprooted for shopping centers and dairy farms have been turned into housing tracts in California. (Right. Prices!)

Perhaps the guiding function of prices is better seen from the businessman's point of view. Higher, more profitable prices bring greater supplies into the marketplace. They also bring new competitors. Prices also guide businessmen into producing what consumers want by signaling an appropriate level of production. In addition, the businessman is affected by the rationing function of price because the amount of resources he buys depends on their prices. Higher prices in the form of wages, interest rates, and rents will influence the businessman's purchase of labor, capital, and raw material.

Note that this guiding function represents society's choice on the *what to produce* and *how to produce* basic questions. Because resources are limited, every society must in some way indicate and choose how such resources are to be used. Now, this guiding function could be served by government control in a five-year plan (remember Chapter 2 and Figure 2-7?) or by traditional roles

FIG. 3–4. Wages (resource prices) affect consumer choice of careers.

and custom. Prices, however, are central to guiding in a market economy, providing incentive to both consumer and businessman to respond to society's desires for their own self-interest. For those of you who've heard of Adam Smith (*The Wealth of Nations*, 1776), this represents his concept of "the *invisible hand*"; that is, by consumer and businessman acting to maximize their own satisfaction and profit, they benefit society as if led by an invisible hand of pricing and competition.

THE FUNCTION OF PRICES

Well, did all of the preceding come through? Let's review again exactly what prices do in our market economy in their effect on the consumer and businessman as well as on product and resource markets.

The Consumer

A *price influences a consumer's decision on whether to make a purchase and how much to purchase.* A price in the United States is stated in dollar terms (prices can also be expressed in pounds, sterling, yen, ounces of tobacco, number of cowry shells, and so on) and represents what you and/or the seller think the article is worth. After viewing, you decide whether to buy or not. We all do this daily. Isn't this what shopping represents?

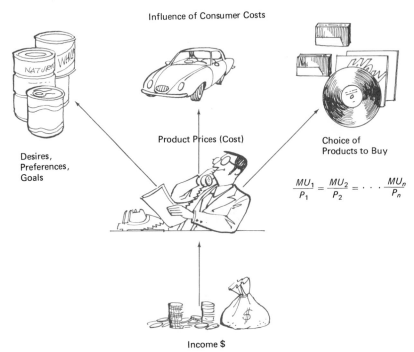

Influence of Consumer Costs

Product Prices (Cost)

Desires,
Preferences,
Goals

Choice of
Products to Buy

$$\frac{MU_1}{P_1} = \frac{MU_2}{P_2} = \cdots = \frac{MU_n}{P_n}$$

Income $

FIG. 3–5. Price affects consumer choice of products.

What does the *worth* of an article mean? Many consumers might agree (do you?) that worth implies the satisfaction derived from the use of the item. How do you go about measuring the satisfaction in dollars and cents or otherwise that you receive from purchasing a record? Although satisfaction is difficult to measure in terms of dollars and cents, all of us, in fact, do just this every time we buy an article. We compare the price of the item with how much satisfaction we would receive from its use, and then we decide to buy or not.

Economists often refer to these consumer satisfaction levels as *utility* and to the additional satisfaction obtained from additional items purchased as *marginal utility* (MU). In their eyes, the "rational" consumer (are you one?) would buy an item if he felt the marginal utility were equal to or greater than the price ($MU \geqslant P$). Of course, each of us places different values on different items, and most of us would tire of the same items after some point. This typical pattern of becoming tired of, or less satisfied by, extra items consumed the economist terms *diminishing marginal utility* (DMU), and it appears as in Figure 3-6. Note that total utility, or satisfaction, may still rise even if marginal utility falls, but would decline if marginal utility became negative.

Let us also not forget our income level when we decide on the purchase of the record. We must weigh not only our satisfaction against price, but also

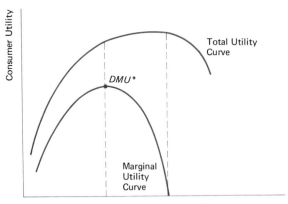

* *DMU*: point at which diminishing marginal utility sets in;
           that is, additional products provide less and less
           added satisfaction.

FIG. 3–6. Typical behavior of consumer utility.

our income level. If you are similar to the authors and to most consumers, your income is limited and will buy only so much. Therefore, when you decide what items to buy, you must take into consideration your income level. When you are making the decision to buy the record or not, you are thinking, "If I buy the record, I can't buy a movie ticket next Saturday night. Is the record or the movie worth more?" Recall the concept of opportunity cost? This really shows the rationing function and decision-making power of a price. Given the price, the consumer balances the satisfaction to be gained from an item against all other possible purchases because of his limited income.

Price affects the income of the consumer. Suppose your wage (a price in the resource market) is $5 an hour. If you work 40 hours a week, your weekly income is $200. If your wage is $10 an hour, your week's work brings in $400. Clearly $400 per week, rather than $200 per week, makes some difference in your purchasing decisions. (See the following sections from the businessman's point of view, if you are bothered by a price being assigned your labor.)

You may well be asking the causes for these wage differences and rightly so. As a simple answer, we'll point to market forces of demand and supply and expand on this in following chapters. Really, though, the higher wage is performing a guiding function in that it signals this labor service is of greater value to society, and it provides incentives to you to upgrade your skill. Yes, there may be market causes (labor unions, discrimination, government, custom, and so on) for wage differences also, and we'll attempt to analyze these later, too.

Price also helps to make decisions in the resource market. What career to choose? Suppose the $5 per hour wage (price) is the current rate for an auto mechanic, and the $10 per hour is for an engineer. Would this price difference influence your decision? (Of course, in your choice of a career you must also consider the expenses of education and your own abilities and interests.) The point is that a price affects the consumer's decisions in the resource market as well as the product market. Price acts as in a rationing function in the product market and as a guiding function in the resource market to the consumer; thus it is vitally important daily.

The Businessman

In the preceding pages we saw how a price helps to form consumer decisions in both the resource and product markets. But price also affects the businessman—in both the product and resource markets. Remember that we must consider both the businessman and the consumer in describing how a market works (business and household sectors of the circular-flow model).

The price of the record, from the businessman's point of view, helps to form his decision "Should I produce, or not? If so, how much?" This decision is important because the businessman gets his gross income from the number of items he sells multiplied by the prices at which he sells these products. At a higher price the businessman may decide to produce a new line of products or to produce more products of an old line. Furthermore, new competitors may enter the market.

Notice, we say *may* decide to produce more items. The qualification is that the businessman wants the highest profits possible, and *profit equals income* (total revenue) *minus costs* (total costs). It could happen that a high income would not be most profitable, if costs are also very high. Which of the choices offered in Figure 3-7 would you prefer, as a businessman? The "rational" businessman, like the "rational" consumer maximizing total utility, would surely choose two items of output for a maximum total profit of $2.

How do we figure costs of operation? The cost of producing a record is the total expense involved in hiring the singers (number $\times$ price = total wages), using plastics and other materials for records (amount $\times$ price = raw ma-

FIG. 3–7. Price affects business decisions.

Output	Price	Total Revenue (Price X Quantity)	Total Cost	Profit (Loss)
1	$5	$5	$4	$1
2	4	8	6	2
3	3	9	8	1
4	2	8	10	(2)

terials cost), using machinery and buildings (number $\times$ price = capital costs), and necessary return to investors or stockholders (profits). Therefore, the prices of these factors of production are involved in computing costs. Consider the many separate costs involved in producing the modern (well, maybe it's not too modern) automobile you own, and you see the complex business decision process of Figure 3-8.

Thus, we see that price, in both the product and resource market, also affects the businessman's decisions: Shall I produce? How much shall I produce? How much labor, natural resources, capital, and managerial talent should I use? The businessman wants maximum profits, profits are equal to income minus costs, and prices are involved in computing both income and costs. Also note that prices guide the businessman in producing preferred consumer items in the product market and ration his resource purchases in the resource market.

FIG. 3–8. Prices (product and resource) affect business decisions.

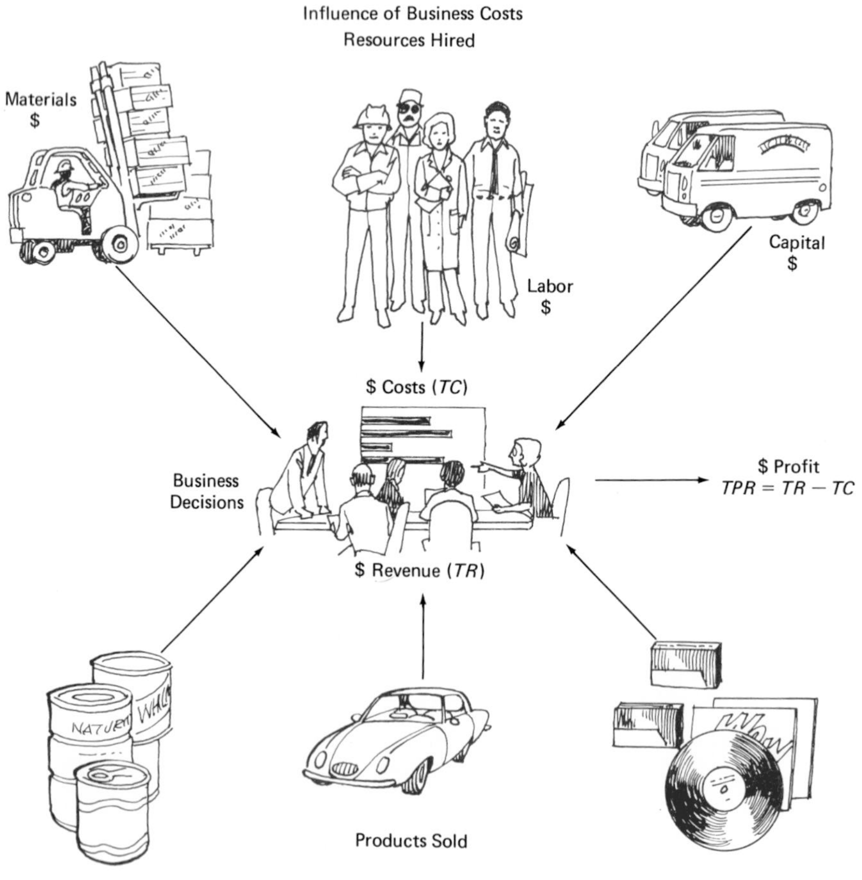

Influence of Business Costs
Resources Hired

Materials $

Labor $

Capital $

$ Costs (*TC*)

Business Decisions

$ Profit
$TPR = TR - TC$

$ Revenue (*TR*)

Products Sold

Summary: The Consumer and the Businessman— Markets and Prices

The U.S. economy consists of many markets, some exchanging products and some exchanging resources for money. There are prices in these markets for both products and resources, and these prices form a basis for decisions made by consumers and businessmen. Product prices ration whether or not and how much the consumer buys and basically guide the type and level of business output. Resource prices determine income levels, guide career choices of consumers, and ration the kinds and amounts of resources the businessman may use to produce his output.

To summarize these price functions by consumer-businessman and product-resource markets:

1. Product prices have a
   a. Rationing effect on consumers, who get maximum satisfaction by choosing among goods on the basis of price.
   b. Guiding effect on businessmen, who get maximum profit by producing those goods with highest prices.

2. Resource prices have a
   a. Rationing effect on businessmen, who get maximum profit by combining resources with lowest prices (minimum cost of production).
   b. Guiding effect on households, which get maximum income by choice of highest-priced job.

This may sound complicated, but these functions are continually performed by prices quite naturally and simply. Perhaps the most important point is that if prices were not there, some other guiding and rationing mechanism would have to be devised by society. Choices must be made (by consumers, by businesses, and by society as a whole), and in a market system prices function daily as essential choice makers. Again, as a good "thought exercise," try to imagine these same choices being made in the U.S. economy without our prices: How would the process go on?

By the way, we've not answered whether all such prices are "fair"—and do not intend to! Frankly, there is no objective definition or answer as to what a "fair" price might be, though economists since St. Thomas Aquinas (1225–1274; still the only "economist" ever to reach sainthood) have argued its appropriateness. The satisfaction, or utility, I receive from a good is different from yours, and businessmen differ in cost efficiency; so fairness may be a vague goal most difficult to define. Going even further, the authors, in line with many other economists, suspect that government bureaucrats cannot define a "fair" price and that the bureaucrats are, therefore, ill-suited to design or administer an equitable or efficient price-control mechanism. We really doubt that frequent government intervention solves many market imperfections.

PRICES AND THE BASIC QUESTIONS

After seeing how both consumer and businessman are affected by prices in both the product and resource markets, let's now try a review of prices and society's choices in general. Recall from Chapter 2 that all societies have to make choices—give answers—of what to produce, how to produce, and for whom to produce. In a market system, prices are a central mechanism in making these choices. Let's examine each of these questions again, emphasizing the role of prices.

What to produce is basically answered in a market economy according to what people will buy. Thus, the high and profitable prices of desired products (homes, compact cars, TVs, for example) guide businessmen to produce these items. Of course, there is some government regulation of what to produce, and the tax rate might be viewed as the price of producing social goods and services. (In 1975 taxes represented the fastest rising consumer "price" of all consumer items!)

How to produce is affected by prices rationing resources to those businesses most able to utilize and profit from them. As the businessman seeks a profit, he attempts to combine those resources and those production methods that are most profitable and is thus guided by prices to maximum efficiency. (Recall the "invisible hand" concept of Adam Smith?) The consumer is also guided by these resource prices into those occupations most rewarding to him or her. Again, government intervention may regulate production methods as a nonprice influence.

The question of for whom to produce involves the rationing effect of prices on the consumer in that if you want and can afford to buy the item, it's yours. Notice that the resource price (wage) guides consumer occupational choice in the resource market and rations consumer product choice in the product market. Government also intervenes to affect income levels, and thus consumer choice ability, with minimum wages, social goods, or welfare payments.

In all of these questions, carefully review the central role of product and resource prices in our society's choice-making process. There are certainly nonprice forces at work, but the role of prices is essential in a market economy.

PRICE DETERMINATION

The discussion thus far should have convinced you that prices are pretty important in our market economy and that they affect you daily. Because prices are such a vital mechanism in the way our economic system answers the basic questions (recall Chapter 2), we shall briefly outline how prices are determined, to return to the issue in detail in Chapters 4-6.

Type of Price	Function of Price	Example of Price Operation
Product	Ration	A person cannot afford an item.
Product	Guide	Businesses produce items most profitable.
Resource	Ration	A business hires the cheapest resource.
Resource	Guide	A person chooses a career of highest wage.

FIG. 3–9. Prices guide and ration to answer basic economic questions.

Basically, product and resource prices are the result of supply-demand forces in the product and resource markets. Demand represents buyers' willingness to buy products or resources, and supply represents what sellers will take for those products or resources. (Remember that in the product market businesses supply and consumers demand products, whereas in the resource market businesses demand and consumers supply resources.) The actual market price is, then, a compromise of supply and demand, in which buyer and seller agree to exchange money for products and resources. Prices, therefore, change if there are changes in either the supply or demand forces.

So much for an overall survey of market operation. Much more about the process is presented in Chapters 4–6, but let us first review the makeup of supply and demand in both the product and resource markets, and, second, look at other factors that also play a role in price determination.

Product Market

When we speak of a product market, we are talking about the exchange of money for goods or services consumers wish to purchase. *Supply* means "the amounts of such goods and services for sale at various prices: *demand* means what consumers will buy at various prices." Remember, we're talking about markets for all sorts of products, from double-knits to tanks, from haircuts to a college education, and from John Denver records to fine wine.

On the demand side of the product market we have four buyer categories: *consumers* (consumer goods), *government* (demands resources to supply social goods), *business* (capital goods), and *foreign* (export goods). All these groups are deeply concerned with prices. You, a consumer, want a car, and the federal government (Defense Department) contracts for jet planes. A business will buy a drill press, and a foreign country will purchase American wheat and lumber. The point is that all these groups want a variety of things; thus, we can speak of many different demands in many separate product markets. Do you see the difference between saying demand and product market in an overall sense, but further analyzing the specific demands in specific markets?

By the way, this breakdown of product demands is also followed in the calculation of *gross national product* (GNP), a much-referred-to statistic we'll discuss further in Chapter 12. Note this carrythrough in Figure 3-10 and projected demand levels for the U.S. economy in 1976.

On the supply side, businesses sell all sorts of goods and services. Some firms sell only to one group (for example, a barber or a hamburger stand sells only to individual consumers), and others sell to many groups (GM makes cars for consumers, produces machinery for businesses, contracts for

FIG. 3–10. Total demand in product market.

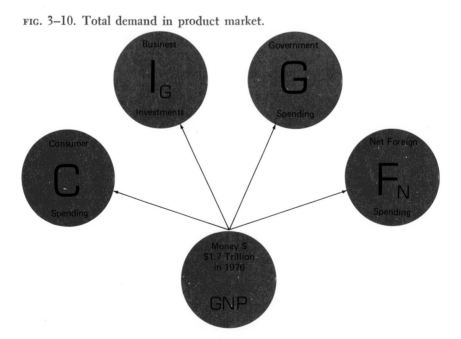

jet engines sold to the federal government, and sells construction machinery to foreign countries). Some firms are small and operate only in one location with a single product, whereas others are huge and sell a great variety of products worldwide. Again, what we're doing here is specifying certain supplies and markets within the overall idea of supply and the product market.

There is one additional point we wish to make about supply in the product market: Some items are supplied from government agencies. For example, the state of California (through its legislature) provides its populace with an extensive public college and university system. Ordinarily, we'd term this a social good (demanded by government; paid for by taxes), but it also constitutes supply of a certain service consumed (used) by the public. Of course, many of the supplies and facilities needed to operate this educational system are purchased by the state from private businesses. But the education supply, or product, itself is from the state. In this same category are the federal government's national defense establishment and local government police and fire services.

Resource Market

Now, let's look at the other side of our economy. You can't produce goods and services without resources, and you know as a consumer that you can't buy products without an income. You also remember that in resource markets the roles are reversed, with buyers (demand) being businesses and sellers (supply) yourself, labor.

On the demand side of the resource market, we have many types and sizes of business firms hiring labor; purchasing raw materials; contracting for machinery; and hiring managers, supervisors, and executives. A large firm, such as GM, may hire 825,000 or more employees (1975), whereas the single-owner hamburger stand, in effect, hires only the proprietor himself. The largest employer of all (some 16 million employees in 1976) is government at all levels.

On the supply side we have you and more than 93 million other Americans in our labor force (1976) standing in line for a paycheck. The amount of hours and acceptable pay rates you and others will work for is, in fact, the supply of labor. (This labor supply will be determined by consumer abilities and preferences, as well as by labor union negotiations and government labor legislation.) In addition, your savings (in banks, savings and loans, and so on) may be used by businesses in buying their capital stock; so you indirectly provide capital stock and receive interest payments in return. Thus, your decisions to consume or save affect the supply of loanable funds (savings) for capital stock uses. The dividends you may receive from stocks or the salary of an independent businessman represents a profit return to you for the management resource you've supplied to the business. If you've received rent or other payment from businesses, you've contributed to the supply of raw materials. In each of these supply roles, the consumer has affected the supply of factors of production (economic resources).

Again, notice we can speak here in overall terms of resource supply and demand, and then specify the specific supplies and markets about which we are talking. For example, the authors are trained as economists and would probably be hired only by businesses, government agencies, or colleges demanding such skills. You probably possess, or are in college to acquire, quite different job skills (how many students in your class work full- or part-time right now?) to supply to business firms or government employers. Can you see that your decisions affect resource supplies? Do resource prices affect your career choices?

Does this discussion aid in bringing supply, demand, and price relationships more into focus? You, the consumer, are on the demand side of product markets and are a supply force in resource markets. The businessman or government agency is a supplier in the product market and is on the demand side in resource markets. Together, *consumer and business decisions constitute the supply-demand market forces* to determine resource and product forces. These decisions also constitute the answers to our basic questions. Review Figure 3-11 to put all of this in perspective.

Other Price-Determining Factors

We have talked extensively about the effect of supply and demand in determining prices. But we also mentioned that *government regulations on supply and demand forces in the product and resource markets have an im-*

FIG. 3–11. Market forces determine answers to the basic questions in the U.S. economy.

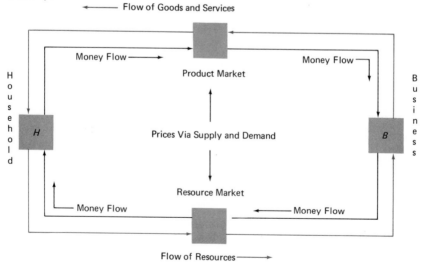

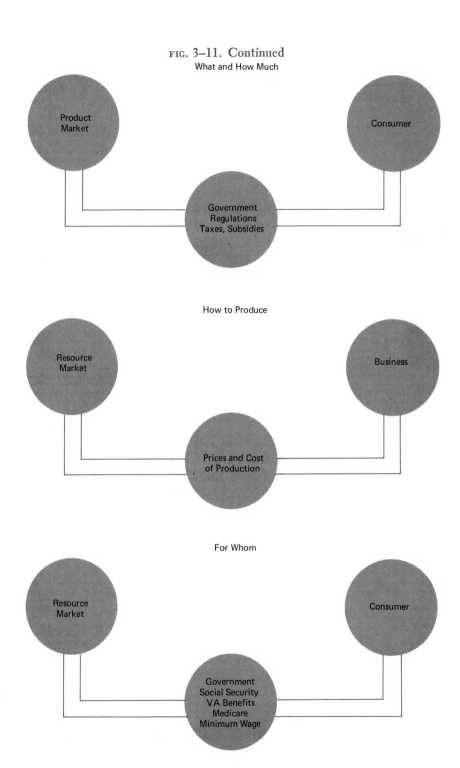

FIG. 3–11. Continued

What and How Much

How to Produce

For Whom

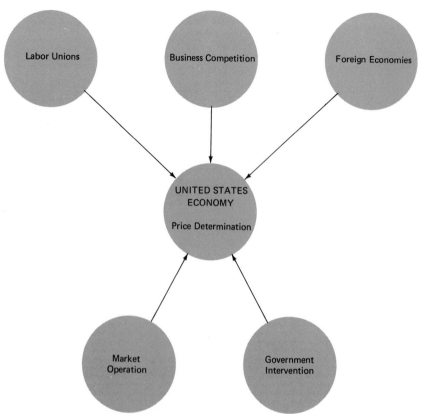

FIG. 3–12. Nonmarket forces also affect prices in the U.S. economy.

pact on price determination. Still other influences at work in the marketplace affect price determination. Among these are competition and labor unions, which exert additional pressures on some prices in some markets.

To get an idea of what we're saying, let's look at the American car market. There are many models and types of cars available at widely differing prices. The demand side is you, the consumer, wanting transportation (plus, perhaps, the status, independence, and so on, that a car implies) with your own preferences for make and model. The supply comes from four domestic manufacturers and a variety of foreign car imports sold through local dealers. The product marketplace is actually you in the dealer's showroom dickering over the sales price!

In this typical situation, price is determined basically by supply-demand forces. Of course, there's not any one price for a car, as there are so many different makes, models, styles, and so on. (Advertisements for one brand once noted that they could supply 2 million different cars!) You can talk of the consumer demand for so many cars as certain prices realizing that this demand really subdivides into demand for each brand and type of car, all determined by consumer preference and income levels. Reference can also be made to the business supply of so many cars at certain prices, again realizing this supply is obtained by adding up domestic and foreign manufacturers output.

One could even analyze the supply of, and demand for, used cars, but that would represent an entirely different car market. Perhaps federal, state, and local government car purchase should be added to the demand side, as a recent proposal would have the 12 million federal government car fleet replaced in 1975–1976 as aid to the ailing auto industry! Still, in all of these market details, supply and demand forces determine car prices, with you and the car salesman agreeing on the final one-to-one compromise.

Now let's consider some other factors that also influence price. On the demand side, your own willingness to buy and the price eventually paid are influenced by *advertising* (buy to "save gas" or join the "smart and sexy" or whatever). Your income level, upon which your ability to pay is based, may depend on *minimum wage rates* or *labor union contracts* specifying your wage. A federal government *income tax* rebate may spur your buying interest, and reduced *interest rates* (with encouragement by Federal Reserve Board policies) may aid your decision. These factors and others indirectly affect price by influencing your desire and ability to purchase (demand).

On the supply side there are also other factors. The supply (amount, price) itself is affected by the *degree of competition* existing in the car market; that is, fewer and larger firms may tend to make prices more similar, though outright price agreements are prosecuted under *antitrust laws*. Perhaps a good example of existing competition is the effort by U.S. producers to design a small car to compete with *foreign imports* in size. The manufacturers' rebates on new car purchases and emphasis on gasoline economy represent a renewed interest in price and nonprice competition.

The prices at which these cars can be sold by the manufacturers depend on costs of production and resource prices. Thus, labor union contracts, minimum wage laws, and pollution and safety standards may all affect the selling price by having an effect on *production costs*. Furthermore, the cost of transporting the cars to your area is affected by federal railway subsidies and rate regulations, state truck license fees, route and rate regulations, and the local dealers' taxes and local business permit charges. (If the city government doesn't grant a zoning permit and business license, you won't even have a car dealer!)

Does the determination of prices sound complicated and confusing? Well, this example was meant to give a full illustration of what is involved in any market (cars, homes, records, and so on) in determining price. In almost all markets, product as well as resource, we'll have supply and demand forces from sellers and buyers, but these forces will themselves be influenced by the other factors noted. We'll talk more about each of these factors in later chapters, but here we summarize the more important factors present in many markets:

1. Indirect price effects, through effect on supply-demand conditions:
   a. Demand. Advertising (desire to buy), labor unions (income), minimum wages (income), welfare funds (income).
   b. Supply. Safety and pollution standards (costs), wage laws (costs), labor unions (costs), degree of competition (amount for sale, variety, prices charged), antitrust laws (price agreements), business income taxes and license charges (costs).

2. Direct price effects, through prices set by regulation:
   a. Minimum prices set by minimum wage laws, "fair trade" laws, state control boards (liquor, haircuts, milk).
   b. Prices directly set through public utility commissions at state level or plane, rail, and fuel charges approved by federal agencies.

Perhaps the best exercise to further your economic understanding is to take any market of particular interest to you (records, cars, your own job, and so on) for study. Write down all factors (supply, demand, other—direct or indirect) that seem to bear on the prices actually charged. You might find there's a lot behind that little sticker price!

PRICES IN OTHER ECONOMIC SYSTEMS

We have gone to great lengths in this chapter to describe the importance of prices in our U.S. market economy. Prices are at the heart of our economic system, and in performing their guiding and rationing functions they affect all of us in answers they provide to the basic economic questions.

We wish to note at this point (review Chapter 2) that prices also exist in many other economic systems, but sometimes serve different functions. If a country has, as the United States does, a market-oriented economy (such as those of Japan, France, and Germany) with limited government intervention, price serves both the rationing and guiding functions. However, in a country with a command-type economic system, price may not serve the guiding function. If a great deal of government intervention exists and centralized government agencies determine what shall be produced rather than let the marketplace make these decisions, price does not serve the guiding function. What to produce is not determined by consumer demand, market prices, business profits, or supply responses, but by some agency such as a central five-year plan. In this case, prices may serve only a rationing function to allocate what is available.

Before you judge such differences as right or wrong, remember we're talking about different economic systems; that is, price does certain things in our economy because of our society's values, traditions, laws, and goals. Different societies, with other values, traditions, laws, and goals go about the allocation of scarce resources in their own manner. It's difficult to judge someone else by your standards instead of theirs.

What we're aiming at here is not judgment but economic understanding: How does their economic system work? Recall that regardless of how a society's economic system operates, it must in some way always answer the basic questions: (1) What and how much to produce? (2) How to produce? (3) Who gets what? Perhaps the best evaluation is how completely any economic system provides answers to these questions.

Perhaps one final illustration is needed to show that the way any system works changes all the time. For example, in America during World War II, prices were fixed by the War Price Administration (WPA), a federal government agency, and a Federal Wage Board-Price Commission control system was instituted by President Nixon from 1971 to 1974 in order to combat inflation. Various proposals (the Liberman Plan) are being tried in the Soviet Union to have factories respond to consumer demand on an incentive basis. (Creeping capitalism?) Furthermore, welfare programs and government intervention have abounded in the United States since the 1930s, and the Soviet Union's five-year plan has allocated increased resources to consumer goods production. It will be interesting to see how both systems are working when your children are studying economics!

TERMS

"Invisible hand." Adam Smith's concept whereby promoting one's self-interest also provides efficiency and productivity for the entire society.

Price. The amount of money necessary to effect the exchange of goods or resources. Prices are really exchange ratios (so many items for so much money).

Product market. The institutional mechanisms by which consumer payments are exchanged for business goods and services.

Profits. The excess of total revenue over total costs, providing business incentive to produce.

Ration. To divide what is available among those who wish the items (one function of price).

Resource market. The institutional mechanisms by which business payments are exchanged for consumer resources.

Utility. Satisfaction resulting from consuming goods or services.

QUESTIONS FOR STUDY

1. Try a lesson in decision making: Suppose you have $10 to spend (income level). Now, walk into a local retail store, or look though a catalog and choose $10 worth of items. Write down why you chose what you did and how you decided to choose that item. (Do you see the rationing function of prices?)

2. What level (high or low) or price do you wish as a consumer in the product market? In the resource market? Now suppose you are a businessman. What level (high or low) of price do you wish in the product market? In the resource market? What conflict of wishes do you see here?

3. If consumers do not purchase standard-sized automobiles in large quantities, what would you predict producers will do? If consumers desire compact, "racy" automobiles, what would you predict American and foreign automobile producers will do? What happened to the convertible? (Do you see the guiding function of prices?)

4. Would auto worker be a "good" career to choose in the late 1970s? Why or why not? Would an engineer's career be a good choice in 1980? Why or why not? What other factors in addition to income affect career choice?

5. What is the directing or *guiding function* of the competitive price system? Contrast the guiding function with the rationing function.

REFERENCES

Heilbroner, Robert L. *The Worldly Philosophers*, Fourth Edition. New York: Simon and Schuster, Inc., 1972. Chapters 1–3.

Radford, R. A. "The Economic Organization of a POW Camp," *Economica* (November 1945), pp. 189–201.

Stigler, George J. *The Theory of Price*, Third Edition. New York: Macmillan Publishing Co., Inc., 1966.

"The U.S. Economy: Special Report," *DuPont Context*. Wilmington, Del: DuPont Company (No. 3), 1973.

Ward, Benjamin. *Elementary Price Theory*. New York: The Free Press, 1967.

4

WHAT IS DEMAND?

SHORT ANSWER. Demand represents the amounts of goods or resources that persons or businesses will buy at different price levels.

A good question to ask yourself in response to the title of this chapter is, "Who cares?" That is, why study the concept of demand to understand economics? After all, isn't demand something you, the consumer, experience daily? And don't you, therefore, understand what it's all about? The authors welcome such a questioning approach throughout this text. For if you are really to understand how our economy works and how it affects you personally, you must constantly try to challenge your understanding. You should relate the concepts and details studied to the big picture of our market-oriented economic system. We wish to convey an understanding of economic theory, not merely put words and graphs in a textbook.

Perhaps a short justification for studying demand, a concept to be explained throughout this chapter, is that we must understand how people choose what to consume if we are to understand how our economic system satisfies those wants. The method by which a market economy makes its choices, especially the *what to produce* question, basically consists of individuals choosing (demanding) those items they feel most desirable. Thus it is your (and other consumers') demand choices and the business response to satisfy such demands that form the basis of our choice-making economic system. Let's see how these choices are made.

YOU AND DEMAND

It is no secret that most of us want almost an unlimited amount of things —cars, clothing, food, a home, stereo tapes, movies, schools, doctors, books, and so on. We all wish to have the highest possible living standard for our-

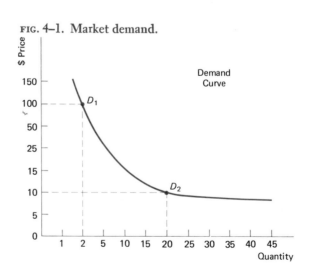

FIG. 4–1. Market demand.

selves and our families. Of course, it is not only Americans who wish to have an abundance of consumer goods, but people the world over. The problem with meeting such wants, as emphasized in Chapter 1, is that no society has sufficient resources to satisfy them all. All societies, therefore, must make choices (answer the basic questions) through their economic systems.

At this beginning point let us not distinguish between an item that is "needed" (must have) or "wanted" (like to have). Obviously, the needs of some people are the wants of others. As an example, you may regard a car as a necessity (need), whereas someone else may view it as a luxury (want). The point is that both wants and needs lead to consumer utility, and thus an economic system regards both categories as consumption items they demand and want to purchase.

Now we arrive at a most important aspect of "choice": What you want and what you will buy may differ greatly. To put it another way, what you will demand depends to a great extent on what it costs. We all know that when we're window-shopping or seriously out to buy an item, the price does make a difference. The reason, of course, is that with a limited income, you want to "get your money's worth" by buying the best item at the lowest price. Therefore, the price of an item is quite important in your buying decision. Do you recall the rationing function of prices from Chapter 3?

We might also note two further aspects of your demand choices—*opportunity cost* and *saving*. The opportunity cost (review Chapter 1) exists because purchasing any one item means you cannot, with the same money, purchase another item; you give up one item by purchasing another. (Isn't this really what you mean when you refer to "shopping for the best deal"?) However, when you do choose to buy, it also means you choose not to save, for you can't do both with the same amount of income. If you choose to save, you choose not to buy. This may sound rather elementary, but it has large implications for our economy:

1. Changes in consumer demand lead to shifts in output, employment, and income as businesses respond to this product market demand.

2. Changes in the proportion of income spent to income saved will lead to shifts in output, employment, and income, for it is spending that stimulates business production. Saving is certainly necessary as a source of business investment funds, but if products are not selling, businesses will seldom invest and expand.

At this point, a somewhat technical note is in order on the consumer choice between spending (demand) and saving. When economists speak of the proportions of income spent or saved, they refer to *average* and *marginal propensities to consume and save*. Although the words may seem a mouthful of picky detail, remember the circular-flow model and the dependence of business output and employee income on spending flows. Given that consumer

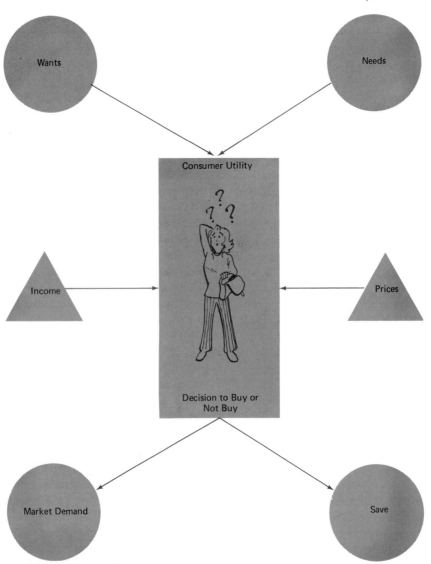

FIG. 4–2. Consumer demand decision.

disposable income (amount left after taxes) in 1976 was $975 billion, per-
haps you see why a small percentage change to spend or save is so important.
Let's try, then, to define these terms a bit more and give a few examples:

1. *Average propensity to consume* (APC = C/DI) is the percentage
   of disposable income spent on final goods and services. At present,
   this averages 93 per cent at all income levels, tending to be greater
   at low income levels and lesser at high income levels.

2. *Average propensity to save* (APS = S/DI) is the percentage of

disposable income not spent on final goods and services. At present, this averages 7 per cent at all income levels, tending to be lesser at low income levels and greater at high income levels.

3. *Marginal propensity to consume* ($MPC = \Delta C/\Delta DI$) is the percentage of change in spending resulting from changes in disposable income (at present, some 66 per cent at all income levels). If your spending increases by $8 when your income rises by $10, your MPC is 80 per cent. As an example, how much did you spend from your 1976 tax rebate?

4. *Marginal propensity to save* ($MPS = \Delta S/\Delta DI$) is the percentage of change in saving resulting from changes in disposable income (at present, some 34 per cent at all income levels). If your saving increases by $2 when your income rises by $10, your MPC is 20 per cent.

By the way, did you notice above that $APC + APS = 100\%$ and $MPC + MPS = 100\%$? Yes, that always happens, for the consumer either spends his income or saves it; so the total must be 100 per cent of his income. To make sure you've got this important demand choice concept, try the tables (termed *Consumption Schedule* and *Saving Schedule*) in Figure 4-3 to test your understanding. We've listed various possible levels of consumer disposable income and various possible spending and saving levels at those income levels and have computed the resulting APC, APS, MPC, and MPS. Do you see how we computed the propensities? What would your own be?

FIG. 4–3. Consumption and savings schedules.

Consumption Schedule

Disposable Income	Consumption	Average Propensity to Consume (*APC*)	Marginal Propensity to Consume (*MPC*)
$100	$120	1.2 or 120%	.8 or 80%
200	200	1.0 or 100%	.67 or 67%
500	400	.8 or 80%	

Saving Schedule

Disposable Income	Saving	Average Propensity to Save (*APS*)	Marginal Propensity to Save (*MPS*)
$100	$−20	−.2 or −20%	.2 or 20%
200	0	.0 or 0%	.33 or 33%
500	100	.2 or 20%	

We have said little new thus far. You all know prices are important and that they limit and help to determine what you will buy. And you know, you divide your income between spending and saving. There is, however, another major consideration because this close tie of what and how much people buy in relation to a price is exactly what the word *demand* means to the economist. When the economist speaks of your demand for, say, a shirt, he's talking about the number of shirts you'd buy at various prices. In Figure 4-4 an example of this logic is given by relating price and quantity.

A word about schedules and graphs: they are not meant to confuse you, but only to illustrate concisely what we have been talking about. Figure 4-4 shows that at different prices you would buy different amounts: four shirts at $1, two shirts at $5, and none when the price is $10. (Do you note here the tendency to buy more items at low prices and fewer items at high prices? Is this the way you would act?) Although you may not think of this purchasing process in exactly these terms of buying more at the lower price when you go shopping, it does represent how you'd choose to spend your income at these prices.

DEMAND BEHAVIOR PATTERNS

The *Demand Schedule* of Figure 4-4 deserves close study by the student and further analysis, for it suggests a number of economic theories regarding consumer behavior. Note first that demand to the economist means a

FIG. 4–4. Consumer demand schedule.

You   Shirt

Demand Schedule

Price	Quantity Demanded
$10	0
8	1
5	2
3	3
1	4

buying behavior pattern—how much will be purchased at various prices; that is, the economist includes various quantities demanded at various prices within his definition of demand because people do buy different amounts at different prices.

Because people buy different quantities at different prices, two further economic theories are suggested by study of Figure 4-4—the *law of demand* and *price elasticity of demand*. Notice in Figure 4-4 that quantity demanded falls when price rises, but quantity demanded rises when price falls. Such an opposite, or *inverse*, relationship of quantity demanded and price is observed so generally that economists term this pattern the *law of demand*. Although a few exceptions may exist (snob appeal, expectation of future price changes, impulse buying, and so forth), this demand behavior pattern usually exists.

Price elasticity (E_D is the symbol used to designate this concept) is a slightly more complex behavior pattern, but also relates to the change in quantity demanded resulting from price changes. Remember that the Law of Demand states that price and quantity demanded are inversely related. Price elasticity quantifies this relationship by measuring exactly how much quantity demanded varies (percentage change) when price varies (percentage change); that is, price elasticity (E_D) equals the percentage change in quantity demanded ($\%\Delta Q_D$) divided by the percentage change in price

($\%\Delta P$), or $E_D = \%\Delta Q_D \div \%\Delta P$.

"So who cares about E_D?"—a perhaps valid challenge by the student, but worth study effort, we feel. Use of the E_D concept may predict changes in sales revenue, estimate unemployment effects, and evaluate the desirability of government intervention in the marketplace. If that news whets your intellectual appetite, let's add a few more details to the concept of price elasticity.

1. First, you should be able to calculate the numerical value of E_D. In Figure 4-5, notice the E_D calculated from data in Figure 4-4. (Polish your fractions a bit?)

2. When the E_D exceeds 1, it is termed an *elastic* demand, which means that people are quite responsive to price changes. But if E_D is less than 1, we have an *inelastic* demand, which means that people do not respond greatly to price changes. Of course, if the buyer response just equals the price change, the E_D will equal 1, and we have a condition of *unitary elastic* demand.

3. There is an inverse (opposite direction) relationship between price and sales revenue (total revenue, *TR*, equals the number sold times price) when demand is elastic, but a direct (same direction) relationship of price and sales revenue when demand is inelastic.

Demand Schedule		Elasticity (E_d)	Sales Revenue Impact			
Price	Quantity Demanded		Total Revenue	= Price $\times$ Quantity Demanded		
$10	0	9	$ 0	= $10 $\times$	0	
8	1	$1\frac{4}{9}$	8	= 8 $\times$	1	
5	2	$\frac{4}{5}$	10	= 5 $\times$	2	
3	3	$\frac{2}{7}$	9	= 3 $\times$	3	
1	4		4	= 1 $\times$	4	

$$E_D = \left|\frac{\% \Delta Q_D}{\% \Delta P_D}\right| = \left|\frac{\dfrac{Q_{D_2} - Q_{D_1}}{Q_{D_2} + Q_{D_1}}}{\dfrac{P_{D_2} - P_{D_1}}{P_{D_2} + P_{D_1}}}\right|$$

Elasticity Computations:

$$\frac{1 - 0 \,/\, 1 + 0}{8 - 10 / \, 8 + 10} = \frac{1}{1/9} = 9$$

$$\frac{2 - 1 \,/\, 2 + 1}{5 - 8 / \, 5 + 8} = \frac{1/3}{3/13} = 1\frac{4}{9}$$

$$\frac{3 - 2 \,/\, 3 + 2}{3 - 5 / \, 3 + 5} = \frac{1/5}{1/4} = \frac{4}{5}$$

$$\frac{4 - 3 \,/\, 4 + 3}{1 - 3 / \, 1 + 3} = \frac{1/7}{1/2} = \frac{2}{7}$$

FIG. 4–5. Price elasticity.

Verify this for yourself from Figure 4-5. Do you see that sales revenue would not change if a unitary elastic demand existed?

If you've mastered the price elasticity concept by now, you can use such economic understanding to make a few predictions:

1. Should a businessman have a sale (reduce price) in a market of elastic demand, his sales revenue would rise, but it would fall if demand were inelastic.
   a. What would happen to sales revenue if he raised prices in an elastic or inelastic demand market (elastic—fall; inelastic—rise)?
   b. Do you see the value of responsive consumers to keep businesses competitive in pricing?

2. Tax revenues (amounts to a price increase) are maximized, bring in the most money, by taxing a product of inelastic demand.

3. Government intervention, such as price controls, minimum wages,

and so on, have greater impact upon quantity demanded when the demand is elastic.

4. Elastic demand is promoted when consumers see many available *substitutes,* when the product's price is a large part of their budget, and when they thoughtfully consider their purchases. How elastic, for example, is your demand for gasoline or shirts or salt or milk or any other item?

There are a few further points to make concerning demand behavior patterns; *determinants of demand* and *market demand.* Determinants of demand refer to the basic factors influencing the consumer's buying behavior; that is, why certain quantities are demanded at certain prices. Because of your income, tastes, sex, age, family or peer-group background, expectations, goals, or whatever else motivates your behavior, you will buy so much of an item at a given price. However, your income, tastes, and so forth, are not identical to those of other consumers (nor even the same for yourself over time—your demand may change). So it's no surprise that at the same prices for the same shirts different people buy different amounts.

Now if we add together the amounts of an item you and all other consumer buy, an economist comes up with what he terms a *market demand* for that item, that is, the amounts all people would buy of this item at various prices. In Figure 4-12 we represent the idea of "adding together" what all people want of some product, constructing a market demand schedule and then a "picture" (another way to look at a graph) of that schedule. Do you see how your choices, combined with those of all other consumers in a general market demand, constitute society's answer to the question of what to produce?

If we now wish to go beyond the consumer's demand for any one product to all the demands of all the economy's sectors (consumer, government, business, foreign) for goods and services, we have an even more expanded concept of market demand. Now we're talking of *gross national product,* or GNP. This is the total market demand (termed *aggregate demand*) for all goods and services by all sectors and is what really provides the market economic system with an answer for the *what to produce question.* (See our economy in action via Figure 4-6?)

In reviewing all we've said thus far about demand, do you see any importance to it? After all, you may say, who cares about the amounts you and others would buy and how much you are willing to pay for them? Well, the businessman, for one, is most interested in what and how much you will buy and what you'll pay for it, for he wants to make a profit. To do so, he must supply (Chapter 5) what you want, when you want it, and at prices you will pay, or there will be another "Out of Business" sign hanging up! If you can see the importance of businesses responding to your consumer spending, you will probably realize the importance of talking here about demand. Your demand choices affect business output—hence the mechanism and answer

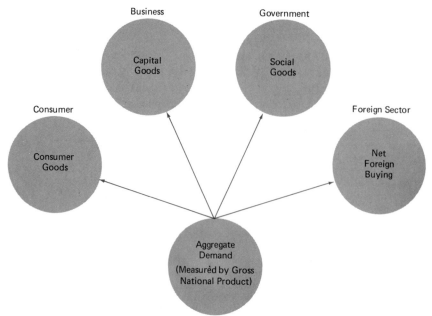

FIG. 4–6. Total market demand (gross national product).

for the question of what to produce. Perhaps you now begin to understand in greater detail how a market-oriented system works?

BUSINESS AND DEMAND

Jumping now to the other side of our circular-flow model—to the business firm—we will look at what demand means to the businessman. We have said that your demand as a consumer is important to a businessman because it tells him how much he can sell to you. In order to supply your *product demand*, the business must purchase resources, thus creating *resource demand*. In our market-oriented economy, therefore, we always speak of two basic types of demands, the *consumers' demand for products and services* and *businesses' demand for resources* to produce those products. Look at Figure 4-8 to see this idea.

Do you see that business resource demand depends upon (is generated by) consumer product demand? Do you also see that the business resource demand generates consumer income, thus providing the basis for consumer product demand? And do you then see how business depends on the consumer and the consumer on the business firm?

Take as an example consumers' demand for automobiles, which amounted

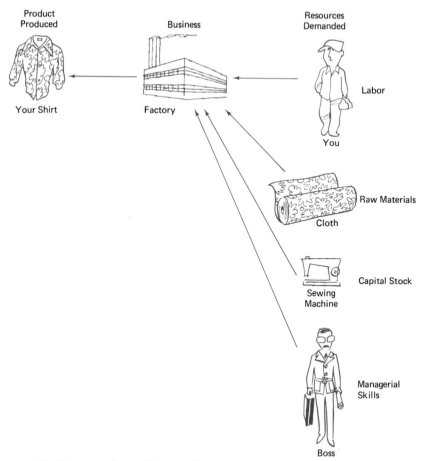

FIG. 4–7. Resource demand for product output.

in 1976 to some 10 million cars of all shapes and sizes sold at a great variety of prices. To produce those cars, the auto manufacturers demanded resources, and the demand for resources to produce an automobile gets pretty complicated when you think about what's involved in putting a car together. As Figure 4-9 shows, just the demand for raw materials alone is a big order. The auto manufacturers demand these products—iron, glass, chemicals, rubber, and so on—from other companies and then assemble them.

Beyond these *natural resources*, the auto companies demand the *capital stock* required to assemble the cars (factory buildings, tools, and machinery). They also demand (employ) *labor* to use the tools and materials in assembly, to design the cars, and to maintain the factories and other capital stock. These companies demand *managerial skills* of people to coordinate the entire operation. The sum of all is quite a process, and all in response to your buy-

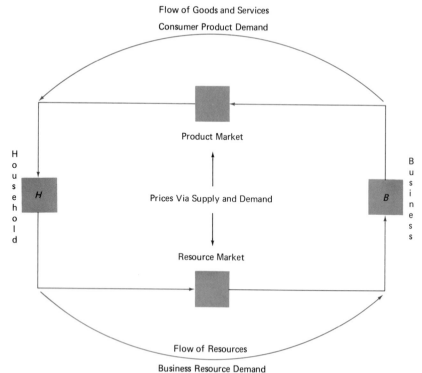

FIG. 4–8. Consumer product demand and business resource demand.

ing a new car! Also realize that each of these demands generates consumer income of various types:

1. Hiring of natural resources provides rental income.

2. Hiring of labor resources provides wage income.

3. Hiring of capital stock (actually consumer savings) resources provides interest income.

4. Hiring of management resources provides profit income.

Remember that a business demands these resources to produce and make a profit in the same way you demand products for your satisfaction. Just as your choices are limited by your income and are influenced by prices, so is the business demand for resources. These resources used by businesses also have a price. Five dollars an hour is wage income to you, but it is also a resource price—a cost of production—to the businessman. What the businessman must do is hire these resources and then sell the resulting products in such amounts and at such prices as to make a profit. It is indeed a complicated process, and those businesses unable to cope with this process usually fail.

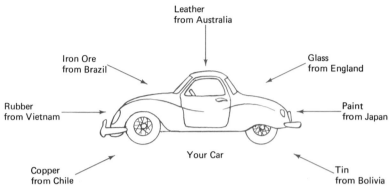

Leather
from Australia

Iron Ore
from Brazil

Glass
from England

Rubber
from Vietnam

Paint
from Japan

Your Car

Copper
from Chile

Tin
from Bolivia

FIG. 4–9. Raw material resource demand.

The complicated process of business decision making, demanding resources, and supplying products for profit is important not only to the individual businessman, but also to our entire economy. When determining the best method (least cost for greater profit) to combine resources in production, each businessman is contributing answers to the basic question of how to produce in our economic system. In other words, the overall society choice for how to produce is, in fact, provided by "adding up" all the 14 million business firms' choices regarding resource demand. Just as the individual consumer demand for products contributes to the question of what to produce, the individual business demand for resources contributes to the question of how to produce. Does this now all tie together for your economic understanding?

There's much more to be said about profit and loss of business firms, and we will do so in Chapters 5, 7, and 8. But for now let us get back to the demand for resources.

As you demand different products (see Figure 4-1), the businessman demands many resources at varying prices. As an example, think back to the shirt you demanded in the product market (Figure 4-4). In producing that shirt, the business firm demands resources in varying amounts depending on the prices of the resources. (See Figure 4-10.) Again, you'll note that business hires fewer resources at high prices, and more at lower prices, just as you do in the product market. Thus, we can apply our previous concepts of *law of demand* and *price elasticity* to business resource demand (total wages fall or rise as prices change rather than sales revenue). We may speak of *determinants of resource demand*, including cost of production, prices of substitute resources, profit expectations, competition, and government regulation.

Just as we added together all consumers like yourself to get a total *product market demand* (Figure 4-12), we can "add together" all business demands to get a *resource market demand* (Figure 4-13). You may asks yourself at this time, "So?" Remember that the business demand for resources creates your job, which gives you an income. In turn, your earnings enable you to purchase

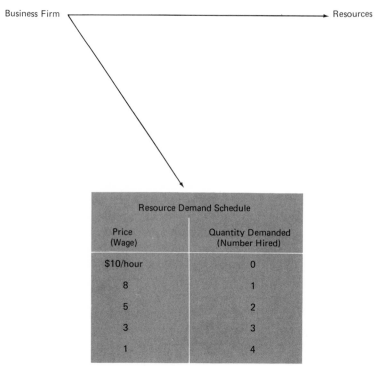

Business Firm ———————————————→ Resources

Resource Demand Schedule

Price (Wage)	Quantity Demanded (Number Hired)
$10/hour	0
8	1
5	2
3	3
1	4

FIG. 4–10. Business demand for resources.

the goods you want. In fact, you should begin to realize that this very important concept (employment theory in Chapter 12) is basically what makes our market economy tick:

1. Business firms want a profit and so produce what consumers buy. Business product supply depends on consumer product demand.

2. Business firms demand resources to produce products. Thus, business resource demand really depends on consumer product demand.

3. Consumer income results from resource demand by business firms. Thus, consumer product demand depends on business resource demand.

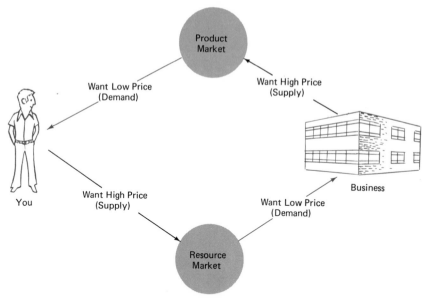

FIG. 4–11. Product demand and resource demand are interdependent.

Can you see an interdependence in these points? Look at Figure 4-11 to review these statements.

SUMMARIZING DEMAND

We have said a great deal about demand thus far, so let's "pull it all together" by referring again to Figure 4-11. On the one hand, we have in our market-oriented economic system a demand for goods and services that you and other consumers desire. This market force is called *product demand* (sold in the product market), and it simply refers to the amounts of these items you would buy if certain prices were tagged on them. This demand depends on your income, desires, goals, and so on. Remember, business firms are very interested in these demands (*market research* is the field that studies these demands), for they provide the sales that generate profits. On the other hand, business firms also have a demand, but it is for resources (factors of production) needed to produce goods and services. These demands, termed *resource demand* (bought in the resource market), determine the amounts of resources businesses will hire at various prices. Resource demand depends on the businesses' costs and sales of production, type of production technique, and so on. The consumer, of course, is also very interested in these resource demands, for they provide employment and income. Furthermore, this income arising from business demand for resources generates consumer demand for products. Do you see the interdependence?

Of course, all we've talked about here are demands for products and resources. It's probably obvious that we'll also have to talk about *supply*, both for products and resources. You must have supply if you're really going to "satisfy" demands. We will talk about supply in Chapter 5, but remember to keep referring to this chapter, as demand and supply interrelate closely.

We might note another point here (we'll say more in Chapter 6), and that has to do with *conflict* in markets. The idea is that you, as a consumer, wish to buy products at low prices, and at the same time you also wish to receive high prices in your job. The businessman wants high prices for his products yet desires to pay low prices for resources hired. Do you see the conflicting demands here? The marketplace must reconcile these conflicts, so that exchanges take place and demands are satisfied.

DEMAND GRAPHS

There is another way to summarize our discussion of demand, and that is graphically. Some people shy away from graphs as complicated devices, but, in fact, all a graph really does is show a "picture" of certain figures and relationships. All the figures do is specify something you have talked about. Therefore, all we're going to do here is summarize in picture form our verbal discussion of demand. Where we "talked" previously, we'll draw "pictures" now!

First, let's look at Figure 4-12. It shows a schedule of products demanded by various consumers, and we "add up" these charts to get a *product market demand*; that is, we add up the quantities demanded of a particular item at various prices to arrive at the total demand from all buyers at all prices for that item. Nothing new, of course, but let's also draw a "picture" (graph) of each of these charts. A graph has two edges (axes). A point on the graph is determined at the meeting place of two lines formed by drawing one line perpendicular to each axis and from a particular point on that axis's scale. For example, one point on chart 1 and graph 1 would be four shirts purchased at a price of $1. (Recall Figure 4-4?) So you put a point directly above 4 (quantity demanded) and straight over from $1 (price). Now, keep doing this, and you'll have a series of points. Connect all the points, and behold, demand curve 1! You can either (1) talk about consumer demand, (2) use a schedule to specify examples, or (3) draw a graph to visualize these relationships. There's nothing different or magic about any method, but perhaps using all three approaches aids in understanding.

Now do the same thing with resource demand in Figure 4-13; that is, you can show a schedule of a business demand for labor, natural resources, capi-

FIG. 4–12. Product market demand.

Demand₁

You

Price	Quantity
$10	0
8	1
5	2
3	3
1	4

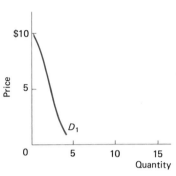

+

Demand₂

Joe

Price	Quantity
$10	1
8	2
5	3
3	4
1	5

+

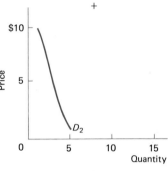

+

Demand₃

Jane

Price	Quantity
$10	2
8	3
5	4
3	5
1	6

‖

+

Demand₁,₂,₃

Consumer
Demand for
Products

Price	Quantity
$10	3
8	6
5	9
3	12
1	15

‖

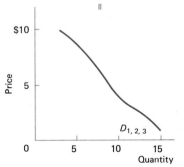

tal stock, and managerial skills and then draw graphs of each. Notice how similar the product and resource demands are?

There is one more "big idea" to discuss, and that relates to what happens when changes occur in product demand or resource demand; that is, when the determinants of consumer demand or business demand change and result in new buying behavior patterns. For consumers do change their spending habits as changes occur in their incomes, desires, goals, or other factors. A businessman may encounter different production costs or a new government regulation or expect different profit results in the future. As an example, if you're laid off work, you may not buy a new car, and you may skip record buying, even if prices in each choice remain unchanged. Or if a businessman discovers a new way to produce a product (would you believe a float method of producing plate glass to eliminate grinding?), he may change his pattern of resource buying. A thought to ponder a minute: Do you see the large changes resulting in our economy since the 1974 increase in crude oil prices by OPEC (Organization of Petroleum Exporting Countries)?

Consumers and businessmen change their minds daily, and this changing modifies product and resource demands. These changes in demand have important effects in our economy in terms of what to produce, how to produce and who gets what. The basic change of consumer demand for more services (haircuts, laundry, all types of recreation, insurance and finance, and so on) has led to other basic changes in how businesses market their products (use of credit cards) and how labor is hired (blue-collar or white-collar workers). It is these changes that lead to a great degree of flexibility within our market system in choice making, yet require the individual consumer and businessman to compete and adjust. It is such changes that provide new or different answers to the fundamental questions. How has the changed degree of U.S. government intervention in the last 40 years affected the for whom to produce question? (Anyone have a case of "future shock" over such changes? Read the book by Alvin Toffler with this same title some time!)

Thus, when the economist speaks of a change in demand, he means far more than just a difference in the quantities demanded if prices change. He is referring to an entirely different set of market attitudes and patterns of spending. He refers more to consumers purchasing steak or eating at restaurants (because of higher incomes) than to buying another pound of hamburger if the price drops 5 cents per pound. In effect, we have a new market behavior.

You may have guessed here that another very important result of changes in demand is that they lead to changes in market price. If consumers do switch from hamburger to steak and restaurants (an increase in demand for steak and restaurants; a decrease in demand for hamburger), this may well cause steak prices to rise and restaurant bills to increase, whereas hamburger prices will tend to fall. Over time this may create additional new businesses to produce steak and new restaurants, and restaurants specializing in hambugers may go out of business.

To be more precise about this concept of "switching" between products

FIG. 4–13. Resource market demand.

Demand for Labor

Price (Wage per Hour)	Quantity
$10	0
8	1
5	2
3	3
1	4

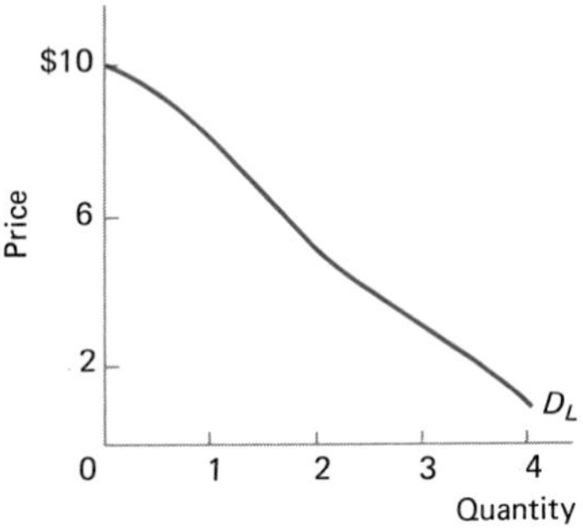

+

Demand for Raw Materials

Price (Cents per Pound)	Quantity
10	0
8	1
5	2
3	3
1	4

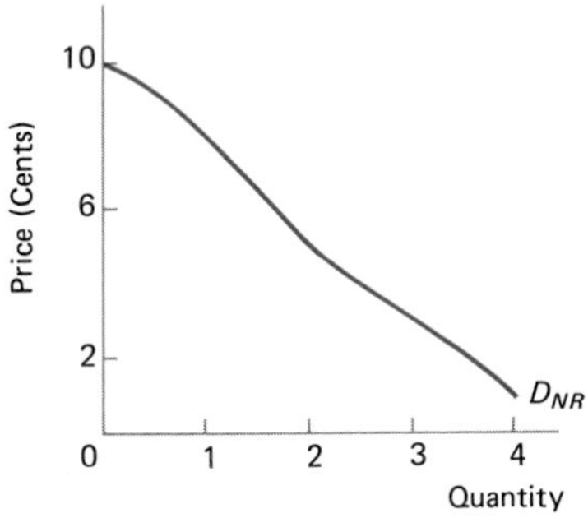

+

Demand for Capital Stock

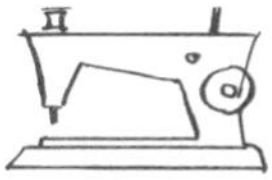

Price (Cost per Machine)	Quantity
$100	0
80	1
50	2
30	3
10	4

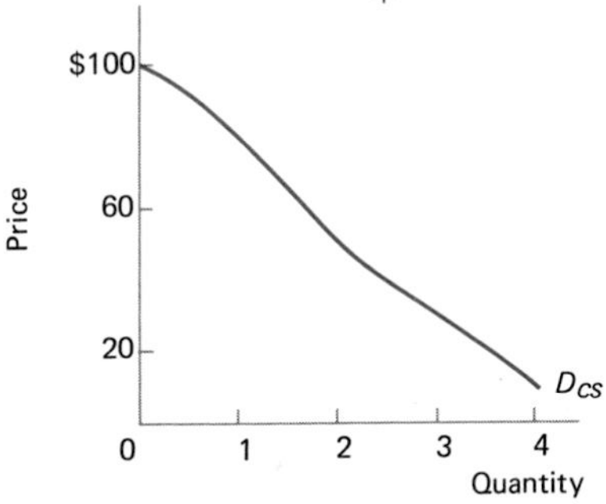

+

Demand for Management

Price (Salary per Month)	Quantity
$1,000	0
800	1
500	2
300	3
100	4

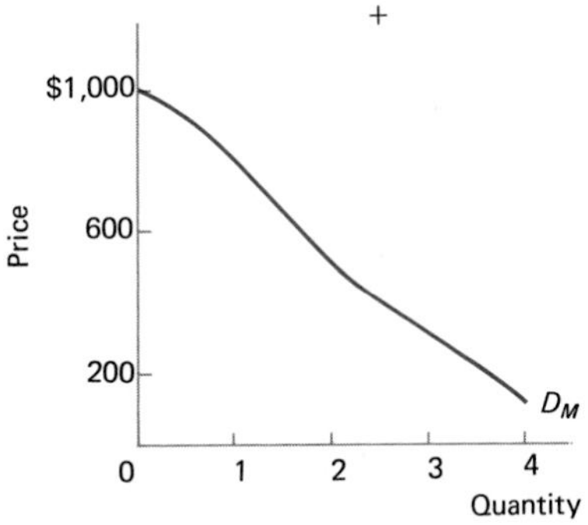

= Total Demand for Resources (Total Employment)

87

(or resources, for businessmen also choose), let us define *substitute* and *complementary* goods or resources. A substitute product (or resource) means that it is interchangeable with another product (or resource); that is, if more of one item is purchased, less of its substitute will be demanded, and vice versa. (See the hamburger-steak substitute here? How about sweaters vs. shirts or labor vs. automated machinery?)

A complement product (or resource), however, is one that goes with another product (or resource); that is, if more of one item is purchased, more of the complement item is also purchased, and vice versa. An example might be hamburger and French fries or tapes and tape decks or automobiles and gasoline. Of course, it should be emphasized that whether a specific item is a substitute or complementary item would largely depend on individual taste and situation.

Substitute and complementary products (or resources) under the concept of demand change relate to price changes; that is, a price change in one product (or resource) will lead to changes in the demand for substitute or complement products (or resources). Trace this price and quantity demanded to a substitute-complement demand relationship in Figure 4-14.

While we are discussing how overall market demands for products and resources change remember where change starts—with you! As you daily buy this or that, you are a part of determining overall market demand. If you ask yourself why you now purchase in a different way than you did a year ago and then multiply your own behavior changes by 215 million other consumers, you'll really get the picture of what we are describing as a change in demand.

FIG. 4–14. Changes in substitute and complement demands result from price changes.

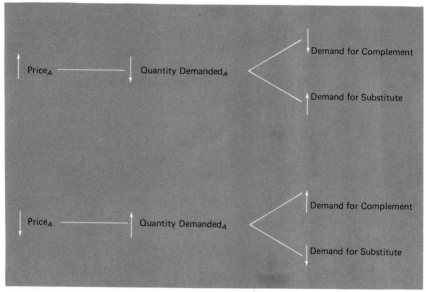

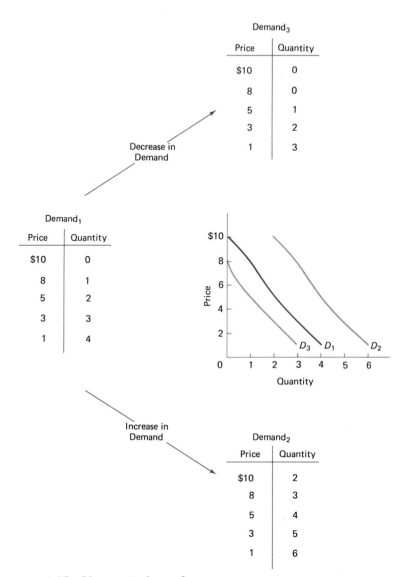

Demand₃

Price	Quantity
$10	0
8	0
5	1
3	2
1	3

Decrease in Demand

Demand₁

Price	Quantity
$10	0
8	1
5	2
3	3
1	4

Increase in Demand

Demand₂

Price	Quantity
$10	2
8	3
5	4
3	5
1	6

FIG. 4–15. Changes in demand.

Graph time again! Just as we drew pictures of our discussion on demand, so we can also graph changes in demand. In Figure 4-15 we show these schedules of demand and a graph picturing the three.

Schedule D_1 shows the initial demand pattern and demand curve D_1 is a picture of that buying pattern. In schedule D_2 we show an increase in demand —a greater quantity demanded at all prices. A picture of such increase is represented by demand curve D_2. On the other hand, schedule D_3 and demand curve D_3 show a decrease in demand.

DEMAND CURVE

In examining these demand curves, let us review a few points:

1. A change in demand appears on the graph as a shift in the position of the demand curve. There is now a new buying pattern; so a new demand curve must be shown.

2. A change in demand is not the same as a change in quantity demanded (a different amount at a different price or merely a slide from one point to another on the same demand curve).

3. An increase in demand means that more quantities will be purchased at all prices (or, alternatively, that higher prices will be paid for the same quantity) and is graphed as a shift to the right.

4. A decrease in demand means that fewer quantities will be purchased at all prices (or, alternatively, that lower prices will be paid for the same quantity) and is graphed as a shift to the left.

5. The downward slope of the demand curve is characteristic and represents the law of demand in action. An inverse relation of price and quantity demanded results in a downward-sloping demand curve as long as price and quantity are always shown on the same respective axis.

You may also wonder what would happen to prices when demand and supply change. Well, in answer, you'd also have to know what changes in supply occurred. (It takes $S + D$ to make a price.) We'll discuss supply in Chapter 5 and then go on to price determination in Chapter 6.

QUESTIONS

1. Do you see how demand curves D_1, D_2, D_3 resulted from schedules D_1, D_2, D_3? Plot the graph points yourself from the schedule numbers.
2. Could you see what "real-life" conditions could have caused such changes—changes in income, style, status, symbols, and so on?

OTHER DEMANDS

Although we have talked at length about the consumer and business sectors of our economy, we should remember that both the government and foreign trade parts of our economy also have demands, both in the product and resource markets. Recall Figure 4-6?

It is true that the consumer buys the largest part, some 64 per cent of our total output of goods and services. Government spending (federal, state, local levels) buys all sorts of products, from tanks to schools to paper clips, the total of which represents about 25 per cent of total demand for output.

Business demands for new plants and machinery, termed *investment,* result in some 10 per cent of total demand from private enterprise. In addition, the foreign trade sector buys from us (chemicals, machinery, grain, and so on, exported), and we buy from them (cameras, motorcycles, watches and radios, raw materials, wines, and so on). Thus, the amount shown is a "net" figure (that is, exports minus imports) and appears quite small at about 1 per cent of total output.

All demands are of concern to you, the consumer, in a number of ways. First of all, purchases they represent create business profits, which create jobs and paychecks. Although the government purchases are often termed *social goods,* the consumer does "use" them. Think about the school you attend, the road on which you drive, the police and fire units at your call—all demanded by government agencies. (You, the consumer, really do pay for these through taxes, but not on an individual basis, as when you buy a new car.)

Business investment creates new factories and machinery to produce more goods and services, and those factories produce more jobs. Not only do foreign demands provide sales and jobs, but our native demand for foreign products also generates a greater product variety and need for more raw materials for our factories. The "oil crisis" of 1974–1975 certainly shows the importance of foreign trade.

FIG. 4–16. Gross national product.

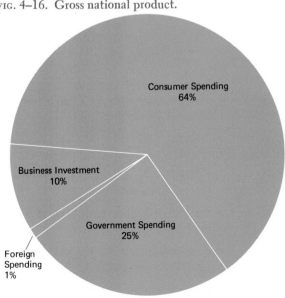

On the other side of the picture, the resource market, government levels also demand large amounts of resources. Civil service provides paychecks for many Americans, including the authors (who teach at a public community college, with funds for our paychecks provided by local property taxes).

One point that should be noted is that these demands differ greatly in demand determinant and market conduct. Consumer demand is determined by income and taste, responds to market price, competes with other consumer demands, and does not set overall market price. Federal government demand for defense goods is based on national security, is financed by taxes, and functions in a unique market arrangement often termed the "military-industrial complex." Business firms' demand for resources is related to expectation of profits. Foreign demand may range from consumer luxuries to government wheat for a starving population. Do you see how these demands vary in type and function? Yet all are part of the American economy, and affect you daily.

We have talked at length about demand in this chapter. It is an important topic, for people want many products in their daily lives. This process of exercising demand (buying products and resources) is basic to the way in which our market-oriented economic system operates. Beyond this, demand and supply (our next topic) together determine market prices. Prices, therefore, play another large role in our daily lives and in out total economic system.

That's about all for this chapter. At this point, your demand for reading about demand is probably more than satisfied! Economists talk about a concept of *diminishing marginal utility* when they wish to note that someone has "had enough" or is "fed up" by consumption of some item (is the third steak as satisfying as the first?). Perhaps this even applies to reading economics.

TERMS

Aggregate demand (AD). Total desire for goods and services in the economy, consisting of purchases by consumer, government, business, and foreign sectors.

Average propensity to consumer (APC). The percentage of disposable income spent on final goods and services $(C \div DI)$.

Average propensity to save (APS). The percentage of disposable income saved or not spent on purchase of final goods and services $(S \div DI)$.

Complement goods. Products (or resources) that are typically used with, or in addition to, other products (or resources).

Consumption. Consumer spending on final goods and services, including durable goods, nondurable goods, and services.

Demand. The behavior pattern relating the quantities of an item that buyers wish to purchase at various possible prices.

Demand curve. The curve showing the relationship between the price of a commodity and the amount of that commodity that consumers wish to purchase. (Assume that income, tastes, and all other prices remain constant.)

Demand schedule. The numerical relationship of prices and quantities demanded.

Determinants of demand. The basic factors that influence the quantities demanded at various prices, including income, tastes, prices of related goods, age, sex, expectations, and so forth.

Disposable income (DI). The amount of money remaining to a consumer after taxes, out of which he may consume or save.

Elastic demand. Buying behavior whereby the quantity demanded changes by a greater degree than the price change $(E_D > 1)$.

Inelastic demand. Buying behavior whereby the quantity demanded changes by a lesser degree than the price change $(E_D < 1)$.

Law of demand. The characteristic inverse relationship of quantity demanded and product price.

Marginal propensity to consume (MPC). The ratio of changes in consumption resulting from changes in disposable income $(\triangle C \div \triangle DI)$.

Marginal propensity to save (MPS). The ratio of changes in saving resulting from changes in disposable income $(\triangle S \div \triangle DI)$.

Price elasticity of demand (E_D). The ratio of per cent change in quantity demanded resulting from per cent change in product price $(\% \triangle Q_D \div \% \triangle P)$.

Saving. The act of not consuming final goods and services, as by using income for time deposits, insurance funds, stocks and bond purchase, or land purchase.

Substitute goods. Products (or resources) that may be used in place of other products (or resources).

Unitary elastic demand. Buying behavior whereby the buyer responds in equal proportion to the price change $(E_D = 1)$.

QUESTIONS FOR STUDY

1. Define demand. Explain the law of demand.
2. Why does a demand curve slope downward?
3. What are the determinants of demand? What happens to the demand curve when each of these determinants changes?
4. Distinguish between a change in demand and a change in the quantity demanded.
5. How would product demand be affected if consumer incomes fell?

6. Define and distinguish APC, APS, MPC, and MPS.
7. Define and give examples of substitute and complement goods.
8. Why are resource demands and product demands interdependent?
9. Draw a demand curve for television sets, based on this information:

DEMAND	
PRICE	QUANTITY
$300	5
200	10
100	15
50	17

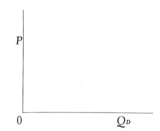

10. Which of the following, according to our demand theory, would tend to increase the demand for rice?
    a. A rise in the price of substitute grain.
    b. A rise in average consumer income.
    c. A change in American tastes involving increased liking for rice.
    d. All would tend to increase demand.
    e. None would increase demand.
11. An increase in the price of bread would lead to
    a. A rightward shift in the market demand curve for bread.
    b. A leftward shift in the market demand curve for bread.
    c. A decrease (slide) in quantity demanded of bread.
    d. None of the above.

REFERENCES

Friedman, Milton. *Price Theory: A Provisional Text*. Chicago: Aldine Publishing Company, 1962, Chapter 2.
Henderson, Hubert. *Supply and Demand*. Chicago: University of Chicago Press, 1958, Chapter 2.
Juster, Francis Thomas. *Consumer Buying Intentions and Purchase Probability*. Columbus, Ohio: Columbia University Press, 1973.
Silk, Leonard. *Capitalism: The Moving Target*. New York: Praeger Publishers, Inc., 1974.

5

WHAT IS SUPPLY?

SHORT ANSWER. Supply represents the amounts of goods or resources that businesses or persons will sell at different price levels.

YOUR INTEREST IN SUPPLY

Chapter 4 discussed demand in the marketplace and found, with no great surprise, that people demand a variety of items. You wish (and will pay) to consume clothes, food, a home, a car, records, education, and so on. Business firms demand resources of all types—labor, natural resources, machinery and tools (capital stock), and managerial talents. In addition, governmental agencies demand goods and services, and foreign nations wish to purchase many of our products. So when we talk of demand, we really have a long shopping list of wants in both product and resource markets.

Let us now talk about *supply* in these markets, for if these demands are to be satisfied, someone must produce the items wanted and get them into consumer's hands. This process involves answering the fundamental question of how to produce, because many choices must be made when combining resources and providing products. The answers to this basic supply question are, in our system, purposefully arranged and carried out by the mechanism of resource and product price influence on business profit. Each business tries to answer the question of how to produce for its own maximum profit. Together, some 14 million of these firms provide us overall societal choices and, one hopes, satisfy society's demands for the question of what to produce.

Again, your interest in supply is probably quite basic and relevant. On the one hand, items you demand must be supplied in the product market

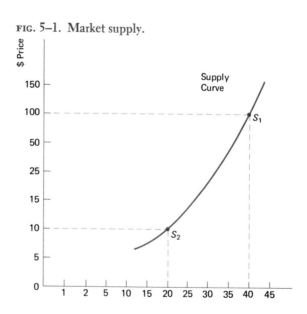

FIG. 5–1. Market supply.

by business firms or governmental agencies. (Remember the distinction between private goods and social goods made in Chapter 4?) On the other hand, you are, in fact, the supply of labor in the resource market. Just as you demand products, businesses demand resources. Just as businesses supply products, you supply resources in the form of labor directly, and, indirectly, you supply capital stock in that your savings are channeled through our financial system to businesses for machinery and plant purchases. (See Figure 5-1.)

Supply is essential, then, in both product and resource markets of the U.S. economy. It is the *daily interaction of supply and demand that determines the product and resource prices* so vital in our economy and, further, provides a feedback incentive for business firms to respond to consumer wishes. One more point about supply is that supply from all sources in our economy comprises the limits on our capability to consume (recall the production possibilities curve of Chapter 1?). This capability, of course, greatly influences our national standard of living.

SUPPLY FROM BUSINESS FIRMS

Most of the goods and services we consume in the United States are produced by private business firms. Although a few people are somewhat self-sufficient in supplying their own needs (have you ever planted a garden from seeds you have produced yourself, baked cookies from flour you have ground yourself, built a shelf, knitted a sweater from wool you have sheared yourself, or fixed a car?), most of us obtain our goods and services in the private marketplace. True, some services do originate from government, such as our public schools and national defense, but even here private business firms often contract to supply the items involved. Although $150 billion in foreign supply (import) flowed to U.S. consumers in 1976, $1.7 trillion, or ten times as much, came from domestic supply sources.

This market supply process illustrates another aspect of our system that we usually take for granted—the lack of self-sufficiency prevalent in our industrial, urbanized society. Very few of us make our own clothes or grow our own food, though perhaps we could if pushed, and perhaps the recent recession is pushing more of us to do so. (The Amish colonies, however, and certain communes are quite self-sufficient.) Instead, most of us work for business firms or government agencies and use the income earned to buy products from these and other firms. Adam Smith referred to this job choice as division of labor and noted the increase in productivity because a person could specialize in one line of work rather than be a Jack-of-all-trades. Smith, of course, was correct. The high U.S. standard of living does indeed depend on our high level of production, which is facilitated by specialization of labor and extensive use of machines. However, the same system that provides the means to satisfy our material needs with relative ease also creates among the vast majority of us a dependence on others. Sometimes that dependence, as in times of recession or inflation, will cause a person's fate to be in the hands of another, as changes in total market demand generate unemployment or rising prices.

Supply Characteristics

Now let us focus our attention on those business firms producing an almost uncountable variety of products. We have in the United States some 14 million business firms, from small "mama and papa" stores to large corporations. You will recall from Chapter 4 that the consumer, government, business, and foreign trade sectors satisfy their demands by allocating their expenditures. Well, the other side of such spending is, of course, the production of the goods and services supplied to them by business firms. Businesses produce cars and tanks, shirts and textbooks, houses and schools, drill presses and chemicals, and so on.

Two additional concepts must be admitted to an examination of the supply of goods and services by business firms. Again, they are points usually taken for granted. The production of many items wanted by society is complicated and requires intermediate suppliers. The finished product (the car on the showroom floor) you buy is the result of many interrelated assembly steps. (Think of what the resource of managerial skills involves in coordinating these steps!) The other point is that for some firms to produce finished products, other firms must produce inputs necessary such as parts, raw materials, and machinery. For example, General Motors may assemble the Camaro, but GM buys steel from the U.S. Steel Corporation and drill presses from Borg-Warner; other firms transport cars to dealers; the dealer stocks cars that you desire; banks or loan companies finance your purchase; insurance companies provide accident coverage; gas stations and garages fuel and repair the machine; and construction firms build roads on which you drive. Quite an interrelated operation when you think about it, and thousands of business firms are involved in various facets of any product we purchase! See the supply process in Figure 5-2?

Another point we should make here is that when we speak of business firms producing products, remember that these products include both tangible goods (such as a can, shirt, or house) and intangible services (such as a ball game, movie or song, insurance, or checking accounts). You, the consumer, demand both goods and services in your daily purchases, and business firms supply both. In fact, as Figure 5-3 illustrates, consumers now spend more on services than on durable goods (cars, TVs, machines, homes and so on— durable goods are sometimes defined as those products that last longer than their payments!) and almost as much as on nondurable goods (food, clothing,

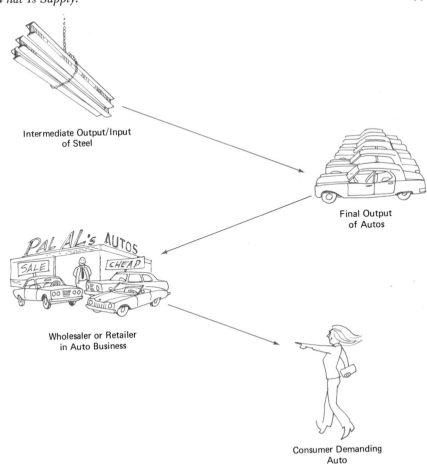

Intermediate Output/Input
of Steel

Final Output
of Autos

Wholesaler or Retailer
in Auto Business

Consumer Demanding
Auto

FIG. 5–2. Supply process.

and so on). This spending pattern illustrates why the United States is now called a *service economy*; it also shows the relative affluence of U.S. consumers.

We should make one further point in this overall view of supply, and this point ties into our discussion of demand in Chapter 4. Which products are supplied depends upon what consumers demand (the *consumer sovereignty principle*); that is, exactly which products are supplied by business firms will be those that can be sold profitably. And you, the consumer, determine what is profitable to produce. For example, if consumers don't buy standard-sized autos, businesses will shift resources to make another size of car.

Figure 5-4 illustrates *dependence of supply on demand in market economy* and reflects our basic question of what to produce in what quantities and how to produce. Interaction of demand and supply of products will determine what to produce, and interaction of demand for resources and supply of products will prescribe how to produce.

Area of Spending	Total Spent in 1974 (billions of 1958 dollars)	Percent of Total Spent in 1974
Durable goods (auto, furniture, etc.)	103	19
Nondurable goods (clothing, food, gas, tobacco, etc.)	224	42
Services (housing, transportation, recreation, etc.)	213	39

Source: U. S. Department of Commerce and *President's Economic Report*.

FIG. 5–3. Categories of consumer purchase.

To understand this dependence better, consider that the supply of your labor depends somewhat on business demand for labor and is, in turn, essentially based on consumer demand for products. Let's outline this relationship, emphasizing the interdependence of supply and demand and the impacts on basic questions:

1. Consumer demand products (depending on income, cost, taste, expectations, and so on). (*What to produce* choice.)

2. Businesses supply products (depending on what people buy). (*What to produce* choice.)

3. Businesses demand resources (depending on what they are producing, thus, on what people buy). (*How to produce* choice.)

4. You supply labor (depending on what you want and are able to do and jobs available) and receive income to spend. (*For whom to to produce* choice.)

This sounds as if "everything depends on everything else" in a market economy, and in a way that's correct. (Recall the circular-flow diagram of our economy in Chapter 2?) Demand and supply, both in product and resource markets, are closely interdependent in our economy. Both of these market forces are involved in the daily responses to our basic questions, and together they determine market prices (see Chapter 6).

SUPPLY FOR PROFIT

We have thus far been talking in general terms about supply in our economy and trying to get a general picture of how it all goes together. Although this is a good approach for general economic understanding, we need now to get a closer look at what supply really means.

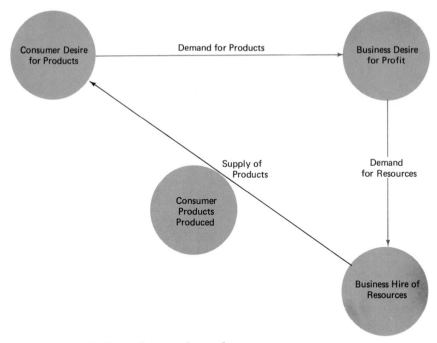

FIG. 5–4. Supply depends upon demand.

When we wish to analyze the supply of any particular item in any particular market, we must realize that the supply represents a particular business decision based on expected profit; that is, the supply of any individual business firm represents a "best guess" of most profitable product type, output level, product price, advertising type and amount, number and combination of resources hired, and so forth. Thus, the concept of market supply involves an analysis of business decision making (choice), and we should, therefore, examine the components of this decision-making process. Study Figure 5-5 to see all the factors involved in the supply choices of any business firm.

When the economist refers to *supply*, he means the *quantities of products businesses will sell at various prices*. (Compare this with the definition of demand in Chapter 4.) For example, in Figure 5-6, a business firm may use its entire factory capacity of 500 cars per day if the selling price is $10,000 per car, but it may shut down if the price is only $1,000. At other prices, other quantities would be supplied, and the entire pattern of price-quantity supplied is termed a *supply schedule*.

The shutdown would occur when the cost of producing the car becomes greater than the income received from selling the cars. The limit of 500 cars depends on the present factory size. Given some more time, the manufacturer might expand capacity if profits were large or try to sell or abandon the factory if it were losing money. Thus, the individual business supply decision

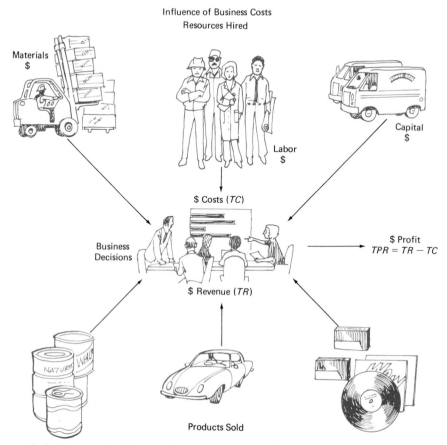

Influence of Business Costs
Resources Hired

Materials
$

Capital
$

Labor
$

$ Costs (*TC*)

Business
Decisions

$ Profit
TPR = TR − TC

$ Revenue (*TR*)

Products Sold

FIG. 5–5. Business decision making.

(the schedule is only an illustration) depends on cost of production, on the one hand, and sales receipts, on the other. The goal is to gain maximum profit.

Figure 5-6 also illustrates that as the price of the cars increases, the amount supplied also increases. (Recall how this was just reversed for demand: higher prices meant fewer purchases.) This direct relationship between price and quantity supplied is termed formally the *law of supply*, showing that price and quantity supplied vary directly (in the same direction).

As with elasticity of demand, we could also compute an *elasticity of supply* (E_s) measure to indicate how responsive business firms are to price changes; that is, we compare the percentage change in quantity supplied to the percentage change in product price.

$$E_s = \%\Delta Q_s \div \%\Delta P = \frac{Q_{s_2} - Q_{s_1}}{Q_{s_2} + Q_{s_1}} \div \frac{P_2 - P_1}{P_2 + P_1}$$

Supply

Price	Quantity Supplied
$10,000	500
6,000	300
3,000	50
2,000	20
1,000	0

FIG. 5–6. Business firm supply schedule.

For example, in Figure 5-6:

1. $\dfrac{300 - 500}{300 + 500} \div \dfrac{6,000 - 10,000}{6,000 + 10,000} = 1$; supply is unitary elastic

2. $\dfrac{50 - 300}{50 + 300} \div \dfrac{3,000 - 6,000}{3,000 + 6,000} = 2.1$; supply is elastic

3. You compute E_s between $3,000 and $2,000, and between $2,000 and $1,000 (2.1 and 3).

Business Decision Making

If we want to get the total number of cars supplied by other firms, we just "add all of them together," as in Figure 5-7. We then have a *market supply schedule*. This schedule represents the total of cars available for sale at all possible prices. The "real-life" illustration of this would be, say, all cars produced at all prices and available to you, the consumer. Quite a range of choices, isn't it? Do you begin to see how overall choices involving what to produce and how to produce come about in our market system? Do you see how actual market price might be arrived at? (Market supply versus market demand results in compromise price.)

Figure 5-7 is what the economist means when he speaks of supply. You see evidence of this daily when you are shopping and are confronted by a large variety of similar products and prices from which to choose. Let's also look at an important "behind-the-scenes" process to determine how a specific amount of goods is produced at the specific range of prices. We wish to see why those particular amounts are decided upon by the business firms.

Recall from our discussion of demand that we said the amounts chosen at various prices depended on your income, likes and dislikes, goals, and a host of other reasons. You have just so much to spend, you want to get the most for your money, and you make your choices accordingly. The demand sched-

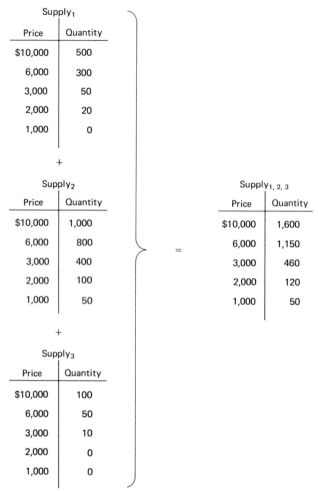

Supply₁

Price	Quantity
$10,000	500
6,000	300
3,000	50
2,000	20
1,000	0

+

Supply₂

Price	Quantity
$10,000	1,000
6,000	800
3,000	400
2,000	100
1,000	50

+

Supply₃

Price	Quantity
$10,000	100
6,000	50
3,000	10
2,000	0
1,000	0

=

Supply₁, ₂, ₃

Price	Quantity
$10,000	1,600
6,000	1,150
3,000	460
2,000	120
1,000	50

FIG. 5–7. Market supply schedule.

ule and demand curve are a pictorial representation of these choices. The same process of choice exists for any business firm. Initially, *maximum profit* is the aim (the same goal as your "satisfaction"). This goal is realized by adding up that which is received from all sales (*total revenue* is the term) and subtracting from this sum all the costs paid out (*total cost* is the term) in hiring the production resources. It is hoped that the result is positive and that a profit is made. But often the result is negative, and there is a loss. (Businesses do fail daily.)

Continuing further into this supply concept from the viewpoint of the single business firm, think what the decision to "supply" really involves. As a consumer, you see the finished product in the marketplace. But to get that supply, every business must decide:

1. What to produce. What specific product will be manufactured or prepared for sale? What areas appear most profitable? Should a new model line be added or an existing one dropped?

2. How much to produce. How many items will consumers buy? At what prices? Are there enough dealer outlets? How strong is the competition? What is most profitable point of production?

3. What price to sell at. Which price level (or levels) will return a profit? What is the competition charging? Are there any government price controls?

4. How to produce. What resources are needed to make goods or services ready for sale? What is the difference in costs of various methods of production? Which is economically efficient, automation or hand labor? What method is most profitable? What government or union regulations must be considered?

As you can see from the preceding list, the term *supply*, as a concept, involves many decisions by every businessman. Although the list may seem complex (the decisions must all interrelate as one depends on another), these supply decisions must be made, or nothing will be produced. Notice also the continued emphasis on profit. If the decisions are made "properly" (depending on you, the consumer), the result is a profit; if they are not, a loss.

Look at this decision-making process more closely; carefully go over Figure 5-8. Let's suppose this is a small suit producer whose present plant size allows him to make from zero to five suits per day. He could charge from $75 to $200 per suit. (Suppose this is the price range of competitors.) Note that we assumed this businessman had already made decisions about what to produce

FIG. 5–8. Business output decisions depend upon revenue and cost.

Quantity Produced	Price	Total Revenue (Price X Quantity)	Total Cost	Total Profit (Loss) (Total Revenue – Total Cost)
0	$200	$ 0	$100	$(100)
1	175	175	135	40
2	150	300	185	115
3	125	375	285	90
4	100	400	410	(10)
5	75	375	560	(185)

and how to produce. What he must do now is pick a price and quantity supplied that maximizes total profit. Given the figures above for illustration, this best profit point is two suits at $150 each for a total profit of $115 and would be this firm's supply decision.

An interesting point is that the best profit position is not necessarily where the selling price is the highest (no one buys a suit) or the cost is the lowest. Although businesses continually aim at increased sales (advertising) and reduced costs (efficiency studies), the overall goal is maximum profit! Changes in revenue and costs must be considered to achieve maximum profit (or minimum loss).

In the illustration of Figure 5-8, the businessman decided on both quantity supplied and product price, and this is often the case. However, if for some reason (competition factors, government price control, and so on) the businessman had no control of price, his supply decision would only be the quantity supplied at some given price. Furthermore, because businesses have different costs, the same price may result in different quantities supplied (review Figure 5-7). Again, notice that total market supply is the result of individual businesses choosing their own supply amounts for maximum profits.

Try to "put together" these various ways of viewing supply. Supply may be represented by a market supply schedule, a business decision to maximize profit, or the variety of products you face in shopping. They all, together, constitute supply in our American economy.

SUPPLY GRAPHS

You guessed it: graph time again. Just as was true of our discussion of demand, everything we've said about supply can be shown in pictures (graphed). We hope that your understanding will be improved by the graphic alternative. One obvious difference for the supply curves is that they are upward-sloping (the demand curves sloped downward). This upward slope is the direct relationship of price and quantity supplied, as expressed by the *law of supply*.

Figure 5-9 should seem familiar by now. We take the supply schedules from Figure 5-7 and have drawn graphs of each. Then we take the total of these three businesses (the market supply schedule) and draw its graph. For example, S_1, S_2, S_3, might represent the amount of cars produced by GM, Ford, and Chrysler (single businesses), and $S_{1,2,3}$ is the total amount of domestic cars available for sale at various prices.

Remember that what these supply curves really represent is the decision-making process of business firms, all making choices for the questions of what *to produce* and *how to produce*. Because different firms have different conditions under which they make decisions, their individual supply curves appear quite dissimilar. (See S_1, S_2, S_3 in Figure 5-9.) Yet "added together," as in Figure 5-9, the individual firms' supply decisions constitute the industry or

FIG. 5–9. Supply schedules to supply curves.

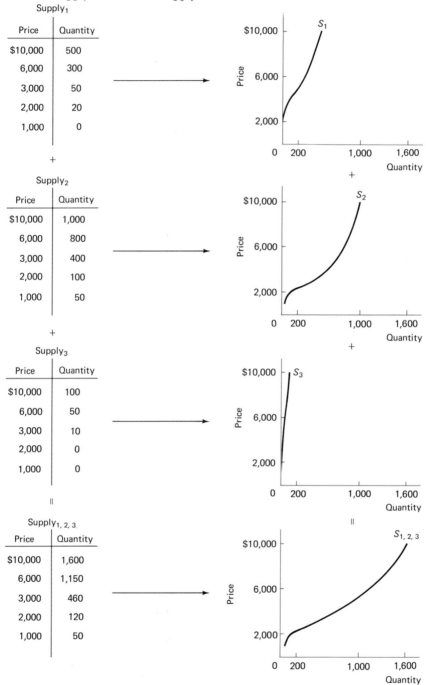

Supply₁

Price	Quantity
$10,000	500
6,000	300
3,000	50
2,000	20
1,000	0

+

Supply₂

Price	Quantity
$10,000	1,000
6,000	800
3,000	400
2,000	100
1,000	50

+

Supply₃

Price	Quantity
$10,000	100
6,000	50
3,000	10
2,000	0
1,000	0

||

Supply₁,₂,₃

Price	Quantity
$10,000	1,600
6,000	1,150
3,000	460
2,000	120
1,000	50

107

market supply of products and are thus pictured by the market supply curve
$S_{1,2,3}$. The other illustration of this supply would be a visit to your local car
dealer, for he's one small part of the total car supply.

Another concept we can show clearly with these supply curves is changes in
supply. Do you recall Figure 4-15, where we showed an increase and decrease
in demand? Well, Figure 5-10 notes the same process for supply: S_2 represents the schedule of a decrease in supply, and supply curve S_2 is its picture;
the S_3 schedule is an increase in supply, and supply curve S_3 is its picture.
Notice that an increase in supply (S_3) means greater quantities supplied at all

FIG. 5–10. Changes in supply.

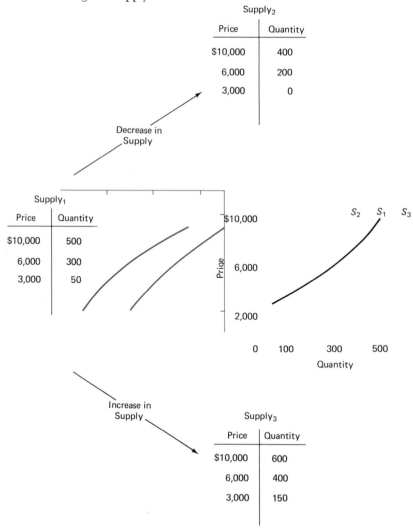

prices and is represented by a rightward shift of the supply curve. A decrease in supply means lesser quantities supplied at all prices and is represented by a leftward shift of the supply curve.

Remember, as was true of changes in demand, that such changes in supply are not just different amounts of goods or services supplied at different prices (this is a change in quantity supplied). Rather, a change in supply is due to an alteration of some basic market determinant, such as different costs of resources or the number of firms leaving and entering the industry or government regulation of profit expectation or some factor influencing basic supply decisions. Such changes in supply are clearly shown by shifts of the supply curve (new curve on graph). A change in quantity supplied means only a different quantity at a different price and is shown by a slide (or movement along) on a given supply curve.

OTHER SUPPLIES

We should note after this long discussion of supply from private business firms that many goods and services we use come from governmental levels. Figure 5-11 shows some of these social goods and services and also the varying governmental levels from which they're supplied. Some of these items are used daily, and there are probably services you use that are not on this list. Some 25 per cent of total output (GNP) arises from these government sectors.

Again, many of the products are directly produced by private busines firms on contract to government agencies. The governmental level then supplies these products to the public, and, of course, the funds used by government to purchase the products for supply are your taxes. You pay a businessman directly when you purchase a consumer good and pay indirectly through taxes for social goods. Perhaps the biggest difference between consumer and social goods is that supply decisions are made for profit by the private business sector, whereas supply decisions by government are based (purportedly) on pub-

FIG. 5–11. Supply of social goods.

Social Goods Supplied by Various Levels of Government		
Federal Level	State Level	Local Level (County, City, School)
Defense	Education	Education
Welfare	Highways	Streets
Agriculture Supports	Welfare	Police
Space Research	Housing	Fire Department
Housing Loans	Parks	Garbage Collect
Banking System	Hospitals	Water
Business Regulation	Business Regulation	Business Permits
Highways		Bus Service
How many of these social goods do you use? Are they "worth" the taxes?		

lic benefit and welfare. The extent, purpose, and desirability of these governmental supplies of goods and services are indeed debatable. But we defer such
debate to Chapter 11.

Another source of supply is from foreign nations. Imports (products sold by
foreign nations to us) are supplied to the United States; the return flow is
exports (products sold by U.S. firms to foreigners). The products often come
from private business in the foreign country and form a part of our daily consumption. (Do you drive a German car, wear a Swiss watch, or listen to a
Japanese radio?) Perhaps Figure 5-12 indicates the size and composition of
these import supplies?

There are also many debatable issues in this import supply area, many of
which we'll defer to Chapter 20. As Figure 5-12 indicates—and the "oil crisis"
impacts of 1974–1975 underscore—import supplies are very important to the
U.S. economy. Many of our industries depend upon imported raw materials
as input for their domestic supply decisions. Many consumers (you?) avail
themselves of products supplied from foreign manufacturers to benefit, we
hope, in quality, variety, and price.

Import supply does entail competition for American industries and workers,
but it also provides greater choices for American consumers. Furthermore, the
foreign incomes earned may then be used to purchase U.S. exports, thus generating domestic jobs and income. Let us think a bit of alternatives and im-

FIG. 5–12. U.S. foreign trade (foreign supply and demand).
Distribution of Commodity Export and Imports

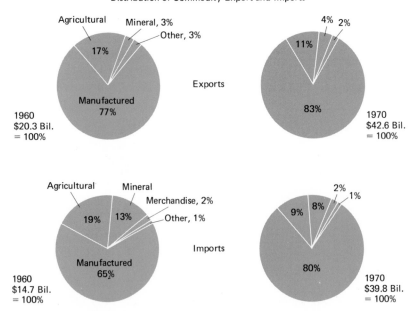

Source: President's Economic Report, 1975, p. 352.

pacts before we decry imports or voice support for tariffs to reduce such foreign trade.

OVERVIEW

We have now discussed both demand and supply. Although these are economists' terms, they also represent the real-life market forces, with which most of you are in daily contact. What we must now do is "put them together," as they always are in market operation. Moreover, we need really to see what is meant by the statement "Demand and supply determine prices." At this point you might review Chapters 2–5 because Chapter 6 combines all the concepts they have introduced.

TERMS

Change in quantity supplied. A movement (slide) from one point on a supply curve to another, resulting from a change in price.

Change in supply. A shift in the whole supply curve so that either more or less is supplied at each price than was supplied previously.

Elasticity of supply (E_s). The ratio of percentage change in quantity supplied to percentage change in price ($E_s = \% \triangle Q_s \div \% \triangle P$).

Imports. Items supplied to the United States by foreign producers.

Intermediate goods. Items that are produced to be used as input to production of final goods or services.

Law of supply. The behavior pattern that states that quantity supplied and price are directly related. It is shown graphically by an upward-sloping supply curve.

Supply. Defined by the economist as the quantities supplied at various prices. It is illustrated by the supply schedule. The supply curve presents a graphic picture of the supply schedule.

QUESTIONS FOR STUDY

1. Define supply. Explain the law of supply.
2. Why does the supply curve slope upward?
3. What happens to the supply curve when determinants change? Distinguish between a change in supply and a change in the quantity supplied. (Draw supply curves of each.)
4. An increase in supply is represented by the shift from S_1 to S_2 in Figure 5-10. An increase in demand is represented by a shift from D_1 to

D_2 in Figure 4-15. Evidently, a rise in demand is represented by an upward shift in the demand curve, whereas a rise in supply is represented by a downward shift in the supply curve. Is this not inconsistent?

5. A rise in the price of leather will probably lead to a(n) _____ in the supply of briefcases. This is represented graphically by a(n) _____ shift in the supply curve.

6. The usual assumption that economists make about the goals of firms is that they seek to _____.

7. As a seller of products, would you supply more or less at higher prices? Explain why. (Do you agree with the law of supply?)

REFERENCES

Gill, Richard T. *Economics: A Text with Readings*, Second Edition. Pacific Palisades, Calif.: Goodyear Publishing Company, Inc., 1975, Chapters 2 and 19.

Henderson, Hubert. *Supply and Demand*. Chicago: University of Chicago Press, 1958, Chapter 2.

Kaplan, A. D., et al. *Pricing in Big Business*. Washington, D.C.: Brookings Institution, 1958.

6

WHAT IS A MARKETPLACE?

SHORT ANSWER. A market is the place or process by which goods, services, or resources are exchanged at various prices between buyers and sellers.

YOU AND THE MARKETPLACE

There are many thousands of marketplaces in the U.S. economy, from the New York Stock Exchange floor to your local commercial bank, from United Auto Workers bargaining with General Motors to your employment at the diner, and from Soviet purchase of millions of tons of grain to your daily shopping tour for groceries. These markets are varied in size, complexity, and types of items sold and purchased. The items may be products (demanded by households; supplied by business) or resources (demanded by business; supplied by households). Examine Figure 6-2.

These various marketplaces do have a basic similarity; an exchange process is taking place. In all of these markets, buyers and sellers are both competing and compromising with other buyers and sellers. There is surely conflict between buyer and seller, and yet exchanges are made representing compromises of wants. Note that these are typically voluntary compromises, for households and businesses benefit from participation in market exchanges.

FIG. 6–1. Price determination in the marketplace.

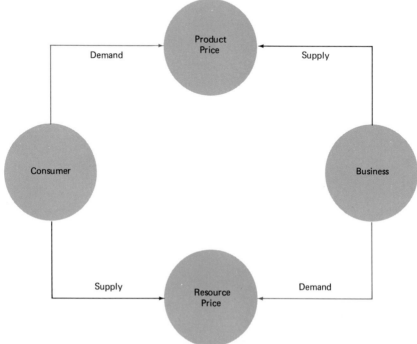

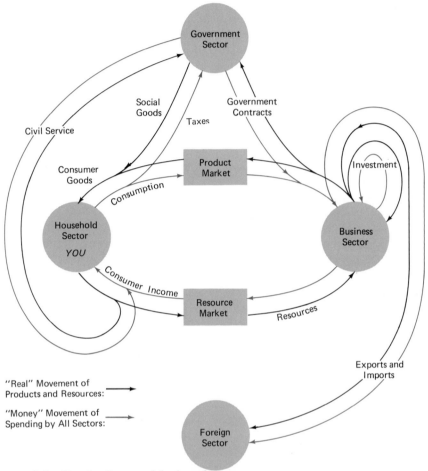

FIG. 6–2. Circular-flow model of market economy.

Another way to illustrate this compromise of wants is that in any marketplace the exchange process involves prices (do you recall the functions of price—ration and guide—from Chapter 3?), either product prices or resource prices. It is this exchange process of the marketplace that determines these market prices; that is, the demand (buyers) and supply (sellers) market forces we've described separately in Chapters 4 and 5 come together in the marketplace to determine prices that result in compromise and exchange. Prices are the heartbeat of our market-oriented economic system. It is through the market mechanism that the daily economic activities of over 215 million producers and consumers within the American economic system are tied together and coordinated.

Appreciation of the importance of the institution called the marketplace and seeing how it coordinates and guides economic activity are necessary for complete understanding of your personal market activity. Furthermore, it is this marketplace activity that provides daily choices for our basic societal questions of what, how, and for whom to produce. Through the process we are about to describe, you will see how a price (of clothes, movies, gasoline, books, your own labor) is determined and how marketplace changes lead to different prices.

HOW DOES A MARKETPLACE WORK?

Undoubtedly, prices make a difference in your purchasing patterns. What if your suit or dress or car costs just a bit less or if you earned $5 an hour rather than $2? Such differences do indeed affect daily economic activity, making prices an important part of our daily lives. The basic function in any marketplace is determining these prices in the process of market exchange. Buyers interact with sellers, goods and services and resources are exchanged, and market prices are determined in the daily operation of any market. Let's look more deeply at these market forces of demand (buyers) and supply (sellers).

Suppose you recently purchased a paisley tie or a pair of black net stockings. Did you realize you were performing the economic act of consumption within a market-oriented economy? As shown in the circular-flow model of the U.S. economic system (Figure 6-2), you are in the household sector and purchase a product from the business sector by paying a price (in terms of money—dollars for the United States) for the good. Your purchase may have seemed like a very simple action at the time, but mull this activity over. Throughout the United States, articles are being purchased by people like yourself from businessmen such as your local retailer. Beyond this immediate action, retail store managers buy from wholesalers, who are, in turn, reselling articles they originally purchased from the manufacturer. The manufacturer is also purchasing factors of production—land, labor capital, managerial ability—to produce the tie you bought. See what you started!

Figure 6-3 shows these links between purchases and sales more clearly, with you, the consumer, in the "driver's seat," making the decision whether or not to buy the tie or socks. This basic fact, that it is the consumer who really determines what and how much is to be produced, is termed *consumer sovereignty*. Although this phase literally means that the consumer is really the boss (by regulating what gets produced and in what quantities), in reality most buying decisions are greatly influenced by the suppliers of the goods and services. Of course, there are other demanders (buyers) in the marketplace (government, business, foreign), as Figure 6-2 illustrates and as we've described in Chapter 4. But the important point is that these demands expressed in the

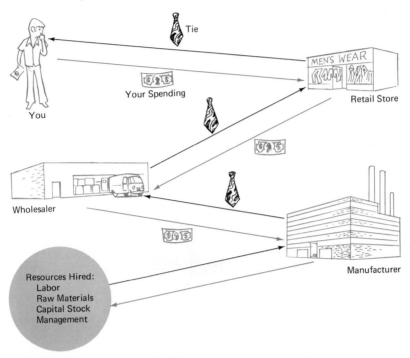

<small>FIG.</small> 6–3. Consumer sovereignty process.

marketplace constitute the essential mechanism in determining the answer to our basic what and how much to produce questions.

Therefore, we define a *market* (or *marketplace*; the phrases are interchangeable) as a "process of exchange." Whether you pay (exchange) money for the ties or stockings in a *product market* or the businessman pays (exchanges) money for your labor in a *resource market*, an exchange is involved. Generally speaking, this exchange involves money for products or resources and at some *exchange rate*, which we term the *price*.

A market is "working," then, whenever an exchange is taking place between buyer and seller. Another way to put it is that market operation involves the interaction of demand and supply forces at some price. It is through such constant interaction that choices are made and answers to our basic questions are provided. Is the importance of market operation quite clear at this point?

THE EXCHANGE PROCESS

We now want to look more closely at this exchange process to see why it lies at the heart of market operation, in which you are daily involved. (Look at Figure 6-4.) Think of the many advantages offered by this market activity.

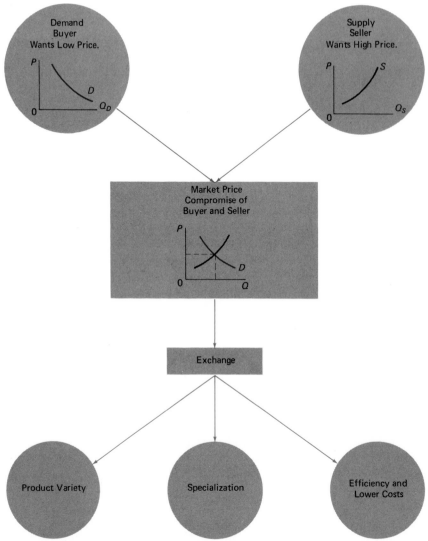

FIG. 6–4. Market activity promotes exchange and specialization.

Recall from Chapter 4 that your exchange for desired products means that you do not have to be self-sufficient, making all the goods you need by yourself. Use of money in exchange provides you with a much greater variety of products. (If you weave all your own clothes, you may be very limited in the variety of patterns you are able to produce.) It also allows specialization. You work at that job at which you are best qualified, using income earned at this particular job to buy products you desire. The businessman of today usually specializes in producing only certain products and often purchases specialized inputs from other business firms.

The amazing thing about this specialization is that everyone gains. The businessman produces at lower cost because he may make more efficient use of productive resources (which may ultimately provide a lower price to you, the consumer), and you earn a higher income because you are more efficient in what you do. Economists often explain such gains from specialization under the heading of the *principle of comparative advantage*; that is, as each person, business, or nation operates in those activities in which he or it is best qualified (where it has a "comparative advantage"), all may benefit. We'll explain the international implications of this process more fully in Chapter 20. Comparative advantage gains apply to international trade, as well as to domestic marketplace activities.

Notice that this specialization could not occur unless there were provisions for exchanging resources and products. This is the function of a market. An essential feature of any efficient market is the existence of some form of money (dollars, yen, francs, shells, or whatever) to provide a *medium of exchange*; that is, buyer and seller will both accept money in their exchange, thus avoiding the necessity for direct barter in their exchange. (Imagine your daily shopping conducted on a barter basis of direct exchanges.) Furthermore, money provides a *standard of value*, in that you may compare your various possible purchases against a common measure (the price of an item may be compared against prices for comparable items), as well as a *store of value*, in that you could save money today to spend in the future. More about money in Chapter 15.

Digging deeper into this exchange process, do you see that there is always *conflict* involved and that exchange represents a compromise of that conflict? That may be a bit heavy, so let's try again. The conflict comes because the buyer generally wants to pay as little as possible and the seller wants to receive as much as possible. In the product market, you, the buyer, probably would like to get a new 360-cc. motorcycle for $200. Conversely, in the resource market you'd like to receive $10 per hour for selling your labor. But the businessman, who is now the buyer, wants to pay you only $1 per hour and charge $2,000 for the motorcycle.

The example may be extreme, but it points out the basic conflict involved between buyer and seller. Both parties act in their own self-interest, and these interests are opposed. Still, both parties benefit if the exchange takes place. You get your motorcycle, and the dealer makes his profit; you receive income to make payments, and the businessman is able to produce his goods and services.

Therefore, in any exchange we have a basic conflict situation, yet one in which both buyer and seller gain by the conflict's resolution. And resolving the conflict is exactly what a market does through the price of the product or resource. The market price at which the product or resource is purchased represents a compromise to which both buyer and seller have agreed. True, you may wish to pay less—but you will pay the price to get the product. (The same goes for the businessman in the resource market.) The seller may wish to receive more, but he'll sell at that price (just as you will in the resource market). So although the motorcycle at $800 is not exactly what either the buyer or seller would like, it is nonetheless agreeable to both if the sale is made at that price.

Notice again that we've described a market as a process of compromise by exchange between buyer and seller. We have not said that it is a physical location, even though most sales occur in stores. A market occurs whenever there are a buyer and seller dickering over terms of exchange (price), be it at the local grocery store, the used-car lot, or the drive-in movie.

Mentioning "dickering" over price (would arguing or haggling be a better term?) brings us to another distinction, that of the individual in the market-place compared to the entire marketplace. You may wonder here to what extent you can actually debate price with a seller. Have you ever argued price in a grocery store, clothes shop, or theater? As an individual buyer, the price is generally set for you by the seller, as a "take-it-or-leave-it" proposition. You can dicker a bit more over a used car or home and even more at a garage sale, but usually prices are set and are a challenge to your budget. In the resource market, especially at a union-contract job, you work at the wages agreed upon by the union and management contract.

The distinction we wish to point out here is that to you, the individual buyer or seller, the price is pretty much predetermined. If you do not wish to pay or accept that price, you usually go without the good or service. This is because as an individual you are a very small part of the whole market. (That is why when it is just you and the car salesman, you have more bargaining power.) Suppose, however, that all buyers do not wish to pay the price set by the salesman. Then either the seller lowers his price to what people are willing to pay or he loses business. This is the essence of competition. Although you as an individual do not affect the selling price, all buyers collectively certainly do. Therefore, when you see prices of products or resources changing, a look behind the scenes will disclose some basic change in habits of buyers and sellers—what economists term *shifts in demand and/or supply.*

DEMAND AND SUPPLY

In describing marketplace activity thus far, we've emphasized its function in facilitating the process of exchange between buyers and sellers. We've also noted that the exchange involves a conflict resolved by exchange at some price. We must now further describe the nature of compromise, which involves the bringing together of the topics of Chapters 4 and 5, demand and supply.

Demand is what the buyer (in product or resource markets) wants; that is, the quantities he is willing to buy at various prices. *Supply* is the quantities the seller (in product or resource markets) is willing to sell at various prices. Again, the buyer wants the lowest price, and the seller wants the highest price, but both parties will agree on an exchange at some price. The particular price that is finally reached depends on the demand and supply conditions for this particular product or resource. The conditions reflect the income level and desires of buyers, amounts and prices of substitute products, costs of production to the sellers, and desires for profits by sellers. (Do you recall the determinants of demand and supply in Chapters 4 and 5?)

Although it is often difficult for seller and buyer to agree, eventually a market price will be reached. The seller will be left with unsold goods (no profit) if the price is too high, or the buyer with no products obtained (no satisfaction) if the price is too low. Somewhere between these high and low extremes exists a compromise price at which buyers are willing to purchase and sellers are willing to unload.

An illustration will clarify this discussion. Figure 6-5 shows a demand schedule and curve and a supply schedule and curve. These schedules are similar to the charts in Chapters 4 and 5, except that here demand and supply are

FIG. 6–5. Supply and demand determine price.

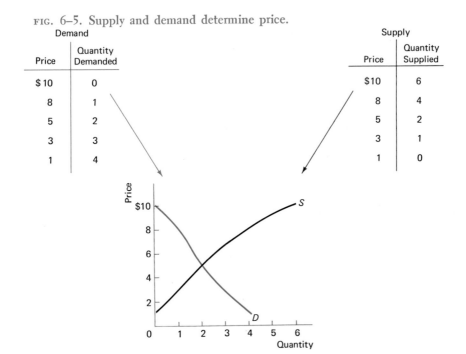

Demand	
Price	Quantity Demanded
$ 10	0
8	1
5	2
3	3
1	4

Supply	
Price	Quantity Supplied
$10	6
8	4
5	2
3	1
1	0

shown together. Notice that at some high prices the quantity supplied exceeds the quantity demanded and a *surplus* results. At low prices the quantity demanded exceeds the quantity supplied, and a *shortage* occurs. Only at one point (X marks the spot) does the quantity demanded exactly equal the quantity supplied. This is the market price at which a compromise occurs, clearing the market of surpluses or shortages. The economist terms compromise the *equilibrium price*, as market price will tend to approach and remain at this level.

Let's review this process of attaining market equilibrium, for it's a basic component of marketplace activity. Suppose, first, that a surplus exists, as at the price of $8 in Figure 6-5. The surplus is three items, as the quantity supplied (4) exceeds the quantity demanded (1). This surplus will exist as excess inventories for the businessman, and he will probably begin to reduce his price and produce less. As price falls, quantity demanded tends to increase. (Recall the concepts of law of demand and of elasticity in Chapter 4?) At some lower price ($5 in Figure 6-5), there will be a tendency for quantity supplied to equal quantity demanded (the market is "cleared"); our market will then be in *equilibrium*, with no further pressure to change prices or quantities. If this market process of reducing a surplus sounds abstract to you, compare the real-life reduction of automobile inventories by dealers in 1975. Price reductions and rebates proliferated to move unsold autos.

Let's also see how market activity would clear a shortage condition. In Figure 6-5 a shortage of two items exists at a price of $3, for the quantity demanded (3) exceeds the quantity supplied (1). Such a shortage entails reduced inventories and perhaps lack of merchandise for businessmen, and eager customers may well pay higher prices to get their desired items ("black market," anyone?). As prices move upward, some decrease in quantity demanded occurs because some customers cannot or do not pay higher prices, whereas quantity supplied may increase in response to the incentive of higher prices. (Do you see the rationing and guiding functions of market price here?) At some higher price ($5 in Figure 6-5), there will be a tendency for quantity demanded to equal quantity supplied. Again, our market has reached equilibrium and will tend to remain at this price-quantity relationship until market conditions change. For a real-life illustration of a shortage condition, consider how rising gas prices appear to resolve a shortage condition.

You may wonder at this point just how close to real life this discussion is. After all, you've never seen these demand-supply curves hanging around like a big X in the sky. You do, however, see prices change, and you do make decisions daily to buy and sell. The surplus of autos (with falling car prices) and shortage of gasoline (with rising gas prices) certainly did exist as real-life market conditions. Once more, what we are describing here is the whole market process, which is something difficult for the individual, who is usually just a small part of that whole process, to see. In addition, this single equilibrium price we describe may take some time to be achieved. With many products there is first a high price, then a low price, with the final equilibrium price being somewhere between the extremes. Pocket calculators have illustrated such price fluctuation in recent years.

Take, as an example, the hamburger market to put this idea in perspective. Many people who like hamburgers are willing to purchase them at various prices (depending on income, taste, hunger, and so on). We have hamburger suppliers of all kinds, from plush restaurants to walk-in stands, each selling hamburgers at many levels of price. We can draw a set of supply schedules and curves to represent these real-life businessmen. There is a restaurant B's hamburger price, of, say, 40 cents, and that is one market equilibrium price. Of course, there are other equilibrium prices too (depending on quality, restaurant atmosphere, and type and amount of meat, if any), ranging from restaurant A's 25-cent price to restaurant C's price of $4. What we are trying to show here is that our demand-supply schedules and curves do represent the real world, although perhaps in an abstract way. They point to forces that exist and to real sellers and buyers munching away. Can you repeat this same market equilibrium process for other goods and services you consume daily?

CHANGES IN SUPPLY AND DEMAND

Does supply or demand determine market price? Replying to this question, Alfred Marshall, a famous economist, answered, "Does the upper or lower blade of a scissors cut the paper?" Of course, both blades of a scissors are required to cut paper—and if you missed the analogy, we remind you again that *both* demand and supply determine market prices.

Chapters 4 and 5 discussed the forces of demand and supply separately. Depending on various determinants, demand and supply forces were defined as the schedules of consumers' willingness to buy and producers' willingness to sell various quantities of goods and services at different prices. In this chapter we have examined supply and demand together, combining supply and demand schedules to see how price is determined. The market price is the result of both supply and demand forces, and thus *any change in demand or supply conditions will result in a new equilibrium price in the market.*

To see why this is true, consider again the concept portrayed by demand and supply schedules. Your demand schedule states that you will buy so many goods at a certain price. When your demand schedule is combined with all other buyers, we have a *market demand schedule* for, say, hamburgers. Given the *market supply schedule*, we will have a certain market equilibrium price and quantity determined. (Review Figure 6-5 again.)

Now suppose the market demand or market supply (or both) schedule changes for some reason. Perhaps you and other consumers grow weary of hamburgers (rather un-American, but possible!), or perhaps steak is cheaper

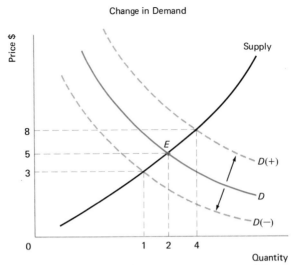

FIG. 6–6. Changes in demand cause new equilibrium prices and quantities.

and you substitute it for hamburgers, or perhaps your income falls. In any case, this would represent a decrease in demand and would lead to a new equilibrium price and quantity, as shown in Figure 6-6. Notice that the new equilibrium price ($3) is lower than before the decrease in demand and that the new equilibrium quantity (1) is also lower.

Actually, this condition of decreased demand and constant supply is only one of a range of market possibilities. The other possible market changes and demand-supply curves to illustrate such conditions include:

1. Demand increases; no change in supply—price rises (Figure 6-7).

2. Demand decreases; no change in supply—price falls (Figure 6-8).

FIG. 6–7. Increase in demand.

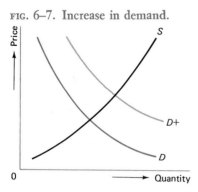

FIG. 6–8. Decrease in demand.

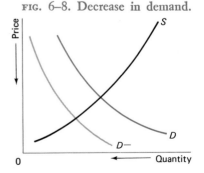

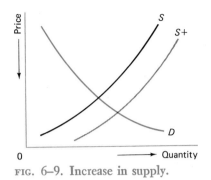

FIG. 6–9. Increase in supply.

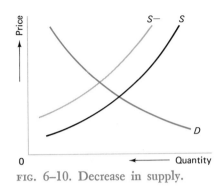

FIG. 6–10. Decrease in supply.

3. Supply increases; no change in demand—price falls (Figure 6-9).

4. Supply decreases; no change in demand—price rises (Figure 6-10).

5. Supply and demand both increase—price may rise, fall, or remain the same (Figure 6-11).

6. Supply and demand both decrease—price may rise, fall, or remain the same (Figure 6-12).

The previous demand-supply curves may appear a bit complex, but are vital for your understanding of market operation and warrant your close review and study. Note that in each market condition, the movement of market price depends on the change in demand and/or supply. In some cases, as shown in Figures 6-11 and 6-12, market equilibrium price may be *indeterminate*; that is, price may rise or fall or remain the same, depending upon the comparative sizes of demand and supply changes. Do you understand each of these possible market conditions? Can you give a real-life example of market activity to illustrate each of these possible market shifts?

FIG. 6–11. Increase in demand and in supply.

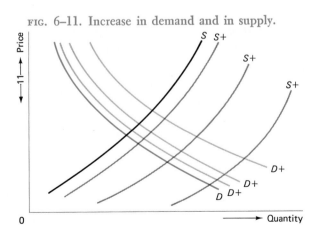

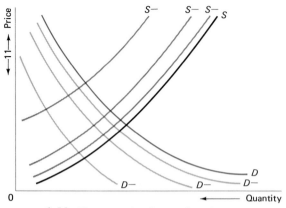

FIG. 6–12. Decrease in demand and in supply.

Let us translate these market conditions to "real life." Have you ever heard, in daily conversation, statements such as the following: "A greater supply of hogs this fall will cause lower pork prices." "I had to pay more for a sports car because everybody wants one." "I think I'll become an engineer because companies are looking for them." Notice that each of these statements connected a change in price with a change in market conditions; that is, a change in either demand or supply or both. These comments exhibit sound economic analysis. Market prices do change in response to supply-demand changes. *An increase in supply tends to lower price,* and *a reduction in supply tends to increase price.* On the other hand, *an increase in demand tends to increase price,* and a *reduction in demand tends to lower price.* Are these principles clear from Figures 6-7 through 6-12?

To see other real-life examples of such price determination, read daily news clippings. Do you see how changes in demand or supply cause new market prices? (Do you also see the other effects of a price change?)

Changes in Supply and Demand vs. Changes in Quantity Supplied and Quantity Demanded

We have described how changes in supply and/or demand will cause market prices to change. But we must be careful to note the difference between a change in demand versus a change in quantity demanded and a change in supply versus a change in quantity supplied.

Remember that a demand schedule represents the quantities consumers (collectively) intend to purchase at different prices. Such a demand schedule is determined by the income of the consumer, his tastes and preferences for the item, his expectations of the future, the number of consumers, and prices of other goods. Thus, a change in demand occurs only when one of these determinants changes, whereas a change in quantity results from a change in the price of the item. For example, the demand for Pacers means the number of these automobiles the consumers will buy at various prices, given their incomes, tastes, and so on. If the price falls, the quantity demanded increases. This is what the demand schedule tells us. If the incomes of people change or if they switch their tastes for small sports automobiles, there will be a change in demand. A different demand schedule now exists in the market, and a new equilibrium price results.

The confusion that sometimes results from attempts to distinguish between the preceding changes is not easily clarified. For instance, it is correct to say that an increase in quantity demanded was caused by a reduction in price. It is also correct to say that a decrease in demand caused price to fall (assuming no change in supply). But it is not correct to say that a fall in price caused demand to increase, because price can affect only the quantity of demand, not the nature of the demand. Do you see the difference? (Make sure you do!)

The same distinction exists between changes in quantity supplied (caused by price changes) and changes in supply (which cause price to vary). A supply schedule shows the various quantities producers intend to supply at different prices. This schedule is determined by costs of production (wages, interest, rent, and so on), the level of technology involved in making the goods, the number of producers, businessmen's expectations of future conditions, and prices of other products. Given certain cost levels, technical knowledge, and so on, producers will increase the quantity supplied in response to a price increase. If the cost of production falls because of lower wages or if a new invention occurs or if more firms enter the market, there will be an increase in supply, and a new equilibrium price results.

These are the basic points to remember:

1. Changes in quantity demanded or quantity supplied are not the same as changes in demand or supply.

2. Quantity demanded is part of a demand schedule; quantity supplied is part of a supply schedule.

3. A change in quantity supplied or in quantity demanded is caused by a change in price. Graphically, this is a slide (movement) on a given demand or supply curve. Also this response in quantity demanded or quantity supplied to a price change is measured by the coefficient computed for elasticity of demand or elasticity of supply.

4. Demand includes the entire demand schedule and curve; supply includes the entire supply schedule and curve.

5. Changes in demand or supply cause price to change. Graphically, this is a shift of the entire demand or supply curve.

Supply and Demand Theory in Economic Analysis

The reader may wonder why so much stress has been placed upon the theory of supply and demand. After all, the last three chapters have been devoted to this topic. This emphasis on supply-demand theory is acknowledgment of the theory's fundamental importance in economic analysis. Many applications of economic analysis to everyday issues depend on this theory. As following chapters indicate, the theory of supply and demand underlies the economic analysis of national income and employment policies, wage determination, foreign trade and foreign exchange rates, and many other areas.

Quite simply put, the reason for our emphasis is that supply and demand determine market price, and it is the functioning of market price that much of economic analysis is concerned with. Remember that economics is the study of a society making choices, specifically, answering the basic questions of what, how, and for whom to produce. In our market economy, prices are essential in answering these questions, for they perform their rationing (for whom) and guiding (what, how) functions daily.

We wish here to repeat that the basic concepts discussed in Chapters 2 to 6 are indeed the heart of economic analysis and are truly the rudimentary tools used by professional economists. The importance of understanding these basic concepts might be illustrated by applying supply-demand analysis to the 1974–1975 oil crisis:

1. The oil embargo by OPEC (Organization of Petroleum Exporting Countries) represented a decrease in supply. Given the continued demand levels, higher oil prices resulted.

2. The decreased supply of crude oil had repercussions for all products derived from oil, thus causing their prices to rise, and resulted in long-term demand-supply reactions:
   a. Gasoline prices rose, and consumers' demand for large, gas-consuming autos fell, whereas demand for economy cars rose. In the long run, this may result in increased demand for mass transit systems and homes closer to metropolitan work areas.
   b. Fertilizer and diesel fuel prices rose, thus increasing farm production costs (decreasing supplies of some foods) and resulting in higher food costs. In the long run, this may result in consumers' substituting lower-priced protein for meat and an in-increased demand for home garden tools and seeds.
   c. Building materials rose in price, thus increasing home building costs, which resulted in higher home prices. In the long run, this may result in consumers' increased demand for apartments, condominiums, and town houses as a substitute for single-family homes.

3. The federal government is now pushing programs (increased demand) designed to develop alternative energy sources for fossil fuels (oil) and is also attempting to reduce demand for imported crude oil. The long-run impacts here are difficult to predict, but may include large changes in energy production and consumption, a battle between environmental and economic growth proponents, and drastic changes in the life-styles of consumers.

Do these types of market reactions and economic impacts convince you of the importance of supply-demand analysis? Can you think of other impacts?

GOVERNMENT REGULATORY EFFECTS

Alas, after all this discussion of supply-demand forces determining market prices, we must add that other forces also contribute to price determination. Government regulation (federal, state, local) is involved in many markets by direct or indirect means. This is not to deny that basic supply-demand forces determine market price (one can't as long as sellers and buyers exist), but it does mean there are other forces to consider.

In stating that government regulations may have direct or indirect effects on prices, we mean that some regulations influence (set) prices directly—such as minimum-wage laws (resource market) or utility prices (product market). Other regulations indirectly influence market operations—such as ruling that some products are illegal for sale (marijuana, impure foods) or prosecuting price fixing by monopolists (antitrust). Many such regulations, from those affecting business licensing to rules enforcing safe working conditions, affect market operations daily. One should note that all levels of government are involved in the regulatory process. The federal government pursues antitrust enforcement, whereas state government agencies set utility rates and special sales taxes (as on liquor, cigarettes, and gasoline), and local governments determine zoning ordinances and grant business licenses.

To apply supply-demand analysis to government regulation, consider Figure 6-13, which illustrates impacts of the California Milk Board (a state agency) on the price of milk. Let's suppose the market equilibrium price of a half gallon of homogenized milk would be 68 cents if demand-supply forces operated freely. However, the Milk Board set a *price floor* (retail price cannot go lower) of 72 cents, thus prescribing higher consumer prices and a surplus of milk. When the control was removed in March of 1975, the price dropped to around 68 cents, and more milk was sold. If you ask the reason for the control to start with, you'll have to argue with milk producers, who contended they needed a minimum price to continue production!

Notice in Figure 6-13 that there is also a 65-cent *price ceiling* control. Although this does not now exist, such a control was suggested to aid low-in-

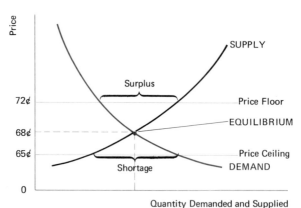

FIG. 6–13. Government regulation affects prices.

come family purchase of milk. The result of this, however, would be a short-age, and some form of rationing (milk tickets, special drawings, black mar-ket?) would then be required.

Although Figure 6-13 is an illustration of milk pricing and control impacts, the same concept could be extended to a variety of other areas:

1. Our minimum wage law represents a price floor ($2.30 per hour in 1976) and appears to result in some surplus labor supplied (unem-ployment owing to elasticity of labor demand).

2. The control of natural gas prices represents a price ceiling and appears to discourage exploration for natural gas (shortage) and encourage use of other fossil fuels.

3. Control of airline fares and trucking or railway rates represents price floors and has resulted in surpluses (empty planes and idle trucks or boxcars), as well as a high degree of market inefficiency and lack of price competition.

Notice that the above examples all show direct government regulation of the market through price floors or ceilings. There are also many indirect mar-ket control impacts through the effect on demand or supply forces themselves. For example, suppose in Figure 6-13 the decrease in supply is due to govern-ment regulation that milk can only be produced from cows at least three years old (perhaps milk "ages"?). Although price is not directly controlled, such a regulation will cause reduced supply, thus affecting market prices. Other, less extreme, examples of such indirect market controls would include safety or health requirements (acts that increase costs and reduce supply); environ-mental standards or restrictions (increased costs and reduced supply); sub-sidies or tax incentives for output (reduced costs and increased supply); pro-hibition of output, such as automatic weapons for private use (reduced supply and reduced demand); or personal income tax exemptions and tax rebates (increased demand).

In all of these examples, the point is that government does affect the market daily, and such controls do have serious and long-term impacts. Remember that our market system is quite interdependent, and a regulation in one particular sector may have wide impact beyond the specific control objective. Perhaps the greatest contribution of supply-demand analysis is prediction of possible impact before regulation is enacted, thus, it is hoped, preventing harmful economic consequences.

We might add here that the U.S. government is not alone in its involvement in market regulation. Many other governments of the world pursue market regulation, and some do so to a much greater degree. The Soviet government, for example, directly sets most product and resource prices, although some free-market operations do exist. Many nations of the world have foreign trade controls (tariffs, quotas, exchange controls, and so on), tax systems to encourage or discourage productive activity, and varying degrees of economic planning to direct output and consumption.

You might well ask, "Does such regulation benefit market operation?" This is a good question, but one you must answer for yourself after considering all sides. (Here is the test of economic understanding!) Economists vary in their opinions as to the effect of governmental regulation: some praise it; some condemn it. Across-the-board answers are very difficult, for many areas and types of regulation are involved. One could support, for example, state regulation of utility rates yet oppose federal levying of tariff rates. Or one could support environmental standards and welfare payments yet oppose government price controls and market restrictions on prostitution and gambling.

This is not an attempt by the authors to sidestep the issue of government regulation. We have our opinions, as all economists do; we tend toward the free-market position. However, the purpose of this book is to help you gain economic understanding and not to promote personal doctrines. Beyond this, the purpose of economic education is to provide you, the student and citizen, with the tools to understand the issues and to draw your own conclusions. What we have attempted to do is to provide you with the tools of demand-supply analysis (Chapters 3-6) so that *you* can evaluate the desirability of alternative market operation and regulation. How you judge such alternatives will depend on *your* goals and values, and *you* must makes choices daily as a participant in our market economy.

TERMS

Comparative advantage principle. Specialization of activity based upon greatest degree of productivity in a certain activity. (An example of this principle would be a person's becoming an economist, where he is most qualified, even though he is also qualified in other fields.)

Equilibrium price. The market price at which quantity demanded just equals quantity supplied, and toward which market conditions will tend to move.

Exchange process. The daily market activity of buyers demanding goods and services and sellers supplying goods and services at some market price.

Money. Some item that provides a medium of exchange, standard of value, and store of value—all necessary for market exchange.

Specialization. The act or process of engaging in a single activity, with resulting gains in productivity and efficiency.

QUESTIONS FOR STUDY

1. Class project: Divide your class into two parts, consumers and producers for some good. Have each group draw up their offers to buy (consumers) and sell (producers) separately; then compare these demand and supply schedules. Is there any equilibrium? How might a compromise be reached?
2. Why do you suppose certain years and models of automobiles sell at a price much different from that of other brands? (Compare a 1965 Ford Thunderbird with a 1965 Plymouth Valiant.)
3. Why might a farmer produce soybeans if the price of corn falls? What would happen to the price of soybeans if this reaction were widespread among farmers? Find out what the "corn-hog cycle" is, and explain it in terms of supply-demand theory.
4. True or false?
   a. If price drops, consumers increase quantity demanded.
   b. If price drops, producers increase supply.
   c. If price rises, consumers decrease demand.
   d. If price rises, producers increase quantity supplied.
   e. A falling price helps to correct a market shortage.
   f. A rising price helps to correct a market shortage.
5. Given these data:

THOUSANDS OF BUSHELS DEMANDED	PRICE PER BUSHEL	THOUSANDS OF BUSHELS SUPPLIED	SURPLUS (+) OR SHORTAGE (−)
10	$3.00	75	
20	2.00	50	
30	1.50	30	
40	1.00	15	

   a. What will be the market or equilibrium price? What is the equilibrium quantity? Using the surplus-shortage column, explain why your answers are correct.
   b. Using the preceding data, graph the demand and the supply.

c. Now suppose that the government establishes a ceiling price of $1. Explain carefully the effects of this ceiling price.

d. Assume now that the government establishes a supported price of $3. Explain carefully the effects of this supported price.

REFERENCES

Adelman, M. A. *The World Petroleum Market*. Baltimore, Md.: The Johns Hopkins Press, 1973.

Carson, R. B., et al. *Government in the American Economy*. Washington, D.C.: Brookings Institution, 1973.

Gill, Richard T. *Economics*, Second Edition. Pacific Palisades, Calif.: Goodyear Publishing Company, Inc., 1975, Chapters 2–3.

Henderson, Hubert. *Supply and Demand*. Chicago: University of Chicago Press, 1958, Chapter 2.

Phillips, Alarmin. *Prices: Issues*. Philadelphia, Pa.: University of Pennsylvania Press, 1970.

7

WHY ARE BUSINESS FIRMS IMPORTANT?

SHORT ANSWER. In the U.S. market-oriented economic system, business firms provide employment and income for employees while producing goods and services for a profit.

YOU AND BUSINESS FIRMS

"The business of America is business." So spoke Calvin Coolidge in describing the role of the business firm in American society. Karl Marx predicted grasping business monopolists would so exploit the worker as to cause eventual revolution and the overthrow of capitalism. Today the business firm is hailed by some as presenting a bulwark of innovation and efficiency and criticized by others as disregarding social problems and obtaining exorbitant profits by gouging. Where, in these viewpoints, the truth regarding business firms lies, you will have to determine for yourself. What we're concerned with in this chapter are the many important aspects of business operation, as indicated by Figure 7-1.

How many times today have you come in contact with some type of private business? How about the breakfast food you purchased or the radio or TV station you turned on or the lunch at the pizza parlor or the movie you plan to attend tonight? All these daily events represent your contact with the product market comprising over 14 million U.S. business firms. These firms are a diverse group in type, size, and location and supply us daily with a great variety of products and services, as indicated in Figure 7-2. And although you perhaps take for granted such contacts ("What's so special about a grocery store?"), recall that such daily consumer-business contacts collectively answer our basic questions of what and how to produce.

FIG. 7–1. Business firms provide output and employment.

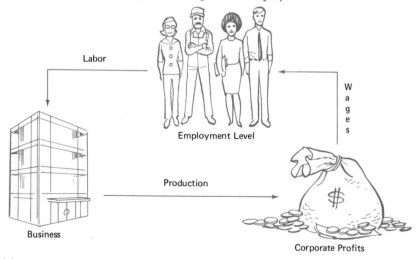

Labor

Employment Level

Wages

Business

Production

Corporate Profits

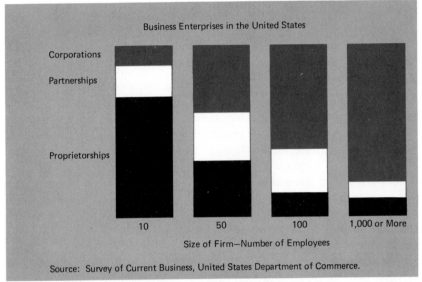

FIG. 7–2. Business structure by type and size.

Besides supplying us with products for consumption, these same firms also generate the paychecks necessary to buy those goods through the hiring of resources in the resource market. (Do you recall the circular-flow model of the U.S. economy in Chapter 2?) Through the generation of this income, the business firm also affects the basic question of for whom to produce. In both the product and resource markets these business firms affect you significantly and continuously.

Given these important influences of business firms in our economic system, we shall discuss in this chapter how businesses are organized, how they compete, and how government regulations affect their operations. We shall also describe the basic decision-making process of a typical business firm. Before we look at specific business structures, however, let's review some basic assumptions underlying the functioning of all U.S. business firms.

As with basic assumptions of most social institutions, we tend to take for granted much of the framework of business operation. For example, the concept of a business firm operating for a profit is the foundation for virtually all U.S. commerce. Simple? But how often do we think to ourselves that profit is what motivates decisions by all our businesses, pushes out the products for your consumption, and generates the paychecks for your income? This driving force of profit depends on the even more basic right to own private property and on its protection under the law. Bluntly put, the businessman can seek a profit because the use of his own property rests on his personal decisions, and protection of both his property and his pursuit of profit is guaranteed by police and fire departments and other government agencies.

In conjunction with the fundamental concept of profit are assumptions of competition (businesses try to outsell their rivals) and consumer sovereignty, whereby the business must please its customers or . . . no sales, no profit, no business!

All these concepts are known and assumed consciously or subconsciously by most of us. Well, that's the way our system operates, and you've lived in the knowledge of these assumptions since you were a youngster. However, by this stage in your economic understanding, we hope you realize that such concepts are not assumed in all economic systems. Command and tradition systems do not operate in this fashion, and many market-oriented systems differ considerably from each other. (See Chapter 2.) Our way is not a universal pattern. We stress this fact because these basic assumptions (profit, private property, protection under the law, competition, consumer sovereignty) are often obscured in discussions of business structures. These concepts are essential, however, in appreciating such structures and in gaining realistic economic understanding.

An experiment in thought: Suppose profit were unknown, although the basic questions facing all societies (Chapter 2) still had to be answered. How would an economic system, in your construction, operate? Or try this the next time you stroll through the local grocery store: Think of the countless business decisions required to operate the store (location, ordering, pricing, hiring, advertising, and so on). How would all these decisions be made without the basic assumptions of profit, private property, and competition?

TYPES OF BUSINESSES

When you begin to analyze all the varying types and activities of business firms, you encounter an amazing variety and complexity. This process can be simplied if you categorize these business firms by describing the different characteristics for which they are noted. By using these categories as guidelines, you can look at a specific example and determine into which slot it will fit. The purpose is not to pigeonhole all businesses, but to aid your understanding of how they're organized and why they operate in a particular manner. Remember that some specific firms may exhibit qualities in a number of categories.

Although many systems might be noted here, there are three groups we'd like to consider: *hierarchy of firms, legal types,* and *market models.*

Hierarchy of Firms

Figure 7-3 illustrates a seldom discussed point about business organization. Business firms operate at different levels in relation to the consumer and in the degree to which they specialize in their function. Some businesses only

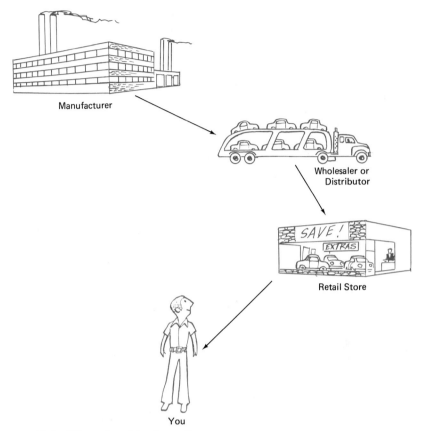

Manufacturer

Wholesaler or
Distributor

Retail Store

You

FIG. 7–3. Hierarchy of business firms.

manufacture products, but leave the actual selling to other firms. Some firms only transport (wholesale) and distribute products to those local retailers actually in touch with the buying public.

Of course, some businesses do all these steps at once, such as the neighborhood hamburger stand, which makes hamburgers and sells them directly to you (but other firms make the buns, catsup, ground meat, and so on, used by the stand). Perhaps another example of an "integrated" business (operates at all hierarchy levels) would be an oil company that has its own oil wells, pipelines, refinery, truck tankers, and service stations. In fact, the term *vertical merger* applies to a business acquiring other firms to have control of production from raw material supply to consumer purchase.

What we're illustrating is that business firms often specialize in a particular relationship to the "consumption process," be it manufacturing, distribution, or wholesale or retail operations. All of these specialized business operations are, of course, important to you, the consumer, as all are necessary to place products at your purchasing command. This interdependence, if you can step back to appreciate it, is amazing because in its generally unregulated fashion it actually works! Imagine, for instance, the many businesses represented by your stroll through the local grocery (retailer).

As we talk below of legal types and market models, you will see that a business firm (1) may be at one level of the business hierarchy, (2) may be of a specific legal type, and (3) may compete according to a specific market model. These three categories of business operation (hierarchy, legal type, market model) overlap, and by their combination and classification you may describe and analyze any business firm fairly well.

Legal Types

When viewing business structure by legal type, you're considering how firms are organized according to the rules and regulations of federal, state, and local government agencies; that is, you're looking at ownership, liability for failure, method of raising operating funds, and regulation of opening and closing. The three legal types of business organization in the United States are the *sole proprietorship, partnership,* and *corporation*. Let us discuss the characteristics of each type and note examples.

The *sole proprietorship* is the most frequent (80 per cent) legal type, found in almost any neighborhood or area in the form of single-owner and operator hamburger stands, family grocery stores, gas stations, other small retail stores, farms, and professional services. These businesses are usually small in sales volume, store size, and number of employees hired; and they usually make direct contact with the consumer. They're probably the type you commonly patronize daily, and they often emphasize personal contact, service, and conversation as you purchase. In fact, you may yourself wish to own and operate this type of business. (A bit risky, as failure rates are high, but you do have pride of ownership, do your own thing, and can't be fired!)

Although the sole proprietorship firm does not sell a great volume or hire many workers, it is a significant factor in daily consumer-business contact. Despite some predictions to the contrary, it will probably be around for some time. And a somewhat new and growing trend may even stimulate the sole proprietorship; franchising. A *franchise business* is one in which a large parent company (such as Kentucky Fried Chicken, AAMCO, McDonald's) grants an individual permission to operate under its well-known name, often providing consulting, training, and advertising services. In return, the individual must pay for the franchise and often must agree to operate according to certain product quality standards, facilities decor, operation hours, and pricing guidelines. A franchise operation may provide a profitable entry for the aspiring business student if he carefully reads contracts and compares "opportunity costs."

Sole Proprietorship
(80% of U.S. Businesses)

Partnership
(8% of U.S. Businesses)

Corporation
(12% of U.S. Businesses)

FIG. 7–4. Legal types of business firms.

In the following list of the specific characteristics of a sole proprietorship, try to recognize examples from your own daily contact:

1. Ownership: One owner—who usually runs and manages the business as well. Provides independence for owner.

2. Finance: Usually, owner's own savings or funds borrowed in his name.

3. Liability: Unlimited—in that failure of business can mean that

the owner's other (personal) property is subject to settlement of debts.

4. Ease of start: Usually easy to start, involving small initial funds and the meeting of usually simple legal requirements limited to city business license.

5. Life of business: Limited—business folds if owner quits or dies without his or her heirs carrying on.

6. Failure rate: Quite high—often caused by inexperience, lack of operating funds, desire for security of paycheck by working for a big firm.

7. Hierarchy: Most often at retail level.

The *partnership* (some 8 per cent of all U.S. businesses) is similar in many respects to the sole proprietorship and is most frequently found in the fields of medicine, law, stock brokerage, real estate, construction, consumer services, and some retail and wholesale lines. You'll often find father and son businesses here, family operations, or persons with specialties cooperating (particularly in medicine, law, and accounting). Again, there is frequent direct consumer contact, though more often in the form of services performed than in goods sold.

How many businesses do you know that have these characteristics of a partnership?

1. Ownership: Two or more owners, usually manager-operators, who may be *full* or *limited* partners. A full partner shares in direct proportion to his or her professional commitment in the finance and operation of a business, whereas a limited—or silent—partner may only contribute financing and receive a percentage return of profits.

2. Finance: Provided by owners' savings or borrowings, with perhaps more available with additional partners.

3. Liability: *Unlimited*—full partners are subect, each personally, for 100 per cent of the debts of the business. Limited partners must settle for stated amounts of profits, but have a stated amount of loss they can suffer.

4. Ease of start: Usually easy, though usually a partnership agreement must be drawn and legally recorded, stating the functions of each partner and his liability.

5. Life of the business: Limited life, as the withdrawal or death of any partner means redrawing of the partnership agreement.

6. Failure rate: Still high, though usually lower than with the sole proprietorship.

7. Hierarchy: Often at the retail level, but sometimes at wholesale level.

Although the *corporation* is a much less frequent legal type (12 per cent of firms) than the sole proprietorship or partnership, it is much more important in terms of sales volume and number of employees hired. Although many small corporations exist, it is the few giant firms that greatly affect our economy. See Figure 7-5 for some idea of the size of these large corporations. Only a few of the "*Fortune* 500" business listings are illustrated here, but perhaps enough to exemplify the size and impacts of corporations. In 1975 these 500 largest industrial corporations accounted for 60 per cent of all sales in the United States (GNP), 15 per cent of the civil labor force, and 35 per cent of all corporate profits. You must combine many small businesses (proprietorships, partnerships) in your daily contact to equal the impact of one of these large corporations.

Another way to look at such bigness is to compare Exxon, with some $45 billion in sales and assets of $33 billion and 137,000 employees, to the 144 members of the United Nations: In 1975 only eighteen nations had annual sales (GNP) larger than Exxon alone. That's a big, big business!

Such bigness, although quite important to our economy in terms of products and jobs, worries many people. They are concerned that these large companies may gobble up smaller firms and thus gain excessive economic power and dominate our economy. And predictions are for fewer, larger businesses with much control of market areas. Other concerns are that such large corporations may achieve great political weight both in our domestic Congress and legislatures and in their international subsidiary operations. (Many of these large domestic corporations are also multinational businesses with worldwide operations.)

There are also arguments supporting such big business operation, often pointing to the lower costs and greater efficiency resulting from large-scale operation and mass production. Also, such size may contribute to output and employment stability and may even spur technological advance through large research and development budgets.

Given such pros and cons of large corporate ownership, it is difficult for the economist or citizen to evaluate corporations on the basis of size alone. Perhaps a more important criterion, frequently adopted even in Supreme Court decisions (the "rule of reason" dictum), is the competitive behavior and consumer impact of these industrial giants, that is, did Standard Oil abuse its oil monopoly powers and reap exorbitant profits during the oil embargo of 1973? Could American Telephone and Telegraph operate more competitively and serve customers more equitably if its size were reduced? These specific types of questions are perhaps more important to evaluate

The 500 Largest Industrial Corporations (ranked by sales)

Rank '75	Rank '74	Company	Sales ($100)	Assets ($100)	Rank	Net Income ($100)	Rank	Stockholders' Equity ($100)	Rank
1	1	Exxon (New York)	44,864,824	32,839,398	1	2,503,013	1	17,024,411	1
2	2	General Motors (Detroit)	35,724,911	21,664,885	2	1,253,092	3	13,082,365	2
3	4	Texaco (New York)	24,507,454	17,262,448	3	830,583	4	8,674,817	4
4	3	Ford Motor (Dearborn, Mich.)	24,009,100	14,020,200	6	322,700	23	6,350,300	8
5	5	Mobil Oil (New York)	20,620,392	15,050,287	5	809,877	5	6,840,997	5
6	6	Standard Oil of California (San Francisco)	16,822,077	12,898,150	7	772,509	7	6,485,062	6
7	9	International Business Machines (Armonk, N.Y.)	14,436,541	15,530,476	4	1,989,877	2	11,415,771	3
8	7	Gulf Oil (Pittsburgh)	14,268,000	12,425,000	8	700,000	8	6,458,000	7
9	8	General Electric (Fairfield, Conn.)	13,339,100	9,763,500	11	580,800	11	4,069,200	12
10	11	Chrysler (Highland Park, Mich.)	11,699,305	6,266,728	17	(259,535)	492	2,409,209	22
11	10	International Tel. & Tel. (New York)	11,367,647	10,407,941	9	398,171	15	4,252,311	11
12	13	Standard Oil (Ind.) (Chicago)	9,955,248*	9,854,099	10	786,987	6	5,584,919	9
13	12	U.S. Steel (Pittsburgh)	8,167,269	8,148,174	12	559,614	12	4,850,143	10
14	14	Shell Oil (Houston)	8,143,445*	7,010,753	14	514,827	13	3,911,364	13
15	18	Atlantic Richfield (Los Angeles)	7,307,854*	7,364,787	13	350,295	17	3,663,558	16
16	16	Continental Oil (Stamford, Conn.)	7,253,801	5,184,581	20	330,085	22	2,134,882	25
17	17	E.I. du Pont de Nemours (Wilmington, Del.)	7,221,500	6,425,000	16	271,800	25	3,834,900	14
18	15	Western Electric (New York)	6,590,116	4,999,944	22	107,308	81	3,209,232	17
19	28	Procter & Gamble (Cincinnati)	6,081,675	3,652,673	32	333,862	21	2,118,147	26
20	19	Westinghouse Electric (Pittsburgh)	5,862,747	4,866,286	23	165,224	45	2,001,692	27
21	22	Union Carbide (New York)	5,665,000	5,740,800	19	381,700	16	2,748,000	18
22	24	Tenneco (Houston)	5,599,709	6,584,204	15	342,936	18	2,400,079	23
23	23	Goodyear Tire & Rubber (Akron, Ohio)	5,452,473	4,173,675	29	161,613	48	1,816,051	34
24	26	International Harvester (Chicago)	5,335,385	3,510,340	33	79,354	120	1,443,863	42
25	20	Occidental Petroleum (Los Angeles)	5,333,919	3,503,372	34	171,956	42	1,200,606	52
26	25	Phillips Petroleum (Bartlesville, Okla.)	5,133,557	4,544,929	25	342,568	19	2,424,299	21
27	34	Union Oil of California (Los Angeles)	5,086,427	3,776,124	30	232,754	32	1,919,441	29
28	21	Bethlehem Steel (Bethlehem, Pa.)	4,977,229	4,591,541	24	241,951	30	2,611,986	19
29	36	Caterpillar Tractor (Peoria, Ill.)	4,963,683	3,386,635	37	398,735	14	1,760,745	36
30	32	Eastman Kodak (Rochester, N.Y.)	4,958,536	5,056,238	21	613,694	10	3,709,079	15
31	35	Rockwell International (Pittsburgh)	4,943,400	2,888,100	47	101,600	90	1,126,900	56
32	27	Dow Chemical (Midland, Mich.)	4,888,114	5,846,731	18	615,662	9	2,450,556	20
33	33	Kraftco (Glenview, Ill.)	4,857,378	1,671,172	93	139,551	55	938,476	72
34	31	RCA (New York)	4,789,500	3,728,400	31	110,000	78	1,179,700	54
35	30	Esmark (Chicago)	4,730,739	1,473,924	110	79,685	119	621,781	132
36	37	Sun Oil (St. Davids, Pa.)	4,389,129	4,383,519	27	220,054	34	2,391,300	24
37	29	LTV (Dallas)	4,312,463	1,962,813	76	13,142	374	360,463	215
38	42	Beatrice Foods (Chicago)	4,191,764	1,658,170	94	134,764	59	871,451	81
39	41	Xerox (Stamford, Conn.)	4,094,032	4,455,649	26	244,307	29	1,906,957	30
40	46	United Technologies (Hartford)	3,877,772	2,701,311	48	117,490	73	957,660	70
41	45	Greyhound (Phoenix)	3,733,291	1,427,964	114	81,220	115	614,969	133
42	40	Firestone Tire & Rubber (Akron, Ohio)	3,724,150	3,180,801	44	134,296	61	1,528,699	39
43	39	Boeing (Seattle)	3,718,852	1,788,896	88	76,347	125	1,010,093	66
44	57	General Foods (White Plains, N.Y.)	3,675,092	1,896,554	79	99,386	93	902,905	77
45	50	Ashland Oil (Russell, Ky.)	3,637,126	1,973,017	73	119,367	70	725,617	109
46	43	Monsanto (St. Louis)	3,624,700	3,450,900	35	306,300	24	1,976,700	28
47	44	W.R. Grace (New York)	3,529,163	2,523,803	52	166,678	43	1,075,013	59
48	49	R.J. Reynolds Industries (Winston-Salem, N.C.)	3,528,895	3,294,322	40	338,673	20	1,899,580	32
49	53	Litton Industries (Beverly Hills)	3,430,168	2,185,731	66	35,280	233	796,598	97
50	47	Lockheed Aircraft (Burbank, Calif.)	3,387,211	1,573,400	101	45,300	191	75,300	465

FIG. 7–5. The "Fortune 500" directory.

than mere corporation size. (You know, there are some shady proprietorships and partnerships around as well!)

These questions are of constant concern to the federal government's Antitrust Division of the Department of Justice, which brings suit against business mergers and business practices that may harm competition and public welfare. The issue of bigness and corporate behavior is one that has been around for some time and poses a large challenge to antitrust legislation attempting

Employees Number	Rank	Net Income as Per Cent of Sales %	Rank	Stockholders' Equity %	Rank	'75($)	'74($)	'65($)	Growth Rate 1965-75 %	Rank	1975 %	Rank	Total Return to Investors 1965-75 Average %	Rank	Industry Code
137,000	12	5.6	142	14.7	128	11.19	14.04	4.80	8.83	175	45.06	269	6.43	154	29
681,000	1	3.5	275	9.6	314	4.32	3.27	7.41	(5.25)	414	95.20	88	0.29	315	40
75,235	31	3.4	284	9.6	316	3.06	5.84	2.35	2.68	326	21.56	386	(0.23)	328	29
416,120	2	1.3	424	5.1	418	3.46	3.86	6.33	(5.86)	418	39.62	294	3.34	219	40
71,300	36	3.9	243	11.8	235	7.95	10.28	3.15	9.70	153	40.70	291	4.75	187	29
38,801	98	4.6	197	11.9	229	4.55	5.71	2.34	6.88	222	41.02	288	2.89	236	29
288,647	5	13.8	10	17.4	60	13.35	12.47	3.53	14.23	74	37.35	306	7.36	136	44
52,100	58	4.9	173	10.8	278	3.60	5.47	2.06	5.74	252	25.97	362	1.78	268	29
375,000	4	4.3	216	14.3	141	3.17	3.34	1.96	4.93	273	42.99	279	0.41	311	36
217,594	6	—	—	—	—	(4.33)	(0.92)	5.53	—		39.69	293	(10.89)	442	40
376,000	3	3.5	276	9.4	323	3.20	3.63	1.79	5.98	246	62.83	189	(1.15)	345	36
46,808	75	7.9	62	14.1	150	5.36	6.86	1.55	13.21	80	2.59	447	9.93	81	29
172,796	7	6.9	95	11.5	249	10.33	11.72	4.62	8.38	185	78.43	133	8.11	115	33
32,496	120	6.3	115	13.2	180	7.59	9.21	3.86	7.00	217	10.38	431	1.65	274	29
28,080	138	4.8	181	9.6	317	6.16	8.36	3.02	7.39	212	2.34	448	11.98	53	29
44,028	86	4.6	199	15.5	104	6.50	6.47	2.13	11.80	104	40.89	289	9.83	85	29
132,235	13	3.8	258	7.1	383	5.43	8.20	8.63	(4.53)	410	41.74	281	(2.55)	376	28
152,677	9	1.6	407	3.3	442	N.A.	N.A.	N.A.	—		—		—		36
51,400	60	5.5	145	15.8	95	4.05	3.85	1.53	10.22	142	11.66	428	12.64	47	43
166,048	8	2.8	329	8.3	354	1.89	0.31	1.43	2.83	323	43.47	272	(4.57)	406	36
106,475	19	6.7	100	13.9	158	6.23	8.69	3.76	5.18	267	53.54	229	3.53	218	28
78,380	28	6.1	122	14.3	140	4.15	4.08	1.81	8.65	179	20.99	391	6.64	150	29
148,225	10	3.0	321	8.9	334	2.24	2.18	1.53	3.89	301	77.47	139	2.91	235	30
104,170	20	1.5	415	5.5	411	2.77	4.46	3.46	(2.20)	385	21.90	384	(1.42)	351	45
33,000	117	3.2	299	14.3	139	2.64	4.74	0.55	16.98	48	17.66	400	6.79	146	10
30,506	129	6.7	102	14.1	147	4.50	5.30	1.91	8.95	169	29.13	346	10.70	72	29
15,668	250	4.6	198	12.1	224	6.81	8.92	3.30	7.51	210	8.79	435	1.47	283	29
112,749	17	4.9	176	9.3	325	5.54	7.85	3.28	5.38	260	43.22	278	3.93	209	33
78,286	29	8.0	60	22.6	22	6.97	4.01	2.85	9.36	160	47.64	253	6.31	158	45
124,000	14	12.4	16	16.5	77	3.80	3.90	1.54	9.45	159	72.06	155	7.82	122	38
122,789	15	2.1	379	9.0	330	2.96	4.14	3.88	(2.67)	389	30.98	336	0.43	310	41
53,121	56	12.6	14	25.1	16	6.65	6.03	1.20	18.68	40	69.23	166	16.40	28	28
47,845	71	2.9	325	14.9	125	5.01	3.41	2.41	7.59	207	27.36	352	4.19	203	20
113,000	16	2.3	364	9.3	324	1.40	1.45	1.70	(1.92)	382	87.25	104	(5.03)	411	36
33,600	109	1.7	405	12.8	189	5.05	4.47	1.08	16.68	53	47.27	257	6.75	149	20
27,848	141	5.0	167	9.2	326	4.20	7.84	2.11	7.13	215	(17.55)	472	2.63	242	29
60,400	43	0.3	460	3.6	438	1.02	10.32	1.84	(5.73)	417	14.10	412	(9.49)	437	20
64,000	39	3.2	300	15.5	107	1.71	1.55	0.64	10.33	140	70.04	164	9.13	96	20
93,532	23	6.0	126	12.8	191	3.07	4.18	0.94	12.56	91	0.73	455	(1.91)	362	38
138,072	11	3.0	316	12.3	217	7.78	6.62	4.61	5.37	261	48.28	251	(1.32)	350	41
53,438	55	2.2	374	13.2	178	1.87	1.37	1.60	1.57	343	38.17	301	1.31	287	20
111,000	18	3.6	267	8.8	341	2.36	2.71	1.51	4.57	280	74.57	146	3.93	208	30
72,600	34	2.1	380	7.6	372	3.60	3.42	4.82	(2.88)	392	61.12	194	(6.86)	430	41
48,000	68	2.7	341	11.0	270	2.00	2.40	1.72	1.52	344	62.40	190	0.20	318	20
27,000	144	3.3	293	16.5	80	4.42	4.45	2.00	8.25	189	26.67	358	1.07	297	29
59,242	46	8.5	53	15.5	105	8.63	9.25	3.74	8.72	177	93.70	93	3.28	222	28
60,200	44	4.7	187	15.5	103	5.31	4.12	2.80	6.61	230	20.13	395	(3.32)	391	28
34,666	105	9.6	39	17.8	57	7.39	6.99	3.27	8.49	183	23.01	377	8.58	105	21
97,000	22	1.0	438	4.4	429	0.87	(1.29)	1.36	(4.37)	408	125.35	35	(12.85)	451	44
57,567	47	1.3	427	60.2	1	3.86	2.04	4.89	(2.34)	386	110.27	53	(16.69)	455	41

to achieve economies of large-scale production in addition to the efficiencies of competition.

Large corporations are seldom in direct contact with the consumer. These firms are usually in the manufacturing end of the business hierarchy, and their products normally reach you, the consumer, through small, local sole proprietorships or partnerships. An example is that of GM, with Chevrolet as one division among many, producing autos and distributing them to local dealers. You see the dealer's showroom, but never the assembly line. (Visit an assembly line sometime for a real experience, or read *Wheels,* by Arthur Hailey!)

Another interesting point about corporations is the *separation of owners from managers.* You may own part of a corporation (as a stockholder), but you don't actually run the daily operations. Take Exxon again as an example. This business is owned by some 1 million stockholders, but is managed and run on a daily basis by professionals who have themselves a minute percentage of ownership. Whether these corporate employees (termed the *technostructure* by John Kenneth Galbraith in his book *Economics and the Public Purpose*) act primarily to serve their own interests or to benefit stockholders is another debatable issue, upon which economists and citizens disagree. Suffice it to say that such corporate managers are the real decision makers within these large corporations, and their decisions greatly affect our American economy. They are often paid rather well for such decision making. Harold Geneen, chairman of International Telephone and Telegraph in 1975, received a total of $766,085 in salary, bonuses, stock options, and benefits!

In summarizing these comments about corporations, compare the characteristics of the corporation with those listed previously for sole proprietorship and partnership:

1. Ownership: Many owners, in the form of common and preferred stockholders. Yet the owners seldom manage, and the managers may own only small amounts of outstanding stock.

2. Finance: Provided by sale of *stock,* common or preferred (actual ownership of business with voting rights), or *bonds* (no ownership or vote, but guarantee of repayment with interest). Through either method large amounts of funds are easily obtained.

3. Liability: *Limited,* in that a stockholder can lose only the value of his stock, but his personal wealth is exempt from attachment by the corporation's creditors. The corporation is itself a *legal entity* (a person?) before the law.

4. Ease of start: Easier to accumulate funds through the sale of stocks or bonds, but more difficult in terms of obtaining a corporate charter (state government usually) and in terms of initial size of business required.

5. Life of business: Unlimited life in that ownership (stock) may frequently change hands (stock market).

6. Failure rate: Usually much lower than that for proprietorship or partnership, as size and financial strength are much greater. But they do fail (Penn Central Railroad).

7. Hierarchy: Most often at manufacturing level.

Market Models

A third way to categorize business firms is to look at the *type of competition* in which they engage; that is, how do businesses vie for the customer's dollar in the particular product field? Are there many competitors or only a few large firms? Do they ignore rivals' decisions, or does each firm attempt to anticipate the other? Do they entice the consumer by offering lower prices *(price competition)*, or are other services offered *(nonprice competition)* such as games or prizes, higher quality, greater variety, better services, and other inducements to buy? As you consider these questions and begin to think about the large variety of competitive business practices, perhaps you see that competition in the business world involves a multitude of complexities and decisions, all of which affect you, the consumer.

We have four market models of competition to discuss: *monopolistic competition, pure competition, oligopoly,* and *monopoly*. Let's summarize the characteristics of each in Figure 7-6 and then discuss the high points. As with many categorical systems, realize that some businesses may exhibit characteristics of several competitive models and may not fit neatly into one of these four categories. Again, the use of such categories is not so much to pigeonhole any one business firm as to analyze and understand more clearly typical business competition.

We can illustrate the characteristics noted in Figure 7-6 by taking a few

FIG. 7–6. Market models of business competition.

Type of Model	Ease of Entry into Industry	Type of Product Made	Price or Nonprice Competition	Degree of Regulation
Perfect Competition	Very easy (finance, license, etc.)	Standard	Little of either (only determine quantity)	Very little
Monopolistic Competition	Very easy	Differentiated	Mostly nonprice, but price also	Very little
Oligopoly	Quite difficult (very costly)	Differentiated	Mostly nonprice	Much federal government action (antitrust)
Monopoly	No entry allowed	Usually standard	No competition but government regulated	Prices usually regulated by state government

daily examples. The many retail stores in which you shop daily (probably of sole proprietorship) are usually of the *monopolistic competition* variety. This odd term, combining monopoly with competition, means that there are many firms, yet they seek to offer their products for sale by appeals so unique or special (differentiated) that you will buy only their brand. These monopolistic competitors thus have some degree of market power and price control (depending on their ability to differentiate or distinguish their product); yet they must also operate in a market with many rivals eager to duplicate or improve these product qualities. You'll find both price (read grocery ads or car lot prices) and nonprice (service, convenience, stamps, attractive facilities, and so on) competition here. In the U.S. economy this is the most frequent market model.

Pure competition seldom actually exists (except, perhaps, in certain agricultural products) because it is difficult to find a product field where all producers sell exactly the same (standard) product to large numbers of buyers at a standard price. The pure competitor would thus have no market control and no pricing control. He can only decide on the best quantity to be sold at a market-determined price. Perhaps small-volume farmers would come close to pure competition (selling a standard grade of corn or hogs at a current market price) or even the small trucking firm operating under standard rates. However, in both of these examples there are significant degrees of federal government control (in price supports and Interstate Commerce Commision trucking rates) that make the existence of pure competition less likely in the modern U.S. economy.

The *oligopoly* market model is another odd term and applies to those product fields where there are only a few very large businesses (auto and aluminum producers are a good example) that produce most—or all—of the output of an industry. Note the large percentage of total industry volume conducted by the largest four firms (termed the *concentration ratio*) in Figure 7-7. Because of this concentration, each firm must react to whatever its rivals do. (*Mutual interdependence* is the formal term.) This reaction is something like a poker game. The firms must respond to each other to maintain their market share, but try to avoid competing with each other on the basis of price. (Can you see how a price war could develop here?) There is, however, much nonprice competition in the form of emphasizing new models and features of products, primarily through the use of advertising. An example would be the recent introduction of new smaller cars by all domestic car firms in response to foreign car competition. Notice also that oligopolists are usually at the manufacturing end of the business ladder and are usually large corporations. Of all market models, the oligopolist is frequently of most concern to the economist because of the large industry impact and concentrated economic and political power. More on this in Chapter 8.

The *monopoly* model is an interesting market area. Although illegal (outlawed by the Sherman and Clayton Antitrust Acts of 1890 and 1914) mo-

Type of Industry	Per Cent of Industry Shipments Accounted for by Largest 4 Firms:
Aluminum	100
Linoleum	87
Copper Smelting and Refining	86
Typewriters	83
Cigarettes	82
Tin Cans and Other Tinware	80
Tires and Tubes	79
Motor Vehicles and Parts	75
Tractors	73
Biscuits and Crackers	71
Distilled Liquors	64
Glass Containers	63
Organic Chemicals	59
Steel Works and Rolling Mills	54
Electrical Appliances	50

Source: U.S. Bureau of the Census, *Survey of Current Business*, 1973.

FIG. 7–7. Concentration ratio, 1972.

nopolies exist, usually as public utilities (telephone, water, electricity, railroad) and some industrial processes (for example, that of Polaroid before Kodak's competing process). Does this sound contradictory? Well, perhaps so, but monopolies that do exist are regulated, with restrictions placed upon them by federal and state government agencies as to prices they may charge and services they may offer. The common practice is to have a government agency (usually a state public utilities commission) grant an exclusive area franchise to only one utility company, but then have the agency regulate the prices and services the company offers to the public.

Although competition is usually desirable for its results of lower prices and better service, monopoly is preferred in the utility field for these same reasons. It's believed that a single, larger company can provide better service at lower prices. This reasoning is based on typical fixed-cost behavior: If it costs a great deal to build a facility (power plant, phone lines, or water pipes), then the more of the product produced, the lower the cost per unit. So you limit the sales to one company in one area, with resulting lower prices. Imagine the

Total Fixed Cost	Number of Units Produced	Fixed Cost Per Unit (Average Fixed Cost [AFC])
$1,000	1	$1,000
1,000	10	100
1,000	100	10
1,000	1,000	1

FIG. 7–8. Fixed-cost behavior.

mess if two or three electricity suppliers in one community had each to provide their own power lines available to every potential customer. Perhaps Figure 7-8 shows reduction of fixed costs more clearly.

This introduction of cost behavior is intended not only to illustrate the possible economic advantages under a regulated monopoly, but to move closer to an analysis of business decision making. For individual business decisions collectively provide answers to our basic economic questions, and these decisions revolve largely around cost and revenue behavior. Let's take a look at costs, revenues, profits, and the business decision process.

BUSINESS DECISION MAKING

We've talked a great deal about the variety of American business firms and the differing approaches by which they can be categorized. But there is an even more important aspect of all business firms that we now examine. They must all make decisions constantly. It is such daily business decisions that are really crucial to the operation of our American economy, for in making these decisions the business firm not only affects its own profitability and existence, but also contributes to our entire economy's answers to the basic questions of *what, how,* and *for whom to produce.* Consider a decision on product prices or output levels made by a major U.S. oil company and the many consequences resulting from such a decision:

1. The company's profit will be affected, so will be the employment, income, and dividends of thousands of employees and stockholders.

2. Consumers will be affected by new (higher?) gas prices and may change their purchase patterns, thus affecting many other businesses and employees (compact cars and UAW layoffs?).

3. New federal government regulations may arise in response, perhaps

affecting excess profits, unemployment benefits, incentives for alternative energy sources, and energy–environment–employment trade-offs.

From such an example (realistic in the late 1970s?), do you see the importance of business decision making?

Although the decisions made by businessmen vary from firm to firm, they usually include what product to produce and sell, how many to sell, what price to charge, what extras (service, stamps, and so on) to offer, how much advertising, how much research or product development, how many people to hire, how much raw material to buy, how to comply with government regulations, and on and on. Sounds like a long list? Well, put yourself in any businessman's shoes, and then ask yourself what has to be done to keep the show running. Also, remember that all of these decisions must be made in the light of what competitors are doing, how consumers' buying patterns are changing, and what new government regulations are legislated.

The next question is, of course, "How are decisions made?" True, the process differs greatly among firms. Sometimes it is one man alone making choices, or it may be done through a highly specialized team approach. All we will do here is touch upon some general principles of decision making that apply to all firms, with the specific factors for a particular firm determining the application of these principles. Whether the business is a small proprietor or a giant, multinational, oligopolistic corporation, these decision principles hinge on *profit, revenue,* and *costs,* which we'll describe in the following paragraphs.

Profit

As everyone is supposed to know (our cultural assumptions?) a business is out to make a profit, which means basically to take in more money than is paid out (total profit = total revenue − total cost, or $TP = TR - TC$). This goal doesn't mean firms are uninterested in product quality or goodwill or customer satisfaction or combating pollution or many other considerations. Businesses are concerned with all these problem areas today (the problems are, in fact, ultimately related to profit), but they must also consider immediate profit, or the business won't be around to worry about these other factors. We should note, however, that it's usually the very large, long-established firms that consider their "social responsibilities" (or, cynically, their "social image") in the areas of pollution, poverty, discrimination, and national welfare.

Many factors bear upon profit calculations, including competition, consumer tastes and income, and government regulation. However, these factors usually enter profit calculation through their effect on revenue and costs. For example, government requirements for preventing pollutant emissions (smog!)

may add to auto production costs, thus affecting profits, thus influencing the response of car manufacturers to such regulations. Perhaps you see a basic debate issue shaping here within our American economy—free-market pursuit of profit versus government intervention in business operation to protect and further consumer welfare? If you do, you're correct: It is a large and continuing issue on which an understanding of the business decision-making process may throw some light.

Generally speaking, a business will aim at maximum profit via maximum revenue and minimum cost. This doesn't always mean that the largest profits occur where sales are the greatest or costs are lowest, for costs of production may be rising even faster than revenues from sales. (See Figure 7-15 and the $MC = MR$ logic in the following paragraphs.) But any decision the business

FIG. 7–9. Corporate profits, 1974.

SOURCE: The Conference Board, *Road Maps of Industry*, No. 1762, May, 1975.

Distribution of

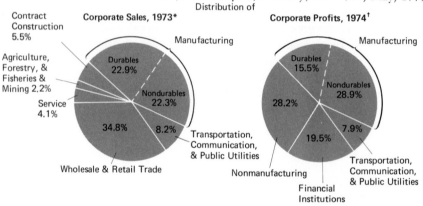

Corporate Sales, 1973*

Total: $2,181.1 Billion = 100%

*Excludes Finance, Insurance and Real Estate.

Corporate Profits, 1974†

Total: $106.0 Billion = 100%

*Profits before Taxes less Inventory Gain.

Disposition of
Total Corporate Profits, 1974

Total: $141.5 Billion = 100%

makes will involve considering the revenue-cost effect and the results in the form of profits. Perhaps Figure 7-9 gives you some idea of the magnitude of such profit results.

There are two basic "decision rules" involved in considering costs and revenue, both designed either to maximize profit or to minimize loss (a loss is a *negative* profit). The first approach is to compare total costs and revenue to see the resulting profit (if any): $TP = TR - TC$; that is, the businessman compares alternative decisions on the basis of their resulting total profit, choosing that alternative with maximum profit or minimum loss.

The second approach is somewhat more complicated, but more applicable to everyday decision making, for seldom can the entire costs and revenues of business operation be compared to make a routine decision. Would the average businessman go through all of his accounting records to determine the advisability of hiring an additional employee, installing a new cash register, or running an ad in a local newspaper? The business manager is more likely to compare the additional costs (*marginal cost; MC*) and additional revenues (*marginal revenue; MR*) resulting from the decision. For example, marginal cost may be the wages of the newly hired employee, whereas marginal revenue would be the added sales made owing to the hiring of that employee.

If the MR exceeds the MC, the business manager will proceed with the change because profit must increase or loss decrease. If MC exceeds MR, the alternative choice, no change, will be made, as profit would thereby decrease or loss increase. In fact, the "ideal" decision level (maximum profit or minimum loss) would be where MR just equals MC ($MR = MC$).

Let's now detail these decision rules further and apply them, analyzing the logic for their statement and exemplifying their application in Figure 7-15.

Revenue

Total revenue (TR) means all the money received from sales made and is equal to the number of items sold, quantity (*Q*), times the price at which the items are sold (*P*), or $TR = Q \times P$. Perhaps another term is *gross receipts*, and businesses often attempt to make these as large as possible to maximize total profit. A business may increase total revenue by selling more at a lower price, making an improved product, offering credit and other extras, and advertising its product—all to attract the customer's dollar. Again, the primary goal is maximum total profit, but increased sales may contribute to this goal only if costs are fairly stable or profit margins are fixed.

Many factors influence decision making, and all of them will affect profits by their effects on revenue. Consumer response to advertising or lower prices, competitors' reactions to sales decisions, or government regulation may affect revenue and profit results.

As an example of revenue behavior impact and decision rule application, a firm may estimate how much sales might be increased by an advertising campaign, how much this campaign would cost, and how profit might be increased even further. The businessman computes total costs and total expected revenues of such advertising and makes his decision on the total profit result ($TP = TR - TC$). As an alternative and a more likely decision-making process, he may compare the additional costs and additional revenues ($MC = MR$) of the advertising program.

In general, the businessman would decide to proceed as long as marginal revenue exceeded marginal cost ($MR > MC$). This latter decision rule is flexible in evaluating whether a venture upon which you decide to embark (increase advertising, introduce a new model, enlarge your store) adds more additional revenue (termed *marginal revenue*, or MR) than the additional costs (termed *marginal costs*, or MC). In even more elementary terms, you decide favorably on an action if it's "worth it" ($MR > MC$), but don't act if it looks like a "loser" ($MR < MC$). The "stopping point" is where $MR = MC$.

By the way, we should review a concept (recall Chapter 4?) in relation to deciding what price to change, that of *price elasticity of demand* (E_D). You might say the higher the price charged, the better, for this means more revenue for the seller. But this doesn't always happen. Recall the *law of demand* (Chapter 3), which states that fewer amounts are purchased at higher prices. If the drop in quantity is very large compared to the rise in price (an elastic demand), you may get less revenue. Consider the example in Figure 7-10. Suppose you're now selling eleven ties per day at $2 each, for a total revenue of $22. Then let us say you raise the price to $3, sell fewer ties (eight), but take in more revenue ($24). So you say, "That's great. Let's go even higher!" But when your price is $4 and only five ties are sold, your revenue drops to $20. The tie buyers now wear turtlenecks. You still do not know which output level is most profitable, as we have not yet compared costs with these revenue results. But with any given cost levels, such revenue behavior is very important.

Your decision to set a particular price must consider the extent to which customers will respond to the price change through changes in the amounts they purchase. This response factor is where the term *elasticity* is derived. An *inelastic* (small) response occurs when the percentage change in quantity purchased is less than the percentage change in price, whereas an *elastic demand*

FIG. 7–10. Elasticity of demand affects revenue.

Price	Quantity Sold	Total Revenue (Price X Quantity)	Elasticity of Demand
$2	11	$22	
3	8	24	Inelastic
4	5	20	Elastic

entails a percentage change in quantity demanded greater than the percentage change in price. (Perhaps you should review Chapter 4 and Figure 4-5.) Play around with this concept a bit, but its importance in decision making should be clear: The price charged does affect the quantity sold; hence it affects the total revenue and the total profit.

Let us go a step further with this elasticity concept. The essence of advertising is to create an inelastic demand, as well as to boost sales; that is, your ad tells the consumer he should prefer your product over all others because of lower price, more desirable features, or other advantageous traits. To the extent that the consumer "believes" the ad, the product now has fewer substitutes, and the consumer's demand is thus more inelastic. As an example, if you really believe "Ford has a better idea!" you many contribute to an inelastic demand for new or used cars, and Ford will have gained a greater degree of pricing control and market power.

Perhaps one further point to add on the revenue side is that government regulation or rivals' reactions may affect business decisions, revenue levels, and resulting profits. For example, the federal wage-price controls of 1971–1974 affected many U.S. business profits by price restraints. As another example, General Motors may roll back announced price hikes largely in response to Ford and Chrysler announcements of small price increases.

In all of this analysis, revenue is certainly important in business decision making. But costs also play an important role (recall Marshall's "two blades of a scissor" analogy?), and we now analyze cost behavior.

Costs

Every business has certain production costs it must pay. The decisions made by businessmen must account for these costs as well as revenue. Many businesses strive continually to maximize profit by reducing costs through improved assembly-line techniques, efficiency studies, improved accounting practices, and so on.

Understanding just how these costs affect decision making requires recognition that there are different types of costs that behave (change) in certain general ways. From an accounting standpoint, total costs are broken into *explicit costs* (must be paid to others as wages) and *implicit costs* (charged only on paper, as depreciation). Total costs are also categorized as *variable costs*, which change as the amount produced changes (labor hired, supplies purchased, and so on), and *fixed costs*, which remain the same regardless of output level (rent of building, depreciation, property taxes, and so on). These variable and fixed costs (which, added together, are called total costs) have an important effect on profit and decision making. This effect is seen in cost change on a per unit or average cost basis.

Suppose, for example, *total fixed cost* (*TFC*) is \$1,000 for rent, licenses, depreciation, and so on. The *average fixed cost*, or fixed cost per unit (*AFC*

Define Costs

A. Types of Costs: Implicit plus explicit equals fixed plus variable.

    1. Implicit – Not Directly Paid Out (Depreciation; Normal Profit).

    2. Explicit – Directly Paid Out (Wages, Materials, Rent, etc).

    3. Fixed – No Change as Output Varies (Rent, Insurance).

    4. Variable – Changes as Output Varies (Wages, Materials).

B. Have fixed costs only in short run (cannot change capacity); have variable costs in short run and all costs variable in long run.

    1. Short Run – Change output level, but not capacity.

    2. Long Run – Change capacity and all productive facilities.

    3. "Law of diminishing returns" operates in short run only (as extra units of variable resources added to fixed resources, beyond some point the marginal product drops). "Economics and diseconomies of scale operate in long run only (size of business organization may become efficient or inefficient).

C. Long-run *ATC* (*LATC*) equals "summation" of short-run *ATC*, termed "planning curve." Reflects "economies and diseconomies of scale."

FIG. 7–11. Business costs.

$= TFC \div Q$), continually declines as more is produced. If you produce one item, the *AFC* is \$1,000; with ten items, it's \$100; with 100 items, it's \$10; with 1,000 items, it's \$1; and so on, as in Figure 7-8. Do you see the effect on decision making? If your business has large fixed costs, you aim for the largest volume possible! This simple concept really explains why many industries have only a few large firms (autos, steel, and so on) and why we have regulated monopolies in the field of public utilities. The more the output, the less the cost per unit, and possibly the lower the price to the consumer.

On the other hand, *total variable cost* (*TVC*) continually increases as more is produced. But *average variable cost*, or variable cost per unit (*AVC* $= TVC \div Q$), first decreases, then increases as more is produced. Although the way in which these costs change will vary by type of firm, in general they vary as shown in Figure 7-12. Notice the S-shape of the *TVC* curve, and the U-shape of the *AVC* curve.

The explanation behind the typical shape of the *AVC* and *TVC* curves is a bit complex, but may add understanding to business decision making. In general, most businesses experience the *law of diminishing marginal productivity* (LDMP, also termed *law of diminishing marginal returns*, or LDMR). This means that as more of the variable factors of production, such as workers, are added to some fixed factor of production, such as set factory size

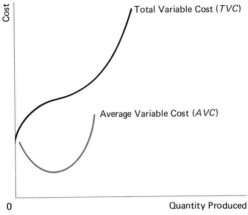

FIG. 7-12. Variable-cost behavior.

and number of machines, the productivity of such variable factors may initially rise to some degree, but then falls. (See Figure 7-13.)

This logic may appear odd, but its reasonableness depends on an appreciation of factors such as time periods, degree of specialization, and overcrowding. For example [let's use Adam Smith's old example in *Wealth of Nations* (1776)], in the production of pins, adding more workers may aid specialization of labor and productivity up to a point. But when too many workers overcrowd the plant size, productivity begins to fall. This change in productivity is illustrated by the marginal productivity curve (MP) of Figure 7-13. Increasing productivity occurs when the MP slopes upward, whereas decreasing productivity occurs when the MP slopes downward.

The relationship of productivity and production costs is also shown in Figure 7-13 in that when productivity is increasing, AVC is falling. When productivity peaks and begins to fall, AVC bottoms out and begins to rise. Although the shape and degree of sharpness of the AVC curve will depend on specific business conditions, such a U-shaped cost behavior is characteristic of most business firms.

One further point to examine about the AVC curve is that the law of diminishing marginal productivity (LDMP) operates only in *short-run* periods of time when both variable and fixed production factors are used. This means that some fixed resource (such as factory size or number of machines) imposes an upper limit on the productivity of additional variable resources (such as labor). Because the fixed resource cannot be quickly changed, the LDMP applies. Given a *long-run* time period (how long will depend on the specific business), all productive factors (factory size, number of machines, labor) are variable. "So is the long-run AVC still U-shaped?" you may ask. The answer is yes, but now for different reasons. There do occur economies of

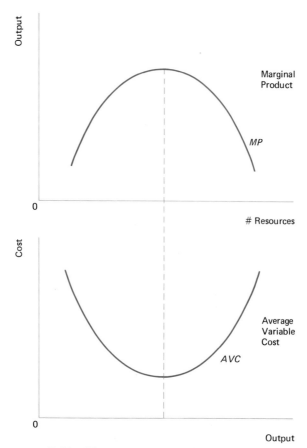

FIG. 7–13. Changes in marginal productivity cause changes in variable costs.

large-scale productiron over time (causing the AVC to fall in the long run), but there is also some inefficiency resulting from management errors in coordinating a large-scale operation (causing the AVC to rise in the long run). Thus, we have a U-shape for the AVC in both short- and long-run time periods.

The value of these cost curves is appropriate in picking an output level where the AVC is falling or at a minimum: This means lowest cost, hence greatest profit, given a certain sales volume. On the other hand, if the business is producing an output level at which the AVC is rapidly rising, the increased revenue may be offset by the increased cost, and profit drops (recall MR <MC?). Again, the full application of business decision making here requires analysis of both revenue and cost behavior.

Figure 7-14 combines and illustrates all the costs described previously. Notice that we have TFC (horizontal), AFC (continually falling), TVC (S-shaped), AVC (U-shaped), TC (S-shaped from adding TFC and TVC),

Cost Behavior in Typical Firm:

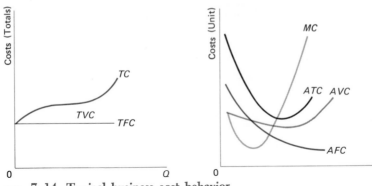

FIG. 7–14. Typical business cost behavior.

ATC (U-shaped, approaching AVC as AFC declines), and MC (U-shaped). Again, such costs represent typical behavior patterns, and individual businesses will have unique cost patterns.

Profit = Revenue − Costs

So much for these interrelated points on revenue and costs. Although the explanations may seem complex, we've only scratched the surface of revenue-cost behavior, and large businesses do considerably more anaylsis in decision making than we've described. The point we've illusrated is that in any business all decisions are made in an attempt to maximize profit. To achieve maximum profit, the effect of any decision on both revenue and costs must be determined. In tying together this discussion of profits and decision making, let's do two final exercises: (1) consider a simple table of revenue and cost data to determine the output level for greatest profit and (2) view a much more complicated real-life decision problem.

The data in Figure 7-15 illustrate a number of possible cost-revenue combinations among which you must decide on the price-output level to achieve the maximum profit. Notice how costs and revenue change at various output levels and thus affect the profit result. Also notice that additional sales do not always result in greater profits and that shutting down (zero output) does not avoid all costs. Well, how would you decide?

Applying either the TP = TR − TC or MR = MC decision rule, we find the best (maximum profit) output level is two units, priced at $150 each, for a total profit of $115. Do you see how the various costs are calculated and how decision rules are applied? What might be the cost-revenue impacts of such effects as higher wages, government controls, or changes in consumer demand?

Quantity (Q)	Price (P)	Total Revenue (TR = P × Q)	Total Fixed Cost (TFC)	Average Fixed Cost (AFC = TFC/Q)	Total Variable Cost (TVC)	Average Variable Cost (AVC = TVC/Q)	Total Cost (TC = TFC + TVC)	Profit or (Loss)
0	$200	$ 0	$100	$ —	$ 0	$ —	$100	$(100)
1	175	175	100	100	35	35	135	(40)
2	150	300	100	50	85	42.50	185	115
3	125	375	100	33.33	185	61.67	285	90
4	100	400	100	25	310	77.50	410	(10)
5	75	375	100	20	460	92	560	(185)

FIG. 7–15. Cost and revenue behavior affect business profit.

Perhaps one further illustration will tie all of these cost–revenue–decision points together—graph the data of Figure 7-16 in Figure 7-17. Do you see the typical cost revenue behavior patterns? Do you also see the $TP = TR - TC$ and $MC = MR$ decision rules applied?

You recall we said real-life business decisions are much more complicated than what we've discussed thus far. Let's illustrate this complexity with the following factors, pertaining to the General Motors Corporation:

FIG. 7–16. Cost-revenue data.

						Cost/Revenue Data for Business Decision							
Input	Output	MP	AP	TFC	TVC	TC	AFC	AVC	ATC	MC	AR	TR	MR	TPR
0	0	—	—	$50	$ 0	$ 50	—	—	—	—	$2	$ 0	—	$–50
1	10	10	10	50	10	60	$5.00	$1.00	$6.00	$1.00	2	20	$2	–40
2	22	12	11	50	20	70	2.27	.91	3.18	.83	2	44	2	–26
3	36	14	12	50	30	80	1.39	.83	2.22	.71	2	72	2	– 8
4	52	16	13	50	40	90	.96	.77	1.73	.63	2	104	2	14
5	67	15	13.4	50	50	100	.75	.75	1.50	.67	2	134	2	34
6	78	11	13	50	60	110	.64	.77	1.41	.91	2	156	2	46
7	84	6	12	50	70	120	.60	.83	1.43	1.67	2	168	2	48
8	88	4	11	50	80	130	.57	.91	1.48	2.50	2	176	2	46
9	90	2	10	50	90	140	.56	1.00	1.56	5.00	2	180	2	40
10	90	0	9	50	100	150	.56	1.11	1.67	—	2	180	2	30

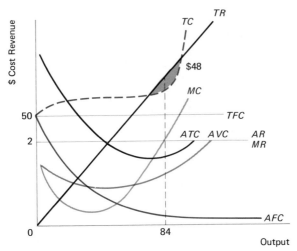

FIG. 7–17. Cost-revenue behavior.

1. How do you organize all the divisions? You're a gigantic operation, with five car divisions (Chevrolet, Pontiac, Oldsmobile, Buick, Cadillac), as well as many other types of products (locomotives, home appliances, diesel engines, defense contracts, and so on).

2. How do you handle federal antitrust suits? You're so big that monopoly is a constant charge.

3. Let us consider just one car division. What "mix" of car models do you plan to produce at what prices? How much material will you buy, and how many people will you hire?

4. How many new model lines do you come out with to meet competition? A new small car is expensive to develop, but you must compete with the small cars of other manufacturers to maintain your market share.

5. How do you meet the federal government's "request" to develop safer cars and better pollution-control devices? Costs are high, but restrictions and public goodwill must be considered.

6. How do you bargain in the upcoming wage negotiations with the UAW (United Auto Workers)? Wage increases add to costs, but a prolonged strike means lost sales. In addition, you must meet demands for increased minority group employment.

We could present more, but these should be enough problems for a "real-life" example of decision making. How would you solve these problems? Don't say "impossible," because such decision making occurs every day.

And it is such business decision making that really affects our daily economic life.

TERMS

Average fixed cost (AFC) Per unit production charges that continually decline as output increases $(AFC = TFC \div Q)$. See Figure 7-8.

Average revenue (AR). The per unit sales amount, also termed *price* $(AR = TR \div Q)$.

Average variable cost (AVC). Per unit production charges that typically decrease as output increases, then begin to increase $(AVC = TVC \div Q)$. See Figure 7-12.

Concentration ratio. The percentage of total industry sales controlled by the four largest firms in the industry. See Figure 7-7.

Explicit cost. Production charges that are paid by the firm to others such as wages and raw material bills.

Franchise. The license granted an individual to operate under a parent company's trade name, usually requiring payment and operation controls.

Hierarchy. A business classification based on relative distance of business operation to the consumer, including manufacturer, wholesaler, and retailer. See Figure 7-3.

Implicit cost. Production charges that are not directly paid out, as depreciation.

Law of diminishing marginal productivity (LDMP). The typical production behavior whereby productivity first increases, then decreases as variable production factors are added to some fixed production factor.

Legal models. A business classification based on legal characteristics, including sole proprietorship, partnership, and corporation. See Figure 7-4.

Marginal cost (MC). The rate of change in total cost or the additional cost of additional output $(MC = \triangle TC \div \triangle Q)$. See Figure 7-14.

Marginal revenue (MR). The rate of change in total revenue or the additional sales amount from additional items sold $(MR = \triangle TR \div \triangle Q)$. See Figure 7-15.

Market models. A business classification based on competitive characteristics, including pure competition, monopolistic competition, oligopoly, and monopoly. See Figure 7-6.

Total fixed cost (TFC). Production charges that do not vary as output changes, such as rent or insurance. See Figure 7-8.

Total revenue (TR). Total sales obtained by multiplying quantity sold by selling price $(TR = Q \times P)$. See Figure 7-15.

Total variable cost (TVC). Production charges that depend upon output levels, such as wages. See Figure 7-12.

QUESTIONS FOR STUDY

1. What are the major legal forms of business organization? Briefly state the advantages and disadvantages of each.
2. How do you account for the dominant role of corporations in our economy?
3. What is the major legal and market model type in American capitalism in terms of (a) the number of firms in operation and (b) the amount of income and employment provided?
4. By what means has big business developed in the United States? What are the pros and cons of big business?
5. Would it benefit the public if the size of corporations were limited?
6. Many stores advertise that their prices are cheaper because they are "discount" stores. What does this mean?
7. Purely competitive producers have little price control, but monopolistically competitive, oligopolistic, and purely monopolistic firms do. Explain.
8. Explain the difference between price and nonprice competition, and give examples.
9. Why is the AVC curve U-shaped in the short run? Why does the AFC curve continually decline?
10. What two business decision rules may be used to maximize profits?

REFERENCES

Averitt, Robert T. *The Dual Economy.* New York: W. W. Norton & Company, Inc., 1968.

Barber, Arthur. *Emerging World Power: The World Corporation.* New York: Warner Modular Publications, 1968.

Cheit, Earl F., ed. *The Business Establishment.* New York: John Wiley & Sons, Inc., 1964.

Fusfield, Daniel R. *The Rise of the Corporate State in America.* New York: Warner Modular Publications, 1972.

Galbraith, John Kenneth. *Economics and the Public Purpose.* Boston: Houghton Mifflin Company, 1973.

————. *The New Industrial State.* Boston: Houghton Mifflin Company, 1967.

Heilbroner, Robert L. *The Limits of American Capitalism.* New York: Harper & Row, Publishers, Incorporated, 1966, Part I.

Luthans, Fred, and Richard M. Hodgetts. *Social Issues in Business.* New York: Macmillan Publishing Co., Inc., 1972.

Mintz, M., and S. Cohen. *America, Inc.* New York: Dial Press, 1970.

The Fortune Double 500 Directory 1975. New York: Time, Inc., 1976.

8

WHAT IS COMPETITION?

SHORT ANSWER. Competition is the condition under which one seller attempts to convince buyers that his good or service is the best buy.

YOU AND COMPETITION

Competition is a word we hear every day. We assume it is almost synonymous with capitalism, and perhaps most of us take it for granted. Although we've talked a bit about this term earlier, let's really analyze its meaning and implications in this chapter.

Perhaps the first question for you to ask is, "Why should I care about competition? What does it do for me?" Ideally, this very practical question is met by a claim of lower prices, better quality, greater variety, extra services, and easy accessibility. In addition, competition is said to spur businesses to reduce costs, to increase efficiency, to develop new technology, and to improve products. Furthermore, competition is supposed to furnish the link between individual consumer choices and social economic answers to the basic question of what to produce. Quite a claim, in all, and the process sometimes falls far short of these ideals. But these consumer benefits are what competition *may* produce and are thus grounds for its operation highly touted in our American economy.

You can see competition in action in many ways, both in type and format. Competitive "types" include price appeals (auto rebates, quantity discounts, "extras" at no added cost, special sales) and nonprice offers (longer warranties, greater variety, higher quality, faster service, trading stamps). Competition comes daily to you, the consumer, in many different formats. You'll see ads in newspapers and magazines and on billboards, neon signs, and radio and TV commercials, all of which urge you to buy this or that product. When you actually do arrive at the store, variety and "specials" abound! In all of these appeal types and formats, notice that the essential feature of competi-

FIG. 8–1. Business competition.
Consumer Decisions

tion is to affect your consumer choice: *Buy me,* not brand X, is the theme of competition.

Whether or not these appeals truly affect your choice, you'll have to determine for yourself. You will also have to decide to what extent competition exists for your benefit. You may also consider to what extent competition really aids or hinders our market answers to the basic economic questions and to what degree government regulation or competition is desirable or detrimental. Let us look, therefore, into the scope and nature of competition in aiding your decisions.

THE MARKET AND COMPETITION

Our previous discussion describing the U.S. economy as a market-oriented system pointed out that consumer choice is a basic mechanism of the entire economy. Consumer preferences play a major role in our economy's answers to *what, how,* and *for whom* products are produced. The whole concept of demand really boils down to what product people want and what they are willing to pay to get it. The businessman's response—supply—ought to be geared to these preferences for the sake of profits. The term *consumer sovereignty* (consumer is king) describes the ideal process well. Businesses either produce what the consumer wants or eventually fail.

There are some citizens and economists (like Galbraith in *The Affluent Society*) who question the validity of consumer sovereignty. They claim consumer taste is manipulated by corporate advertising and that the consumer only chooses from available output. You must evaluate these criticisms, but the authors would at least point out the response of General Motors to consumer preference for compact cars. The Chevette was introduced in 1975 to comply with consumer preference, just as consumer sovereignty would predict.

This necessary business response under a market economy to consumer desires and "dollar choices" is precisely where competition comes in. Because each business wants you to buy its product rather than a similar one from another firm, it tries to outdo its rivals to gain the consumer's preference and dollar vote. It may "campaign" for your vote by offering a product that is lower-priced longer-lasting, of higher quality, of greater variety, and so on. Or the business may offer all sorts of extras with the product, such as better service, more locations in which to buy, cleaner stores, gifts, bonus games, and so on.

These appeals must, of course, be communicated to the consumer, so *advertising* (in all the types and formats previously mentioned) is used to influence and persuade. As we noted in Chapter 7, the purpose of advertising is to increase demand for the product, as well as to make the product appear more unique (fewer substitutes possible, so elasticity of demand is lower). Putting competition aspects all together, we get a picture of consumer choice something like that in Figure 8-2.

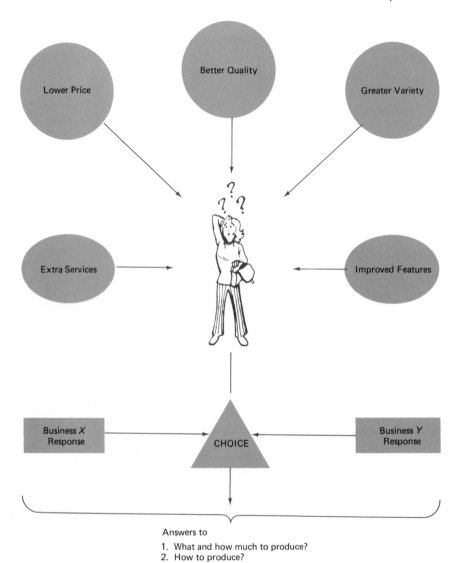

Answers to
1. What and how much to produce?
2. How to produce?
3. For whom to produce?

FIG. 8–2. Advertising affects business competition.

Let's take one case study to show competition in action, with consumer choice and business response affecting our entire economy:

1. Through the 1950s, American automobiles tended toward large size, high horsepower, much chrome, and high "sex appeal." Advertising appeals pushed these features, and consumers appeared to respond.

2. Foreign compacts began a serious penetration of the U.S. auto market in the late 1950s and had very different attractions. Many consumers began to prefer a smaller, more economic, more responsive, less showy means of transportation.

3. U.S. auto manufacturers at first had little response to the foreign competition. American Motors had pushed the small, economy car (Rambler) without significant success and was moving toward larger autos in the early 1960s. The "partial" competitive response by Ford and Chevrolet—the Falcon and Corvair—was judged adequate to meet U.S. tastes. Evidently, the Detroit auto manufacturers believed the compact demand to be insignificant or of short duration.

4. Although foreign compact sales increased during the 1960s, especially with new Japanese rivals and "Americanized" styling, little new competitive response came from American auto companies. Again, it was felt (and appeared true) that the majority of the U.S. auto market did prefer larger autos and had the income to pay the rising prices and that a large switch to compacts would not be profitable.

5. Then came the environmental concerns of the 1970s, the energy crisis of 1973, and rising prices of gasoline and autos in 1974–1975. Now there appeared to be a large change in consumer auto demand: The gas-saving, less expensive, less polluting, compact auto was "in"! The foreign compacts were ready with new and better models, whereas U.S. manufacturers produced models that did not appear to compete adequately with the small foreign compacts. Other domestic manufacturers expanded their small-car offering beginning in the mid-1970s.

6. The result of this "competitive lag" of U.S. auto manufacturers in responding to a shift on consumer demand has been plummeting U.S. auto sales, rising import sales (almost 20 per cent of the market in 1975—see Figure 8-3), great unemployment of U.S. auto workers, and a considerable contribution to the serious U.S. economic recession of the mid-1970s.

Perhaps you feel we have gone to excessive lengths to nail down exactly where competition fits into our American economy. The authors' reasoning is that the consumer typically is bombarded by so many advertising claims daily that it may be necessary to back off and see just why the whole show comes about. Put simply, business firms want your dollar, and they try to outdo their rivals for your preference. That's the essence of competition. It's an integral

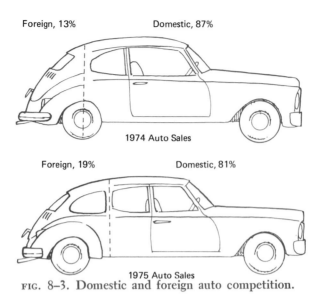

Foreign, 13%   Domestic, 87%

1974 Auto Sales

Foreign, 19%   Domestic, 81%

1975 Auto Sales

FIG. 8–3. Domestic and foreign auto competition.

and important part of our economy's workings, and you, the consumer, are in the driver's seat.

Before we look at the various types of competition, a few side notes are in order. One qualification is that although competition is generally preferred in our economy, there are areas where monopoly is typical, as in providing certain services through government-regulated public utilities. (Recall the discussion on fixed costs in Chapter 7?) Such monopoly may achieve lower production costs; lower, regulated prices (the role of the state government agency); and thus greater consumer benefit. Even under such monopoly conditions, there is some *interindustry competition* possible, for example, electricity versus gas or telephone versus telegraph and mail serivce. Most people are aware of *intraindustry competition* (compete with firms in the same industry producing similar products) daily, but the concept of interindustry competition does apply to consumer choice and further extends the range of available substitutes and opportunity cost considerations.

There are also certain "costs" to competition. Not only do advertising expenses (perhaps) raise prices, but advertising often results in unsightly billboards and idiotic commercials. Although competition is basic to our economy and generally regarded as beneficial and desirable, it is not an unmixed blessing. Could the $30 billion now spent by American businesses on advertising per year be better spent on, for instance, rebuilding slum housing? Would total social well-being increase if the consumer were not constantly urged to purchase energy-consuming, polluting autos, but strongly encouraged to support and utilize a mass transit system? These are serious questions to which we will return, but let's first define and detail competitive practice in the U.S. economy.

TYPES OF COMPETITION

Remember, the name of the game in competition is, "Buy my product instead of my rival's." The obvious method is to convince you, the consumer, that a certain product is "a better deal" than another. Think about any recent ad or commercial you've seen, and this method becomes fairly evident. Now the appeal can vary widely, but basically there are two types of appeal (or methods of competition) used: *price* and *nonprice* competition. As we discuss these types, recall ads or commercials you've seen or heard, and classify them. Also, review the "market models" we described in Chapter 7, for we'll note what types of competition frequently occur in each type.

Price Competition

The appeal in price competition is lower price; that is, a product is more attractive as it costs less than a rival one of comparable quality. Numerous examples of price competition occur daily in retail operations—food markets, gas stations, car lots, clothes shops, and so on. In all these instances the consumer is urged to buy the less expensive product and thereby receive "more for his money"—at least, he is so urged by purveyors of the cheaper products. Perhaps the most obvious use of price competition is the auto manufacturers' rebates of 1975, which were designed to spur lagging sales and compete with foreign imports. Note that rebates were used by manufacturers rather than a

FIG. 8–4. Price competition.

Brand *A*   Brand *B*

Margin Level	Cost	Price	Profit/Unit	Number Sold	Total Profit
Very high (exclusive shop or brand)	$1.00	$1.50	$0.50	100	$50
Very low (discount store)	1.00	1.25	0.25	300	75

FIG. 8–5. Margin level affects profits.

direct price reduction, so as to maintain price levels while encouraging consumer purchase. The "suggested" auto price thereby remained the same even
though the consumer paid less. Another growing example of price competition is the "basic homes" now advertised without many extras (cabinets, tile,
and so on) to sell at a price within the reach of a medium-income family.

From the businessman's viewpoint, lower prices often add to total profits
through larger sales volume. (Recall the law of demand and elasticity of demand from Chapter 4? People buy more at lower prices.) Thus, even if the
profit per item (termed *margin*) is less, total profits may be higher with
greater sales, as in Figure 8-5. Lower prices also often force the business continually to reduce production costs, as by cutting costs in packaging, buying of
cheaper supplies, lowering payrolls, offering fewer "extras," and reducing
maintenance. Thus, you may go to a store offering lower prices and find few
sales clerks, no bonuses or stamps, and fewer parking spaces.

This point about services and extras versus lower prices is a good one for
the daily shopper, yourself, to consider. Your purchasing pattern usually takes
into account not only price, but all the other "product features" of convenience, service, store appearance, quality, brand name, and a host of other
extras (nonprice competition). If you want these "extras" in a product you'll
probably have to pay higher prices. If, however, you prefer a lower price, don't
always expect all the other features. See the trade-off?

Consumer choice between lower prices and greater services has an important impact for both the individual consumer and our entire economy. For
this price–nonprice competition trade-off choice by the consumers determines
the nature of the interaction between oligopolists and monopolistic competitors. If the consumer prefers (or at least offers little sales resistance) nonprice product qualities, advertisements will tout special features, quality, sex
appeal, and so on of the 1960s. If consumers begin to emphasize lower prices
in their selections, both large and small businesses may respond with the rebates or discounts (from autos to toasters), sale ads, and price wars of the
middle 1970s. Consumer preference and choice, in fact, may directly affect
the nature of business competition, Vance Packard (see the reference at end
of the chapter) and advertising textbooks not withstanding.

Actually, most ads and commercials may push lower prices as well as other features. As food market ads note, they offer not only lower prices, but fast and courteous service, large variety, fresh products, and attractive parking lots and store front. It's also true that most price competition occurs at the local retail store level of business hierarchy and goes on mainly in the market models of pure competition and monopolistic competition. You will see, though less frequently, lower prices advertised at the manufacturer level (like auto rebates) and in the market models of oligopoly and monopoly. The oligopolist usually fears a "price war" possibility (and thus prefers nonprice appeals), and the monopolist has no close competitors to undersell him.

Two other trends that have spurred price competition in the U.S. economy are *foreign imports* and *differentiated branding*. Although consumer preference for imported items may well be for reasons of quality or unique features, very often the foreign item offers the consumer a lower-priced option to a comparable domestic product. Again, there is debate here as to the desirable impact on American employment and wages, but the imported item has often forced lower prices and product variety. (Witness autos, electronic calculators, bicycles, and steel.) Would there have been a Pacer or Chevette without a Volkswagen and Datsun?

By *differentiated branding* we mean "the practice of a large manufacturer's producing similar items for a variety of different brand names." For example, the mother of one of the authors worked in a bicycle factory that produced bicycles under its own brand name, as well as for eight other brand names. (Her task was to apply different striping on similar bicycles on the same assembly line.) Or consider the perhaps 100 brand names of tires you may have seen, all originating from perhaps six major tire manufacturers. And there are two large producers of compressors supplying the basic components for many brands of refrigerators, and two transmission manufacturers who supply transmissions to producers of diesel buses.

Without getting into an argument over quality differences (there are sometimes different production standards applied to a name brand washer and the similar washer with a less-well-known brand name attached), let us concede that different brands sell at widely different prices. There may be some quality differences among them, but such differences are often insignificant in relation to price variations betwen major and minor brand names. These price variations increase price competition and consumer benefit, and the differentiated branding production encourages the economies of large-scale production and retailer variety of product line. One tip on consumer choice: You don't always "get what you pay for." A higher-priced brand name is not always superior in quality (or at least the quality difference is not as great as the price difference) to a lower-priced and less-well-known brand. Read *Consumer Reports*.

Putting all this together, we conclude that a great deal of price competition still exists in the American economy, benefiting you as a consumer. This price

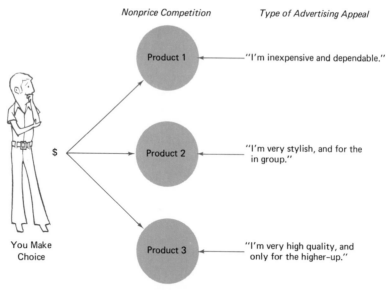

FIG. 8–6. Nonprice competition affects consumer choice.

competition often includes nonprice appeals (that is, service, stamps, location) and occurs mainly at the local retail store level at which you purchase daily. Bluntly, the American consumer loves a bargain and generally responds quickly to businesses advertising them. In fact, the authors would further claim that the vitality of American competition really depends on the extent to which the American consumer chooses products on the basis of price and quality features. Auto manufacturers will try rebates and compact cars if consumers will not buy the high-horsepower tanks.

Nonprice Competition

As Figure 8-6 illustrates, nonprice competition attracts the consumer's dollar by emphasis on a product's "special features." These special features may involve higher quality, longer life, better warranties, greater convenience or comfort, more prestige and status, and other intangible benefits that ownership of the product will convey to the consumer. Although the price of the item may or may not be mentioned, the promotion emphasis is on these special features (what the product "will do for you") and not on a lower price. In fact, a higher price may even be used to convey "snob appeal," prestige, or quality. ("For pennies a day more you can impress your friends.")

Another way to view this nonprice competition is through *brand name identification.* The seller wishes you to remember his product as so unique and special that when you're shopping, you'll choose it over competing brands. Perhaps you recall the market model of monopolistic competition

(Chapter 7) and see the tie-in to brand names here? If the customer feels the product (including the item itself plus all services, extras, atmospheres, and so on) is unique among similar products, the seller will, in fact, have a monopoly as far as that buyer is concerned (an inelastic demand). The businessman has achieved some degree of market and price control. Such market control may be even more important in the market model of oligopoly, for the oligopolists can avoid detrimental price wars through this form of nonprice competition.

The method for convincing you of these special brand name features is through advertisements. Think of the appeals made to you by newspapers, magazines, TV, radio, billboards, and junk mail; and consider why you are supposed to buy the product advertised. As noted earlier, the ad may stress quality, special features, or other benefits, all of which accrue to you on purchase. True, you may say, "These silly ads have no effect on my buying patterns!" But consider why you pick one brand among many cereals or soaps on the grocery shelves or why you happen to hum a certain ad tune. As with a tried and true teaching approach, the repetition of advertising slogans seems to achieve its purpose. [See how many classmates can identify a popular ad slogan. Read *The Hidden Persuaders* by Vance Packard (reference at the end of the chapter).]

By the way, we're not saying price competition and nonprice competition exist always in a "pure" form, separate from each other. Often you'll see ads noting both special features of the product (nonprice competition) and low price (price competition). But, in general, the price competition aspect of an ad will be emphasized at the retail or local dealer level, and the nonprice competition aspect will be emphasized at the manufacturing level. Do you recall our earlier discussion in Chapter 7 on monopolistic competition business structure (retail level) versus oligopoly (manufacturing level)? As an example, look at the difference in appeals made by the ads in your local newspaper.

Advertising and Competition

Advertising itself is "big business," and large amounts (some $30 billion in 1976) are spent for advertising. This advertising budget is a definite cost of production for many companies, justified on the assumption that increased sales resulting from the ads will more than make up for the advertising cost. (See Figure 8-7.)

Another point about advertising, stressed in every marketing class (are you interested in this career choice?), is that the composition of any ad should be based on a specific and manipulative approach; that is, first determine your market: What groups are you aiming for in selling your product? What are the specific qualities and status symbols of a particular group (reading level, emphasis on success, common goals)? Then compose an ad to emphasize these features (wording, length of sentences, colors, types of pictures, and other appeals). You may consider this to be exploitation of the consumer, but the approach is firmly based on the ways people are known to respond. People react in certain, somewhat predictable, patterns to certain appeals, and an ad takes advantage of this. (Doesn't this approach carry over to political campaigns and your own dealings with others?)

You might ask at this point just who pays for the cost of advertising? As we noted earlier, advertising represents a cost of operation for the businessman, just like rent, wages, and raw material supplies. So the businessman pays the cost, but then charges a price that will cover all costs and return a profit. Thus, you, the consumer, must ultimately pay. There is another point to consider, though, and it involves the cost-of-production behavior we discussed in Chapter 7.

Recall that per unit production costs (AFC, AVC, MC) change as output level varies. Fixed cost per unit continually falls as output increases, whereas variable and marginal costs per unit generally fall to some low point, but then begin rising as output increases. (Refer to Figure 7-17.) Now an advertisement will probably be a fixed cost (so much charged for a certain type run a certain number of times) and will increase total costs. But if this ad causes a large increase in the number of products sold, the cost per unit will actually fall, so that a lower price may be charged!

Let's try to illustrate this idea in Figure 8-7. The graph illustrates fixed

FIG. 8–7. Advertising affects output and costs.

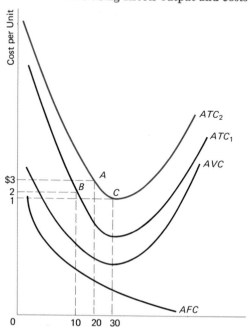

cost per unit (AFC) falling, variable cost per unit (AVC) falling and rising, and total cost per unit ($ATC = AFC + AVC$) also falling and rising. Now, suppose that before this firm advertises, it is producing ten items. Its production-cost behavior is described by ATC_1. When it advertises, its cost per unit rises at all levels to ATC_2. However, the cost per unit may then rise or fall, depending on the increase in sales:

1. If there are moderately increased sales to twenty units (point A), the cost rises to $3. There were more sales, but not enough to off-set the increased cost. (For advertising, $MC > MR$.) The price will probably rise, so that ad will cost you money.

2. If there is a large increase in sales to thirty units (point C), the cost falls to $1. The large increase in sales more than offsets the cost rise. (For advertising, $MC < MR$.) Thus, the price may fall, and you'll pay less.

Which of these results will prevail? That's hard to predict, although the businessman, of course, hopes for the second alternative. However, when all firms advertise, the increased sales to any one firm may be small, thus causing a cost increase. Such ads are still required just to "meet the competition" from other firms.

One other point that is sometimes raised regarding advertising is its social effect; that is, because most advertising extols the virtues of purchasing consumer goods, society may not devote enough resources to purchase social goods. Consider the number of ads you've seen to buy automobiles versus the number for schools or parks or mass transit systems? This thesis of "social poverty" amidst "private wealth" is argued by John Kenneth Galbraith in *The Affluent Society* and appears valid to the authors. Given our society's general high standard of living (there are still real questions of equality, or for whom) and given increased concern for environmental protection, human resources, and energy use, perhaps a societal rethinking of the consumer goods versus social goods choice (what to produce) is in order. What is your viewpoint?

GOVERNMENT ROLE IN COMPETITION

In our discussion of competition within the American economy, we cannot forget the existence of government regulations. There are varying restrictions placed by all levels of government (federal, state, local) on business operations, and such restrictions have existed for long periods in our nation's history. Governmental regulation of business existed even before our nation officially began (there were colonial regulations on tobacco-container size in the colony of Virginia during the 1750s!), and there exists a confusing mixture of regulations today.

Figure 8-8 illustrates the vast bureaucracy of regulatory agencies that currently administer a most complex web of regulations on our nation's businesses and households. These agencies have a very definite impact on our economy and on how we answer the basic questions. Not only do these agencies represent a significant taxpayer expense (an estimate by President Ford is that the average family may pay as much as $2,000 higher prices in 1976 caused by government regulation), but their operation and impact is increasingly criticized and has been under recent congressional investigation. This "fourth branch" of government, as the regulatory agencies are sometimes referred to, may well be drastically changed in future years if the growing reform movement is carried through. (Ever hear about the "Yak Fat" ruling by the Interstate Commerce Commission?)

Keep in mind while trying to analyze these complex governmental regulations that the basic intent is *consumer benefit*. Although business regulation by government takes many forms, from antitrust suits to zoning ordinances, the main goal declared for all is that the restriction is to benefit, protect, or aid the consumer in some way. It is important to remember this laudable intent because there is such a great and confusing array of laws and regulations that it is simetimes difficult to pinpoint exactly what benefit a particular regulation seeks.

In general, the following basic goals are sought by varying types of governmental regulation (note the consumer benefit aspect in each):

1. To *promote competition*. Business combinations may be prevented or new business encouraged and subsidized to help ensure lower prices, better quality, and greater variety through competition.

2. To *protect consumers*. Products and procedures must meet certain standards to protect consumer health, safety and purchasing.

3. To *protect society* as a whole. Emission standards and auto pollution laws are to ensure health levels for all citizens.

Although there are a great number of regulations, let's examine a few major areas under these headings.

Promoting Competition

Generally speaking, we in the American economy value competition among businesses because such activity tends toward lower prices, better quality, greater variety, technological advance, product innovation, and producer incentive through profit motivation. Therefore, the federal government has, in general, acted to promote competition through antitrust legislation. Since the late 1800s the federal government has aimed at preventing "unduly large"

Latest Tally of Federal Regulators	
A summary of rough estimates by the Office of Management and Budget shows this breakdown of employes in regulatory agencies and workers with regulatory jobs in other agencies—	
Agriculture Department (animal and plant-health inspection; Forest Service; stabilization, conservation, and marketing services; commodity-credit functions)	25,187
Environmental Protection Agency	11,208
Department of Health, Education and Welfare (food and drug rules, medicare regulation)	9,000
Treasury Department (tax regulation; Comptroller of the Currency; Bureau of Alcohol, Tobacco, and Firearms)	7,705
Labor Department (employment standards, occupational safety)	4,790
Commerce Department (Maritime Administration, Patent Office)	4,724
Interior Department (mine safety, land management)	3,713
Federal Energy Administration	3,257
Federal Deposit Insurance Corporation	2,966
National Labor Relations Board	2,404
Department of Transportation (traffic safety, marine safety)	2,285
Equal Employment Opportunity Commission	2,220
Nuclear Regulatory Commission	2,141
Interstate Commerce Commission	2,076
Federal Communications Commission	2,060
Securities and Exchange Commission	1,959
Federal Trade Commission	1,622
Army Corps of Engineers (inland-waterways regulation)	1,500
Federal Reserve Board	1,488
Federal Home Loan Bank Board	1,435
Federal Power Commission	1,316
Consumer Product Safety Commission	1,098
Department of Housing and Urban Development (housing regulations, federal insurance rules)	826
Justice Department (Antitrust Division)	768
Civil Aeronautics Board	718
Other agencies	2,514
TOTAL	100,980

FIG. 8–8. Government regulatory agencies.

SOURCE: U.S. Office of Management and Budget: *U.S. News & World Report*, September, 1975.

Act	Date	Intent
Sherman Act	1890	Illegal to monopolize trade; outlawed all combination or conspiracy in restraint of trade.
Clayton Act	1914	Outlawed price discrimination, tied contracts, interlocking directorates, and mergers that lessened competition (excluded labor as commodity in sense of antitrust).
Federal Trade Commission (FTC) Act	1914	Investigate, hold hearings, issue cease-and-desist orders on antitrust issues.
Robinson–Patman Act	1936	Outlawed competitive chain-store practices and actually reduced competition.
Miller–Tydings Act	1937	Enforced retail price maintenance (fair trade) agreements and actually reduced competition.
Cellar–Kefauver Antimerger Act	1950	Prevented mergers to reduce competition via acquisition of assets.

FIG. 8–9. Antritrust legislation.

business combinations, price fixing, or "unfair" competitive practices. Review these government actions in Figure 8-9.

Much of this antitrust action has been aimed at *business merger* (not only combinations of the "horizontal and vertical"type, as shown in Figure 8-10, but the more recent type of conglomerate merger). Whether such action has really prevented business merger is debated, as mergers continue at a somewhat constant rate and degree of concentration (percentage of total industry business conducted conducted by the largest four firms) has changed little. The idea in all of this antitrust action is to prevent large business firms from gaining market power to "exploit" the consumer. Of course, the offsetting factor to consider is that larger firms may also attain lower costs and prices by their large-scale production. Do you see the possible contradiction arising in the prohibition of mergers and why antitrust action is brought against some mergers (higher prices anticipated), whereas other combinations are encouraged (lower prices expected)?

Although the general trend of federal regulation has been to increase competition, there have also been instances where less competition was desired. In some cases, as in airline and railroad franchise and subsidy, the idea was that fewer firms could attain lower costs and prices for the public. In other cases, such as "fair trade" laws and "cutthroat competition" acts, the idea was to prevent long-term market control gained by temporary lower pricing to eliminate competitors. In still other instances, as with the National Industrial Recovery Act (NIRA) of 1933, the goal was to increase employment by ac-

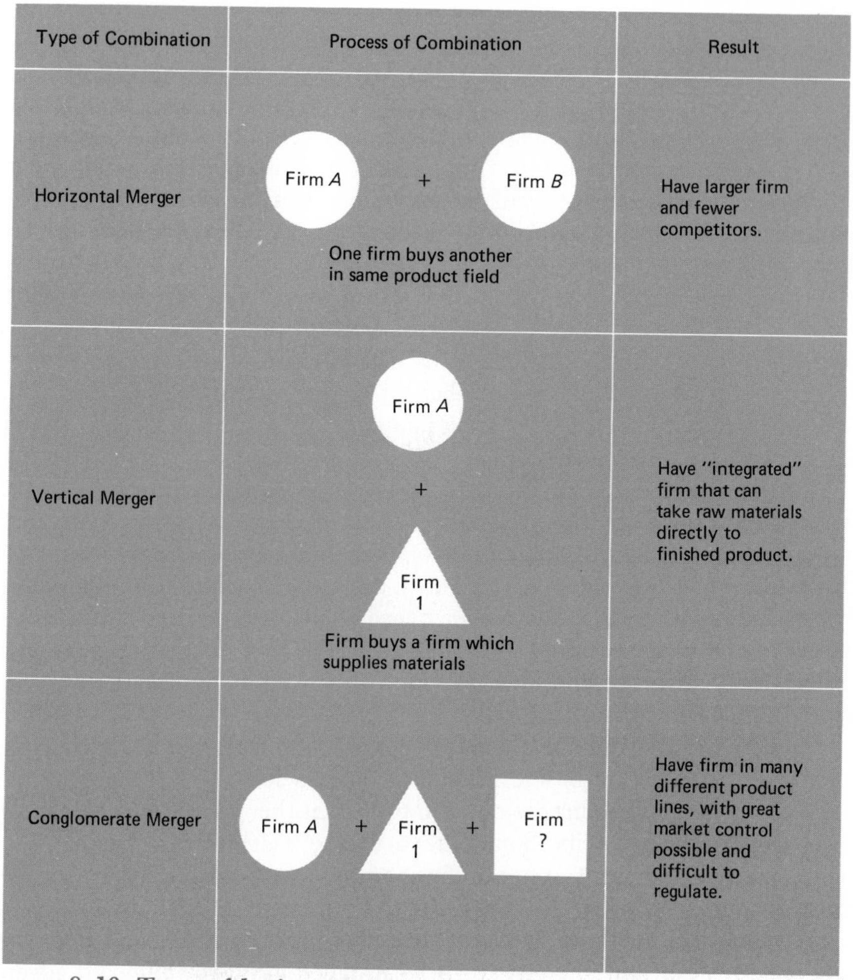

Type of Combination	Process of Combination	Result
Horizontal Merger	Firm *A* + Firm *B* One firm buys another in same product field	Have larger firm and fewer competitors.
Vertical Merger	Firm *A* + Firm 1 Firm buys a firm which supplies materials	Have "integrated" firm that can take raw materials directly to finished product.
Conglomerate Merger	Firm *A* + Firm 1 + Firm ?	Have firm in many different product lines, with great market control possible and difficult to regulate.

FIG. 8–10. Types of business mergers.

tually preventing competition under "blanket pricing codes" enforced on businesses. (This act was declared unconstitutional by the Supreme Court in 1935.)

In addition, the United States has a long history of tariff legislation, dating from colonial days to the present, which basically seeks to ensure that foreign goods shall enjoy no undue advantage of lower price over domestic products. The purpose of such tariff legislation has been stated as protecting American jobs, promoting higher wages and living standards, guaranteeing existence of strategic industries, and protecting infant industries (more about tariffs in Chapter 20). In yet other areas, such as farm price-support programs or minimum wage laws, market competition is purposely reduced in order to ensure higher income levels for those industries or persons covered.

There are even some areas in which U.S. government regulation is extremely difficult to apply to any pupose, as in the multinational corporation. These large business firms, such as International Telephone and Telegraph or Gulf Oil, operate worldwide, and thus much of their operation is not under U.S. government purview. Regulation of these giant businesses, if desirable, may require diplomatic cooperation or even the framing of a new international legal system.

"Quite confusing picture," you may say at this point, and you're right. However, recall again that the basic goal of regulation is consumer benefit, which may be attained in various ways. Competition is generally promoted, not for itself, but for the consumer benefit competition usually produces. In cases where "noncompetitive" practices promote consumer benefit to a greater degree, we have allowed monopolies to exist, although in a regulated form.

To make this point clearer and to involve the state governmental levels, consider the public utilities (telephone, water gas, electricity) in your area. In most cases, these are regulated monopolies. The state public utilities commission or equivalent body has granted an exclusive franchise to the business, thus excluding other competitors, but it also regulates the prices that may be charged. Large-scale operation for public utilities is said to achieve lower cost of operation and better consumer service. (How would you like ten gas and ten telephone companies from which to choose?)

Moreover, local governments, through, for example, their city councils, really determine the extent of business competition in a local area when they approve or deny a business license or permit or when they set zoning ordinances to regulate business activity. Sometimes a license is denied or a zoning ordinance changed to prevent unsightly businesses or overcrowding or to provide other "consumer benefits." A most interesting example of such action was a local city council's ruling to outlaw billboards within the city limits. The purpose was to "clean up" the city for the consumer, although billboard advertisement competition was thus voided and the sign company was put out of business. How would you have voted?

Protecting the Consumer

In addition to the quantity of competitors, another large governmental regulation area is that of *standards and impacts of competition.* We are concerned about the health and safety standards that must be met by business products and about the manner and impact of business competition. Thus, regulation might prevent rat hairs in candy bars (quality of product) or use of installment loan contracts that fail to inform the customer of true interest rates (manner of conduct). You might say that government acts as the consumers' spokesman and protector to ensure that no business product or procedure causes harm to the buyer because of poor ingredients or fraudulent intent.

Again, this area of regulation has long roots in our nation's economic history, especially with the Pure Food and Drug Act of 1903. This piece of federal legislation came in response to so-called muckraking demands (Upton Sinclair exposed low health standards practiced by the meat packing industry in *The Jungle,* thus stirring public interest in reforms through government regulation) and has created a constant watchguard on product quality. This regulation assures that products meet certain health standards prior to being offered for sale. Although it can be pointed out that unsafe products still reach the market (such as diet pills with tapeworms in them or candy bars with rat hairs or cars with faulty brakes), the incidence is probably much less than it would be with no regulation. And consumer "muckrakers" still abound, in case you haven't heard of Ralph Nader or read *Unsafe at Any Speed.*

One might also view the Environmental Protection Agency at the federal level and "environmental impact statements" at the local level as an example of health and safety standards. However, this is a different kind of consumer protection because pollution requirements benefit society at the cost of the individual consumer. This regulatory area has become especially large in the 1970s and represents both a costly (some $8 billion of federal budget in 1975 and perhaps $20 billion in private expenditures) and extremely vital (smog can kill!) impact on our economy. We'll discuss this environment question further in Chapter 18; however, the basic issue is the extent to which environmental protection should be carried to serve the consumer interest. For example, should a polluting strip-mine operation in Virginia be closed down even if it means increased unemployment? Congress said yes, whereas the president said no in 1975. What is your view?

In recent years there has been a tendency for federal government legislation to move into the realm of business practices, such as advertising claims. These regulations are intended not merely to prevent unsafe products, but also to prevent the manufacturer from offering products for sale in a manner that misrepresents the product's features. Thus, the federal government legislation would prevent misleading packaging techniques (no large boxes with smaller packages inside) and prosecutes false advertising claims (no "instant-result" diet pills, no unsubstantiated ads by name personalities, no "more of the pain relievers doctors recommend"). Between the Pure Food and Drug Commission and the Federal Trade Commission, many areas of fraudulent practice have been exposed and corrected.

Another area of business practice now regulated is that of purchasing on credit terms. Such terms (down payment, interest rate, total price, number of payments, conditions, and penalties for nonpayment) must now be stated on installment loan contracts, and advertisements must contain similar information. In addition, unsolicited credit cards cannot be mailed, loss from credit card use by others is limited, and credit acceptance or denial is not to be based on discriminatory practice (race, sex, or age). Consumer financial interests are further protected by long-standing regulations to ensure commercial bank stability and by more recent legislation to ensure stability of pension funds.

Lest we forget the state and local government levels, there exist numerous regulations guarding consumer health and safety at these levels. Health permits and operating licenses must be obtained for various types of employment (food service and preparation) from state agencies, and local ordinances may require operation in certain prescribed methods to avoid contamination. Also, state and local building codes are designed to ensure quality construction and occupant safety, and police and fire regulations prevent occupation of hazardous buildings. Unsafe or unsanitary working conditions are prevented not only by federal legislation, but also by state and local rulings and enforcement. And there are state and local environmental agencies that enforce antipollution standards and weigh growth vs. environmental impact considerations.

A further regulation area deserves recognition. This aspect is that of legal prohibition of some product deemed unsafe for the consumer or of products not socially acceptable. Products and services in this category include marijuana, drugs, prostitution, abortion, and pornographic books or movies. The real question is the extent to which society can and should decide consumption standards for the individual or the success of legal enforcement of such prohibition. How would you vote on legalization of such products and services? What results would you predict from their legalization?

TERMS

Advertising. Presentation of product appeal to the consumer—for example, via the media of television, radio, newspaper, magazine, and billboard.

Differentiated branding. The practice in which a single manufacturer produces simliar products under different names and contracts for competing sellers.

Nonprice competition. Business attempt to induce consumer purchase through the appeal of product quality, variety, service, extra features, or atmosphere.

Price competition. Business's attempt to induce consumer purchase via appeal of lower prices.

Profit margin. The difference between cost and revenue.

QUESTIONS FOR STUDY

1. What is nonprice competition? Give some examples and evaluate.
2. Is price or nonprice competition more beneficial to you as a consumer?
3. "Advertising may lead to lower or higher prices." Explain this statement.
4. Is business competition aided or hindered by government regulation?
5. What is the basic purpose of government regulation? Has this purpose been achieved?
6. What types of legislation tend to increase consumer protection?
7. List the arguments for and against federal and state laws on environmental protection.
8. Should the extent of regulatory agency power be expanded or contracted at the federal level?

REFERENCES

Adams, Walter, and Horace M. Gray. *Monopoly in America*. New York: Macmillian Publishing Co., Inc., 1955.

Freeman III, A. Myrick, et al. *The Economics of Environmental Policy*. New York: John Wiley & Sons, Inc., 1973.

Galbraith, John Kenneth. *The Affluent Society*. Boston: Houghton Mifflin Company, 1958.

Morgan, E. V., and A. D. Morgan. *The Economics of Public Policy*. Chicago: Aldine Publishing Co., 1972.

Nader, Ralph, ed. *The Consumer and Corporate Accountability*. New York: Harcourt Brace Jovanovich, Inc., 1973.

Noll, R. G., et al. *Economic Aspects of Television Regulation*. Washington, D.C.: Brookings Institution, 1973.

North, Douglas C., and Roger Leroy Miller. *The Economics of Public Issues*, Second Edition. New York: Harper & Row, Publishers, Incorporated, 1973.

Packard, Vance. *The Hidden Persuaders*. New York: Pocket Books, Inc., 1957.

Weiss, Leonard W. *Case Studies in American Industry*, Second Edition. New York: John Wiley & Sons, Inc., 1971.

9

WHAT ARE LABOR UNIONS?

SHORT ANSWER. Labor unions are legally organized groups of workers who organize and cooperate to improve their wages, hours, and working conditions.

YOU AND LABOR UNIONS

"Why bring up the topic of labor unions at this point in the text? I'm not a labor union member. So why worry?" These are valid questions you may raise. Perhaps Figure 9-1 gives one answer, for "big labor" does indeed affect the modern American economy and you as an individual consumer. John Kenneth Galbraith introduced the concept of *countervailing power* some years ago to emphasize the importance of these segments (big labor, big business, big government) in our economy's operation and in our daily consumer choices.

To begin to understand the importance of labor unions, consider their impact on answers to the basic economic questions. Labor unions certainly affect the question of for whom by their contract negotiations for wage rates and hence workers' income levels and also, as a corollary, the goods and services

FIG. 9–1. Labor unions and countervailing power.

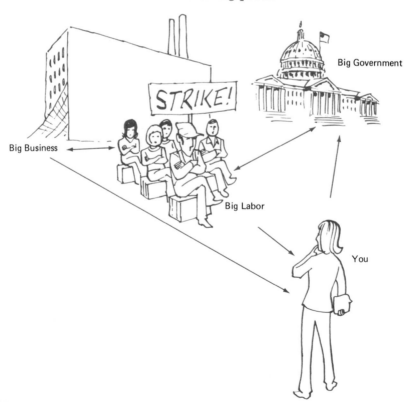

affordable by the union member. Negotiations also involve work rules and procedures, which directly affect the question of how to produce. Labor unions may even affect the question of what to produce through the indirect impact of production costs on business decisions or the direct impact of political lobby pressure for tariffs and other government subsidies.

But let's be even more particular. Let us consider the possible economic consequences of a nationwide labor union strike on, for example, railroads:

1. The strike would affect all businesses dependent on rail transit either for shipping of finished goods or receiving of inputs for manufacture. A prolonged rail strike would cause these businesses to reduce output and employment.

2. The strike would lower railway employees' incomes (because strike fund and unemployment benefits would usually fall short of regular paychecks) as well as those of other workers, as noted in item 1, and hence their spending levels and the revenue and employment patterns of oher business firms.

3. By affecting incomes received and retail sales generated, the strike would affect the tax revenues of local, state, and federal government agencies and, possibly, their spending levels.

These economic consequences of a labor union strike are perhaps dramatic, but many more subtle consequences occur daily. Such consequences include wage impacts on nonunion employees, work conditions and employee satisfaction and participation attitudes (morale), and political results of labor union lobbying activities. The point we're making about the importance of labor unions in the U.S. economy is that business decisions, government legislation, consumer choices, and our economy's answers to the basic questions are all affected by labor union operation. Given such importance, we need to define and clarify the operation of labor unions in the U.S. economy.

U.S. LABOR UNIONS

Perhaps your only contact with labor unions is when you see a strike exercised. On the other hand, you or your parents may carry a union card, as more than 24 million Americans do. There are many types of United States labor unions in various fields and of differing membership sizes—from the Teamsters, with some 1.6 million members, to racetrack horseshoers, with a few hundred. Figure 9-2 illustrates the types and membership strength of various major unions, and Figure 9-3 points out the change in total labor union membership over time.

Although there are great differences among labor unions, there are also

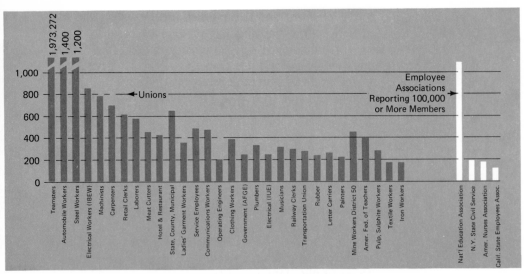

Source: *Finance Facts*. National Consumer Finance Association, September, 1975.

FIG. 9–2. Labor union membership by union, 1970.

basic similarities. Let's examine these similarities as definitions of labor unions, emphasizing that we're defining general patterns of all labor unions. As you read these definitions, try to recall real-life contact you have had with the points mentioned.

> 1. A labor union is an association of workers who cooperate in order to secure economic gains.

FIG. 9–3. Growth of labor union membership.

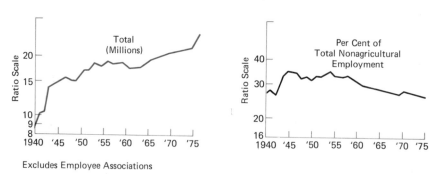

Excludes Employee Associations

Source: The Conference Board, *Road Maps of Industry*, No. 1702, November 15, 1972

2. Economic gains desired by unions include higher wages, cost-of-living adjustment, improved working conditions, job security, and "fringe benefits" (insurance, pension, medical care, paid vacations, and so on). There may also be certain political gains desired, such as elimination of price–wage controls, increased tariffs or protection from foreign products, or reduction in environmental protection standards that aggravate unemployment. As an example, the fishing industry workers have much interest in securing a 200-mile territorial-waters limit.

3. Labor unions emphasize collective (united) actions in order to win economic gains from business and government employers. Examples of collective action are a strike (no work), a boycott (no buying of products), a slowdown (less effort at work), and legal action (court cases on terms of labor contract).

4. Labor unions have leaders (elected by members) who act as representatives, supported often by retained lawyers, in collective bargaining with business firms in determining the union contract. This contract sets wages, work conditions, and so on, for a specified time period and binds workers and employers in agreement.

The student should realize that although these characteristics may be found in all labor unions, their nature and practice vary widely. Some unions are quite powerful on a nationwide basis (United Auto Workers), and their collective bargaining results determine the guidelines for all associated locals. Other unions are quite small within a specific industry and affect only one employer and union local in contract negotiations. In addition, some labor unions deal only with certain skilled groups (Carpenter's Union), whereas other unions include a great variety of skilled, semiskilled, or unskilled employees (Teamsters Union). And some unions include only professional groups (American Federation of Teachers) in public employment, though most unions deal with privately employed workers.

As Figure 9-4 illustrates, labor union strength is not evenly distributed in the United States. Some states have "right-to-work" laws (Section 14-b of the Taft–Hartley Act of 1947), which permit workers the choice of joining or not joining a labor union. Many states, however, approve a *union shop*, meaning that the worker may be employed prior to joining the labor union, but must then join the union within a time period (usually thirty days) to keep the job. Some states also have an *agency shop*, whereby the employee is not required to join the labor union, but must pay the regular dues and fees because he or she receives the benefits of labor union contract negotiations. However, states cannot allow a *closed shop* condition under the Taft–Hartley Act, which requires a worker to join the union before employment. Although the legal provisions of the Taft–Hartley Act apply to all states, the regional impacts of

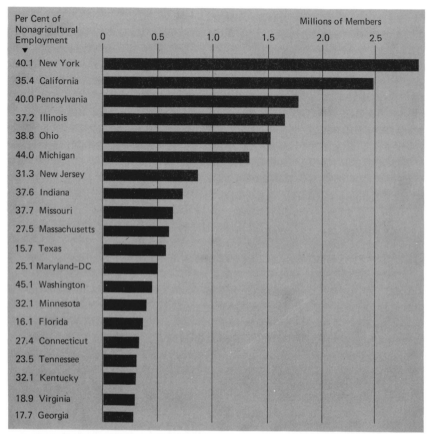

FIG. 9–4. Labor union membership by state.

labor unions often depend on legal enforcement, degree of union organization, and public attitudes. For example, one may find unions harassing nonunion construction firms in Florida or unions practicing nondiscriminatory
membership recruitment under the "Philadelphia Plan."

These descriptions are selected and brief, but should point out the important aspects and rich variety of labor union operation in the modern U.S.
economy. In order to appreciate more fully these characteristics and impacts
of labor unions, let's review the history of labor unions in the United States.
The virtue of a historical outline is to put the present in perspective, and such
outlines are a frequent and useful teaching technique especially valuable to an
understanding of labor unions. Tremendous changes have occurred very
quickly in American labor unions—recognition, growth, and economic power.
A full understanding of currrent labor union "problem issues" (at the end of
the chapter) requires a historical warm-up.

LABOR UNION HISTORY

Perhaps the areas of pay benefits and work conditions best illustrate what our historical survey of labor union growth is intended to emphasize: There's been a great change! Not only have pay levels, working conditions, and public respect for the working man changed and improved greatly, but there's also been a tremendous shift in the legal status of the labor union itself.

Although labor unions have been around a long time in the United States (the Federal Society of Journeymen Cordwainers, established in Philadelphia in 1794, is perhaps our first trade union), their large membership and impact on our national economy are of rather recent origin. These developments may be traced to legal recognition, economic conditions, social reform movements, and changing social values. In looking over this whole range of labor union history, three periods may be noted to summarize such changes:

1. From the year of the first unions (1790s) to the 1930s. Labor unions were very low in social esteem, were prosecuted in courts as a conspiracy in restraint of trade, and had few members.

2. From the 1930s through World War II. Labor unions grew tremendously, aided by favorable federal legislation, increased worker desire or job security, and favorable public attitude toward union membership.

3. From the end of World War II to the present. Public concern over labor union practices and economic effects brought new controlling legislation and a leveling of union membership gains.

Let's look at each of these historical phases a bit to see reasons for such great change.

1790–1930

Remember that "economic production" prior to the 1840s in the United States (our industrial revolution) was usually of small-scale, nonassembly-line, owner-worker variety (see Chapter 7). There was at first little worker desire for unions, and the public attitude was one of mistrust toward such organized groups. When workers began seriously pushing for labor union bargaining in response to large business formation of the early 1800s, they were met with charges of "criminal conspiracy!" That is, the mere association of two or more workingmen to improve their working conditions was *in and of itself* a criminal activity, even if no other "normally" criminal methods were used. The courts followed with severe antilabor union policies until the 1842 verdict in the *Commonwealth* vs. *Hunt* case (Massachusetts), which held that labor unions in and of themselves were not illegal. But labor unions were still generally distrusted by the public and were prosecuted under the 1890 *Sherman Antitrust Act* as a "conspiracy in restraint of trade." (Although this act was designed to combat such large business monopolies as railroads and oil, it was most frequently used against unions in injunction proceedings.) During this period, business tactics against labor union organization were often brutal, and strong-arm methods were used frequently, but business was generally supported by public and court responses. The bloodshed in the Tompkins Square riot (1874, New York), the Haymarket Square riot (1886, Chicago), the Homestead strike (1892, Pennsylvania), the Pullman strike (1894, Illinois), and the Ludlow massacre (1914, Colorado) was indeed discouraging to labor union formation.

One might wonder, with such obstacles, if (and why) any labor union activity occurred prior to the 1930s. Nevertheless it did, and a strong base was laid for the meteoric increase in labor union growth after the 1930s. Although local labor unions (New York, Philadelphia, Chicago) were forming all through the early 1800s and aiming at workingmen's political parties, the first large movement was that of the National Labor Union, which was formed in 1866. This group included all workers (skilled and unskilled), espoused demands for general social reform (aid to the poor, public health, direct vote, and other issues) and was led by William H. Sylvis. Such concern or social and political reform spread the union leadership thin and led to worker disinterest, with the NLU "replaced" by the Knights of Labor in 1869. In leading the KOL, Uriah S. Stephens also pushed an all-worker concept aimed at social and and political reform, and he also lost worker support.

At this point a new labor philosophy of "business unionism," emphasized by Samuel Gompers, led to the formation of the American Federation of Labor in 1886. This group, the forerunner of many present-day unions, emphasized demands for direct worker benefit (better pay, hours, work conditions) and shunned direct political involvement and social reform. It also emphasized the *craft union* concept, in that only skilled workers of specific trades (carpenters, cigar makers, tailors, and so on) were included. This left the unskilled worker shortchanged; and it was not until 1936, under the Congress of Industrial Organizations (CIO) led by John L. Lewis, that industrial unions were formed. The AFL concept proved generally successful, with some 4 million members prior to World War II, and generally formed the base for later labor union gains. Although there were other labor groups during this period, like the Industrial Workers of the World (ever hear of radical "Wobblies" and "Big Bill" Haywood?), the AFL is the first and most prominent organization of the period.

World War I proved generally favorable to labor union growth; there was recognition of, and cooperation with, labor by both the National War Labor Board and the Wilson administration. In addition, the Progressive movement of the early 1900s swung public opinion toward support of labor union organization through its emphasis on reform of social, economic, and political inequities. However, the bloom of labor growth was short-lived. War's end brought renewed court injunctions, business reprisals, and a short but severe depression in 1921–1922. With the later 1920s' boom period of higher wages and improved economic conditions, worker interest and agitation for union membership waned.

So much for a synopsis of labor union history of the turbulent 1800s and early 1900s. Although the end of this era saw labor union membership in retreat, note that labor union organization was an established concept and that labor demands centered on the "bread and butter" issues of the AFL. Remember also that this very bitter period of union formation was only some forty to fifty years ago. Things have since changed a great deal in regard to labor union acceptance and importance.

1930–1945

The 1930s were the years of the Great Depression, when some 25 per cent of the labor force was unemployed; and many others, underemployed. It was a low point for union organization. Yet this depression showed the worker his need for labor union job protection. Labor legislation of Franklin Roosevelt's "New Deal" provided the base for the great climb in labor union membership.

The tremendous gain in labor union membership started with the passage of the Wagner Act of 1935 (formally, the National Labor Relations Act). Previously, the Clayton Antitrust Act of 1914 had specified that labor unions were not conspiracies in restraint of trade. Section 7A of the National Industrial Recovery Act of 1933 further stated that all workers had the fundamental right to form labor unions of their own choosing. (NIRA was, however, declared unconstitutional in 1935.) The Wagner Act was really the Magna Charta (do you know this term?) of American Labor!

The basic importance of the Wagner Act to labor union growth and of its great encouragement to membership gains was that:

1. Workers had the basic right to form unions for collective bargaining purposes. Unions were now "legal, official, and encouraged."

2. Employers could not interfere with union organization and had to recognize member-elected representatives in collective bargaining procedures. No blacklisting (firing for union activity), yellow-dog contracts (hire only if the worker promised in writing not to join a union), company unions (company-sponsored groups to sidestep unions), or coercive tactics were allowed.

3. The National Labor Relations Board was set up to enforce provisions of the act and to regularize and evaluate elections to determine properly elected union representation of workers. This

agency makes sure business management recognizes and cooperates with unions and acts as an appeal board for complaints.

Although the Wagner Act gave great force to the labor union movement, two other events also spurred membership gain: the formation of the CIO and World War II. Recall that the American Federation of Labor included only skilled, specific craft workers. But the great mass of unskilled and semi-skilled assembly-line workers were not organized until the formation of the Congress of Industrial Organizations in 1936. Led by John L. Lewis, the CIO grew very rapidly (3.7 million members in 1937 against 3.4 million for the AFL) and took in all workers of a particular industry, such as coal mining, steel, oil, auto, and so on. Although the CIO and AFL engaged in bitter disputes through the 1930s and 1940s (they merged in 1955), the existence of both craft and industrial union membership provided union entry for many American workers.

World War II also bolstered labor union status and gains because it emphasized the important role of labor in wartime and provided employment and wage gains for many of those who were unemployed in the 1930s. In fact, the War Labor Board included labor union representation and was formed to smooth labor disputes and increase war goods production.

All in all, this period from 1930 through the end of World War II saw tremendous labor union progress in both public acceptance and membership gains. Labor indeed became an economic power, and business–labor union collective bargaining was an accepted fact.

World War II to the Present

Since the end of World War II, something of a reversal in public opinion and government legislation has occurred in regard to labor unions. Whereas encouragement was the word in the 1930s and 1940s, cooling down might be used to describe public attitudes in the 1950s and 1960s. Instead of supporting labor union protection of worker interests, the public demanded regulation of the unions' large economic impact and internal practices. One might say the scales have been tipped the other way in an effort to control and regulate labor union activity.

The first of these control measures was the Taft–Hartley Act of 1947 (formally, the Labor Management Relations Act). This act came in response to severe and frequent work-stoppage strikes following World War II and to employer and worker complaints of "unfair labor union practices." Notice the features controlling labor unions in the act's provisions:

1. Unfair labor practices were spelled out, protecting the worker himself against his union. No restraint on worker choice of union representation, no forcing of union participation, no closed shops (must join union before being hired) were allowed, but union

shops (join after hire in stated time period) were allowed. Excessive union membership fees were prohibited.

2. Business received protection against "unfair" union practices. No secondary boycotts (picket a company because it uses products of another company being struck), no jurisdictional strikes (strike over what union represents workers), no featherbedding (pay for services not performed or unnecessary) were officially allowed.

3. The public was protected in case of work stoppage on a large scale in critical-service-public-interest industry areas. If the flow of essential goods and services were threatened by a strike, an eighty-day cooling-off period (back to work and negotiation) could be ordered by the president, and mediation (a third party attempts to resolve differences between the positions of the labor union and the employer) services could be offered to resolve disputed labor contract points.

4. The so-called *right-to-work provision* (Section 14-b) was included, giving state governments permission to outlaw local union-shop contracts. Thus, a worker could be hired without the requirement of joining a union.

These provisions of the Taft–Hartley Act should illustrate issues that are still with us today and that are of concern to many who are aware of the economic power of labor unions. The public interest issue, whereby union bargaining for member pay gains may endanger public service, is still unsolved, basically because government arbitration (government requirement that business and labor agree on contract terms determined by a third party) is generally not welcome in our present market economy. The worker vs. union issue remains a problem because we want union protection of worker interest, yet do not want workers subject to union abuse.

In addition, public concern was, and is, widespread over union use of membership funds. Control of such funds was the intent of the Landrum–Griffin Act of 1959 (formally, the Labor–Management Reporting and Disclosures Act). This act stipulated that

1. Unions must have a constitution, noting membership requirements, fees and dues, handling of union funds, and bargaining and strike procedures.

2. Union members must have the right to participate in union business affairs, to control union officials, and to make court appeals on union discipline actions.

3. Unions must file financial reports with the secretary of labor on all business and financial activities.

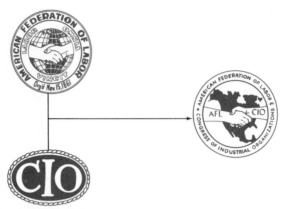

FIG. 9–5. Merger of the AFL and CIO in 1955.

4. Both unions and businesses must limit organizing and union pre-vention tactics, respectively.

One other major event that should be noted in this period is the merging of the AFL and the CIO in 1955, with George Meany as president. This merger ended years of feuding between the two labor groups, thus giving greater labor unity and producing a labor union organization of some 15.5 million workers (9.5 million in the AFL and 6 million in the CIO). The independent unions (Railway Brotherhoods, United Mine Workers, Team-sters, and so on) had at the time some 2.5 million members.

SUMMARY

We end this section on labor union history by again emphasizing the great change and growth of the American labor movement in a relatively short period of time. Figure 9-6 summarizes the major pieces of labor legislation, and reference to Figure 9-3 should summarize the long-term changes in labor union membership. We also point again to the unanswered issues generated by such rapid growth: how to control the large economic power of labor unions, how to protect the worker in a huge labor organization, and how to promote benefits and simultaneously protect public interest? Consider these problems yourself and some possible solutions to them.

CURRENT LABOR ISSUES

While you're still considering the preceding problems, let's turn to some other current questions facing the labor union movement and the American economy. No final "answers" are given here; our purpose is to show economic

1600s	Working Day of 14–16 Hours, Week of 6–7 Days
1633	Skilled Worker Legally Limited to 50 Cents for a Day 14–16 Hours
1600s–1700s	Courts Said "No" to Better Work Conditions, Higher Pay, and Shorter Hours
1835–1850s	10-Hour Day for Men Established
1852	First 10-Hour Law for Women (Ohio)
1860	Children Under 14 at 10-Hour Day
1866	National Labor Union for 8-Hour Day
1868	8-Hour Day in Federal Service
1916	Adamson Act Set 8-Hour Day in Railroads
1924	Amendment to Regulate Child Labor
1932	Norris-LaGuardia Act Denied Federal Power to Issue Injunctions against Unions
1935	National Labor Relations Act (Wagner Act) Promoted Equality of Bargaining Power between Employees and Employers
1938	Fair Labor Standards Act Set Minimum Hourly Wage of 25 Cents and Regulated Child Labor
1940	8-Hour Day and 40-Hour Week
1947	Labor–Management Relations Act (Taft–Hartley Act) Forbade Featherbedding and Promoted Industrial Peace
1959	Landrum-Griffin "Labor Reform" Act
1963	Minimum Legal Wage of $1.25 per Hour
1968	Minimum Legal Wage of $1.60 per Hour
1973	Minimum Legal Wage of $2.00 per Hour
1976	Minimum Legal Wage of $2.25 per Hour

FIG. 9–6. Labor union legislation.

pressures facing labor unions, as well as labor union effects on the American economy.

First, labor unions want higher pay for their workers (not a new demand since the early days of the AFL and S. Gompers) and are worried about inflation eating up pay gains. Hence, escalator clauses are added to union contracts to compensate for inflationary loss of purchasing power. (This means automatic increases in worker pay as the cost-of-living index rises.) In addition, labor unions have more frequently demanded that fringe benefits be added to union contracts. Fringe benefits include all types of nonwage provisions, among them medical and dental care, retirement plans, insurance packages, stock options, and so on.

Now, as you might guess, these union demands for direct wage or fringe benefit increases mean cost increases to businessmen. If such cost increases outstrip productivity increases (output per man-hour rises less than wage cost per man-hour), cost of production rises; then either product prices remain the same, and profit margins are lowered, or product prices are pushed up by wage-cost inflation pressures. Either way, someone is going to be unhappy, and we're in danger of an inflationary spiral, with wages rising to beat prices and prices rising to cover higher wages. This tendency is of real concern in current federal government fiscal policy attempts to level inflationary pressures. (More about this in Chapter 13.) The use of price-wage controls from 1971 to 1974 did not appear to resolve the problem, for many complaints were voiced during controls of inequitable rulings, and wages and prices greatly increased as soon as the controls were lifted.

Not only is this wage-cost inflation spiral of concern to the businessman, the consumer, and the government, but there's another, "hidden" concern to the union leader and worker; that involves automation to avoid labor cost increases. Let's recall our supply-demand tools of Chapters 4 to 6. (Refer to Figure 9-7.)

1. Suppose market supply-demand for labor results in fifty workers hired at $2 per hour, or $100 per hour total wages.

2. Suppose, now, that a higher wage is forced by contract and the business responds by hiring fewer workers. Forty workers are hired at $3 per hour, or $120 per hour total wages.

3. Suppose again, because of higher costs, the business later replaces certain workers with machines to do their jobs, thus reducing worker demand to D_2. Now only thirty workers are hired at $3 per hour or $90 per hour total wages. (The change in total wages depends upon elasticity of business demand for labor. The more elastic the business demand, the more will increased wages result in decreased total wages. Recall Chapter 4?)

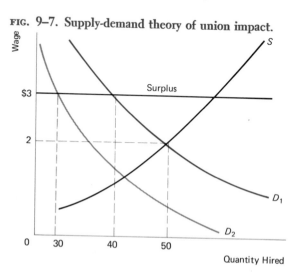

FIG. 9–7. Supply-demand theory of union impact.

Can such shifts occur? Of course, and they do daily, as illustrated by automation in the fields of agriculture, dock loading, and auto production. This fear of being priced out of a job is a simple result of supply-demand forces, relationships between wages, productivity, costs, and business desire for profit. If you add to these causes the pressure of lower foreign wage costs (in certain cases) and import competition, you've got a real problem.

Before you become an adversary of automation, however, remember that automation will itself create new job opportunities (someone must produce the machines), as well as increase labor productivity, reduce production costs and prices, and possibly spur greater sales. The big problem is that the "displaced" worker may possess neither the new skills required in the new jobs (longshoremen may not have machinist skills for producing the automated dock loading equipment) nor the financial and personal flexibility resources to acquire such training. We then have a problem of structural unemployment (unemployment due to lack of job skills demanded), which is a very real issue today. People are unemployed and seek jobs, and jobs requiring specific skills go unfilled.

Another issue of concern to labor leaders is that of organizing new fields in the labor force. Current labor union membership is 24 million out of 93 million in the total labor force, or 26 per cent. One challenge, therefore, is how to organize the other 74 per cent. Well, this is a bit difficult, as those other groups are often white-collar service workers (government, finance, recreation, service, and so on). These groups traditionally haven't favored labor union affiliation. If one considers that such "service" jobs are the areas of expanding employment, you see the challenge for labor leaders.

On the other hand, there have been many inroads made by labor unions in these traditionally nonunionized groups of government workers and teachers. Such unions are the American Federation of State and County Municipal Employees and the American Federation of Teachers. Both claim large organizational gains. And, increasingly, we have slowdowns and strikes by such public employee groups as garbage collectors, bus drivers, policemen, firemen, and teachers. Now the issue here is whether government workers can strike. Even if they do so against the law, can you arrest everyone and still get the job done? Can you arrest all firemen or teachers if they strike? Again, some unsolved questions.

Perhaps the largest issue of all is the extent to which labor unions actually do influence our economy; that is, is it proper in the U.S. "market economy" for government to reduce or limit union power at some point to avoid problems of inflation, public discomfort, or political power imbalance? If it is proper to limit union power, what is the "proper point" of limit? If it is not proper, can a market economy operate successfully when so much "monopoly power" is possessed by one group (labor or business)?

Well, we've thrown much labor union history and a number of current labor issues at you in this chapter, so it's about time to "wrap it up." The purpose was, of course, not to confuse you, but rather to develop economic understanding of such problems and to induce you to tackle some real current issues. Did we succeed?

TERMS

Agency shop. A business in which the worker is not required to join a union but must pay union fees and dues.

Automation. The replacement of labor with capital stock (machinery).

Binding arbitration. A process in which a third party makes a settlement that binds two other parties in a negotiation dispute.

Closed shop. A business in which a worker must be a member of a particular union in order to be employed (illegal under the Taft–Hartley Act).

Countervailing power. A term coined by John Kenneth Galbraith, referring to the tendency of one market group (such as big labor or big government) to offset the market power of another group (such as big business).

Craft union. A labor group composed of members possessing specific skills, exemplified by the American Federation of Labor.

Escalator clause (also called cost-of-living clause). A union contract provision tying wage rates to changes in the cost of living, as indicated by changes in the Consumer Price Index.

Industrial union. A labor group composed of members with no specific craft skill, exemplified by the Congress of Industrial Organizations.

Mediation. A process by which a third party attempts to compromise (no binding authority) a negotiation dispute between two other parties.

Union shop. A business in which a worker must join a union within a certain period of time after beginning work.

QUESTIONS FOR STUDY

1. What proportion of American workers are members of labor unions?
2. Why have many workers failed to join unions of either the AFL or CIO?
3. Account for the turnaround in public and government attitudes toward unions from 1900 to 1935 and from 1935 to 1947.
4. Briefly contrast the antiunion and prounion views on organized labor.
5. Should public employees (your teachers) be allowed to organize? To strike?

6. Would it be advisable for states to pass laws requiring compulsory arbitration of all labor disputes?

REFERENCES

Bakke, E. Wight; Clark Kerr; and Charles W. Anrod, eds. *Unions, Management, and the Public*, Second Edition. New York: Harcourt Brace Jovanovich, Inc., 1960.

Chamberlin, Edward H. *The Economic Analysis of Labor Union Power*. Washington, D.C.: American Enterprise Association, 1958.

Dulles, Foster Rhea. *Labor in America*, Second Edition. New York: Thomas Y. Crowell Company, 1955.

Galenson, Walter. *A Primer on Employment and Wages*. New York: Vintage Books, 1966.

Killingsworth, Charles C. "Organized Labor in a Free Enterprise Economy," in *The Structure of American Industry*, Third Edition. Edited by Walter Adams. New York: Macmillan Publishing Co., Inc., 1961, p. 570.

Morgan, Chester A. *Labor Economics*. Homewood, Ill.: The Dorsey Press, Inc., 1962.

Nickson, Jack W., Jr. *Economics and Social Choice: Microeconomics*. New York: McGraw-Hill Book Company, 1975, Chapters 11 and 12.

Rayback, Joseph G. *A History of American Labor*. New York: The Free Press, 1966.

10

HOW TO
"GET YOUR
MONEY'S WORTH"?

SHORT ANSWER. Compare all purchases for quality and price; analyze all savings decisions for liquidity, return, and risk; and evaluate tax impacts on both spending and saving.

YOU AND "CONSUMER ECONOMICS"

Do you know anyone in financial difficulties, whose income is strained to meet expenses and whose debt is mounting? How do you suppose this person got in such difficulties? Can you avoid these problems yourself? Is there really a theory of wise saving and buying? Do you manage your income according to the "Savings Pyramid" of Figure 10-1? (We discuss this in more detail later in the chapter!) These are questions of consumer economics, and their answers are probably of concern to you.

Thus far in this text we have discussed "standard" economic theory in an attempt to convey how our American economy operates. We have emphasized continually your own role in our economy and why and how its workings affect you. We've not yet discussed directly how you might manage your own finances. In fact, few economics texts mention the very practical

FIG. 10–1. Savings pyramid.

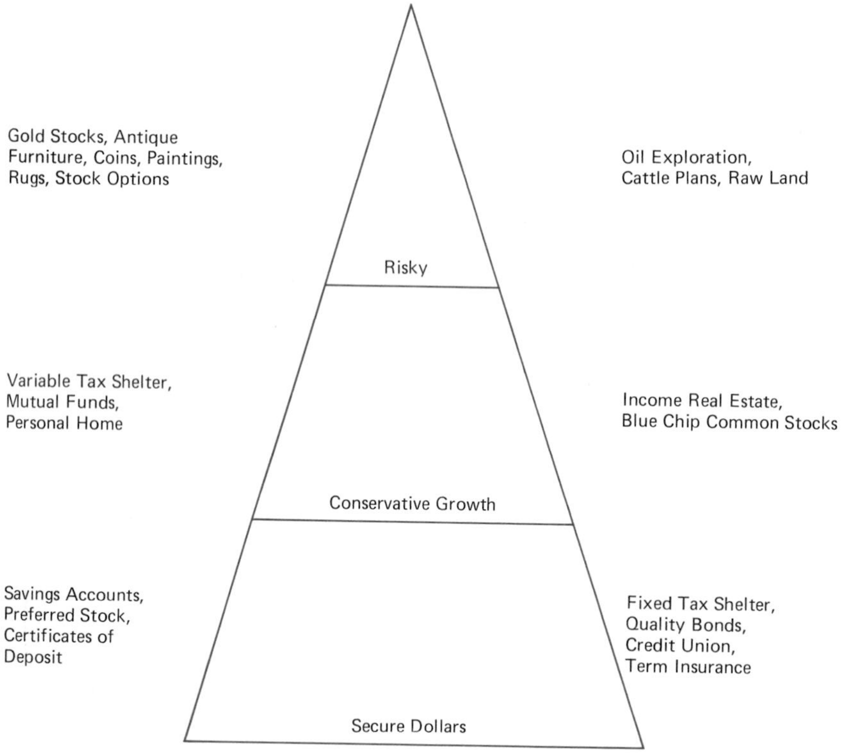

Gold Stocks, Antique Furniture, Coins, Paintings, Rugs, Stock Options

Oil Exploration, Cattle Plans, Raw Land

Risky

Variable Tax Shelter, Mutual Funds, Personal Home

Income Real Estate, Blue Chip Common Stocks

Conservative Growth

Savings Accounts, Preferred Stock, Certificates of Deposit

Fixed Tax Shelter, Quality Bonds, Credit Union, Term Insurance

Secure Dollars

area of consumer economics, because their province is economic theory, not personal finances, and because it is difficult to tell anyone exactly how to buy and save wisely. We cannot tell you precisely how to buy or save either. Your purchase decisions are your own business, and your decisions involve personal factors that we cannot anticipate. But we can discuss some basic points of personal finances in the hope of alerting you to the important effect your buying and saving decisions have on your financial standing. Although everyone's finances are unique, principles of consumer economics may be applied in some degree by all consumers.

CONSUMER CHOICE

As a general introduction and to provide perspective to the topic of consumer economics, let's re-emphasize the effect consumer buying habits have on the total economy. Recall (Chapter 2) that the economy is greatly affected by how the consumer chooses to apportion his or her income among types of spending (durables, nondurables, services) and saving. The consumer (allegedly) rules! Consumer spending and saving choices create jobs and incomes for others and greatly affect whether we have inflation or a depression in our economy. Consumer choice, therefore, affects others.

We also indicated (Chapter 4) that consumer choice in buying depends on various demand determinants: income, tastes, values, expectations, goals, and so on. Shifts in consumer demand (caused by changes in determinants) affect market prices, output and employment levels, and consumer income itself. So, in a sense, we've emphasized the importance of consumer buying patterns on the economy as a whole. One example of the importance of consumer purchase behavior is the attention paid to indexes of consumer optimism and intention to buy (Figure 10-2). If consumers are optimistic and confident about the economy as a whole and about their personal finances as well, their high levels of spending aid overall prosperity. But if consumers are pessimistic and unsure of the economy and their own income stability (as in 1975), serious deficiencies in consumer spending may force a recession.

We haven't really looked yet at why spending and saving are very important to you. Consider how whether people rent or buy their homes affects the economy. (Product demand for home construction creates resource demand for carpenters.) That decision is also of great relevance to you on an individual basis. Whether to own or rent one's residence (be it a single-family home, condominium, townhouse, or apartment) involves questions of personal preference, type of leisure-time use, desire for privacy, income tax impacts, and family life-style and needs. All of these issues are of prime importance in consumer economics, although the resulting consumer choice

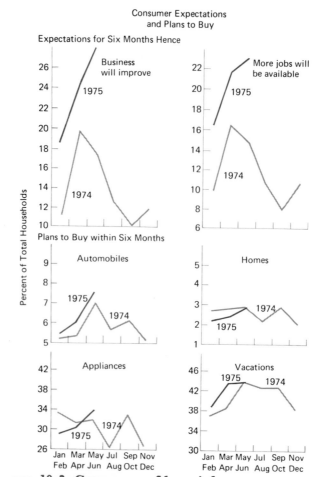

FIG. 10–2. Consumer confidence index.

SOURCE: *Finance Facts.* National Consumer Finance Association, September 1975.

itself would be of great importance to standard economic theory. Although there are these differences between "standard economic thory" (effect on economy) and "consumer economics" (effect on you), both areas are important to your economic understanding and can affect your daily economic activity.

In this chapter we'll look at how considerations and impacts divide consumer incomes between *spending* and *saving.* (Anything else you can think of to do with that paycheck?) Again, we can't (and wouldn't want to) tell you precisely how to spend or save, but we'll try to outline general strategies to benefit the typical consumer.

CONSUMER INCOME

One approach in consumer economics is to consider consumer income as given (use what you have), and concentrate on how best to spend and save this amount. Although we'll do this later in this chapter, there are a few points to be made about generating this income itself. This is a large issue, for the average wage earner will earn some $500,000 in his lifetime, although you, as an individual, may be well above or below this average.

Let's first note that career choice makes a large difference in your potential income. Figure 10-3 gives some idea of the income range possible in different occupations. Some digging in your own college placement center should add detail. Of course, income alone is not the only factor in career choice. We hope you will choose a career (or retrain for one) that suits your abilities and beliefs, for which you can afford training costs, and that provides you with challenge and personal growth. But you should reailze that job opportunities change over time and that you need a combination of specific, marketable job skills as well as the background and flexibility to adapt to new career directions and opportunities. For example, accountants are currently much in demand (as are machinists and computer technicians), al-

FIG. 10–3. Wage comparisons.

SOURCE: *Orange County Employment Handbook*, Orange County, California, 1974.

Occupation	Monthly Wage, Entry Level, 1976
Accountant	$1,000
Advertising Salesperson	725
Air Pollution Control Technician	1,000
Airline Pilot	2,200
Architect	1,100
Electronics Assembler	700
Auto Mechanic	960
Bank Clerk	575
Bank Officer	1,000
Carpenter	925
Chemist	1,000
Computer Operator	800
Civil Engineer	1,300
College Faculty	1,075
Home Economist	800
Machinist	975
Economist	1,200

though you might broaden your accounting degree to include some management and marketing background. The point we're making is that career choice should not be viewed as a once-and-for-all decision. You should develop a variety of job and personal skills.

Another important point to realize about income earned is that "satisfactory" income levels change over time. Although the income level you desire ($14,400 was the average family income in 1976) depends on your needs and goals, recognize that this level will probably be affected by *inflation* over time, as Figure 10-4 illustrates. The challenge is to maintain and perhaps improve your income position—first, through your choice of career and, second, by judicious saving and spending to make your income work for you. Let's now look at this aspect of "wise" buying and saving.

CONSUMER SPENDING

Let us assume that you're a typical wage earner who will generate a lifetime income of some $500,000 and that you spend some 93 per cent of your income (as most consumers do); you will later dispense about $465,000 in your lifetime. This is no small responsibility. In fact, it is one requiring a professional consumer approach. By this we mean that consumer spending is an important and demanding undertaking worthy of much attention, effort, and homework. The authors' view is that spending your income is perhaps more important than earning it. Your personal satisfaction and life-style are significantly affected by your spending decisions. Thus, a sloppy or careless spending habit should not be tolerated. The consumer must plan purchases, evaluate alternatives (do homework), and work constantly at making spending decisions.

Perhaps the first thing to emphasize is that your spending gets the "most for your money" only when you have a *definite spending plan* when you shop. By "definite spending plan," we mean something more than merely a shopping list for one trip to the store, although such a list is recommended. (Impulse buying will hurt your budget.) What we're getting at is that the consumer should sit down, alone or with his or her family, and think over what the *spending priorities* are overall: to eat better, dress more flashily, drive a newer car, live in a plush apartment, travel more, go to school in the future, and so on. Plan ahead!

Spending money is serious business and should involve more than just a wild guess in the aisle of a store. "Getting the most for your money" requires comprehensive spending plans (the shopping lists are the daily carry-through on these plans), and this means thought and effort. As an illustration, consider the decision to attend college and to spend money to do so:

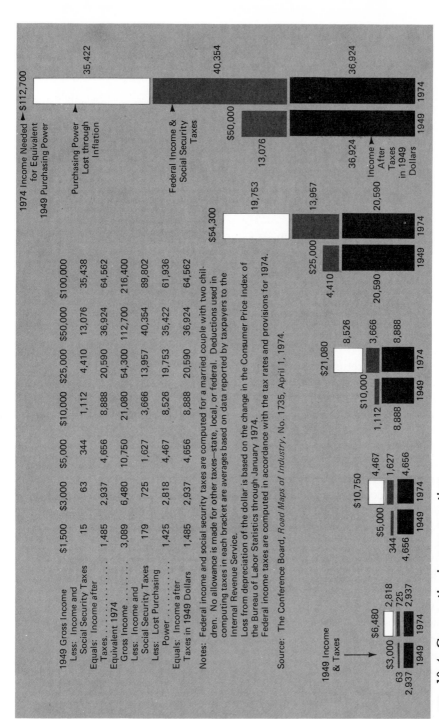

FIG. 10-4. Comparative income over time.

1. What are your goals and life ambitions? What career and life-style do you wish to pursue?

2. Does your career choice require a college degree, and will future careers be benefited by such?

3. What type of college curriculum best satisfies immediate job skills and provides long-term flexibility?

4. What does college cost in terms of both direct charges and income not earned (opportunity cost again) because you're in class instead of working?

5. How do different colleges compare in cost and quality of education provided? What employment prestige does each provide?

6. Should you attend full-time or part-time while working?

7. Should you go into debt for your college education?

8. What is the relative return for a college-degree job compared to that for the job requiring no college education?

9. Is the return greater than the cost?

Of course, college attendance aims not only at advancing in a career, but also at broadening the individual's perspective and culture. College attendance is not a decision based on money alone, although that's the point of first coming up with a spending plan. If you have a long-run goal of college graduation, then the choice is how best to allocate your finances to achieve that goal. Notice that in this example we illustrated the existence of *opportunity cost* in college attendance. The money or nonmoney cost of any action is not being able to do something else at the same time. College class means not working full-time, and a new car means no new wardrobes or stereo systems with the same dollars. We again emphasize (recall Chapter 2?) opportunity cost because it's often forgotten in consumer buying plans, but it is of real importance if you're to be a "professional consumer." (How seriously do you really take your role as a consumer?)

After you've decided on an overall spending plan, consider another major question: How serious are you about the specific items you buy? Do you compare prices and quality between brands and stores? Do you believe just what the ad says? Do you, for example, read *Consumer Reports* and judge quality? Do you really do your homework in shopping for products, or do you just pick up what's easiest? Do you know when stores generally have sales on particular items (linen sales in January, appliance discounts in April, auto sales in September, and summer clothing in October)? Do you compare *unit prices* (how much per ounce or gram) on alternative products when you shop? Do you clip coupons and buy in quantity, anticipating when you can really use the item? And do you frequently consider substitutes or alternative combinations to the products you typically purchase?

If you can't say yes to most of these questions, you're not "getting the most for your money," and you need more effort before and during your shopping sprees. Let's face it. There are many similar products around, and if you don't compare them, you are shirking your role as a consumer and probably hurting your budget as a result. Besides, the real challenge and enjoyment (do you enjoy being a consumer?) of purchasing are the shopping and comparisons made before you buy the product.

Get all the information available on a product, but make your own decision! Read the ad, listen to your neighbor's experiences, compare brands, and look at *Consumer Reports*, if available. But remember, you are consuming it, and your needs and tastes are not the same as those of others. If possible, try to avoid status symbol purchases or peer group buying pressures. Buy (live also?) on a pattern that does the most for you, and you'll probably be a long way ahead. On the other hand, you may benefit from joint purchasing with others, especially if you can then purchase in large quantities and secure volume price discounts. This is possible through arrangements with friends or family (purchase of a side of beef rather than a few pounds) or by joining a consumer cooperative designed to coordinate and reduce the cost of consumer purchases (usually you can make bulk food purchases for lower unit prices).

And now, how about the way you pay for that product—for example, the use of *credit?* Many consumers have pressing debt problems, perhaps because buying on time is just too easy and attractive and because the use of credit is a rapidly expanding habit. (See Figure 10-5.) The use of credit allows product use now (at a cost, of course!) and may be essential for large items such as a home or an auto. But remember that your purchases, whether for cash or for credit, should not exceed your income capacity. Again, you have to make the choice.

Now, you are, of course, aware that there is a cost to the use of credit, varying according to the type of credit instrument used. This may be the ever-popular *credit card* or an *installment sales contract* with costs (interest rate) stated (now required by law). The first thing to do is to find out just what the *credit cost* will be on a purchase. Is this credit cost justified by your expected satisfaction from the use of the product? Shop around to see if a lower credit cost is available. A direct *bank loan* is usually cheaper than an installment contract, and a *credit union* is less costly than a credit card or *charge account*.

Is buying on time worth it? Well, that's up to you, of course. Credit buying does give product use much sooner than cash purchase, and you pay for this time convenience. Also, in a time of rapid inflation, buying on credit may even be less costly than buying in the future for cash. You may even wish to buy on credit now so as to establish credit availability for future use. What

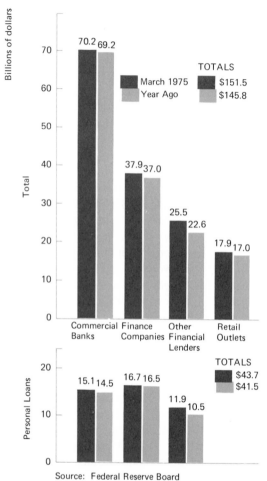

FIG. 10–5. Consumer installment debt.

SOURCE: *Finance Facts.* National Consumer Finance Association, June 1975.

we are emphasizing is that you should (1) determine buying priorities, (2) realize the credit cost involved, and (3) decide if the extra cost is worth it to you.

Debt accumulation is probably the biggest problem area for most consumers, and we want to emphasize its consideration. Don't rush into credit buying or forget about costs and future repayments. Don't buy "over your head"; that is, beyond your ability to repay. Just what the over-your-head amount is depends on your income, but don't go into debt right up to your monthly income ($1,000 per month earnings to cover $1,000 per month recurring bills is a pressure-cooker situation) and leave no flexibility or margin for miscalculation. As an ending note, you might read *The Devil and Daniel Webster, The 2000% Rule,* or *Merchant of Venice* to review future consequences of debt.

One further point to review in evaluating your spending decisions is the possible income tax impact of purchases; that is, there may be tax advantages (allowable deductions) by purchasing in particular patterns and according to certain timing or by buying particular items that should affect your decisions. For example, if you have a home office, the purchase of a calculator, typewriter, or desk will qualify as a deduction, as would a portion of your utility bills and home maintenance charges. Some of your clothing purchases or travel expenses may qualify as tax deductions if your occupation requires a "uniform" or sales visits. Although all of these possibilities should be evaluated by referring to a tax booklet or a tax consultant for allowable deductions, you must keep accurate purchase records and sales receipts to substantiate your deduction claims. The point is this; if you're going to spend, try to do it in order to "count" at tax time.

CONSUMER SAVING

Now we shall analyze the second important consumer decision, that of saving. Again, this decision is vital to the entire American economy. (See Figure 10-6.) The decision allows business firms to expand productive capacity, other consumers to purchase items on credit (such as houses and autos), and governments to provide social goods. All of these spending activities are to some extent based on the savings decisions of consumers. Output, employment, and income levels are thus affected by savings decisions.

FIG. 10–6. Consumer saving.

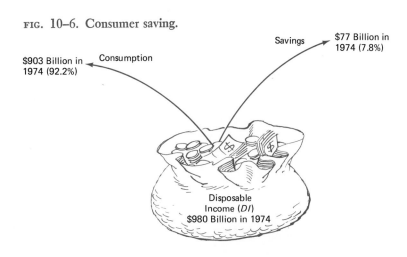

Savings → $77 Billion in 1974 (7.8%)

$903 Billion in 1974 (92.2%) ← Consumption

Disposable Income (*DI*) $980 Billion in 1974

We should again take note of the economist's distinction between *saving* and *investment*, for the two are often interchanged in daily conversation, and an important difference is involved. *Saving* is defined by the economist as consumer expenditure taken from disposable income (disposable income being income remaining after personal income taxes are removed) and used in some manner other than for purchase of final goods and services. Consumer purchases of stocks and bonds, real estate (other than personal housing), gold coins or bullion, payoff of debt, and so on, are all considered acts of saving by the economist (though many of you perhaps call them investments). For the economist, if the consumer is not spending on final goods and services, he is saving.

The economist defines *investment* as creation of new capital stock (tools, machinery, and factory buildings or *social capital* such as schools, transit systems, and hospitals or parks) that increases the productive capacity of the economy. And this *change in productive capacity* is the important distinction: Your buying a share of GM does not directly change productive capacity, but a utility company purchasing an electric generator does expand the economy's ability to produce. Do you see the difference?

FIG. 10–7. Savings pyramid.

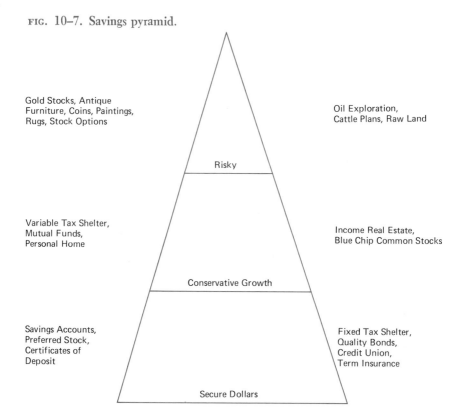

Gold Stocks, Antique
Furniture, Coins, Paintings,
Rugs, Stock Options

Oil Exploration,
Cattle Plans, Raw Land

Risky

Variable Tax Shelter,
Mutual Funds,
Personal Home

Income Real Estate,
Blue Chip Common Stocks

Conservative Growth

Savings Accounts,
Preferred Stock,
Certificates of
Deposit

Fixed Tax Shelter,
Quality Bonds,
Credit Union,
Term Insurance

Secure Dollars

This is not to deny the importance of consumer saving. As we've noted, consumer saving may enable businesses to invest or aid other consumers to spend on credit. From a consumer economics approach, saving is most important to your present and future financial stability. If we again assume the typical $500,000 life-income amount and a typical savings level of 7 per cent of such income, you may be making savings decisions amounting to $35,000 in your lifetime. This is, indeed, a large and important choice and requires a "professional consumer" approach to achieve full benefits; that is, to save effectively requires the consumer to define goals, evaluate alternatives, and carry out a regular and planned savings procedure.

Just as with spending, the most important point for your savings decisions is to have an overall savings plan. This plan will depend on your own income, expectations, goals, and so on. But a few general guidelines are in order:

1. Plan for a definite savings purpose. This may be for future spending (home, car, college, retirement, and so on), for possible emergencies (a "rainy day," sickness, unemployment), for income gains (interest earned), or for retirement (future income provision).

2. Plan to save on a regular basis. Certain amounts (suited to your income ability and savings goals) should be saved weekly or monthly by some mechanism (many are available) to achieve a certain goal at some time in the future.

3. Compare savings mechanisms (bank, savings account, stocks, insurance, syndications, real estate, bonds, and so on) that best meet your needs.

THE SAVINGS PYRAMID

To put these general savings guidelines in a form for daily application, let's review the savings pyramid of Figure 10-7. What the pyramid illustrates is a long-term "building block" approach for your saving decisions; that is, you "move up" the pyramid according to your own savings goals, amounts, desired risk, and preferred savings alternatives. Although the amount and placement of your savings in this pyramid is your choice, the overall strategy of saving is the primary concern and general guideline applicable to all consumers.

For most consumers, the first saving goal is to build a base of "secure dollars." This base should not only offer some degree of liquidity (able to be quickly cashed in), but also be fairly low in risk. In addition, this level may provide long-run protection and financial security for the individual and family. Although it may be difficult for any one savings alternative to offer all of these features, note that Figure 10-7 offers a variety of possible alternatives. Savings accounts (commercial banks, savings and loan associations, credit

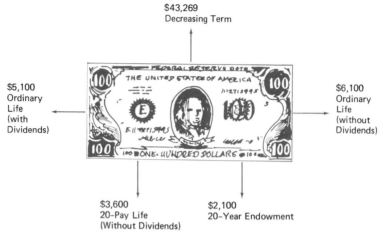

$43,269
Decreasing Term

$5,100
Ordinary
Life
(with
Dividends)

$6,100
Ordinary
Life
(without
Dividends)

$3,600
20-Pay Life
(Without Dividends)

$2,100
20-Year Endowment

FIG. 10–8. Cost of insurance. Courtesy of W. D. Renter & Associates, Corona Del Mar, California.

unions) offer both liquidity and a low risk, whereas stocks, bonds, and endowment-type insurance may provide security for retirement or family protection. One must recognize that such "secure dollars" may produce an interest return less than current inflation rates, thus resulting in reduced purchasing power of savings.

Even on this "secure dollar" level of the savings pyramid, let us emphasize the importance of evaluating and comparing savings alternatives for the "best value" choice. For example, *endowment-type* (often termed *whole life*) insurance offers long-term financial security, but at a very low rate of return, and it is really a fairly expensive method of protection, as Figure 10-8 points out. Perhaps a much better choice would be *term* insurance (only death protection; no savings buildup) for protection, with a fixed tax shelter for buildup of savings. The choice is yours, but always compare.

If you're unfamiliar with "tax shelters" noted previously, we should explain and emphasize their importance. Although there are many types of tax shelters (from individual retirement accounts to oil drilling), the basic points of each are to minimize tax liability on income earned. If you are at the "risky" level of the savings pyramid, your interest in the type of tax shelter would be quite different from your interest at the "secure dollars" level, but reducing taxes is still the purpose. For our example at the "secure-dollars" level, a fixed tax shelter might be an *individual retirement account* (IRA) set up with a commercial bank or insurance company whereby nontaxable amounts are put into some type of fund with a fixed and guaranteed rate of interest (also not taxed). Under such a plan you have the advantage of saving *before* taxes, low-risk buildup of secure dollars, and the possibility of later converting the same funds to a higher-yield savings alternative. Does this make sense? (In such a plan, you really need to see an investment counselor, financial broker, or finance agency.)

Notice that we urge you to save before taxes (have income deducted for a savings plan prior to taxes) and continually to consider alternative savings plans even at this "secure dollars" level. Your savings amounts are much greater, and your income tax liability is less, if you reduce your income by saving prior to tax application. A number of alternative savings plans will achieve this result, requiring your choice. You want financial security, liquidity, and a low risk (the specific combination must be your choice), but the number of qualified savings alternatives requires that you "shop around." Perhaps you may accumulate a large amount of secure dollars and then decide to indulge in the "conservative growth" level of the savings pyramid.

After you have satisfied your "secure dollars" goals, the "conservative growth" level of Figure 10-7 presents many more savings alternatives, all designed to increase future income streams and asset amounts. Although there may be some risk at this level and lesser liquidity, there are many income and tax advantages in the alternatives listed. Again, the importance of a systematic process of saving before taxes is to be emphasized, as is the need for evaluating savings alternatives. Purchase of income real estate (apartments, condominiums, business) offers an excellent *inflation hedge* (the asset usually increases with the general price level) and also offers many *tax deductions* (and tax liabilities!). Variable tax shelters (pretax savings in funds with varying rate of return) and mutual funds provide inflation protection and future income security.

We should explain the inflation hedge aspects of savings alternatives, for many consumers have unfortunately found their life savings inadequate upon retirement. Inflation itself means a rise in the general price level (see Chapter 12 on causes) and results in the decreased puchasing power of consumer income and savings. Many consumers have public (Social Security or state employee) and private (company or union) pension funds, but these fixed amounts must often be supplemented by additional income (as from your "secure dollars" or "conservative growth" plans) to maintain acceptable consumption standards. Review Figure 10-4 to see this inflation pressure on savings plans, and follow the calculation of Figure 10-9 in evaluating your savings plans. By saving before taxes, you increase savings amounts and reduce tax liabilities. By putting your savings in tax-free plans, you increase the savings yield. A tax-free return of 6 per cent is equivalent to a 12 per cent return after taxes if you are in the 50 per cent tax bracket. Taxes have risen faster than any other "cost-of-living index" component in the 1970s!

Whether you may ever get to the "risky" level of the savings pyramid depends upon your decisions, goals, opportunities, financial skills, and savings

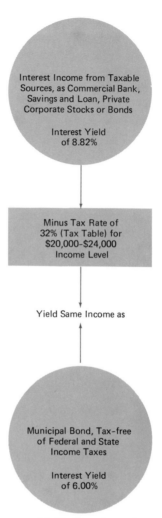

FIG. 10–9. Tax impact on
interest income.

amounts. At this level the purpose is to incur *greater risk in the prospect of
higher returns* with frequent *income tax and inflation hedge advantages*. However, the savings alternatives at the "risky" level in Figure 10–7 should not be
viewed as alternative to those at the "secure dollars" level. Although there
may be some mixture of alternatives among the three levels of the savings
pyramid, the best consumer saving strategy is, in general, to move from the
bottom to the top. Make sure you have "secure dollars" and "conservative
growth" levels completed to your satisfaction before you leap to the "risky"
level.

Savings Review

After all of these general guidelines on saving, you may still question what type of savings plan to pursue. Should you set up a savings account in a commercial bank or savings and loan association, buy government bonds, purchase common stock or mutual funds, or perhaps make a little hole in your mattress? Again, the final choice is up to you, but we offer a few points to consider:

1. What degree of safety must you have? Generally, higher interest rates are earned to compensate for greater risks taken. If you can afford a loss, fine. But don't save in a risky fashion if you really can't stand a loss.

2. What liquidity must you have? If you need your savings for spending use in a hurry, you'll probably want a savings account instead of stock or some other less liquid form of saving.

3. Are you saving in a manner that minimizes taxes, thus affording the highest saving return possible? A tax shelter plan through your investment broker or purchase of municipal bonds and income real estate provides such a feature.

4. Do your savings provide an inflation hedge over time to guarantee adequate income levels? You must consider both future and present purchasing power of savings to evaluate the adequacy of your retirement or family protection plans.

5. Do you really have a saving strategy? Is your saving done systematically and in specific plans designed to achieve stated goals in stated time periods, and do your savings really "work for you" (secure previous advantages)?

6. Recall that some saving is probably "automatically" done for you. Many are covered by Social Security or by company retirement plans, and the withholding tax may result in a refund at the year's end. (Don't "overwithhold," for you then forfeit the interest opportunity cost and lose through inflation!)

Choosing what savings method to use based on the preceding guidelines should involve a "professional consumer" approach; that is, just as in your spending, you should compare interest offered (an aspect similar to product price) and the quality of the type of saving (risk, liquidity, tax, and inflation features are similar to product standards and guarantees). Some of these savings plans, such as stocks and especially bonds, require large initial cash amounts that you may not have, but that you may accumulate by systematic saving in an easily convertible savings plan. Again, the word is that you must shop around and choose a savings method that best meets your overall savings plan.

THE PROFESSIONAL CONSUMER

What we've offered in this chapter are general guidelines on consumer economics. We can't offer specific buying and saving recommendations, for such advice depends on your particular financial condition, goals, expectations, and so on. (In fact, we strongly recommend your talking to an investment adviser or financial broker regarding your savings strategy and possible savings alternatives.) But we have emphasized that you should approach your buying and saving actions in a definite and deliberate manner and should do your homework beforehand. You need (1) to be aware of what's involved in these choices, (2) to keep current on changing buying and saving conditions, and (3) to pursue your spending and saving decisions as a "professional consumer" determined to achieve the "most for his money."

We hope that this chapter helped in the first instance to analyze general guidelines involved. Our advice on the second point is to spend time daily reading price ads, to subscribe to *Consumer Reports* or some other shopper's guide, to keep up on general business conditions through newspapers and magazines (*U.S. News & World Report, Business Week, Newsweek* or *Time* business section, and so on), and to seek out professional opinions on spending and saving possibilities.

As for the third principle mentioned earlier, it is up to you to become (are you now?) a professional consumer, achieving full value from all spending and saving decisions. We can only strongly recommend this approach in your daily spending and saving decisions: Know where you're going (overall plan), have information available (do your homework), and carry through on a regular and planned basis. (You might "blow" a few coins once in a while too, just to avoid being a drudge! Doing this will add immensely to your psychic income, even if your normal income is, on the surface, somewhat diminished.)

TERMS

Credit. A finance plan allowing the consumer to purchase something and pay for it (plus interest) later. Types include bank loans, installment contracts, charge accounts, and credit cards.

Inflation hedge. A savings plan that provides an increase in dollar value equal to increases in consumer price levels, thus preserving the purchasing power of the asset.

Investment. The purchase of capital goods, usually made by business firms. (Investment is not the same as saving, in which the consumer refrains from buying goods and services.)

Liquidity. The quality of being quickly convertible from savings into spendable cash.

Opportunity cost. The loss (e.g., in money, goods, or time) resulting from choosing one alternative over another.

Pretax savings. Savings not subject to income tax.

Tax shelter. A means of saving that minimizes income tax liability.

QUESTIONS FOR STUDY

1. Make a budget for yourself or your family, comparing your monthly purchases of all types against your monthly income. How much of a gap (plus or minus) is there between spending and income?

2. What spending and saving priorities did you have in mind when you made this budget? Do your choices reflect these priorities?

3. Add up all credit now extended your family. Then add up all interest charges paid. What percentage of interest charges are you paying? Have you shopped around to see if lower interest charges are available?

4. To what extent do you follow the savings pyramid of Figure 10-7? What types of savings alternative do you now have?

5. What percentage of interest do you currently receive on your savings? Have you shopped around to see if higher rates are available?

6. Do your saving (and spending) decisions provide tax advantages and inflation hedge protection? What alternatives would provide these features?

7. Are you a "professional consumer" now? Do you wish to be?

REFERENCES

Donaldson, Elvin F., and John K. Pfahl. *Personal Finance,* Fifth Edition. New York: The Ronald Press Company, 1971.

Mandell, Lewis. *Economics from the Consumer's Perspective.* Palo Alto, Calif.: Science Research Associates, Inc., 1975.

Miller, Roger LeRoy. *Economic Issues for Consumers.* St. Paul, Minn.: West College Text Division, 1975.

Niss, James F. *Consumer Economics.* Englewood Cliffs, New Jersey: Prentice-Hall, Inc., 1974.

Rathall, Denis T., and Anthony D. Bilick. *Money Management for the Consumer.* Boston, Mass.: Little, Brown and Company, 1975.

Reilly, Frank K. *Readings and Issues in Investments*. Hinsdale, Ill.: The Dryden Press, 1975.

Schultz, Theodore W. *Economics of the Family*. Chicago: The University of Chicago Press, 1974.

Swagler, Roger M. *Caveat Emptor: An Introductory Analysis of Consumer Problems*. Lexington, Mass.: D. C. Heath and Company, 1975.

11

EVER CONSIDER THE ECONOMIC EFFECTS OF GOVERNMENT ACTIONS?

SHORT ANSWER. Although the lunch may be "free" to you, somebody, some-where, at some time must pick up the tab—TANSTAAFL! [1]

[1] There ain't no such thing as a free lunch.

THE ROLE OF GOVERNMENT

As Figure 11-1 illustrates, the role of government in the modern U.S. economy is large and involves federal, state, and local government regulation in much of our daily lives. In the preceding ten chapters we've described government influence to some degree, but we'll analyze its effects even more so in the following nine chapters. Our purpose in this chapter is to survey this pervasive government influence and to stimulate your thinking on some practical and philosophical issues of the "proper" role for government.

The questions we'd like you to consider, both in review and in reading the following chapters, are as follows:

1. How have governmental policies expanded their influence within the U.S. economy?

2. What forces have promoted the expansion of government economic policy?

3. Is the present government economic policy role "proper," or is more or less government influence desirable?

4. What future directions for government policy appear most likely or most desirable?

FIG. 11–1. Government role in the economy.

| Price Controls | Factor Prices |
| (Air Fares, Milk) | (Minimum Wage) |

Unemployment Policies	Taxation
Environment and Pollution Standards	Welfare Spending
Antitrust Policies	Discrimination and Equal Opportunity Legislation
Energy Policies	Regulations for Public Health and Safety
Tariffs and Foreign Trade Policies	Inflation Policies

These are significant questions and most important in evaluating impacts on our economy and your own daily activities. Although the authors may not answer such questions completely to your satisfaction (the third question is, of course, a value judgment, and any answer depends on the respondent's goals and attitudes), they hope to stimulate your interest and thought. You must realize that the role of government has changed a great deal in the United States over the last forty years and will probably continue to change in the decades to follow. Our first purpose, therefore, is to examine these changing patterns of government economic activity and influence.

GOVERNMENT IN THE U.S. ECONOMY

Microeconomics Review

In the previous ten chapters, which analyzed the various sectors of the U.S. economy and covered topics of microeconomics, we frequently analyzed the impact of government policy. Although we may have basically a market type of economic system (recall Chapter 2?), the U.S. economy is daily affected by government "command" elements. Thus our economy may actually be closer to what Robert Heilbroner once termed *guided capitalism*, involving market forces overseen by government policy control and direction.

Reviewing our previous analysis of government policy impacts on market operation, recall the many instances in which government policy affected decision making of consumers and businesses:

1. Some products are prohibited from sale whereas others are subsidized and otherwise encouraged.

2. Products must meet health and safety standards, must be properly labeled, and must not be deceptively advertised.

3. Finance charges are regulated, and installment contracts must clearly indicate interest rates and total charges.

4. Business competition is usually encouraged, and antitrust suits seek to prevent anticompetitive tactics or actions detrimental to consumer welfare.

5. Business production methods must meet certain pollution standards; energy conservation and exploration for alternative sources of energy are encouraged.

6. Minimum-wage laws attempt to set income guarantees, as do income security (transfer payments) programs such as social security, unemployment compensation, and aid to families with dependent children.

7. Some market prices are directly controlled by government rule, whereas others are indirectly affected through supply and demand influences.

8. Foreign import competition may be reduced or eliminated through tariff or quota legislation, whereas export products may be subsidized.

9. Tax legislation and deductions are designed to encourage certain activities and discourage other pursuits and often benefit special interest groups.

10. The large bureaucracy of government regulatory agencies attempts to control or modify business practices for consumer welfare, although the benefits of this goal and the high consumer costs it seems to produce are increasingly questioned and criticized.

This list is rather long, but this enumeration only briefly summarizes a wide range of government influences. There are numerous examples and specific agencies involved in each preceding summary point, with powers sometimes duplicated among federal, state, and local government agencies. Indeed, extensive government regulation of microeconomic functioning has been estimated (Council of Economic Advisers—1975) to cost the taxpayer-consumer some $130 billion annually!

Now, of course, the question is whether such governmental regulation is "worth it?" or do the costs outweigh the benefits? Could some "unncessary" regulation (and who is to say what is "unnecessary"?) be eliminated, while still preserving areas essential to consumer protection and welfare? Should the future direction of such regulatory practices be toward contraction (politically possible?) or expansion (revenue source and cost impacts)? Is our economic system of "guided capitalism" (how would *you* describe it?) becoming more of a "command capitalism" (implications?), and does it make any difference?

The answers to such very difficult questions depend on individual value judgments in many instances. There have been, of course, numerous economic cost-benefit studies (match added costs against added gains to see the market impact), but many of them are without significant conclusions. Many economists agree that government regulation (especially in areas of trade, transportation, energy use, and pricing) has often been ineffective at best and detrimental to consumer interest at worst. Although it constitutes a value judgment area, the authors would conclude that much of such direct market intervention by government policy is unjustified and that such intervention's stifling effect on market operation actually harms consumer welfare in the long run.

Now that the authors have pronounced their value judgment on government microeconomic policy (macroeconomic policy is defined and evaluated in the following section), let us further pursue the logic of our criticism, remembering that this is a "philosophy" chapter. Market operation, you will recall, is basically our economy's chosen process for resource allocation; and spending patterns, the profit motive, and market prices are the prime determinants in this process. Recall also the pervasive interdependence of our market system, and perhaps you will begin to see the logic of our objections to government intervention. If resource allocation based on consumer choice and the efficient use of resources are the desired goals, then free market operation—unhampered by government intervention, distortion, and bottlenecking—should be maintained. Frequent tampering with such an interdependent mechanism by government legislation may (and often does, in our opinion) create a patchwork result of ineffective market results and bureaucratic inefficiencies.

On the other hand, there are some areas where government intervention may be desirable if efficiency and consumer choice are not the only goals of society. Such situations arise where *social welfare goals* and *externalities* are present. An example of a social welfare goal would be the elimination of discriminatory employment practices or housing sales or perhaps the bolstering of income levels through minimum-wage laws or rent controls. (Rent control, however, may cause urban deterioration, as in New York City.) Notice that a cost-benefit analysis of such intervention is difficult because the goal is not one of efficiency or consumer choice. Even here, however, one may question whether present government bureaucracies effectively achieve the stated social welfare goals. (Perhaps discrimination is better reduced through government employment or education, and income maintenance is better effected through a "negative income tax"?)

The definition of an *external economy* or *external diseconomy* (externalities) is that some economic impact (benefit or detriment) occurs because of business operation, but does not directly affect that operation. Other sectors of society, however, are affected. For example, a steel mill may pollute the air with its production process, but the "external diseconomy" of pollution is borne by society at large, not by the steel firm through increased costs. In such cases, this separation of private costs (the steel firm's production expenses) and social costs (the detrimental pollution) may justify governmental intervention. Pollution standards, filter requirements, or close-down injunctions may be used to reduce this external diseconomy if such reduction is a stated social goal. Perhaps a good example of an external economy would be public financing of education on the grounds that overall social benefits are achieved through a more skilled, intelligent, and aware citizenry. (Economic understanding for all?)

What we're attempting to set forth is the thesis that unhampered market operation is preferable when the goals of efficiency and free consumer choice predominate. But when other social goals have priority, effective government intervention may be justified. Of course, the trick is still to discover these priorities and match proper intervention with desired results. But we hope we've fully challenged your thought thus far.

Macroeconomics Survey

The following nine chapters will examine the various topics of macroeconomics (analyze economic operation in its entirety) and will frequently analyze the role of government in economics. We aim here to survey only the areas, issues, and impacts of government policy in the functioning of the U.S. economy as a whole. The purpose is to challenge your philosophy (do you have one?) of "proper" government macroeconomic policy and to alert you to the complex issues involved.

Perhaps a simple way to survey government macroeconomic policy impact is to review the *circular-flow model* of the U.S. economy (recall Chapter 2?). By inspection of this model and by thinking of news accounts you've read, do you see these "impact areas" of government macroeconomic policy?

1. *Income levels.* Government taxation and transfer payment (income maintenance programs) policies attempt to equalize or maintain disposable income levels.

2. *Employment levels.* Government spending rates, subsidies, and tax incentives attempt to achieve full employment rates.

3. *Inflation rates.* Government spending and taxation policies (budget results) attempt to achieve stable prices.

FIG. 11–2. Government in the circular-flow model.

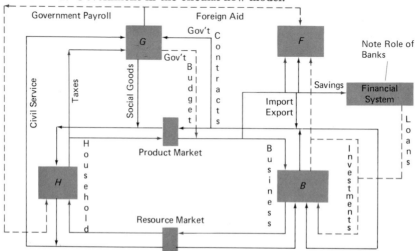

4. *Energy use and supply.* Government spending, taxation, price controls, oil tariffs, exploration subsidies, and ration control policies all aim at conserving present energy supplies and developing new, alternative energy sources.

5. *Environmental protection.* Government production controls and pollution standards aim at conserving natural resource beauty and public health levels.

6. *Economic growth.* Government spending and taxation policies are designed to promote increased total output and resource productivity both in the domestic U.S. economy and in underdeveloped economies.

7. *Foreign trade.* Government tariff and foreign aid policies affect export and import movements, thus affecting domestic and foreign output, employment, income, and price levels.

The preceding list of macroeconomic policy impact areas is a long and complex one and requires much analysis to evaluate the issues involved. The topics are developed in detail in the following chapters, and we ask here only that you be aware of such issues as you read forward.

In attempting to focus your attention on this multitude of macroeconomic policies, notice that the basic purpose is to modify aggregate economic activity (total levels of output, employment, income, prices) so as to increase consumer welfare. This basic goal is, therefore, similar to microeconomic policy, although the intervention and impacts occur throughout the entire economy rather than in specific markets. Thus, although the policy mechanisms of macroeconomics and microeconomics are quite different, many of our previous evaluation points on microeconomic policy also pertain to macroeconomic policy.

As an example of evaluating the impact of macroeconomic policies, one might ask if full employment, price stability, economic growth, environmental protection, alternative sources of energy, and increased foreign trade flow goals have been achieved. (Given the "embarrassing" results of 1974–1975, an economist hesitates to answer!) Economists no less than citizens would surely disagree among themselves, and a clear-cut reply is virtually impossible. During the middle 1960s it appeared that such goals had been achieved by macroeconomic policies, and thus government planning enjoyed strong support. However, the subsequent recession combined with inflation during the 1970s has created much doubt in the success of macroeconomic policy. What do you think of economic results illustrated by Figure 11-3?

The authors themselves would criticize macroeconomic policy, but for reasons different from those supporting their previous criticism of microeconomic policy. The problem is not so much a distortion of the resource allocation process by market operation as it is the lack of definite policy goals, the

Year	Output		Umemployment Rates All Workers Per Cent	Disposable Income 1958 = $100 Billion	Prices Consumer Prices Index (All Items) 1967 = 100
	GNP 1958 = $100 Billion	Industrial Production 1967 = 100			
1950	$355.3	44.9	5.3	$249.6	72.1
1955	438.0	58.5	4.4	296.7	80.2
1960	487.7	66.2	5.5	340.2	88.7
1965	617.8	89.2	4.5	435.0	94.5
1970	722.5	106.6	4.9	534.8	116.3
1975	931.1	113.8	8.5	668.9	161.2

Source: *President's Economic Report*, 1975.

FIG. 11–3. Economic performance, 1950–1975.

poor and inadequate design and timing of policy application, and the frequent reversal of policy emphasis. If this appears a heavy charge to you (it is!), realize that our point is not that macroeconomic policy is detrimental, but rather that it has been badly designed and applied and that the goals of macroeconomic policy have been often lost in the thicket of political compromise and bureaucratic procedure.

Our previous mention of social welfare and externality considerations applies especially to the evaluation of macroeconomic policy. Much of macroeconomic policy is not directed to resource allocation or use efficiency as such, but rather to elevating consumer welfare and maintaining national interest. The authors' criticism here, again, is not against the goals, but rather against the shoddy application of policy that seeks to achieve them.

An "overhaul" of our macroeconomic policies seems in order, involving (a) statement of definite policy goals in quantitative terms, (b) in-depth economic analysis of policy impact in short- and long-run periods, (c) speedy and direct policy implementation, and (d) periodic evaluation of goal achievement. Such an overhaul might greatly improve macroeconomic policy operation, and some movement by Congress in this direction has already occurred (the 1974 Budget Reform Act).

FUTURE GOVERNMENT ROLE

At this point the authors ask you to evaluate present and predict future trends in government. This is difficult and of doubtful success, for such projections are based on past history, present trends, and future guess. Many economists and citizens predict ever-growing government intervention in

U.S. economic, social, and political life. (Given our previous criticism, perhaps you see the authors' concern?) What is your prediction?

The prediction of increased government intervention is based on the seemingly endless demand for government programs to respond to social welfare claims, the increasing complexity of our technological industrial society, the increasing need to resolve and reduce conflict among societal groups, and the growing pressure to fulfill society needs for energy and social goods without increased costs to the individual consumer. All of these pressures exist at present, and all appear to point toward growing government intervention. True, we have now some public question of regulatory agency efficiency (e.g., the FEA, which oversees natural gas prices, and the CAB, which regulates air fares) and the invasion of privacy by the CIA, FBI, and army, but such current pressures do not appear sufficient to divert the longer-run trend of increased government economic influence.

Whether this prediction materializes we can only wait to see. We've at least raised some questions (have we in your mind?) as to government policy and stimulated analysis of policy issues throughout this text.

TERMS

Externalities (external economy or external diseconomy). An economic impact originating in the operation of a particular business or industry, without effect on its source but affecting society as a whole. (The impact is not usually considered [or counted as cost or gain] by the originating business in output decisions.)

Guided capitalism. Heilbroner's description of the U.S. economy, implying a basic market system overseen by governmental control and direction.

Macroeconomic policy. Government actions to influence the overall economy levels of output, employment, income, and prices.

Microeconomic policy. Government actions to affect directly or indirectly specific market operation and resource allocation patterns.

QUESTIONS FOR STUDY

1. How does government microeconomic policy differ from macroeconomic policy? Give daily examples of each policy type.

2. To what extent is your own daily life affected by government intervention? How do you evaluate this impact?

3. What is an external economy (external diseconomy)? How does it affect policy evaluation?

4. Pick some macroeconomic policy in which you're interested. Then

(a) state the specific goals of that policy, (b) find out how long the policy took to develop and become enacted, and (c) state what evaluation procedure is used to review policy success. Do you have any criticisms? 5. Do you feel government intervention should increase or decrease (in what areas?) in our future U.S. economy? Do you estimate government intervention will increase or decrease in the future?

REFERENCES

Carson, R. B., et al. *Government in the American Economy.* Boston: D. C. Heath & Co., 1972.

Eulan, H. *Micro-Macro Political Analysis.* Chicago: Aldine Publishing Co., 1968.

Galbraith, John Kenneth. *Economics and the Public Interest.* Boston: Houghton Mifflin, 1973.

Heilbroner, Robert L. *An Inquiry into the Human Prospect.* New York: W. W. Norton & Company, Inc., 1974.

Miller, Roger LeRoy, and Raburn M. Williams. *The Economics of National Issues.* San Francisco: Canfield Press, 1972.

Morgan, E. V., and A. D. Morgan. *The Economics of Public Policy.* Chicago: Aldine Publishing Co., 1972.

Soule, George H. *Planning: U.S.A.* New York: Viking Press, 1966.

WHAT CAUSES INFLATION AND DEPRESSION?

SHORT ANSWER. In general, when total spending exceeds a full employment level of output, inflation occurs. When total spending is insufficient to purchase a full employment level of output, recession or depression occurs.

WHAT DO YOU CARE ABOUT
INFLATION OR DEPRESSION?

The causes of inflation and depression are of central importance in the study of macroeconomics and affect your own economic activities daily. Understanding the causes not only sheds much light on the operation of our complex economic system, but also illuminates the reasons for much of government macroeconomic policy. If an economist (or you) can explain why inflation or depression occurs, he is then in a position to recommend (and you can evaluate) economic policies to alleviate these conditions. This chapter seeks to promote such economic understanding so that you are familiar with the impacts, statistical record, and causal theory of inflation and depression.

You've probably seen graphs of business cycles (like Figure 12-2), especially these last few years. And you've probably heard people quoting statistics and using the terms *inflation, recession,* and *unemployment.* Perhaps you've noted the great concern, including legislation, arising from such problems. But do you see the issue of inflation versus depression as directly affecting yourself and your own living standards and life-style? Perhaps you feel that concern over inflation and depression is only for economists and politicians and doesn't relate to your daily economic activity. If so, you are wrong. Moreover, these issues are not too complicated to understand.

Initially, let's define both *inflation* and *depression* (*recession,* if unemployment is mild; *depression,* if severe) in terms of their effects on the average person. By reviewing this "definition by effect," you should see very quickly why these economic conditions affect you.

FIG. 12–1. Causes of inflation and depression.

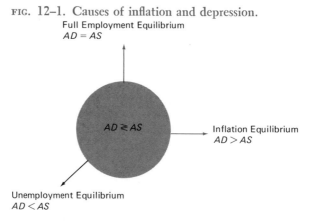

Full Employment Equilibrium
AD = AS

AD ≷ AS

Inflation Equilibrium
AD > AS

Unemployment Equilibrium
AD < AS

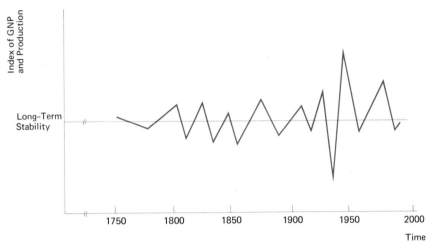

FIG. 12–2. The business cycle.

1. *Depression.* A condition in which the actual output of the economy is low compared to potential output at full employment.
   a. The amount of goods and services produced is low compared to the economy's ability to produce (perhaps 70 per cent capacity).
   b. Factories shut down or reduce output and employment.
   c. Unemployment is large (above 4 to 5 per cent of the labor force, which is now more than 95 million).
   d. People want to work but businesses aren't hiring.
   e. Family incomes fall, people can't spend as much, and must "make do."

2. *Inflation.* A condition of generally rising prices, with the value and purchasing power of currency falling.
   a. It takes more money to buy the same amount of goods and services. (Your paycheck doesn't go as far as it did.)
   b. Costs, prices, and taxes appear to increase continually.
   c. Fixed-income groups (e.g., those living on Social Security and pensions) must do without certain goods and services.
   d. Everyone wants higher wages to "catch up" with the high prices now! Businesses raise prices to maintain profits; labor unions demand *escalator clauses*. (Wages rise automatically with changes in the cost-of-living index.)

Do these descriptions seem important to you? Do you see how you are directly affected by the present state of the economy? In fact, the U.S. economy of the early and mid-1970s has experienced inflation and recession simultaneously, with inflation at some 12 per cent in 1974 and unemployment around 9 per cent of the labor force in 1975. These are grim statistics and have affected many Americans adversely. Many families, both in the United States and abroad, have found themselves confronted by soaring food and housing prices, unemployment, and rising taxes (personal income taxes rose some 28 per cent in the United States during 1974!) and have demanded government policy action.

By now we hope to have conveyed the impression that inflation-recession issues are critical and do affect you directly. Going on, let's now trace the inflation-recession record in the U.S. economy to get some historical perspective on where we've been and then develop a theory to explain the causes of recession or inflation. With an understanding of the theory, you should have inflation-recession issues pretty well in hand. You'll also be in a good position to move on to Chapter 13, where we analyze policy measures (*fiscal policy* in Chapter 13, *monetary policy* in Chapter 17) to deal with these problems. Does this sound like a logical attack to maximize understanding?

INFLATION AND UNEMPLOYMENT

Inflation

Inflation is definitely a current macroeconomic problem and has existed in our economy over recent years. Prices historically have risen, and they rose even faster in the 1970s (although the inflation rate of 12 per cent in 1974 dipped to about 6 per cent in 1975). Our long-term inflation rate of 1 to 2 per cent annually has been exceeded, and many citizens now consider inflation "public enemy number 1"! The direct impact of this rise in prices is that your dollars don't go as far in purchasing what you want: The decision on how to spend your dollars becomes more difficult. (Remember Chapter 10?)

Another way to express the inflation problem is to show the *purchasing power* of your dollar declining over time, illustrated in Figure 12-3. Think what a squeeze this puts on the retired or other fixed-income person as his dollar shrinks in purchasing power, requiring more dollars to buy the same amount of products.

With so much policy attention given this problem (more about this in Chapter 13), you'd think we could solve the problem of inflation (rising prices). We haven't, but at least we can aid you here in understanding the terms tossed around in newspapers in discussing the problem of inflation. A very common term is *consumer price index*, which is a statistic used to describe comparable prices through the years. Figure 12-4 illustrates what is involved in setting up such a table. The exact procedure involves the Bureau

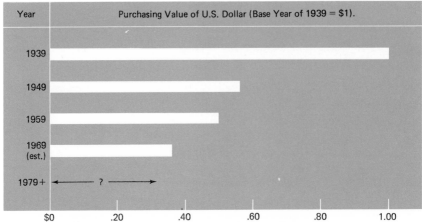

FIG. 12–3. Decline in purchasing power of U.S. dollar.

of Commerce's gathering price data on 400 items in its "market basket" of consumer purchases, then comparing price changes and computing the consumer price index results. Figure 12-5 is the result.

Don't be confused by these tables or that nasty-sounding term *statistics*. To understand what's going on in the inflation battle, you need to be familiar with their data. All we're doing is comparing *index numbers*, which show how all years compare against a common base of 100. Some year is chosen as the *base year* (=100) to measure all other years against. Then any year with a lower value (in prices, wages, or whatever else is being compared) than the base year has an index number less than 100, and any year with a greater value than the base year has an index number over 100. In

FIG. 12–4. Derivation of a price index.

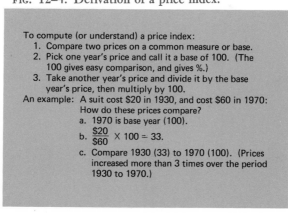

Year	Consumer Price Index Number (1967 = Base of 100)	Change in Value of U.S. Dollar
1940	42.0	-------
1950	72.1	Increase
1960	88.7	Decrease
1970	116.3	Decrease
1974	147.7	Decrease
1975	161.2	Decrease

Source: *President's Economic Report*, 1976.

FIG. 12–5. Consumer price index measures purchasing power.

Figure 12-5, the meaning is that $42 in 1940 would have purchased what $100 did in 1967 or what required $147.70 in 1974.

It's not difficult to see from these charts that prices have risen. Of course, to see how you really stand vis-à-vis prices, you also have to consider how

FIG. 12–6. Money income vs. real income.

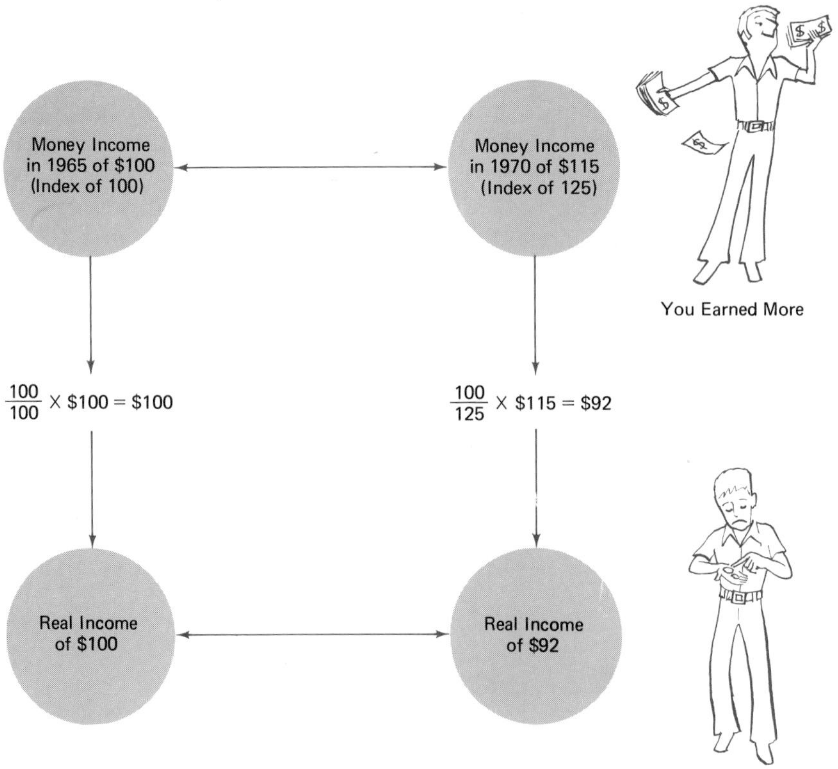

Money Income in 1965 of $100 (Index of 100)

Money Income in 1970 of $115 (Index of 125)

You Earned More

$\frac{100}{100} \times \$100 = \$100$

$\frac{100}{125} \times \$115 = \$92$

Real Income of $100

Real Income of $92

much your income has risen. Economists are fond of talking about *real income* or purchasing power (which is adjusted for price changes) versus *money income* (which is not adjusted). As Figure 12-6 illustrates, an increase in money income (a larger paycheck) may still be a reduction in real income (less purchasing power). The importance of such figures will perhaps be more real to you when you think of the case of persons on a fixed income, that is, those living on pensions, Social Security, and so on. Consider also how those on Social Security are faring when their income remains constant (legislative pressures for benefits increased). In fact, the real income of the average factory worker declined from 1973 through 1975!

Unemployment

The U.S. economy has also experienced recurrent unemployment over time, as evidenced in Figure 12-7. Serious unemployment occurred in the 1930s (some 25 per cent of the labor force) and has again risen during the 1970s (some 9.3 per cent in 1975). In evaluating the impact of such unemployment, you should consider the output not produced by unemployed workers and idle factories (an estimate of $200 billion in 1975) and the economic and psychological damages to families resulting from job loss.

There are several terms the student should be familiar with to understand unemployment policy debates. To begin with, *full employment* is defined by most economists to exist when only 4 to 5 per cent of our civilian labor force do not have jobs. This allowance is to cover *frictional unemployment* resulting from geographical patterns that continually occur within our labor

FIG. 12–7. U.S. unemployment rate record.

*Unemployment as Percent of Civilian Labor Force; Quarterly.

Source: Department of Labor.

force of more than 95 million workers (students who seek summer jobs, for example).

But when unemployment exceeds this 5 per cent level, we may be experiencing *deficient aggregate demand unemployment* as a result of lack of total spending. If spending is insufficient to maintain output at existing production levels, unemployment of this excessive type results. Another, perhaps more serious condition is that of *structural unemployment*, meaning a lack of job skills. This type of unemployment is most difficult for economic or governmental policies to counteract as job vacancies do exist, but the unemployed are not properly trained to fill them.

In the 1970s, both inflation and unemployment have, surprisingly, increased, creating economic pressures on American families and political pressures for government macroeconomic policies. Let us now review the statistics and then analyze theoretical causes of these statistical variations in employment and inflation.

GROSS NATIONAL PRODUCT

A close examination of business cycles, inflation, and unemployment statistics shows that inflation and recession have existed for some time in the United States. Realize that these statistics represent the economic performances of the U.S. economy, that is, the long-term changes in the levels of output (O), employment (E), income (Y), and prices (P) in our economy. But an even more general and widely used economic indicator is that of *gross national product* (or GNP).

GNP statistics (See Figure 12-8) show that in some years (upswing) our economy was quite prosperous, with high output, low unemployment rates, high family incomes, and rising prices. During other years (downswing, depression) the performance was reversed (especially in the 1930s and in 1975), with low output levels, high rates of unemployment, low family incomes, and falling (in the 1930s but not in 1975) prices. Put simply, the U.S. economy has had recurring "boom and bust" experiences over many years, though such fluctuation has subsided somewhat since World War II. These GNP statistics not only report economic performance, but also establish a policy basis to signal when offsetting government actions are required.

This frequently quoted gross national product statistic is actually only one component of the *national income accounting system.* Basically, this means that there is a conventionally adopted accounting system by which to measure just how well an economy is doing (dollar volume of goods produced). Now we're not here to make you an expert in this field or to introduce all the technicalities of national income accounting. But we should look a bit at the system in order to (1) give you an understanding for reading news ar-

					Government Purchases of Goods and Services					Per Cent Change from Preceding Period, Total Gross National Product
							Federal			
Year or Quarter	Total Gross National Product	Personal Consumption Expenditures	Gross Private Domestic Investment	Net Exports of Goods and Services	Total	Total	National Defense	Other	State and Local	
				Billions of Dollars						
1929	103.1	77.2	16.2	1.1	8.5	1.3	1.3		7.2	- - - - -
1933	55.6	45.8	1.4	.4	8.0	2.0	2.0		6.0	−4.2
1939	90.5	66.8	9.3	1.1	13.3	5.1	1.2	3.9	8.2	6.9
1940	99.7	70.8	13.1	1.7	14.0	6.0	2.2	3.8	8.0	10.2
1941	124.5	80.6	17.9	1.3	24.8	16.9	13.8	3.1	7.9	24.9
1942	157.9	88.5	9.8	.0	59.6	51.9	49.4	2.5	7.7	26.8
1943	191.6	99.3	5.7	−2.0	88.6	81.1	79.7	1.4	7.4	21.3
1944	210.1	108.3	7.1	−1.8	95.5	89.0	87.4	1.6	7.5	9.7
1945	211.9	119.7	10.6	−.6	82.3	74.2	73.5	.7	8.1	.9
1946	208.5	143.4	30.6	7.5	27.0	17.2	14.7	2.5	9.8	−1.6
1947	231.3	160.7	34.0	11.5	25.1	12.5	9.1	3.5	12.6	10.9
1948	257.6	173.6	46.0	6.4	31.6	16.5	10.7	5.8	15.0	11.3
1949	256.5	176.8	35.7	6.1	37.8	20.1	13.3	6.8	17.7	−.4
1950	284.8	191.0	54.1	1.8	37.9	18.4	14.1	4.3	19.5	11.0
1951	328.4	206.3	59.3	3.7	59.1	37.7	33.6	4.1	21.5	15.3
1952	345.5	216.7	51.9	2.2	74.7	51.8	45.9	5.9	22.9	5.2
1953	364.6	230.0	52.6	.4	81.6	57.0	48.7	8.4	24.6	5.5
1954	364.8	236.5	51.7	1.8	74.8	47.4	41.2	6.2	27.4	.1
1955	398.0	254.4	67.4	2.0	74.2	44.1	38.6	5.5	30.1	9.1
1956	419.2	266.7	70.0	4.0	78.6	45.6	40.3	5.3	33.0	5.3
1957	441.1	281.4	67.9	5.7	86.1	49.5	44.2	5.3	36.6	5.2
1958	447.3	290.1	60.9	2.2	94.2	53.6	45.9	7.7	40.6	1.4
1959	483.7	311.2	75.3	.1	97.0	53.7	46.0	7.6	43.3	8.2
1960	503.7	325.2	74.8	4.0	99.6	53.5	44.9	8.6	46.1	4.1
1961	520.1	335.2	71.7	5.6	107.6	57.4	47.8	9.6	50.2	3.2
1962	560.3	355.1	83.0	5.1	117.1	63.4	51.6	11.8	53.7	7.7
1963	590.5	375.0	87.1	5.9	122.5	64.2	50.8	13.5	58.2	5.4
1964	632.4	401.2	94.0	8.5	128.7	65.2	50.0	15.2	63.5	7.1
1965	684.9	432.8	108.1	6.9	137.0	66.9	50.1	16.8	70.1	8.3
1966	749.9	466.3	121.4	5.3	156.8	77.8	60.7	17.1	79.0	9.5
1967	793.9	492.1	116.6	5.2	180.1	90.7	72.4	18.4	89.4	5.9
1968	864.2	536.2	126.0	2.5	199.6	98.8	78.3	20.5	100.8	8.9
1969	930.3	579.5	139.0	1.9	210.0	98.8	78.4	20.4	111.2	7.6
1970	977.1	617.6	136.3	3.6	219.5	96.2	74.6	21.6	123.3	5.0
1971	1,054.9	667.1	153.7	−.2	234.2	97.6	71.2	26.5	136.6	8.0
1972	1,158.0	729.0	179.3	−6.0	255.7	104.9	74.8	30.1	150.8	9.8
1973	1,294.9	805.2	209.4	3.9	276.4	106.6	74.4	32.2	169.8	11.8
1974	1,396.7	877.0	208.9	2.0	308.8	116.4	78.6	37.9	192.4	7.9

Source: *President's Economic Report*, 1975.

FIG. 12–8. Gross national product (GNP).

		Personal Consumption Expenditures				Gross Private Domestic Investment						
							Fixed Investment					
								Nonresidential				
Year or Quarter	Total Gross National Product	Total	Durable Goods	Nondurable Goods	Services	Total	Total	Total	Structures	Producers' Durable Equipment	Residential Structures	Change in Business Inventories
				Billions of 1958 Dollars								
1929	203.6	139.6	16.3	69.3	54.0	40.4	36.9	26.5	13.9	12.6	10.4	3.5
1933	141.5	112.8	8.3	58.6	46.0	5.3	9.7	7.6	3.3	4.3	2.1	−4.3
1939	209.4	148.2	14.5	81.2	52.5	24.7	23.5	15.3	5.9	9.4	8.2	1.2
1940	227.2	155.7	16.7	84.6	54.4	33.0	28.1	18.9	6.8	12.1	9.2	4.9
1941	263.7	165.4	19.1	89.9	56.3	41.6	32.0	22.2	8.1	14.2	9.8	9.6
1942	297.8	161.4	11.7	91.3	58.5	21.4	17.3	12.5	4.6	7.9	4.9	4.0
1943	337.1	165.8	10.2	93.7	61.8	12.7	12.9	10.0	2.9	7.2	2.9	−.2
1944	361.3	171.4	9.4	97.3	64.7	14.0	15.9	13.4	3.8	9.6	2.5	−1.9
1945	355.2	183.0	10.6	104.7	67.7	19.6	22.6	19.8	5.7	14.1	2.8	−2.9
1946	312.6	203.5	20.5	110.8	72.1	52.3	42.3	30.2	12.5	17.7	12.1	10.0
1947	309.9	206.3	24.7	108.3	73.4	51.5	51.7	36.2	11.6	24.6	15.4	−.2
1948	323.7	210.8	26.3	108.7	75.8	60.4	55.9	38.0	12.3	25.7	17.9	4.6
1949	324.1	216.5	28.4	110.5	77.6	48.0	51.9	34.5	11.9	22.6	17.4	−3.9
1950	355.3	230.5	34.7	114.0	81.8	69.3	61.0	37.5	12.7	24.8	23.5	8.3
1951	383.4	232.8	31.5	116.5	84.8	70.0	59.0	39.6	14.1	25.5	19.5	10.9
1952	395.1	239.4	30.8	120.8	87.8	60.5	57.2	38.3	13.7	24.6	18.9	3.3
1953	412.8	250.8	35.3	124.4	91.1	61.2	60.2	40.7	14.9	25.8	19.6	.9
1954	407.0	255.7	35.4	125.5	94.8	59.4	61.4	39.6	15.2	24.5	21.7	−2.0
1955	438.0	274.2	43.2	131.7	99.3	75.4	69.0	43.9	16.2	27.7	25.1	6.4
1956	446.1	281.4	41.0	136.2	104.1	74.3	69.5	47.3	18.5	28.8	22.2	4.8
1957	452.5	288.2	41.5	138.7	108.0	68.8	67.6	47.4	29.1	29.1	20.2	1.2
1958	447.3	290.1	37.9	140.2	112.0	60.9	62.4	41.6	16.6	25.0	20.8	−1.5
1959	475.9	307.3	43.7	146.8	116.8	73.6	68.8	44.1	16.2	27.9	24.7	4.8
1960	487.7	316.1	44.9	149.6	121.6	72.4	68.9	47.1	17.4	29.6	21.9	3.5
1961	497.2	322.5	43.9	153.0	125.6	69.0	67.0	45.5	17.4	28.1	21.6	2.0
1962	529.8	338.4	49.2	158.2	131.1	79.4	73.4	49.7	17.9	31.7	23.8	6.0
1963	551.0	353.3	53.7	162.2	137.4	82.5	76.7	51.9	17.9	34.0	24.8	5.8
1964	581.1	373.7	59.0	170.3	144.4	87.8	81.9	57.8	19.1	38.7	24.2	5.8
1965	617.8	397.7	66.6	178.6	152.5	99.2	90.1	66.3	22.3	44.0	23.8	9.0
1966	658.1	418.1	71.7	187.0	159.4	109.3	95.4	74.1	24.0	50.1	21.3	13.9
1967	675.2	430.1	72.9	190.2	167.0	101.2	93.5	73.2	22.6	50.6	20.4	7.7
1968	706.6	452.7	81.3	197.1	174.4	105.2	98.8	75.6	23.4	52.2	23.2	6.4
1969	725.6	469.1	85.6	201.3	182.2	110.5	103.8	80.1	24.3	55.8	23.7	6.7
1970	722.5	477.5	83.8	206.5	187.2	103.4	99.5	77.2	23.7	53.5	22.2	3.9
1971	746.3	496.4	92.5	211.3	192.6	111.1	105.8	76.7	23.2	53.5	29.1	5.3
1972	792.5	527.3	104.9	220.2	202.2	125.0	118.0	83.7	23.8	59.8	34.3	7.0
1973	839.2	552.1	113.6	228.6	209.9	138.1	127.3	94.4	25.4	69.0	32.9	10.8
1974	821.1	539.9	103.4	223.8	212.8	126.3	118.1	94.1	26.2	67.8	24.0	8.2

FIG. 12–8. Continued.

ticles, (2) allow the development of some theory base for analyzing problems, and (3) indicate a source of reference for you to look up facts as needed.

The complete national income accounting system includes five accounts, but the most universally quoted is the *gross national product*, or GNP. GNP, almost a household word now for politicians and newspapermen, measures the total amount of final goods and services produced in any year. This figure is obtained, as shown in Figure 12-9, by adding up the amounts spent by each of our spending sectors of the U.S. economy (expenditures method) or by adding up all incomes earned in producing that output (incomes method). Thus GNP is both an output and income measurement and also indicates associated levels of employment and prices.

The statistics-gathering process itself is a large field of study, involving several government agencies, thousands of government employees, countless business reports, and computer time to coordinate. The Bureau of Commerce publishes many of the GNP statistics, with information gathered from processing retail sales totals, wage and salary reports, and other financial reports. For the interested reader, the *Survey of Current Business* describes the GNP accounting process.

Notice that we said GNP measures only output of final goods and services; that is, *no resale or used items* sold are included in GNP, nor are intermediate products that are components of final products (such as steel in autos). In addition, no nonmarket output is included in GNP, such as your home garden produce or the services of a homemaker or "honeydo" ("Honey, do

FIG. 12–9. Components of GNP

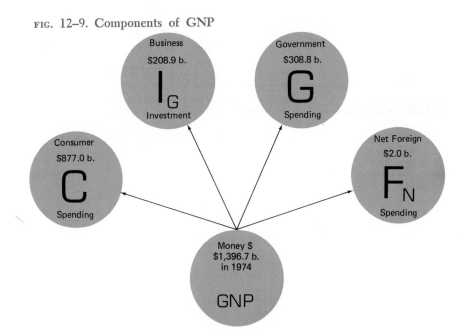

Year	Money GNP in Billions	Price Index 1958 = 100	Real GNP in Billions
1940	$ 99.7	43.87	$227.2
1950	284.8	80.16	355.3
1960	503.7	103.29	487.7
1970	977.1	135.24	722.5
1974	1,396.7	170.11	821.1

Source: *President's Economic Report*, 1975.

FIG. 12–10. Money GNP vs. real GNP.

this?") labors. These exclusions mean that much more spending actually occurs than the 1.5 trillion of the U.S. GNP for 1975.

Another important point about GNP is that it is only a "quantity" measure: No "quality" distinctions are made; that is, GNP measures total final output through total spending without regard to the differing social benefits that may result from equal spending for education or bombs. This deficiency is important in evaluating the impact of GNP changes and becomes more vital as our society debates the "trade-off" of economic growth for more material goods versus conservation of resources and environmental protection. Some economists have proposed methods to achieve a "quality" measure of total output (the Nobel Prize–winning economist Paul Samuelson has suggested a *net economic welfare*—NEW—measure.), but the statistical problem is that of differing value judgments on resulting benefits.

One additional point to remember in evaluating GNP statistics is the distinction between *real* GNP and *money* GNP. Money GNP is simply the total spending of a society, is reflected in Figure 12-9 and the left-hand column of Figure 12-10. But recall from our discussion of inflation that the purchasing power of the dollar changes over time. Thus a dollar spent in 1975 is not comparable to a dollar spent in 1955, and such purchasing power changes seriously affect the validity of GNP comparisons. *Real GNP* corrects for this change in purchasing power (see the right-hand column of Figure 12-10) by use of the following formula:

$$\text{GNP}_{\text{real}} = \text{GNP}_{\text{money}} \cdot \frac{100}{\text{Price Index}}$$

If you recall our previous discussion of price index application, you may see that real GNP comparisons are more important to examine.

You might ask, "But how does one use GNP?" Well, you can analyze national accounting records to see changes in economic performance over time. Or you can compare outputs between countries in a discussion of economic growth and further project GNP to see future levels of output and income. Perhaps the greatest use of the GNP account is the basis for economic policy, both as an indicator of needed action and as an evaluation of policy impact. Again, GNP has several deficiencies described previously, yet it is perhaps the most vital and useful economic indicator available.

Well, that's a lot on GNP, a term that is used almost daily in news releases as the basic measure of overall economic performance. However, there are also four other accounts in the national income accounting system. These accounts are

1. *Net national product* (NNP). Dollar value of all new goods produced (no depreciation amounts).

2. *National income* (NI). Amount of income earned by all resource suppliers or costs of production in producing total output.

3. *Personal income* (PI). Total income received by households from all sources.

4. *Disposable income* (DI). Household income, after taxes, to divide between consumption (C) or saving (S).

Note that these other four accounts are all derived from GNP by making the appropriate adjustments, as outlined in Figure 12-11. Although these accounts are not as widely used or known, they do give useful information for specific purposes. Disposable income, for example, is often the central reference point in discussions of income inequality and poverty.

Well, perhaps that's a long description of U.S. economic performance over time, but economic history takes a while. The point to recognize is that fluctuations in our national economy have been occurring for some time, and there are standardized statistics (such as GNP) for recording the changes. We must now analyze what economists term *national income and employment theory* for an explanation of these economic changes. We emphasize the importance of this theory in the following section. It's one thing to record changes, but it's even more important to be able to explain them, for then you can hope to predict and even prevent or alter such changes. National income and employment theory is, therefore, the foundation for fiscal and monetary policy.

NATIONAL INCOME AND EMPLOYMENT THEORY

The decade of the 1970s has proved to be most troublesome to both economic theorists and government macroeconomic policy makers. We have had, simultaneously, rapid inflation and high unemployment. (Some economist wags have termed this condition of simultaneous unemployment and inflation one of *stagflation*.)

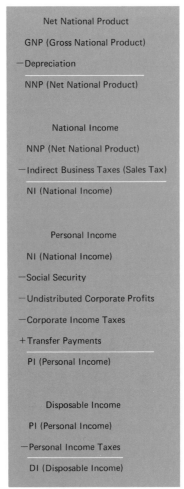

FIG. 12–11.
National income accounting system.

Ordinarily, examining business cycle experience in the past, one would expect inflation during prosperity, but also full employment. The excessive spending that causes inflation would also be expected to provide a high degree of employment and worker income. Or, if unemployment were large in a recession, one might see stable or falling prices. One would expect lower spending levels to lead to factory shutdowns, reduced payrolls, and lower prices to encourage sales. This typical inverse relationship of inflation and unemploy-

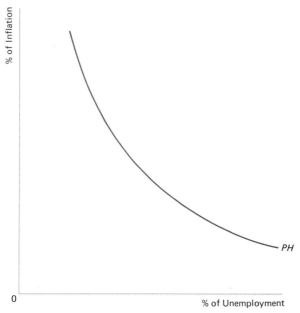

Fig. 12-12. The Phillips curve.

ment (usually illustrated by the *Phillips curve, as in* Figure 12-12) has been upset in the 1970s, and we need to explain the causal factors.

The typical relationship of low unemployment and high inflation has occurred because the high spending levels that generate output and employment also tend to cause rising prices as producers strain to supply high consumer demand *(a demand-pull inflation)*. When spending sags, causing unsold products and increased unemployment, the pressure on prices abates and inflation slows *(a deficient aggregate demand unemployment)*. Such relationships have been observed over long periods in many market economies, and the Phillips curve, based on such observation, serves to describe them.

Inflation may also occur when unemployment is quite high, as has happened in the 1970s. In addition to large spending levels (government deficits, rising exports, business investment), the U.S. economy experienced commodity shortages (crop failure and high foreign demand), increased oil prices (causing increased costs and prices in all oil-based production), and wage increases exceeding productivity gains *(a cost-push inflation)*. The price-wage controls of 1971–1974, although perhaps temporarily slowing inflation, probably caused production bottlenecks and economic distortions that contributed to further inflation. Given all such factors, it is perhaps no surprise that inflation rose rapidly through 1974 (reaching an annual increase of some 12 per cent in the consumer price index) as unemployment also soared (exceeding 9 per cent in 1975).

The oil price increases have proved especially inflationary (perhaps contributing 3 per cent to 5 per cent of the 12 per cent inflation in 1974) and illustrate the circular-flow nature of the U.S. economy. Increased oil prices result not only in increased gasoline and fuel oil prices, but also in increased costs and prices for all industries using oil derivatives as raw materials. Thus utility prices rose (oil is burned to generate electricity), fertilizer prices soared (causing increased food prices), production costs and prices of building materials and plastics rose, and chemicals of many types soared in price (further pushing up other product prices). A large wave of inflation rolled through the whole U.S. economy as a result of higher oil prices.

Notice that in the explanation of inflation-recession during the 1970s, much emphasis is placed on the relationship of spending levels and output and employment levels. The importance of the relationship between *aggregate demand* and *aggregate supply* has not always been recognized.

As you might well guess, people (especially economists, businessmen, and politicians) have been asking for a long time *why* changes occur in levels of output, employment, income, and prices. They've wanted to know exactly what causes inflation and unemployment and how our economy moves into periods of prosperity and depression. Obviously, if one can specify the cause of some result, he may then take actions to avoid such results or secure other desired results. Explanations of business cycle fluctuation have long been sought in order to design policy proposals to avoid such fluctuations!

As might be guessed, there have been many explanations of business cycle (GNP) fluctuation. Some of the theories were quite crude, such as the sunspot theory. (Sunspots cause weather changes; weather changes cause crop failures; crop failures cause depression.) Other theories, such as the *classical employment* theory, were much more sophisticated and workable and did the job fairly well until the 1930s. The classical employment theory stated that the market economy would not suffer a long-term, severe, worldwide depression. This classical theory conclusion was based on assumptions that wages were flexible downwards, that rates of investment and saving would harmoniously adjust to changes in interest rates, and that no structural rigidities existed in the economy. The market economy always "automatically" regains stability with full employment; there is no need for federal government "intervention" (budget deficits, public employment, or welfare programs) in the economy to alleviate unemployment and stop inflation. You might imagine the "credibility gap" such a theory suffered in the worldwide depression of the 1930s.

We needed a better explanation with the 1930s experience, and along came John Maynard Keynes. A good point to recall is that economic theory, like all theories, must explain the real-world happenings. (No "ivory tower" or theory vs. practice here.) If one theory doesn't do the job, then you work up a new and better theory. Keynes did just that. Although there have been many refinements in Keynesian economic theory since Keynes's 1936 book *The Gen-*

eral Theory of Employment, Interest, and Money, most present economic theory is based on a Keynesian framework. True, public policy implications drawn from such theory may differ greatly, and there is at present an increasing attention to monetary factors on GNP swings, but Keynesian theory is pretty well accepted. It is this theory we now must analyze and relate to our question of *why there are changes in the business cycle and GNP*.

Keynesian Economic Theory

The "New Economics." You may recall from our earlier paragraphs that the classical employment theory said (1) that the market economy was self-adjusting, (2) that such adjustment would always result in full employment, and (3) that there's no need for government intervention in this adjustment process. As a starter, let us try to summarize what Keynes said:

1. The market economy was not perfectly adjustable and flexible. Prices do not easily adjust downward, labor was often immobile, and savers and users of money did not always respond to interest rate shifts.

2. Full employment was not always an "automatic" result of market activity. Aggregate demand may equal aggregate supply (*equilibrium* position, as theory terms it) at a level below full employment (unemployment and recession-depression) or even "above" full employment (rising prices and inflation in "prosperity").

3. If full employment is the goal, government intervention may be required. Spending levels may be influenced so as to reduce unemployment or reduce inflation through government policies of spending and taxation. The *federal government budget* (surplus or deficit budget to meet inflation or recession, respectively) could be used to promote full employment and stable prices, thereby smoothing out the business cycle; hence the term *countercyclical fiscal policy:* offset the business cycle by changes in government spending and taxation policies. (See Chapter 13 for the mechanics of this.)

That's quite a skimpy summary of a very sophisticated piece of economic theory, and we've glossed over many fine points. But you should be able to see how different Keynes's conclusions are from those of the classical employment theory. You should also be ready to appreciate the big policy debate his theory immediately stirred: Was government's proper role that of a "balance wheel" in the economy? Well, we debate daily what it is proper for the government (federal, state, or local) to do in our economy. Do note, however, that the implications of government policy are weighed in terms of Keynes's economic theory; that is, government activity should result if the goal of full employment were desired because full employment is not always an automatic result of market activity. Have you got that relationship of theory and public policy straight? Put the case another way. Theory aids in explaining how things work and how one may secure certain goals, but theory does not determine such goals. They are to be determined only by the value systems of the particular society.

We stated the conclusions of Keynesian theory, but Keynesian theory itself revolves around the relationship of total spending and the levels of output, employment, income, and prices. Looking at Figure 12-13, follow the process described by Keynesian theory. As we observed in a previous section and as Keynesian theory emphasizes, the explanation of inflation and depression lies in the level of *aggregate demand* (AD—total spending by all sectors) in relation to a full-employment level of *aggregate supply* (AS—business production of all products). When AD is less than AS at full employment, unemployment and recession occur. But if AD exceeds AS at full employment, inflation takes place.

To make sure you have this Keynesian analysis straight, review Figure 12-13, and trace the following adjustment consequences:

1. *Total spending* or aggregate demand (consumer, government, business, and foreign—in symbols this is stated as $C + G + I_G + F_N$ $= AD$) causes changes in *output* levels. As more or less is spent, more or fewer goods and services are produced by business to match this AD level.

2. As *output* rises or falls, *employment* of resources will increase or decrease. Greater production creates new jobs, but reduced output leads to layoffs and unemployment.

FIG. 12–13. Spending determines output and employment levels.

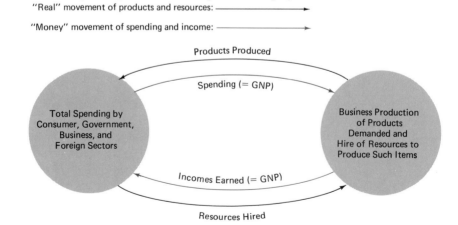

"Real" movement of products and resources: ────────────▶

"Money" movement of spending and income: ────────────▶

Products Produced

Spending (= GNP)

Total Spending by Consumer, Government, Business, and Foreign Sectors

Business Production of Products Demanded and Hire of Resources to Produce Such Items

Incomes Earned (= GNP)

Resources Hired

3. As *employment* rises or falls, consumer (and business) *income* increases or decreases. Steady work means fatter paychecks, but unemployment means little money to spend.

4. If *income* rises or falls, consumer *spending* increases or decreases. This fluctuation again leads to changes in output, employment, and income; and the cycle repeats and repeats!

5. *Inflation* results when buyers try to purchase greater amounts than current productive capacity allows (AD exceeds AS at full employment). Recession occurs when buyers do not purchase sufficient output to maintain the current employment level (AD falls short of AS at full employment).

If you gather from this elementary analysis of Keynesian theory that "aggregate demand calls the tune" and that "everything depends on everything else," you're on the right track. In a market economy, spending, output, employment, income, and prices all interact. In fact, Keynes termed such interaction the *multiplier effect*, meaning that any initial changes in spending lead to a much greater change in total spending and income, either up or down. This multiplier effect adds much to understanding national income and employment theory and has significant implications for macroeconomic policy impact. Let's explain the multiplier effect a bit more.

Suppose you receive a $10 wage increase this week: How much additional spending will you do because of the additional income? Suppose you spend $9 more and save $1 from the $10 change in your income. The economist would say your *marginal propensity to consume* ($MPC = \Delta C \div \Delta DI$) is 90 per cent, as your spending changed by 90 per cent of the change in income. And your *marginal propensity to save* ($MPS = \Delta S \div \Delta DI$) is 10 per cent, because your saving changed by 10 per cent of the change in income. Do you recall these terms from Chapter 4?

But now think of what your additional spending leads to. Your $9 increased spending represents an $9 increase in income to someone; and if that person's MPC is also 90 per cent, he or she will spend an additional $8.10. That $8.10 added spending also results in $8.10 added income to someone else, which (if the MPC continues to be 90 per cent) will lead to an additional spending of $7.29, and so on. The added spending thus far is $9 plus $8.10 plus $7.29 plus all the further (though successively smaller) spending increments. If you see that the total added spending amounts to far more than the initial change of $10 in income, you have grasped the multiplier effect. Remember, though, that the multiplier works for decreased spending as well as increased spending.

The multiplier effect itself is limited only by the marginal propensity to save, as you'll note in the previous example that each spending round is 10 per cent (the MPS here) less than the previous change. Thus, the greater the

An "extra" for those students who cotton to theory and mathematics:
1. The multiplier indicates the extent to which total output and spending will change, given some initial change in spending.
2. The multiplier is computed via the formula $M = 1/MPS$, where M is the multiplier effect and MPS is the Marginal Propensity to Save.
3. The Marginal Propensity to Save measures the change in saving (and, thus, in spending) resulting from changes in income. That is, MPS = change in saving divided by change in income.
4. An example: Suppose the MPS is 20% (20% of changes in income is reflected by changes in saving) and government spending rises by $5 billion. By how much might GNP change?
    a. $M = 1/MPS = 1/.20 = 5$.
    b. Initial change of $5 billion multiplied by 5 gives an increase in GNP of some $25 billion.

FIG. 12–14. The multiplier effect.

MPS, the less the multiplier. Rather than continually compute these successive spending chains, however, a simple formula to compute the multiplier effect (M) is $M = 1 \div MPS$. (In our example, $M = 1 \div 0.1 = 10$, or a multiplier effect of 10.) For an extra review and an introduction to estimation of economic policy impact, study Figure 12–14.

To put this inflation-recession explanation perhaps more simply and to use some Keynesian theory terms, try comparing the entire U.S. economy with a single market for goods and services. (Recall Chapters 4 to 6?) Recall that we analyzed a single market of *demand* by the consumer or business (product or resource markets), *supply* by the business or household (product or resource markets), and the resulting *equilibrium price* determined by such supply and demand forces. Suppose we now consider all goods and services produced by all business firms as *aggregate (total) supply* and all spending (consumer, government, business, foreign) for such goods and services as *aggregate demand*. Viewed in this light, the level of aggregate demand will determine the levels of output, employment, and income because businesses will produce the aggregate supply to match such spending. Does this make sense to you? Would you do otherwise as a businessman? Do you see that these two forces, AD and AS, will produce an *equilibrium level* of output, employment, and income? If AD rises, AS will increase (output grows), causing employment to climb, incomes to grow, and consumer spending (a part of AD) to rise, again causing AD to rise, causing. . . . Can you follow the *multiplier effect?*

Of course, things can spiral down as well as up. Think for a minute how a depression could result from cuts in spending, as decreased spending would cause reduced output, leading to increased unemployment, therefore generating less income, and so leading to further reductions in spending. Perhaps you can also see why businesses, economists, politicians, labor unions, and so on, are greatly interested in the yearly forecasts of spending predictions (GNP

statistics). Depending on the amounts of spending (AD), industries will supply certain output levels (AS), thus employing so many resources, thus paying
out so much income, thus leading to so much spending, and so on.

A basic point and a conclusion of Keynesian theory is that any given level
of AD will buy a certain level of AS, thus supporting a certain level of employment, income, and prices. But this level need not be one of full employment! The AD level may be far short of buying that amount of AS needed
for full employment. (Unemployment and recession result.) Or the AD level
may be much greater than the AS level possible at full employment, and
prices rise in all markets accordingly. (Is inflation the price of prosperity?)
There is no reason why the AD and AS levels must at any one time equal
each other at full employment. Hence, we have Keynes's conclusion of possible *unemployment or inflation equilibrium* and the implied need for government action to attempt equilization of AD and AS at the full-employment
level.

Let us now put our Keynesian analysis in graphic terms, Figure 12-15. To
summarize the basic points of this "Keynesian cross" diagram:

> 1. AS is graphed as an upward-sloping 45° line, indicating that out-
>   put will match spending up to some full-employment level.

FIG. 12–15. Aggregate demand and aggregate supply determine national
output and employment.

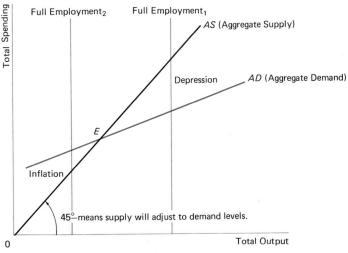

Given the *AD/AS* equilibrium at point *E* above:
  1. There will be depressionary pressure (unemployment) if the economy
     has a full–employment ability of Full Employment$_1$.

  2. There will be inflationary pressure (rising prices) if the economy
     has a full–employment ability of Full Employment$_2$.

2. AD is graphed as an upward-sloping line, showing that spending increases as the output-employment-income level rises. (AD could be broken down into components of consumption, government, investment, and net foreign spending lines.)

3. The equilibrium (E) output-employment-income level is determined by the intersection of AD and AS (AD $=$ AS for equilibrium) lines.

4. The multiplier effect is evident if you draw in a new AD line (increase or decrease) and compare the change in AD with the resulting change in total spending and output. The resulting change is larger—the multiplier effect—than the initial change.

Notice in Figure 12-15 that the $AD = AS$ equilibrium is not the same point as full employment. If the Full Employment $_1$ level is considered, we have a condition of unemployment and depression because AD will fall short of purchasing sufficient output. If the Full Employment $_2$ level is considered (AS could not really exist beyond this level), a condition of inflation is present because the AD level exceeds the ability of the economy to produce. Try manipulating this graph to see that sufficient increase in AD could eliminate the depression condition, whereas sufficient reduction in AD would wipe out the inflation gap.

Public Policy Implications

Perhaps all of this Keynesian employment theory has seemed a bit heavy, and you may wonder at its value. Well, it gives an explanation of inflation-recession causes: Changes in AD cause changes in AS, output; hence changes in employment, income, and prices. It suggests fiscal policy measures if full employment is wanted without price inflation. Put very simply, *countercyclical fiscal and monetary policy* attempts to vary the levels of AD to eliminate depression and inflation conditions (as suggested in the previous paragraph and in Figure 12-15).

TERMS

Aggregate demand. Total purchases of goods and services from consumer, government, business, and foreign sectors.

Aggregate supply. Total output of goods and services from all business firms.

Business cycle. A periodic variance of output, employment, income, and prices, as charted by relating gross national product levels against time.

Consumer Price Index. A Bureau of Commerce statistic that computes the purchasing power of currency against some base-year value.

Cost-push inflation. Rising prices resulting from wage increases in excess of productivity gains.

Countercyclical policy. Governmental policy that attempts to avoid inflation and recession by manipulation of budget and money stock levels in counteraction to the prevailing business cycle.

Demand-pull inflation. Rising prices that result when the desire to purchase goods exceeds available supply.

Depression. An economic state in which high (over 10 per cent) levels of unemployment and falling income levels result from reduced output levels and unused productive capacity.

Equilibrium. A static condition existing when aggregate demand equals aggregate supply.

Frictional unemployment. Unemployment due to moving, retraining, seasonal labor, or time lost between jobs, usually accounting for some 4 to 5 per cent of unemployment.

Full employment. An employment condition viewed by many economists to exist at a 4 per cent to 5 per cent level of unemployment.

Gross national product (GNP). The money value of all final goods and services produced in an accounting period, measured by adding up the components of consumption, government, investment, and net foreign spending.

Inflation. Increase in the general level of all prices.

Multiplier. The cumulative effect of an initial change in spending leading to a larger change in total spending ($M = 1 \div MPS$).

Real income. Income adjusted for changes in the purchasing power of money.

Recession. An economic condition in which output is reduced and unemployment is above normal.

Structural unemployment. Unemployment resulting from a lack of job skills among the otherwise employable.

QUESTIONS FOR STUDY

1. What is the basic cause of inflation and depression?
2. Define *aggregate demand*, *aggregate supply*, and *equilibrium*.
3. If this economy has a labor force of 95 million, will full employment always result? Explain.

4. How does structural unemployment differ from frictional unemployment?

5. How does demand-pull inflation differ from cost-push inflation?

6. What factors other than aggregate demand might cause inflation or unemployment?

7. If consumers attempt to increase their rate of saving, a recession may result. Explain.

8. What is the multiplier effect? Of what use is this concept?

9. If the *MPC* equals 75 percent and the *MPS* is 25 per cent, what is the multiplier?

10. Is is true that full employment means that everyone in the labor force has a job?

11. The Department of Labor announced recently that unemployment *and* employment rose last month. Explain how this occurs.

REFERENCES

Adams, F. Gerald. *National Accounts and the Structure of the U.S. Economy.* New York: General Learning Corp., 1973.

Barrett, Nancy Smith. *The Theory of Macro-economic Policy,* Second Edition. Englewood Cliffs, N.J.: Prentice-Hall, Inc., 1975.

Gill, Richard T. *Economics: A Text with Readings,* Second Edition. Pacific Palisades, Calif.: Goodyear Publishing Company, Inc., 1975, Chapters 7–10.

Heilbroner, Robert L. *The Worldly Philosophers,* Third Edition. New York: Simon and Schuster, Inc., 1967, Chapter 9.

Lekachman, Robert. *National Income and the Public Welfare.* New York: Random House, 1972.

Nordhaus, W., and J. Shoven. "Inflation 1973: The Year of Infamy," *Challenge,* May-June, 1974, pp. 14–22.

WHAT IS
FISCAL POLICY?

SHORT ANSWER. Fiscal policy is federal government manipulation of aggregate demand, through taxes and government spending, to secure desired goals of full employment and stable prices.

$T\uparrow \rightarrow DI\downarrow \rightarrow C\downarrow \rightarrow AD\downarrow \xrightarrow{PL} GNP\downarrow, \ldots$

$\Delta G_3\uparrow \rightarrow AD\uparrow \rightarrow GNP\uparrow \rightarrow DI\uparrow \rightarrow C\uparrow \rightarrow \ldots$

YOU AND FISCAL POLICY

Current news clippings illustrate the importance of fiscal policy to you as student and citizen. Consider the following topics: inflation (what prices you pay), unemployment (will you get a job?), energy use (what is available, and can you afford it?), and environmental protection (how healthy is the air you breathe or the water you drink?). Fiscal policy involves all these major issues of national economy and countless smaller ones. It affects each of us in his or her daily pursuits. In encouraging economic understanding on this topic during the next few pages we aim to give you an idea of the determinants of fiscal policy—how it works (or doesn't) and what some of the problems in formulating this policy are. After studying this chapter, you still may not be able to set up a national budget, but you should be able to analyze and evaluate many significant economic issues. Your decisions as a citizen will, we trust, benefit by such understanding.

We should first define exactly what we mean by *fiscal policy*. We're referring to the determination (through decisions by Congress) of the levels of federal government spending and taxation to effect some specific desired result in our economy. This last sentence really refers to the changes in spending and taxing rates of the federal government, for these changes normally cause a change in aggregate demand. (Recall Chapter 12?) To illustrate this first part of fiscal policy definition, study Figure 13-2. Notice the changes in expenditure (spending) and revenue (taxes) occurring over the period from 1967 to

FIG. 13–1. Fiscal policy control of the business cycle.

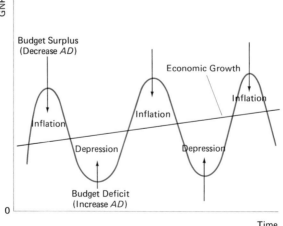

1976, both in *total amount* and in *composition* of the budget. The importance of fiscal policy lies not only in the change of total spending within the budget and the economy, but also in what output and employment areas these changes occur. For example, a large budget deficit (over $56 billion) in fiscal 1976 probably tended to increase aggregate demand and to prevent unemployment from increasing. An increase in the percentage of spending toward the more effective social programs and environmental protection would affect income inequality and the quality of daily life.

But let us also emphasize the second part of our fiscal policy definition, the idea of a definite effect to be achieved by particular spending changes. The object of fiscal policy is to do more than merely collect enough taxes to pay the bills. The amounts collected, as well as the type of spending, have the direct purpose of affecting the levels of output, employment, income, and prices. Put more bluntly, Congress attempts to set tax collection and spending priorities to avoid inflation or recession—hence the term *countercyclical fiscal policy*. Refer to the introductory Figure 13-1 (fully explained later in this chapter) for a visual illustration of these desired impacts. Do you see that the term *countercyclical* refers to the attempt to dampen fluctuations of inflation and depression?

You may have detected a "conflict" within this definition of fiscal policy thus far, the *trade-off of policy objective*. Because the achievement of one policy goal (such as reduced unemployment) may interfere with securing another policy goal (such as reduced inflation), priorities must be assigned to these desired policy goals. We will discuss this issue at length in the following section, but we should at this point note that this unavoidable conflict exists. The goals of fiscal policy are both numerous and often contradictory. For example, the closer the economy is to full employment, the greater the inflationary pressure. The wish for both full employment and stable prices, as embodied in the Employment Act of 1946, has rarely been achieved in the three decades since the act was passed. Policy trade-offs must be continually weighed. One of the large policy issues of 1976 is how far expansionary (increased spending) fiscal and monetary policy may be carried to reduce unemployment before renewed inflationary pressures begin. The nature of fiscal policy is that it involves choices among alternative objectives, with the achievement of one goal frequently coming at the expense of another.

One additional definition of fiscal policy should be noted (it is evident in Figure 13-2). The *fiscal year* calendar is used in the budget process. Until recently the federal budget year (like that of most state and local governments) ran from July 1 of one year to June 30 of another. The fiscal 1976 budget illustrated runs from July 1, 1975 to June 30, 1976. But future fiscal years were shifted at the federal level from October 1 to September 30 (part of the congressional budget reform legislation in 1974), to begin on October 1, 1976.

As an example of this fiscal policy definition and trade-off process varying

Description	1966	1967	1968	1969	1970	1971	1972	1973	1974	1975	1976
					Actual					Estimate	
Receipt by Source											
Individual Income Taxes	55.4	61.5	68.7	87.2	90.4	86.2	94.7	103.2	119.0	117.7	106.3
Corporation Income Taxes	30.1	34.0	28.7	36.7	32.8	26.8	32.2	36.2	38.6	38.5	47.7
Social Insurance Taxes and Contributions	25.6	33.3	34.6	39.9	45.3	48.6	53.9	64.5	76.8	86.2	91.6
Excise Taxes	13.1	13.7	14.1	15.2	15.7	16.6	15.5	16.3	16.8	19.9	32.1
Estate and Gift Taxes	3.1	3.0	3.1	3.5	3.6	3.7	5.4	4.9	5.0	4.8	4.6
Customs Duties	1.8	1.9	2.0	2.3	2.4	2.6	3.3	3.2	3.3	3.9	4.3
Miscellaneous Receipts	1.9	2.1	2.5	2.9	3.4	3.9	3.6	3.9	5.4	7.7	10.9
Total Receipts	130.9	149.6	153.7	187.8	193.7	188.4	208.6	232.2	264.9	278.8	297.5
Outlays by Function											
National Defense*	55.9	69.1	79.4	80.2	79.3	76.8	77.4	75.1	78.6	85.3	94.0
International Affairs	4.6	4.7	4.6	3.8	3.6	3.1	3.7	3.0	3.6	4.9	6.3
General Science, Space and Technology	6.8	6.3	5.6	5.1	4.6	4.3	4.3	4.2	4.2	4.2	4.6
Natural Resources, Environment, and Energy	3.1	3.4	3.6	3.5	3.6	4.4	5.0	5.5	6.4	9.4	10.0
Agriculture	2.4	3.0	4.5	5.8	5.2	4.3	5.3	4.9	2.2	1.8	1.8
Commerce and Transportation	9.0	9.2	10.6	7.1	9.1	10.4	10.6	9.9	13.1	11.8	13.7
Community and Regional Development	1.5	1.7	2.2	2.5	3.5	4.0	4.7	5.9	4.9	4.9	5.9
Education, Manpower, and Social Services	4.1	6.0	7.0	6.9	7.9	9.0	11.7	11.9	11.6	14.7	14.6
Health	2.6	6.8	9.7	11.8	13.1	14.7	17.5	18.8	22.1	26.5	28.0
Income Security	28.9	30.8	33.7	37.3	43.1	55.4	63.9	73.0	84.4	106.7	118.7
Veterans Benefits and Services	5.9	6.9	6.9	7.6	8.7	9.8	10.7	12.0	13.4	15.5	15.6
Law Enforcement and Justice	.6	.6	.6	.8	1.0	1.3	1.6	2.1	2.5	3.0	3.3
General Government	1.4	1.6	1.7	1.6	1.9	2.2	2.5	2.7	3.3	2.6	3.2
Revenue Sharing and General Purpose Fiscal Assistance	.2	.3	.3	.4	.5	.5	.5	7.2	6.7	7.0	7.2
Interest	11.3	12.5	13.8	15.8	18.3	19.6	20.6	22.8	28.1	31.3	34.4
Allowances†										.7	8.0
Undistributed Offsetting Receipts	−3.6	−4.6	−5.5	−5.5	−6.6	−8.4	−8.1	−12.3	−16.7	−16.8	−20.2
Total Outlays	134.7	158.3	178.8	184.5	196.6	211.4	231.9	216.5	268.4	313.4	349.4

FIG. 13–2. Federal budgeting.

Budget Receipts by Source and Outlays by Function, 1966-76 (in billions of dollars)

Description	1966	1967	1968	1969	Actual 1970	1971	1972	1973	1974	Estimate 1975	1976
Receipt by Source											
Individual Income Taxes	55.4	61.5	68.7	87.2	90.4	86.2	94.7	103.2	119.0	117.7	106.3
Corporation Income Taxes	30.1	34.0	28.7	36.7	32.8	26.8	32.2	36.2	38.6	38.5	47.7
Social Insurance Taxes and Contributions	25.6	33.3	34.6	39.9	45.3	48.6	53.9	64.5	76.8	86.2	91.6
Excise Taxes	13.1	13.7	14.1	15.2	15.7	16.6	15.5	16.3	16.8	19.9	32.1
Estate and Gift Taxes	3.1	3.0	3.1	3.5	3.6	3.7	5.4	4.9	5.0	4.8	4.6
Customs Duties	1.8	1.9	2.0	2.3	2.4	2.6	3.3	3.2	3.3	3.9	4.3
Miscellaneous Receipts	1.9	2.1	2.5	2.9	3.4	3.9	3.6	3.9	5.4	7.7	10.9
Total Receipts	130.9	149.6	153.7	187.8	193.7	188.4	208.6	232.2	264.9	278.8	297.5
Outlays by Function											
National Defense*	55.9	69.1	79.4	80.2	79.3	76.8	77.4	75.1	78.6	85.3	94.0
International Affairs	4.6	4.7	4.6	3.8	3.6	3.1	3.7	3.0	3.6	4.9	6.3
General Science, Space and Technology	6.8	6.3	5.6	5.1	4.6	4.3	4.3	4.2	4.2	4.2	4.6
Natural Resources, Environment, and Energy	3.1	3.4	3.6	3.5	3.6	4.4	5.0	5.5	6.4	9.4	10.0
Agriculture	2.4	3.0	4.5	5.8	5.2	4.3	5.3	4.9	2.2	1.8	1.8
Commerce and Transportation	9.0	9.2	10.6	7.1	9.1	10.4	10.6	9.9	13.1	11.8	13.7
Community and Regional Development	1.5	1.7	2.2	2.5	3.5	4.0	4.7	5.9	4.9	4.9	5.9
Education, Manpower, and Social Services	4.1	6.0	7.0	6.9	7.9	9.0	11.7	11.9	11.6	14.7	14.6
Health	2.6	6.8	9.7	11.8	13.1	14.7	17.5	18.8	22.1	26.5	28.0
Income Security	28.9	30.8	33.7	37.3	43.1	55.4	63.9	73.0	84.4	106.7	118.7
Veterans Benefits and Services	5.9	6.9	6.9	7.6	8.7	9.8	10.7	12.0	13.4	15.5	15.6
Law Enforcement and Justice	.6	.6	.6	.8	1.0	1.3	1.6	2.1	2.5	3.0	3.3
General Government	1.4	1.6	1.7	1.6	1.9	2.2	2.5	2.7	3.3	2.6	3.2
Revenue Sharing and General Purpose Fiscal Assistance	.2	.3	.3	.4	.5	.5	.5	7.2	6.7	7.0	7.2
Interest	11.3	12.5	13.8	15.8	18.3	19.6	20.6	22.8	28.1	31.3	34.4
Allowances†	.....	.....	.....	.....	.....	.....	.....	.....	.....	.7	8.0
Undistributed Offsetting Receipts	-3.6	-4.6	-5.5	-5.5	-6.6	-8.4	-8.1	-12.3	-16.7	-16.8	-20.2
Total Outlays	134.7	158.3	178.8	184.5	196.6	211.4	231.9	216.5	268.4	313.4	349.4

*Includes civilian and military pay raises for the Department of Defense.
†Includes energy tax equalization payments, civilian agents, pay raises, and contingencies.

Source: *President's Economic Report*, 1975.

FIG. 13–2. Continued

spending and tax levels, review Figure 13-2. Initially, such figures reflect "proposed" policies by the president. You'll notice a 1976 deficit (outgo more than income) specifically designed to reduce unemployment by raising total spending levels. Of course, the size of the final deficit will depend on congressional decision, for Congress may decide on different spending and tax levels from those suggested by the president. Although President Ford desired a limited expansionary budget deficit to reduce unemployment, many congressmen wanted to increase the deficit further. The president vetoed many congressional spending proposals, which illustrates again the inherent conflict referred to previously.

One other item to consider is that we're talking mainly of *federal-level* spending and tax decisions in our references to fiscal policy. Although state and local governments spend and tax in large amounts (New York City's budget in fiscal 1977 was over $12 billion), their budgets are not calculated to offset inflation or depression in our economy. States do not usually aim to minimize business cycle fluctuations; they are instead, concerned with attempts to meet their rapidly rising bills. One problem area of federal countercyclical fiscal policy, in fact, is that its impact may be offset to some degree by state and local government budgetary decisions (state budget reduction during a depression, for example). A recent (began in 1973) federal attempt to aid states in their financial problems is *revenue sharing,* an apportioning of federal revenues among state and local government programs.

THE GOALS OF FISCAL POLICY

The Employment Act of 1946, a perspective piece of federal economic legislation, places definite responsibility on Congress to achieve full employment and price stability (no or little inflation). In addition, Congress is to maintain economic growth (increase in output produced yearly) without violating economic freedoms within a market economy. Beyond the goals

FIG. 13–3. Fiscal policy goals.

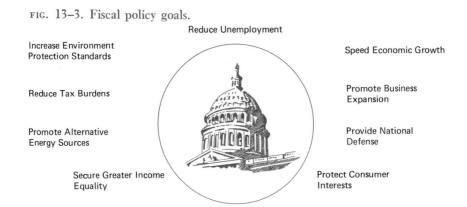

Reduce Unemployment

Increase Environment
Protection Standards

Speed Economic Growth

Reduce Tax Burdens

Promote Business
Expansion

Promote Alternative
Energy Sources

Provide National
Defense

Secure Greater Income
Equality

Protect Consumer
Interests

stated by this particular act, government has in recent years pursued a large number of other goals that also involve spending and tax rates. These include the War on Poverty (programs to improve low-income family economic conditions) and reduction of hunger conditions, rebuilding urban inner-city areas, elimination of discrimination in all forms, improvement of educational levels for all, aid to the elderly, advancement of scientific discovery (especially in space exploration), and, recently, improvement of environmental condition and development of alternative energy sources.

That's quite a challenge for fiscal policy to achieve and probably an abbreviated list at that. There are 535 congressmen and senators who also have their individual specific goals as representatives of particular voting areas! You'll realize, therefore, that a clash of these goals on the floor of Congress is easy. Actual legislation is, consequently, often a series of compromises. Regional economic interests may be more basic to a congressman's vote than national economic welfare, and personal value judgments are legion as to what constitutes economic welfare. Perhaps the basic problem is that for the long list of fiscal policy goals there is no consensus of *priority* for achievement. There are significant differences in value interpretation and emphasis for trade-offs of policy. Of course, such undefined priorities for fiscal policy make it very difficult to evaluate fiscal policy's success, for who defines the outstanding priority to evaluate?

These fiscal policy goals are also often contradictory. As previously stated, full-employment conditions tend to be quite inflationary as there is little labor flexibility and workers have relatively large incomes to spend. Recall our aspirations to both full employment and price stability. (Do you see any problem here?) Another element of such goal conflicts, wage-price guidelines, might aid in reducing inflation, but might also undermine market operation and economic freedom within the economy. (How would you respond?) Protection of the environment may necessitate legislation that reduces employment or hinders the achievement of national energy independence. As noted in Chapter 2, fiscal policy must choose among goals, considering the opportunity costs of alternative policies and producing politically and economically acceptable trade-off compromises.

As a bit of economic history at this point, we might add that few of the goals listed previously were relegated to federal government responsibility prior to the 1930s. The "countercyclical" concept of government as a *balance wheel* was not widespread in the early 1900s or before. The philosophy was basically that of *laissez-faire*; market operation was supposed to solve any problems. However, the federal government did eventually begin to enlarge its role in our economy and continues to do so. Such intervention was typically in response to public demand, such as the Progressive movement reforms of the early 1900s, relief measures of the early 1930s, economic stability demands of the 1940s, and consumer and environmental protection movements of the 1960s and 1970s. Now there is severe criticism of the federal government's impact.

Fiscal Year	Receipts	Outlays	Surplus or Deficit (−)	Federal Government† Debt
1929	3,862	3,127	734	16.5
1933	1,997	4,598	−2,602	24.3
1939	4,979	8,841	−3,862	42.6
1940	6,361	9,456	−3,095	44.8
1941	8,621	13,634	−5,013	56.3
1942	14,350	35,114	−20,764	101.7
1943	23,649	78,533	−54,884	154.4
1944	44,276	91,280	−47,004	211.9
1945	45,216	92,690	−47,474	252.5
1946	39,327	55,183	−15,856	229.5
1947	38,394	34,532	3,862	221.7
1948	41,774	29,773	12,001	215.3
1949	39,437	38,834	603	217.6
1950	39,485	42,597	−3,112	217.4
1951	51,646	45,546	6,100	216.9
1952	66,204	67,721	−1,517	221.5
1953	69,574	76,107	−6,533	226.8
1954	69,719	70,890	−1,170	229.1
1955	65,469	68,509	−3,041	229.6
1956	74,547	70,460	4,087	224.3
1957	79,990	76,741	3,249	223.0
1958	79,636	82,575	−2,939	231.0
1959	79,249	92,104	−12,855	241.4
1960	92,492	92,223	269	239.8
1961	94,389	97,795	−3,406	246.7
1962	99,676	106,813	−7,137	253.6
1963	106,560	111,311	−4,751	257.5
1964	112,662	118,584	−5,922	264.0
1965	116,833	118,430	−1,596	266.4
1966	130,856	134,652	−3,796	271.8
1967	149,552	158,254	−8,702	285.5
1968	153,671	178,833	−25,161	291.9
1969	187,784	184,548	3,236	289.3
1970	193,743	196,588	−2,845	301.1
1971	188,392	211,425	−23,033	325.9
1972	208,649	231,876	−23,227	341.2
1973	232,225	246,526	−14,301	349.1
1974	264,932	268,392	−3,460	364.1
1975*	278,750	313,446	−34,696	389.6
1976*	297,520	349,372	−51,852	493.1

*Estimate.

Note. Data for 1929–39 are according to the administrative budget and those for 1940–76 according to the unified budget. Certain interfund transactions are excluded from receipts and outlays beginning 1932. For years prior to 1932 the amounts of such transactions are not significant.
Refunds of receipts are excluded from receipts and outlays.

†Net Federal Government and agency debt is the outstanding debt held by the public, as defined in the "Budget of the United States Government, for the Fiscal Year ending June 30, 1976."

Sources: Department of the Treasury and Office of Management and Budget.

FIG. 13–4. Federal government expansion.

Federal government economic responsibilities have continued to expand since the early 1900s. The public has asked the government to regulate large monopolies, restrict child labor, prohibit unsafe food and drugs, aid farmers, help in public construction and education, aid the poor, subsidize the established and infant industries, end discrimination, and clean up the environment.

As you may imagine, this expansion of federal government intervention in the economy has demanded allocation of numerous economic resources. Figure 13-4 indicates some of the consequences of fiscal policy expansion (increased spending, taxes, national debt), and government employment now involves one out of every six workers in our labor force. Although such expansion of intervention in our economy is not without its opponents, criticism of it often centers on the method rather than on the practice; that is, we're more likely to criticize how some program is administered than whether we should have the program at all. *Welfare spending* (transfer payments) is an example of such disagreement. Many support the concept of aiding those unable to help themselves, but questions and criticism abound on payment mechanism, payment levels, and program prerequisites.

This question of exactly what the role of federal (or state and local) government in our economy should be is extremely difficult to answer. What the government does is, in our politicoeconomic system, dependent on what the members of the public wish and express through their elected representatives. (Assume majority views to be represented by elected legislators and minority interests to be represented by lobbying pressures and protected by law.) If the public wants less defense spending, more mass transit, a minimum annual family income, a cleaner environment, an end to the variety of discriminatory practices, a space trip to Mars, or even a bigger (or smaller?) military establishment, the government responds accordingly. Perhaps this answer begs the question of a "proper" governmental economic role, but it points out, nonetheless, that the answer is basically an evolutionary process rather than a hard-and-fast reply.

Evolutionary is a term that is, in fact, accurately descriptive of the changes over the last fifty years: As public and economic pressures changed, so did the federal government's role. As these pressures change in the future, the role will change further. Your economic understanding will aid in both understanding and participating in the future process.

THE MECHANICS OF FISCAL POLICY

We've stated quite a number of fiscal policy goals, but how do we attain these objectives? This is really what the mechanics of fiscal policy involve. How do we put the process in motion? How do we know what impacts may

occur? Furthermore, how may fiscal policy be suited to specific goals? In analyzing these questions, let's go back to our national income theory of Chapter
12 and review "Keynesian economics" again.

Chapter 12 stated that the economy's levels of output, employment, income, and prices depend basically on the volume of total spending (or *aggregate demand* interacting with *aggregate supply*). If total spending rises or
falls, the result is an increase or decrease in output, employment, income, and
prices, respectively. Remember that this effect is a "multiplied" one (*multiplier effect*), with final spending and output changes greater than initial
spending changes. (Again, review Chapter 12, especially Figures 12-14 and
12-15.) In order to achieve desired changes in output, employment, income,
and prices, fiscal policy must affect such spending components of aggregate
demand as consumption, government, investment, and net foreign levels.

Fiscal Policy Logic

With this review and introduction, you should see more clearly the logic
of fiscal policy:

1. Total spending volume determines the levels of output, employment, income, and prices.

2. Changes in output, employment, income, and prices are brought
   about by changes in the components of aggregate demand.

3. Changes in government spending change total spending *directly—*
   whereas changes in government taxation affect total spending
   through consumption and investment *indirectly.* (Recall GNP
   $= C + G + I_G + F_N.$)

4. Government spending and taxation are varied according to economic conditions to obtain desired levels of output, employment,
   income, and prices, but actual successes are becoming less frequent.

Another way to put this same logic and mechanics of fiscal policy is shown
by Figure 13-5. Notice the changes in government spending (ΔG) or taxation (ΔT) causing changes in total spending (ΔAD) and thus changes
in the levels of output, employment, income, and prices ($\Delta O, E, Y, P$).

Now, Figure 13-5 oversimplifies things (see "Problems" in a later section
of this chapter), but the logic should be clear:

1. A change in government spending (ΔG) directly causes changes in
   total spending (ΔAD), which thus causes changes in output, employment, income, and price levels ($\Delta O, E, Y, P$). (Remember
   multiplier effect—M—here.)

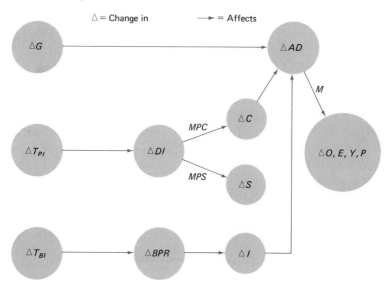

FIG. 13–5. The mechanics of fiscal policy.

How about some terms?

G = Government Spending	C = Consumption spending
T_{PI} = Personal Income Taxes	S = Saving
T_{BI} = Business Income Taxes	I = Investment spending
DI = Disposable Income	AD = Aggregate Demand
BPR = Business Profits	O = Output level of economy
MPC = Marginal Propensity to Consume	E = Employment level of economy
MPS = Marginal Propensity to Save	Y = Income level of economy
	P = General price level
	M = Multiplier

2. A change in government taxation (on personal income ΔT_{PI}; on business income ΔT_{BI}) causes a change in disposable income levels (ΔDI) or a change in business profits (ΔBPR). A change in disposable income is then split between a change in consumption and a change in saving, denoted respectively by the marginal propensity to consume ($MPC = \Delta C \div \Delta DI$) and the marginal propensity to save ($MPS = \Delta S \div \Delta DI$). Although the change in saving (ΔS) is a "leakage" that has no effect on total spending, the change in consumption (ΔC) does cause a change in total spending (ΔAD) and, consequently, a change of output, employment, income, and price levels ($\Delta O, E, Y, P$).

3. On the business side, the change of investment (ΔI), depending on business profits (ΔBPR), causes a change in total spending (ΔAD) and thus changes output, employment, income, and prices ($\Delta O, E, Y, P$).

Estimating Fiscal Policy Impact

Although Figure 13-5 and the previous enumeration lay out the crude logic of fiscal policy impact, it is vital to understand the impact in terms of particular *size and timing*. Suppose a tax cut of $22 billion ($17 billion in personal income and $5 billion in corporate income taxes) occurred, as it did in 1975. How large an economic impact is to be expected, and on what timetable?

The general impact one would expect from a tax cut may be followed in Figure 13-5: Tax cuts mean increased consumption and investment, hence increased output, employment, and income. (Prices may rise also, depending upon capacity level and other nonspending factors previously discussed.) For a more speific forecast of impact, the following "rough estimate" formula may be used:

$$\Delta T \cdot MPC \cdot M = \Delta GNP$$

This formula is read as: the change in taxes times the marginal propensity to consume times the multiplier equals the resulting change in gross national product. (Notice that the Δ, or delta sign, stands for "a change in.") If we take our personal tax cut of $17 billion and assume an economywide *MPC* of $\frac{2}{3}$ and a resulting multiplier of 3 (do you see from Figure 12–14 how the 3 results?),

$$\Delta T \cdot MPC \cdot M = \Delta GNP$$
$$\downarrow\$17 \text{ billion} \cdot \tfrac{2}{3} \cdot 3 = \$34 \text{ billion increase}$$

This result is, of course, very rough and does not consider consumer optimism, timing impact (probably eighteen months to occur), or investment response (both from the $5 billion corporate income tax cut and in response to increased consumer spending). The change in investment spending because of changes in consumer spending (businesses anticipate possible impact on future profits) may be quite significant and is termed the *accelerator effect*. But our simple estimate gives some indication of the powerful impact of fiscal policy.

Let us also state a rough estimate formula for government spending, as *spending changes* are even more potent (economically and politically) than changes in taxation, and such federal budget outlays rose by $35 billion in fiscal 1976. This simple formula and the corresponding estimate for 1976 (*MPC* of $\frac{2}{3}$, multiplier of 3 again assumed) is:

$$\Delta G \cdot M = \Delta GNP$$
$$\uparrow\$35 \text{ billion} \cdot 3 = \$105 \text{ billion increase}$$

Again, this estimated spending impact is very imprecise, for it does not consider consumer optimism, business investment reaction, the differing impacts between *types* of spending (food stamps versus defense spending), and unemployment or inflation barriers. But you do get some general idea of expected policy impact (perhaps over a twelve-month time span)? Given the expected impact these tax cuts and spending increases would produce, perhaps you see why some economists feared a renewal of inflationary pressures.

Notice that we used our rough estimate formulas to go from "cause to effect" previously; that is, we estimated the ΔGNP (effect) from a given fiscal policy (cause). And such procedure is often valuable for the citizen or politician to consider predicted policy results in evaluating the desirability of any given policy. But suppose we now wish to go from "effect to cause." That is, suppose we wish to know what magnitude of fiscal policy is required (cause) in order to achieve a desired ΔGNP (effect)? We use our same formulas, but work "backward"!

Suppose we wish GNP to increase by $200 billion so as to reduce unemployment to 5 per cent (the Council of Economic Advisers estimates that each $50 billion in GNP affects employment level by 1 per cent, and we're now at 9 per cent unemployment). Suppose also that MPC is $\frac{3}{4}$ and the multiplier is 4. Let us first see the spending increase required to achieve this result and then compute the tax reduction necessary:

$$\Delta G \cdot M = \Delta GNP$$
$$\Delta G = \Delta GNP \div M$$
$$\$50 \text{ billion increase} = 200 \div 4$$
$$\Delta T \cdot MPC \cdot M = \Delta GNP$$
$$\Delta T = \Delta GNP \div (MPC \cdot M)$$
$$\$66.66 \text{ billion decrease} = 200 \div \left(\tfrac{3}{4} \cdot 4\right)$$

These estimates of required policy change are again quite rough, but give an approximation of levels required to achieve the stated goal. (You may not agree that $200 billion increase in GNP is desirable.) Notice also that these previous calculations illustrated that a tax cut is not as "powerful" (size of economic impact) as an increase in government expenditures. (Recall the "leakage" of saving, which occurs under tax cut conditions?)

We hope that this long and detailed tracing of fiscal policy mechanics enables you to see "what causes what." Do you see the process at this stage? If not, back up, get national income theory straight, and take another run through the preceding figures and detailed enumerations.

COUNTERCYCLICAL FISCAL POLICY

If you understand the logic and estimates of fiscal policy, we can go on to its *countercyclical aspect*. Recall, if you will, that we are after, among other goals, full employment and stable prices. We must, therefore, vary govern-

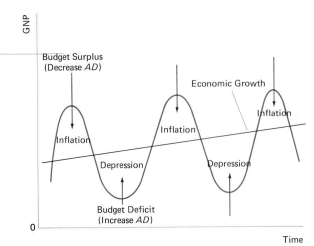

FIG. 13–6. Fiscal policy control of the business cycle.

ment spending and taxation levels to offset undesired results (inflation, recession) and achieve the desired goals. Perhaps Figure 13-6 will illustrate this "countercyclical" aspect of fiscal policy in reaching such goals. By realizing a *budget surplus* (taking in more from tax revenues than is spent) to reduce inflation and by running a *budget deficit* (spending more than tax revenues produce) to alleviate unemployment, *countercyclical fiscal* policy attempts to stabilize the economy in an upward direction toward controlled economic growth.

To be more specific, countercyclical fiscal policy attempts deliberately to offset or counter actual economic conditions (cycles) by "moving the economy" in a different way: to lower total spending ($\downarrow G, \uparrow T$) during inflation and to raise total spending ($\uparrow G, \downarrow T$) in a recession. Trace the effects of such changes in spending and taxation on total spending and output, employment, income, and price levels by referring to Figure 13-7. The federal government, under this countercyclical theory, acts consciously as a balance wheel by neutralizing economic conditions. Fiscal policy is varied both to cool off inflationary measures ($\uparrow T + \downarrow G \rightarrow \downarrow AD \rightarrow \downarrow O, E, Y, P$) and to bolster recessionary sags ($\downarrow T + \uparrow G \rightarrow \uparrow AD \rightarrow \uparrow O, E, Y, P$). Again, the logic should be clear:

1. If you wish to affect the levels of output, employment, income, and prices, you must change their determinants.

2. Total spending increases cause upward changes in output, employment, income, and price levels, with decreased spending having the opposite effect.

3. By altering government spending and taxation practices to cause

In Order to Offset	Fiscal Policy Should (*Theory*):		Therefore, the Budget Result Is
	Spending	*Taxation*	
Inflation (want to lower *AD*)	Decrease	Increase	Surplus (income greater than outgo)
Depression or Recession (want to raise *AD*)	Increase	Decrease	Deficit (outgo greater than income)

FIG. 13–7. Countercyclical fiscal policy operation.

changes in total spending, a "countercyclical" effect occurs to achieve desired goals of full employment and stable prices.

PUBLIC DEBT

There is another important issue "hiding" in Figure 13-7 beyond that of the mechanics described, and that is *budget deficit* and *public debt*. Notice that in past inflationary periods a *surplus budget* (revenue greater than spending) was purposely developed to reduce total spending and to limit price advances. By the same principle, countercyclical fiscal policy calls for a *budget deficit* (spending greater than revenue) in times of recession to increase total spending and reduce unemployment. Do you follow that logic? We are still concerned with the basic relation of total spending to output, employment, income, and price levels and shifts of total spending to achieve goals of full employment and price stability.

In economic conditions of either inflation or recession, however, countercyclical fiscal policy calls for an *unbalanced budget!* A *surplus* is a positive imbalance to offset inflation; a *deficit* is a negative imbalance to offset recession. The entire concept of countering economic conditions requires a counterpoise measure, that is, an unbalanced budget! In order to work correctly, countercyclical fiscal policy cannot be neutral. A balanced budget (spending equals revenue) is essentially of neutral effect. (There is a fine theoretical aspect of some effect even with a balanced budget—the *balanced budget multiplier*—because changes in government spending have a greater effect on GNP than the effect of equal changes in taxes.)

An unbalanced budget may make all sorts of theoretical sense, and there is nothing "ivory tower" about it either. But there may well be severe political and public reaction to the effects of such unbalanced budgets, particularly a deficit budget. Although a surplus budget is "troublesome" in the sense of public demand for tax reduction and return of monies, a budget deficit usually garners much more adverse reaction. (Consider the jokes about "bigger than the national debt.") *A budget deficit means an increase in public debt.* (You might run the government printing presses or default on bills to finance the deficit, but borrowing through debt creation has been our chief method.) Increased public debt is definitely an unpopular issue. Reduced taxes creating the deficit may be fine, but the resulting debt is not well taken. (Yes, there may be an "inconsistency" here.)

There are a great many reasons for the critical reaction to public debt. The main objections arise from (1) comparison to private debt, (2) fear of "burdening" future generations, (3) concern about absorbing interest payments on debt from higher taxes, (4) worry over inflationary pressures, and (5) suspected noncontrol of government spending. On the other hand, one can reply that (1) public debt is not the same thing as private debt (we owe it to ourselves—*an internal debt*), (2) future groups receive benefits of debt creation as well as the debt assets themselves, (3) interest payments contribute to public income and thus generate spending, and (4) government controls are available at the ballot box. (Vote out the big spender!) How do these arguments appear to you? Can you add more ideas pro or con? Do you own any securities representing part of the national debt? (A savings bond is one form.)

To give more perspective and analysis to the preceding debate, study Figure 13-8. Our U.S. public debt (over $500 billion in 1975) has been rising for some years, with exceedingly rapid accelerations in the rate of increase during World War II and the "Great Society" and Vietnam War period of the 1960s. It is the acceleration of debt increase that alarms many citizens and economists rather than the size of the debt itself. Actually, U.S. public debt as a percentage of GNP has declined since 1950 and is now some 33 per cent

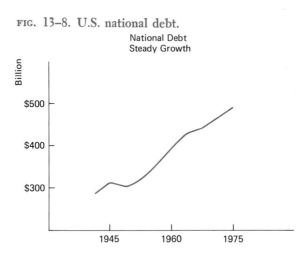

FIG. 13–8. U.S. national debt.

of GNP. (Can many families claim that their total debt is only one-third of their annual income?)

The alarm of some over the rate of debt increase grows from concerns at (1) congressional lack of control over expenditures, (2) inflationary pressures of debt increase, and (3) finance complications involved in borrowing these monies. In analyzing the lack of control concern, some economists see the continual and ever larger (some $70 billion in fiscal 1976) budget deficits during a peacetime economy as evidence that Congress cannot control its spending habits. In fact, the uncontrollable spending percentage of our federal budget appears to grow yearly with little congressional revision or control. "Uncontrollable spending" refers to programs that have set spending limits per recipient, but no limit to the number of new recipients, as in the case of many of our social welfare programs. Although a truly countercyclical fiscal policy approach might balance budget surplus against deficit in the long run, only a budget deficit appears to gain popular political appeal, and budget control is overlooked in the shouting.

The inflationary pressure alarm of debt increase is closely tied to the lack of control concern, for increasing government spending from budget deficits may create a demand-pull inflation. If the rate of productivity and capacity growth is exceeded by the rate of increase in government spending, with no offsetting spending reductions in other components of aggregate demand, inflationary pressure must result. In addition, the incomes earned from government spending for social goods are, typically, spent for consumer goods, thus adding to inflationary pressures.

Finance complications concerns of economists over public debt borrowing arise from several factors. Some economists are concerned over the increasingly short-term nature of the public debt; that is, rather than borrowing for periods longer than five years (bonds) or even one year (notes), the U.S. Treasury borrows much of our public debt on a less-than-one-year basis (bills). This short-term borrowing means that the U.S. Treasury is continually engaged in the money markets and is incurring high interest costs (some $34 billion in fiscal 1976) for such borrowing.

A further finance complication to many economists is that very large borrowing by the U.S. Treasury may deny credit to private business. In effect, these private borrowers are "crowded out" of the money markets (less risk on larger amounts for the U.S. Treasury), thus limiting business investment and expansion of productive capacity. In fiscal 1976, Treasury borrowings amounted to approximately $70 billion in new debt and $200 billion in refunding present debt. Such amounts may well present competitive finance pressures to private businesses.

The preceding objections and concerns are hotly debated in academic circles, Congress, barber shops, and bars around the United States and, perhaps, abroad. Although many economists denigrate the negative effect of public debt, others (the authors included) share the concerns previously discussed. Budget deficits play a valuable role in countercyclical fiscal policy, but uncontrolled spending has few merits. At this point we challenge you to form your own opinion as to a *cost-benefit analysis* of U.S. debt existence and manipulation.

PROBLEMS OF FISCAL POLICY

In case the preceding description of fiscal policy mechanics appears a simple and automatic method of modifying business cycles, it's not all that easy in real life. It may seem simple to say cut or raise spending, cut or increase taxes, or run a surplus or deficit budget; but problems of politics, value differences, timing, and so on, add their weight to the issue

One of the largest problems of fiscal policy (in a democracy?) is that there are so many people and political issues involved in the process. Economic policy formation involves the cooperation of many groups and individuals. Study Figure 13-9 to see the federal budget preparation and administration process. And, of course, each of these groups has its own best answer to solve problems. What we often end up with, if a bill does pass the process of the committee hearing, floor vote, compromise committee, and presidential signature is some basic proposal with much modification and perhaps many nonassociated riders. (A *rider* is a clause tacked onto a main bill, generally for some unrelated purpose, in order to secure sufficient vote support.) Although such a legislative process may have political appeal and illustrates our "checks and balances" political structure, the resulting bills often fall short from the standpoint of economic theory.

To illustrate the difficulty of fiscal policy decision making, let's illustrate the question with an example of current concern. A bill passed in 1975 to control strip-mining practices (the mining of coal by removal of topsoil to reveal the coal seam) for a greater degree of environmental protection. Although many might support this environmental goal of fiscal policy, President Ford vetoed the bill on the basis of its unfavorable unemployment impacts and negative energy considerations. (Some coal mines may close under the bill's standards, contributing to increased unemployment and reduced coal output.) Enough congressmen must have shared the president's same priorities of fiscal policy goals, for the veto was not overridden. Now, economic decision maker, how would you have voted? How do you propose a compromise on such goals to pass a measure involving them? How do you predict the national effects of such a bill, let alone state reactions?

This political problem brings in the associated *problem of timing;* that is, for greatest effect, countercyclical fiscal policy measures should be taken in step with general economic conditions. However, economic conditions may often be subordinate to committee hearings, floor maneuvering for votes, and

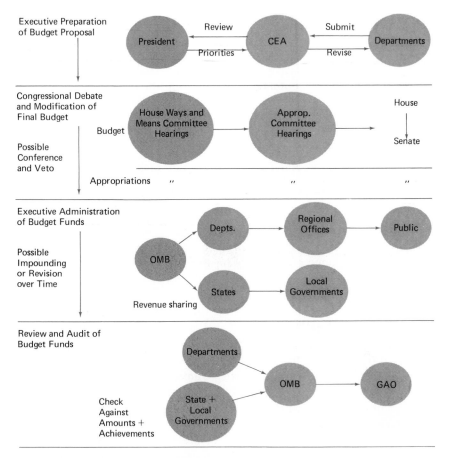

Terms: CEA—Council of Economic Advisors
OMB—Office of Management and Budget
GAO—General Accounting Office

FIG. 13–9. Federal budget process.

political campaigning. Add to these distractions the genuine *disagreement over value orientation* (what is really the best thing to do?) and you have a real stalemate. Perhaps the best example of such conflicts is appreciated by reviewing the inflation buildup of recent U.S. economic history. In 1975 recessionary economic conditions led to passage of spending increases and a tax cut designed to raise spending and reduce unemployment. Although this policy appears to be slow in working, there is growing concern that its increased spending volume may lead to renewed inflation. For various reasons (value differences, budget problems, political maneuvering, and so on), any anti-inflation policies may now be quite slow in adoption.

Perhaps one way to reduce these timing-and-value conflict issues is through greater use of our *automatic stabilizers* of fiscal policy; that is, we could adopt more *nondiscretionary fiscal policy* that changes expenditure of tax revenue levels automatically whenever certain economic conditions occur. For example, the federal progressive income tax (increased tax rate for larger incomes) automatically counteracts inflation (greater taxes reduce higher incomes) and recession (reduced taxes alleviate falling incomes) without a congressional vote required. This same *automatic stabilizing impact* (maintenance of aggregate demand) occurs in such programs as Social Security, unemployment compensation, and even food stamps. The real challenge of these programs is to develop a preliminary sound program structure and then to be implemented by Congress (forming thus, initially, a *discretionary fiscal policy*).

Another problem for fiscal policy is that of conflicts with other policies; that is, policies to implement fiscal policy goals may hinder goals set for monetary policy, balance-of-payments policies, environmental concerns, or a host of other economic goals (more on these policy goals and mechanics in following chapters). Fiscal policy proposals either may not be as effective owing to contradictory impact of other policies or may be modified from primary goals in a compromise with other aims.

One additional fiscal policy issue is that forecasting is often scientific guessing, which implies that the effects of fiscal policy are often difficult to predict. Of course, estimates are made and analyzed in order to evaluate the policy proposed, but such predictions are imprecise, particularly if concern is with several goals, some of which are actively opposed (as, for example, full employment and stable prices). This imprecise prediction of effects can cause much disagreement.

In addition to all of these conflicts, federal countercyclical fiscal policy may well be offset by state and local government fiscal policy, as noted previously. The state and local governments aim mainly to meet public needs without concern for business cycle offsets and thus may run counter to federal policies. States sometimes increase spending when federal policy attempts to reduce inflation and vice versa.

In closing this catalogue of fiscal policy problems, let us conclude by challenging your evaluation of a new addition to fiscal policy tools: *price-wage controls*. Although the United States has experienced price-wage controls in wartime economies, the use of such controls during our 1971–1974 peacetime economy was somewhat unique. Political and inflationary pressures contributed to the institution of such controls.

The "game plan" of price-wage control use was that traditional fiscal and monetary policies (expansion of aggregate demand) were to be used to reduce unemployment from 1971 onward. But the expected inflationary pressure (recall the Phillips curve?) was to be contained by the price-wage control structure. In this manner, the U.S. economy was supposed to achieve both full employment and stable prices, as had been experienced during the early

1960s. Although evaluations differ on the degree of success (or reasons for failure) of such controls, most economists do not give high marks to this particular fiscal policy approach. The control agencies were understaffed, proper planning appeared lacking, consistent administrative support did not occur, and control was often sporadic and uncoordinated.

Although some economists (like John Kenneth Galbraith) debate that a "properly" developed and administered price-wage control program will achieve fiscal policy goals, the authors are doubtful. Given the complex interdependence of the modern U.S. economy and assuming that the past ineptitudes of government bureaucracy will continue, we doubt that price-wage controls will reduce inflation without consequential market distortions and production bottlenecks. But we leave our analysis, personal point of view, and Figure 13-10 (study for price-wage impact record) to your evaluation.

FIG. 13–10. Price-wage controls result.

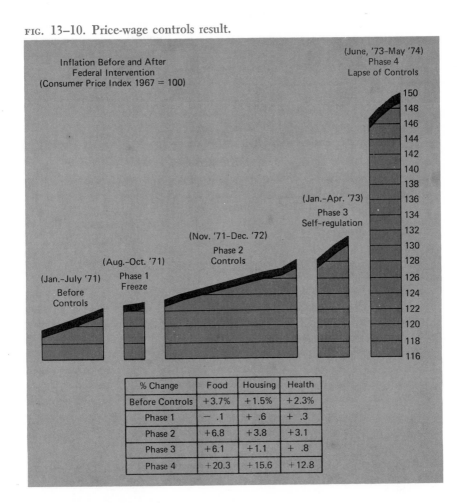

% Change	Food	Housing	Health
Before Controls	+3.7%	+1.5%	+2.3%
Phase 1	− .1	+ .6	+ .3
Phase 2	+6.8	+3.8	+3.1
Phase 3	+6.1	+1.1	+ .8
Phase 4	+20.3	+15.6	+12.8

Well, these are perhaps enough problems for any budding economist or politician. (Any of you considering these careers?) The point has been to illustrate the difficulty of implementing what may seem simple cookbook procedures. Countercyclical fiscal policy can be (and has been) effective, but there are many associated problems. A problem to leave you with: What fiscal policy (or combinations?) would you propose when inflation and unemployment occur at the same time? The authors modestly propose (1) reduced personal and business taxes, (2) reduced government regulation of daily marketplace activity, and (3) increased emphasis on job training at high school and college levels. What is your view?

TERMS

Accelerator effect. The change in business investment in response to changes in consumer spending.

Automatic stabilizer (nondiscretionary fiscal policy). A fiscal policy that changes expenditures or tax revenue levels without a required congressional action.

Countercyclical fiscal policy. The attempt by Congress to affect levels of employment and income by deliberate changes in the amounts of federal government spending and taxation.

Econometric models. Mathematical models used to forecast national economic performance that would result from proposed changes.

Fiscal year. A budget period, usually extending from July 1 of one year to June 30 of the next year. (October 1 to September 30 is the recent federal fiscal year.)

Multiplier effect. The process by which initial changes in spending and taxation cause larger changes in final spending and output.

Revenue sharing. An intergovernmental transfer of revenue whereby the federal government tax revenues are dispensed to state and local governments.

Unbalanced budget. An expenditure-revenue result showing either a surplus or a deficit.

Uncontrollable spending. Expenditures that occur because of presently adopted program payments to an increasing number of recipients.

QUESTIONS FOR STUDY

1. Explain how a government deficit may reduce unemployment.
2. Assuming a government spending increase of $20 billion ($MPC = \frac{4}{5}$), GNP may be roughly predicted to ＿＿＿＿ (increase, decrease) by $＿＿＿＿ billion.

3. Assuming a tax increase of $20 billion ($MPC = \frac{4}{5}$),GNP may be roughly predicted to _____ (increase, decrease) by $_____ billion.

4. To reduce an inflationary pressure of $60 billion ($MPC = \frac{3}{4}$),

    a. Government spending must _____ (increase, decrease) by $_____ billion.

    b. Government taxes must _____ (increase, decrease) by $_____ billion.

5. How do private and public debts differ?

6. Is countercyclical fiscal policy a "proper" role for our government?

7. State and evaluate three problems limiting the effectiveness of fiscal policy operation.

8. How effective do you feel price-wage controls are in achieving fiscal policy goals?

9. "It is quite easy for fiscal policy to maintain full employment and prevent inflation." Do you agree with this statement?

REFERENCES

Blinder, Alan S. *Fiscal Policy in Theory and Practice*. New York: General Learning Corp., 1973.

Economic Report of the President (Fiscal 1976). Washington, D.C.: U.S. Government Printing Office, 1975.

Friedman, Milton. *Dollars and Deficits*. Englewood Cliffs, N.J.: Prentice-Hall, Inc., 1972.

Kogiku, Kuchiro. *An Introduction to Macroeconomic Models*. New York: McGraw-Hill, 1974.

Mishan, E. J. *Economics for Social Decisions*. New York: Praeger Publishers, 1972.

Morgan, E. V., and A. D. Morgan. *The Economics of Public Policy*. Chicago: Aldine Publishing Co., 1972.

North, Douglas C., and Roger LeRoy Miller. *The Economics of Public Issues*, Second Edition. New York: Harper & Row, Publishers, 1973.

O'Connor, J. *The Fiscal Crisis of the State*. New York: St. Martin's Press, 1973.

Silk, Leonard. *Nixonomics*, Second Edition. New York: Praeger Publishers, 1973.

WHY PAY TAXES?

SHORT ANSWER. Taxes are levied (1) to pay for government services, (2) to allocate social goods while redistributing income, and (3) to act as a stabilizing effect on economic fluctuations.

"The only sure things in life are death and taxes!" —A Cynic.

YOU AND TAXES

Although we discussed taxes in the previous chapter, that analysis of fiscal policy did not specifically enter into the many issues related to our U.S. tax structure. Besides making the big hole in your pocketbook, the impact of taxation on the U.S. economy is considerable and involves many diverse issues. (Reread this chapter's short answer, and study Figure 14-1.) Taxes may moderate business cycle fluctuation (Chapter 13), may shift economic resources between social goods and consumer goods, and may affect some income distribution (the *for whom* question). Let's analyze these tax issues in this chapter with emphasis on personal impact.

FIG. 14–1. Taxation impacts.

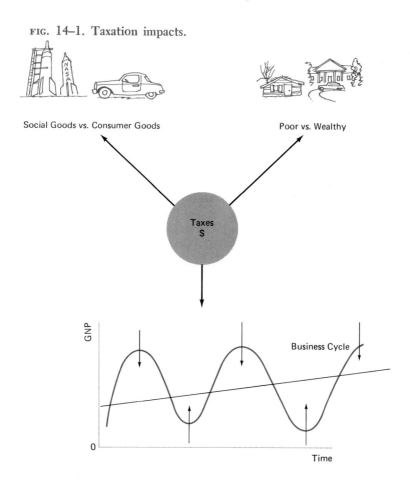

How does your or your parents' tax bill (all federal, state, local taxes combined) compare to the typical U.S. tax load in Figure 14-2? How greatly have your taxes increased (about a 28 per cent increase for all taxes in 1974), especially compared to the growth of your income? Have you gotten your money's worth from taxes; that is, do the benefits you receive from tax payment (social goods and services, transfer income, community impacts) compare favorably to the costs (amounts paid) of taxes to you?

The questions suggest the importance of taxes in your daily economic activity as well as in our national economic system. Their important impact should be further understood. Your tax bill represents an *opportunity cost* (recall Chapter 2?) in that taxes paid represent consumer goods not purchased. This trade-off (illustrated by the *production possibility curve*) occurs throughout our economy, as tax expenditures direct resources from the production of consumer goods to the production of social goods. The amount of disposable income (income after taxes to spend or save) you and other consumers receive will be influenced by the amount, type, and structure of tax levies.

You should remember that you receive benefits from the provision of social goods; thus the taxes you pay are not a total loss. Compare, for example, the

FIG. 14–2. Tax load.

Mounting Burden of Taxes

All Taxes—Federal, State and Local—as a Share of National Income in U.S.

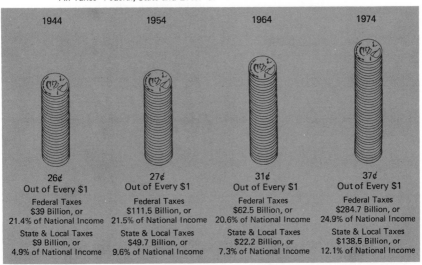

1944	1954	1964	1974
26¢ Out of Every $1	**27¢** Out of Every $1	**31¢** Out of Every $1	**37¢** Out of Every $1
Federal Taxes $39 Billion, or 21.4% of National Income	Federal Taxes $111.5 Billion, or 21.5% of National Income	Federal Taxes $62.5 Billion, or 20.6% of National Income	Federal Taxes $284.7 Billion, or 24.9% of National Income
State & Local Taxes $9 Billion, or 4.9% of National Income	State & Local Taxes $49.7 Billion, or 9.6% of National Income	State & Local Taxes $22.2 Billion, or 7.3% of National Income	State & Local Taxes $138.5 Billion, or 12.1% of National Income

In Three Decades: The tax take in the United States is nearly nine times what it was in 1944, climbing from a total of $48 billion, or 26 per cent of the national income, to $423 billion, or 37 per cent of national income in 1974. A cut in federal income taxes this year may slow or halt the increase in the tax burden—but fast-rising state and local taxes point to resumption of boosts in the tax load in years ahead.

Source: Internal Revenue Service.

tuition charges (and quality?) at private schools (elementary, secondary, college) to those at public schools supported by tax levies. Or how about the "value" of the beach, local park, or national forest you use? What about the time the fire department put out the garage fire, and the police department recovered your stolen camera? What we're trying to show is that the provision of social goods in some part repays the opportunity cost of taxes.

We have a good many tax issues in this chapter to analyze, so let's start. We hope we've impressed upon you the important economic effects of taxes (try a cost-benefit analysis of your own taxes?), and we will examine these effects in greater detail. You may be interested in a comparison of U.S. tax burdens with those of other nations (Figure 14-3). Notice that as a percentage of GNP the U.S. tax take is much below those of other nations! It is true that U.S. income taxes on individuals and corporations exceed those of other nations on a percentage basis (but not Sweden for individuals or Japan for corporations). However, U.S. Social Security taxes and sales taxes are much below those of other nations. Of course, a valid cost-benefit analysis would compare social goods and services provided against taxes paid in each country.

TYPES OF TAXES PAID

Let us first consider the types of taxes you pay, as your total tax burden is composed of several tax types from the various levels of government. You pay these many types of taxes daily; some you may not even realize you're paying. There are *income tax* (state, federal, some local), *sales tax* (mostly state, but some federal excise tax), and *property tax* (local). Income taxes are

FIG. 14–3. Comparative tax loads.

	Direct Taxes (on Incomes, Corporate Profits, Estates, Gifts)	Indirect Taxes (Sales and Property Taxes, Excises)	Social Security Taxes	Total Taxes
United States	14.2%	8.9%	5.2%	28.3%
Sweden	20.1%	13.7%	7.1%	40.9
France	6.4%	17.5%	14.8%	38.7%
Norway	13.6%	15.5%	8.8%	37.8%
Netherlands	13.8%	10.7%	12.6%	37.1%
Austria	12.7%	15.6%	8.1%	36.3%
West Germany	10.4%	14.6%	10.3%	35.3%
Britain	12.8%	15.1%	4.8%	32.7%
Denmark	14.7%	15.4%	1.9%	32.0%
Belgium	9.4%	13.5%	8.6%	31.5%
Italy	6.9%	13.2%	10.7%	30.8%
Canada	11.5%	15.1%	3.3%	29.9%
Japan	7.8%	7.5%	3.6%	18.9%

Note: Based on 1967 data, latest available, for national, state, and local levies.

usually quite obvious in payment, especially when collected on a withholding basis from your paycheck. Sales taxes are included in the final purchase price of products and you may not see the separate tax amount, as on a gallon of gas (a four-cent federal tax, perhaps a seven-cent state tax, and sometimes a one-cent local tax). If you pay rent for your home or apartment, you may not realize that part of your rental charge goes toward a property tax payment. But to analyze taxes, we need to view them from several angles.

We can first look at taxes on the basis of the level of government to which they're paid. Note from Figure 14-4 that there's quite a difference in the "importance" of the type of tax by governmental level and also in the type of expenditure a particular level of tax is used to finance. At the federal level the most important tax is the personal and corporate income tax, which is used mainly for defense spending and transfer payments. At the state level, the sales tax is usually the biggest revenue item; and education, highways, and local government aid (states give funds to local governments for use in roads, education, and welfare) are big expenditures. But at the local level, property taxes are the main revenue source, and education is the largest expense item.

Although these general categories of taxation and expenditures hold for all states, some state and local governments may have unique tax-spending patterns. There is also a good deal of *intergovernmental transfer* of taxation and spending, whereby one level of government collects tax, but another governmental level spends it. One example of such transfer is state collection of gasoline, retail sales, liquor, and cigarette taxes, with moneys therefrom remitted to local governments for their spending. Another much publicized transfer example is that of the federal *revenue sharing* plan (started in 1972), by which federal tax revenues are expended by state and local governments. These transfers are to bolster state-local government revenues and to meet pressing social goods needs. This program now runs some $6 billion annually (about $60 per state resident, although there exist large differences among amounts the various states receive), and allocation of spending is illustrated by Figure 14-5.

Another way a tax can be viewed—and perhaps a more important perspective for analytical purposes—is the percentage change in tax rate in accordance with income level change. On this basis of percentage change, a tax may be termed *progressive, proportional,* or *regressive.* A progressive tax is one for which the tax rate percentage increases as the income level rises, as in the federal income tax. For example, the income tax rate might be 18 per cent on an income of $10,000, but increases to 22 per cent at an income of $15,000. A proportional tax maintains the same tax rate percentage at all income levels and is exemplified by property tax. All property would be taxed at the rate of, say, $12 per $100 assessed valuation (about 25 per cent of market value). A regressive tax means the tax rate percentage rises as the income level falls, so that those with lower incomes pay higher tax rates. A sales tax is often termed regressive because lower income groups pay a higher

	General Revenues by Source†							General Expenditures by Function†				
Fiscal Year*	Total	Property Taxes	Sales and Gross Receipts Taxes	Individual Income Taxes	Corporation Net Income Taxes	Revenue for Federal Government	All Other Revenue†	Total	Education	Highways	Public Welfare	All Other
1927	7,217	4,730	470	70	92	116	1,793	7,210	2,235	1,809	151	3,015
1932	7,267	4,487	752	74	79	232	1,643	7,765	2,311	1,741	444	3,269
1934	7,678	4,076	1,008	80	49	1,016	1,449	7,181	1,831	1,509	889	2,952
1936	8,395	4,093	1,484	153	113	948	1,604	7,644	2,177	1,425	827	3,215
1938	9,228	4,440	1,794	218	165	800	1,811	8,757	2,491	1,650	1,069	3,547
1940	9,609	4,430	1,982	224	156	945	1,872	9,229	2,638	1,573	1,156	3,862
1942	10,418	4,537	2,251	276	272	858	2,123	9,190	2,586	1,490	1,225	3,889
1944	10,908	4,604	2,289	342	451	954	2,269	8,863	2,793	1,200	1,133	3,737
1946	12,356	4,986	2,986	422	447	855	2,661	11,028	3,356	1,672	1,409	4,591
1948	17,250	6,126	4,442	543	592	1,861	3,685	17,684	5,379	3,036	2,099	7,170
1950	20,911	7,349	5,154	788	593	2,486	4,541	22,787	7,177	3,803	2,940	8,867
1952	25,181	8,652	6,357	998	846	2,566	5,763	26,098	8,318	4,650	2,788	10,342
1953	27,307	9,375	6,927	1,065	817	2,870	6,252	27,910	9,390	4,987	2,914	10,619
1954	29,012	9,967	7,276	1,127	788	2,966	6,897	30,701	10,557	5,527	3,060	11,557
1955	31,073	10,735	7,643	1,237	744	3,131	7,584	33,724	11,907	6,452	3,168	12,197
1956	34,667	11,749	8,691	1,538	890	3,335	8,465	36,711	13,220	6,953	3,139	13,399
1957	38,164	12,864	9,467	1,754	984	3,843	9,250	40,375	14,134	7,816	3,485	14,940
1958	41,219	14,047	9,829	1,759	1,018	4,865	9,699	44,851	15,919	8,567	3,818	16,547
1959	45,306	14,983	10,437	1,994	1,001	6,377	10,516	48,887	17,283	9,592	4,136	17,876
1960	50,505	16,405	11,849	2,463	1,180	6,974	11,634	51,876	18,719	9,428	4,404	19,325
1961	54,037	18,002	12,463	2,613	1,266	7,131	12,563	56,201	20,574	9,844	4,720	21,063
1962	58,252	19,054	13,494	3,037	1,308	7,871	13,489	60,206	22,216	10,357	5,084	22,549
1963	62,890	20,089	14,456	3,269	1,505	8,722	14,850	64,816	23,776	11,136	5,481	24,423

FIG. 14–4. Government budgeting.

Year or Quarter	Receipts					Expenditures							Surplus or Deficit (−), National Income and Product Accounts
	Total	Personal Tax and Nontax Receipts	Corporate Profits Tax Accruals	Indirect Business Tax and Nontax Accruals	Contributions for Social Insurance	Total*	Purchases of Goods and Services	Transfer Payments To Persons	Transfer Payments To Foreigners (Net)	Grants-in-aid to State and Local Governments	Net Interest Paid	Subsidies Less Current Surplus of Government Enterprises	
1962–63	62,269	19,833	14,446	3,267	1,505	63,977	8,663	14,556		23,729	11,150	5,420	23,678
1963–64	68,443	21,241	15,762	3,791	1,695	69,302	10,002	15,951		26,286	11,664	5,766	25,586
1964–65	74,000	22,584	17,118	4,090	1,929	74,546	11,029	17,250		28,563	12,221	6,315	27,447
1965–66	83,036	24,670	19,085	4,760	2,038	82,843	13,214	19,269		33,287	12,770	6,757	30,029
1966–67	91,197	26,047	20,530	5,826	2,227	93,350	15,370	21,197		37,919	13,932	8,218	33,281
1967–68	101,264	27,747	22,911	7,308	2,518	102,411	17,181	23,598		41,158	14,481	9,857	36,915
1968–69	114,550	30,673	26,519	8,908	3,180	116,728	19,153	26,118		47,238	15,417	12,110	41,963
1969–70	130,756	34,054	30,322	10,812	3,738	131,332	21,857	29,971		52,718	16,427	14,679	47,508
1970–71	144,927	37,852	33,233	11,900	3,424	150,674	26,146	32,374		59,413	18,095	18,226	54,940
1971–72	166,352	42,133	37,488	15,237	4,416	166,873	31,253	35,825		64,886	19,010	21,070	61,907
1972–73	190,177	45,283	42,047	17,994	5,425	181,615	39,256	40,172		69,573	18,615	23,582	69,316
Fiscal Year:													
1949	40.0	16.3	11.0	8.0	4.8	39.6	19.3	8.1	5.0	2.1	4.3	0.8	0.4
1950	42.0	16.5	11.9	8.2	5.5	42.4	19.0	11.3	4.3	2.4	4.4	1.0	−.5
1951	60.8	23.2	21.5	9.5	6.6	44.6	25.1	8.1	3.1	2.4	4.6	1.3	16.2
1952	65.1	28.8	19.3	9.7	7.3	66.0	46.6	8.5	2.6	2.5	4.8	1.1	−1.0

* Fiscal years not the same for all governments. See footnote ‖.

‖ Excludes revenues or expenditures of publicly owned utilities and liquor stores, and of insurance-trust activities. Intergovernment receipts and payments between state and local governments are also excluded.

Includes licenses and other taxes and charges and miscellaneous revenues.

Includes expenditures for health, hospitals, police, local fire protection, natural resources, sanitation, housing and urban renewal, local parks and recreation, general control, financial administration, interest on general debt, and unallocable expenditures.

Data for fiscal year ending in the 12-month period through June 30. Data for 1963 and earlier years include local government amounts grouped in terms of fiscal years ended during the particular calendar year.

Note.—Data are not available for intervening years.

| Year or Quarter | Receipts | | | | | Expenditures | | | | | | | Surplus or Deficit (−), National Income and Product Accounts |
	Total	Personal Tax and Nontax Receipts	Corporate Profits Tax Accruals	Indirect Business Tax and Nontax Accruals	Contributions for Social Insurance	Total*	Purchases of Goods and Services	Transfer Payments To Persons	Transfer Payments To Foreigners (Net)	Grants-in-aid to State and Local Governments	Net Interest Paid	Subsidies Less Current Surplus of Government Enterprises	
Fiscal Year:													
1953	69.3	31.4	19.7	10.7	7.5	75.8	56.1	9.3	2.1	2.8	4.8	.9	−6.5
1954	65.8	30.3	17.3	10.4	7.8	74.2	53.2	10.5	1.7	2.9	5.0	1.0	−8.5
1955	67.2	29.7	18.7	10.0	8.7	67.3	43.9	12.1	2.1	3.0	4.9	1.3	−.1
1956	75.8	33.6	21.1	10.8	10.2	69.8	45.2	12.8	1.8	3.2	5.1	1.7	6.0
1957	80.7	36.7	20.6	11.7	11.7	76.0	47.7	14.4	1.9	3.7	5.5	2.8	4.7
1958	77.9	36.3	17.8	11.6	12.2	83.1	50.7	17.8	1.7	4.7	5.7	2.5	−5.1
1959	85.4	38.2	21.5	11.9	13.8	90.9	54.7	19.8	1.8	6.2	5.9	2.4	−5.5
1960	94.8	42.5	22.3	13.2	16.7	91.3	52.7	20.6	1.8	6.8	7.0	2.3	3.5
1961	95.3	43.6	20.3	13.3	18.1	98.0	55.5	23.6	2.1	6.9	6.8	3.2	−2.7
1962	104.2	47.3	22.9	14.2	19.9	106.4	60.9	25.1	2.1	7.6	6.8	3.8	−2.1
1963	110.2	49.6	23.5	15.0	22.1	111.4	63.4	26.4	2.1	8.4	7.5	3.6	−1.2
1964	115.5	50.7	25.7	15.6	23.5	116.9	65.7	27.3	2.2	9.8	8.1	3.8	−1.4
1965	120.5	51.3	27.7	16.9	24.6	118.5	64.4	28.3	2.2	10.9	8.5	4.1	2.0
1966	132.8	57.6	31.0	15.7	28.5	131.9	71.7	31.8	2.3	12.7	9.0	4.5	.9
1967	147.2	64.5	31.2	15.8	35.7	154.5	85.3	37.2	2.2	14.8	9.9	5.1	−7.3
1968	160.6	71.4	33.7	17.1	38.3	172.5	94.9	42.7	2.1	17.8	10.9	4.1	−11.9
1969	190.4	90.0	37.4	18.6	44.4	185.7	99.4	48.5	2.2	19.2	12.3	4.1	4.7
1970	195.2	93.6	33.3	19.2	49.1	195.9	98.0	54.8	2.0	22.6	14.0	4.7	−.7
1971	192.5	87.5	32.3	20.1	52.6	212.4	95.8	67.4	2.3	26.8	14.3	5.7	−19.8
1972	213.2	100.7	34.1	20.0	58.5	232.9	103.2	75.7	2.8	32.6	13.4	5.3	−19.7
1973	240.4	106.8	41.2	20.7	71.7	255.4	105.3	86.7	2.7	40.2	14.5	6.7	−15.0
1974	273.6	123.1	45.6	21.6	83.3	278.3	110.3	101.3	2.9	41.5	17.4	4.7	−4.7
1975†	287.6	122.1	41.0	33.1	91.4	323.7	121.1	128.2	3.5	47.0	19.8	3.7	−36.1
1976†	305.1	111.1	39.9	54.7	99.4	361.0	136.1	143.0	4.0	50.8	23.0	4.1	−55.9
Calendar Year:													
1949	38.9	16.1	9.8	8.0	4.9	41.3	20.1	8.7	5.1	2.2	4.4	.8	−2.4
1950	49.9	18.1	17.0	8.9	5.9	40.8	18.4	10.8	3.6	2.3	4.5	1.2	9.1

FIG. 14–4. Continued.

Year													
1951	64.0	26.1	21.5	9.4	7.1	57.8	37.7	8.5	3.1	2.5	4.7	1.3	6.2
1952	67.2	31.0	18.5	10.3	7.4	71.0	51.8	8.8	2.1	2.6	4.7	1.0	−3.8
1953	60.0	32.2	19.5	10.9	7.4	77.0	57.0	9.5	2.0	2.8	4.9	.8	−7.0
1954	63.8	29.0	17.0	9.7	8.1	69.7	47.4	11.5	1.8	2.9	5.0	1.1	−5.9
1955	72.1	31.4	20.6	10.7	9.3	68.1	44.1	12.4	2.0	3.1	4.9	1.5	4.0
1956	77.6	35.2	20.6	11.2	10.6	71.9	45.6	13.4	1.9	3.3	5.3	2.4	5.7
1957	81.6	37.4	20.2	11.8	12.2	79.6	49.5	15.7	1.8	4.2	5.7	2.6	2.1
1958	78.7	36.8	18.0	11.5	12.4	88.9	53.6	19.5	1.8	5.6	5.6	2.7	−10.2
1959	89.7	39.9	22.5	12.5	14.8	91.0	53.7	20.1	1.8	6.8	6.4	2.1	−1.2
1960	96.5	43.6	21.7	13.5	17.7	93.0	53.5	21.5	1.9	6.5	7.1	2.5	3.5
1961	98.3	44.7	21.8	13.6	18.2	102.1	57.4	24.9	2.1	7.2	6.6	3.8	−3.8
1962	106.4	48.6	22.7	14.6	20.5	110.3	63.4	25.5	2.2	8.0	7.2	4.0	−3.8
1963	114.5	51.5	24.6	15.3	23.1	113.9	64.2	27.0	2.2	9.1	7.7	3.6	.7
1964	115.0	48.6	26.4	16.1	23.8	118.1	65.2	27.8	2.2	10.4	8.3	4.2	−3.0
1965	124.7	53.8	29.3	16.5	25.1	123.5	66.9	30.3	2.2	11.1	8.7	4.3	1.2
1966	142.5	61.7	32.1	15.7	33.0	142.8	77.8	33.4	2.3	14.4	9.5	5.4	−.2
1967	151.2	67.5	30.7	16.3	36.7	163.6	90.7	40.0	2.2	15.8	10.2	4.6	−12.4
1968	175.0	79.7	36.7	18.0	40.7	181.5	98.8	46.1	2.1	18.7	11.7	4.1	−6.5
1969	197.3	94.8	36.6	19.0	46.9	189.2	98.8	50.3	2.1	20.3	13.1	4.6	8.1
1970	192.0	92.2	31.0	19.3	49.5	203.9	96.2	61.0	2.2	24.4	14.6	5.5	−11.9
1971	198.5	89.9	33.4	20.4	54.6	220.3	97.6	72.3	2.6	29.0	13.6	5.2	−21.9
1972	227.2	108.2	36.6	20.0	62.5	244.7	104.9	80.1	2.7	37.4	13.5	6.6	−17.5
1973	258.5	114.1	43.7	21.2	79.5	264.2	106.6	92.9	2.6	40.5	16.3	5.3	−5.6
1974	291.1	131.2	49.1	22.0	88.7	298.6	116.4	114.4	2.6	43.7	18.8	2.1	−7.6

Seasonally Adjusted Annual Rates

1973: I	249.1	107.9	42.8	20.9	77.4	260.2	106.4	89.9	2.1	41.2	14.8	6.1	−11.2
II	255.0	110.3	44.7	21.4	78.6	262.4	106.2	91.5	3.3	40.1	15.9	5.4	−7.4
III	261.8	116.7	43.8	21.0	80.2	263.4	105.3	93.9	2.7	39.8	16.8	5.0	−1.7
IV	268.3	121.6	43.5	21.3	81.8	270.6	108.4	96.3	2.5	41.0	17.6	4.8	2.3
1974: I	278.1	124.1	45.9	21.5	86.7	281.0	111.5	104.0	2.7	42.9	17.9	2.2	−2.8
II	288.6	129.4	49.2	21.9	88.1	291.6	114.3	110.8	2.7	43.2	18.7	1.3	−3.0
III	302.8	134.8	55.4	22.5	90.0	304.7	117.2	118.4	2.4	43.4	19.1	2.7	1.9
IV	—	136.6	—	22.2	90.0	317.3	122.8	124.4	2.7	45.5	19.7	2.3	—

*Wage accruals less disbursements have been subtracted from total. These were (in billions of dollars at seasonally adjusted rates) .1, −.1, .0, and .0 in the 4 quarters of 1973 and .0, −.6, −1.5, and .0 in the 4 quarters of 1974.
†Estimates.

FIG. 14–4. Continued.

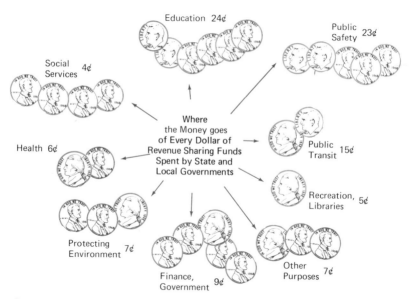

Source: U.S. Department of the Treasury.

Federal Revenue-Sharing Funds Distributed from Jan. 1, 1972, When the Program Started to June, 1974					
	Total	Per Person		Total	Per Person
Alabama	$216,841,000	$61	Montana	$49,438,000	$69
Alaska	$16,076,000	$49	Nebraska	$93,358,000	$61
Arizona	$125,409,000	$61	Nevada	$27,940,000	$51
Arkansas	$131,155,000	$64	New Hampshire	$40,372,000	$51
California	$1,361,428,000		New Jersey	$398,843,000	$54
Colorado	$132,586,000	$54	New Mexico	$80,154,000	$72
Connecticut	$160,298,000	$52	New York	$1,415,209,000	$77
Delaware	$38,066,000	$66	North Carolina	$326,436,000	$62
District of			North Dakota	$53,095,000	$83
Columbia	$57,422,000	$77	Ohio	$507,017,000	$47
Florida	$360,932,000	$47	Oklahoma	$141,746,000	$53
Georgia	$263,477,000	$55	Oregon	$125,685,000	$56
Hawaii	$56,509,000	$68	Pennsylvania	$655,120,000	$56
Idaho	$52,086,000	$68	Rhode Island	$57,677,000	$59
Illinois	$652,412,000	$58	South Carolina	$173,416,000	$64
Indiana	$271,802,000	$51	South Dakota	$57,672,000	$84
Iowa	$180,655,000	$62	Tennessee	$237,802,000	$58
Kansas	$124,103,000	$54	Texas	$599,988,000	$51
Kentucky	$208,758,000	$62	Utah	$74,964,000	$65
Louisiana	$293,292,000	$78	Vermont	$35,706,000	$77
Maine	$76,801,000	$75	Virginia	$252,544,000	$52
Maryland	$254,097,000	$62	Washington	$185,393,000	$54
Massachusetts	$401,291,000	$69	West Virginia	$124,610,000	$69
Michigan	$539,112,000	$60	Wisconsin	$319,799,000	$70
Minnesota	$251,782,000	$65	Wyoming	$24,085,000	$68
Mississippi	$211,637,000	$93	United		
Missouri	$236,577,000	$50	States	$12.7 billion	$61

Note: Amounts distributed by the federal government are determined by formula that takes into account—in addition to population—per-capita income and the effort made by State and local governments to raise taxes on their own. Hence the differences in per-capita revenue sharing among states.

Source: U.S. Department of the Treasury.

FIG. 14–5. Revenue sharing.

percentage of tax on purchases. For example, suppose a person making $100 per month and one earning $1,000 per month each purchase a $100 item and pay $6 in sales tax. The tax is 6 per cent for the low-income worker, but only 0.6 per cent for the high-income worker. See Figure 14-6 to clarify these tax terms.

If you question the importance of such tax analysis, the answer lies in the impact of taxes on social goods allocation, income distribution effect, and

FIG. 14–6. Progressive, regressive, and proportional taxes.

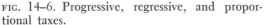

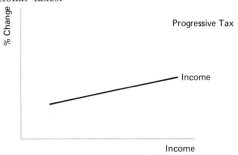

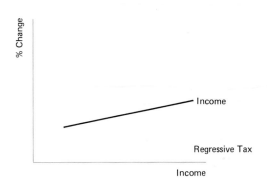

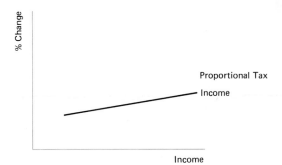

equity in tax administration; that is, depending on the relative weight of progressive, proportional, or regressive taxes in our overall U.S. tax structure, various income groups bear different tax burdens. Whether these tax burdens are in proportion to the social goods and transfer payments received by the income groups will then have a large effect on the net income received by them. Many economists claim, for example, that the sales tax (regressive) impact significantly offsets the impact of income tax (progressive) on low-income groups, thus permitting little increase in equality of income distribution over time. Lower-income groups pay lower income tax rates (progressive) but higher sales tax rates (regressive) than high-income groups, so the total tax impact is not to alter significantly the gap between lower- and higher-income groups. Do you understand these issues? (More on this in the Tax Reform section later in this chapter.)

Another way to analyze a tax—and also one that considers the "fairness" of the tax—is to determine if a given tax is based on *benefits-received* or *ability-to-pay* principles. A benefits-received tax, such as admission fees to a county museum, means that you pay the tax only if you use the service. You don't pay if you don't use the service taxed. On the other hand, an ability-to-pay tax, such as the income tax, is set up so that higher-income groups pay an increasing tax rate percentage in relation to lower-income groups, whether or not they use the items the tax finances. Of course, there are some taxes that are difficult to classify under either of these headings, such as property tax. Is this tax paid for benefits received (police, fire, sewer services), for ability to pay (a measure of wealth), for the ability of *other* persons to pay (market value of property, not purchase price), or for all or for none?

Again, the importance of such description is tax impact on social goods allocation and equality of income distribution. Emphasis on the ability-to-pay principle tends to promote greater income equality, whereas emphasis on the benefits-received principle directly affects allocation of social goods. As an illustration, consider the issue of school finance reform in which many states may be required to modify tax and expenditure patterns to provide greater education revenues to low-income school districts. Property taxes as an education base cause wealthy communities to have more money to spend on schools. Use of the benefits-received principle would surely hinder such reform, but is exclusive reliance on the ability-to-pay principle a "fair" approach? Another example might be the low-income camper who enjoys a public campground, although the wealthy stay-at-home pays more taxes for the campground upkeep. What is "fair" taxation in this case?

Another question in tax analysis is *tax incidence*; that is, who really pays the tax? How far may a tax burden be "shifted" from one group of taxpayers to another group? For example, a property tax on apartment buildings may be transmitted through the landlord to the tenant, so that the tax incidence is actually a concern of the tenant. A corporation sales or income tax (what would you term a pollution control fee?) may be shifted to consumers of the corporation's products. This issue of tax incidence becomes most important in debate over tax reform, especially if the intent of reform is to equalize disposable income distribution.

Perhaps the basic issue here is what constitutes an equitable system for levying taxes. Well, you'll have to debate that one yourself; it's been argued for a long time and the tax reform debate continues today. Perhaps the bitterest questioning arises when tax revenues are used to finance some social good intended for groups not being proportionately taxed, for example, low-income housing, food-for-poor programs, or public schools. Is it really "fair" to tax some groups who feel they receive no direct benefits in order to aid other groups who, presumably, cannot in their own right afford the good or the tax? Notice that in this introductory analysis of tax types, you're already into a heated economic policy issue. Ask any legislator.

WHERE DO TAXES GO?

After all this discussion of the sources and impacts of taxes collected, an obvious question is "Where are all the dollars going?" There are many issues of debate in a federal budget of $413 billion (fiscal year 1977) or in a state budget (California—fiscal year 1977) of $12.6 billion. Let's analyze such issues, noting problem areas.

In the analyzing of Figure 14-7, defense spending is, and has been for some time, the largest single item of tax expenditure in our federal government budget ($101 billion out of $413 billion total budget for fiscal 1977). If "related" expenditures (veterans' payments, national debt interest, and so on) are considered, the superiority of the defense budget is even greater. However, the largest category, as opposed to single item, in our federal budget is that of *transfer payments* (also termed income maintenance or human service programs), including the Social Security, debt interest, health, education, and welfare items. As one might expect, there are disagreements over the division of funds; some say the slice for national defense is too large, whereas others say it is too small. Although such debate over allocation is basically a conflict of value judgments, it should be pointed out (study Figure 14-8) that there have been significant shifts in the allocation over time. Notice that even though a spending item (like defense) may be increasing in *absolute* amount, it may still be decreasing in *relative* (percentage) comparison (compare Figure 14-7 against Figure 14-8). We have had much increased emphasis on human needs in our federal budget in the last ten years, although opinions may vary on the adequacy of such budget shift.

This question of how to cut the pie becomes even more crucial as new needs emerge in the late 1970s. There are at present urgent cries for in-

Description	Actual									Estimate	
	1966	1967	1968	1969	1970	1971	1972	1973	1974	1975	1976
Receipts by Source											
Individual Income Taxes	55.4	61.5	68.7	87.2	90.4	86.2	94.7	103.2	119.0	117.7	105.3
Corporation Income Taxes	30.1	34.0	28.7	36.7	32.8	26.8	32.2	36.2	38.6	38.5	47.7
Social Insurance Taxes and Contributions	25.6	33.3	34.6	39.9	45.3	48.6	53.9	64.5	76.8	86.2	91.6
Excise Taxes	13.1	13.7	14.1	15.2	15.7	16.6	15.5	16.3	16.8	19.9	32.1
Estate and Gift Taxes	3.1	3.0	3.1	3.5	3.6	3.7	5.4	4.9	5.0	4.8	4.6
Customs Duties	1.8	1.9	2.0	2.3	2.4	2.6	3.3	3.2	3.3	3.9	4.3
Miscellaneous Receipts	1.9	2.1	2.5	2.9	3.4	3.9	3.6	3.9	5.4	7.7	10.9
Total Receipts	130.9	149.6	153.7	187.8	193.7	188.4	208.6	232.2	264.9	278.8	297.5
Outlays by Function											
National Defense*	55.9	69.1	79.4	80.2	79.3	76.8	77.4	75.1	78.6	85.3	94.0
International Affairs	4.6	4.7	4.6	3.8	3.6	3.1	3.7	3.0	3.6	4.9	6.3
General Science, Space, and Technology	6.8	6.3	5.6	5.1	4.6	4.3	4.3	4.2	4.2	4.2	4.6
Natural Resources, Environment, and Energy	3.1	3.4	3.6	3.5	3.6	4.4	5.0	5.5	6.4	9.4	10.0
Agriculture	2.4	3.0	4.5	5.8	5.2	4.3	5.3	4.9	2.2	1.8	6.3
Commerce and Transportation	9.0	9.2	10.6	7.1	9.1	10.4	10.6	9.9	13.1	11.8	13.7
Community and Regional Development	1.5	1.7	2.2	2.5	3.5	4.0	4.7	5.9	4.9	4.9	5.9
Education, Manpower, and Social Services	4.1	6.0	7.0	6.9	7.9	9.0	11.7	11.9	11.6	14.7	14.6
Health	2.6	6.8	9.7	11.8	13.1	14.7	17.5	18.8	22.1	26.5	28.0
Income Security	28.9	30.8	33.7	37.3	43.1	55.4	63.9	73.0	84.4	106.7	118.7
Veterans Benefits and Services	5.9	6.9	6.9	7.6	8.7	9.8	10.7	12.0	13.4	15.5	15.6
Law Enforcement and Justice	.6	.6	.6	.8	1.0	1.3	1.6	2.1	2.5	3.0	3.3
General Government	1.4	1.6	1.7	1.6	1.9	2.2	2.5	2.7	3.3	2.6	3.2
Revenue Sharing and General Purpose Fiscal Assistance	.2	.3	.3	.4	.5	.5	.5	7.2	6.7	7.0	7.2
Interest	11.3	12.5	13.8	15.8	18.3	19.6	20.6	22.8	28.1	31.3	34.4
Allowances†										.7	8.0
Undistributed Offsetting Receipts	−3.6	−4.6	−5.5	−5.5	−6.6	−8.4	−8.1	−12.3	−16.7	−16.8	−20.2
Total Outlays	134.7	158.3	178.8	184.5	196.6	211.4	231.9	246.5	268.4	313.4	349.4

*Includes civilian and military pay raises for Department of Defense.

†Includes energy and equalization payments, civilian agents, pay raises, and contingencies.

Source: *President's Economic Report, 1975.*

FIG. 14–7. Federal government spending.

Receipts	1969	1975
Individual Income Taxes	43%	42%
Social Insurance	22	28
Corporation Income Taxes	18	16
Excise Taxes	9	6
Borrowing	4	3
Other	4	5
	100%	100%
Spending		
National Defense	44%	29%
Benefits to Individuals	25	37
Other Federal Operations	13	10
Grants to States and Localities	11	17
Net Interest	7	7
	100%	100%

Source: *President's Economic Report*, 1975.

FIG. 14–8. Government budgeting.

creased tax monies for urban renewal; more health services; improved educational facilities; aid to the aged, the poor, and the disadvantaged; expanded pollution control and pollution research; expanded energy exploration; and so on. The basic economic question—how to allocate limited resources among competing alternative wants—arises in two aspects:

1. Given a fixed government budget, more funds to one need means fewer funds in another area. How and to what degree do we shift these funds?

2. If more funds are desired for all areas, then taxes must rise to provide a greater budget. But this means a shift from consumer goods to social goods. What is the proper balance?

These are indeed crucial choices and ones faced daily by our national congressmen. The problem is compounded when you consider that 535 congressmen, all representing competing interests and value judgments, must "compromise" on a single decision! You may call it politics, but it is also economics in action.

Now to the issue of state and local tax expenditures, where the choices may be even more difficult. State and local spending is estimated to be $215 billion in fiscal 1977 (compared to a federal budget of $413 billion), and state-local taxes are increasing even faster than federal taxes. Deficit spending is not easily available to state and local governments, so the balancing of revenue and expenditures is a continuous challenge. Major state expenditure areas are education, welfare, highways, and aid to local governments. At the local level the big expenditures are for education; roads; and police, fire, and welfare. In comparing Figure 14-9 to Figure 14-7, do you see the significantly different spending emphasis among government levels? Actually, one should expect these differences in federal, state, and local budgets because, as the

Calendar Year or Quarter	Receipts						Expenditures					Surplus or Deficit (—), National Income and Product Accounts
	Total	Personal Tax and Nontax Receipts	Corporate Profits Tax Accruals	Indirect Business Tax and Nontax Accruals	Contributions for Social Insurance	Federal Grants-in-aid	Total*	Purchases of Goods and Services	Transfer Payments to Persons	Net Interest Paid	Subsidies Less Current Surplus of Government Enterprises	
1946	12.9	1.5	0.5	9.3	0.5	1.1	11.0	9.8	1.7	0.3	—0.7	1.9
1947	15.3	1.8	.6	10.6	.6	1.7	14.3	12.6	2.3	.3	—.8	1.0
1948	17.6	2.1	.7	12.1	.7	2.0	17.4	15.0	2.9	.3	—.8	.1
1949	19.3	2.4	.6	13.3	.8	2.2	20.0	17.7	2.9	.3	—.9	—.7
1950	21.1	2.6	.8	14.5	1.0	2.3	22.3	19.5	3.5	.3	—.9	—1.2
1951	23.3	2.9	.9	15.8	1.2	2.5	23.7	21.5	3.0	.3	—1.1	—.4
1952	25.2	3.1	.8	17.3	1.3	2.6	25.3	22.9	3.2	.3	—1.1	†
1953	27.2	3.4	.8	18.7	1.5	2.8	27.0	24.6	3.3	.3	—1.2	—.1
1954	28.8	3.7	.8	19.7	1.7	2.9	29.9	27.4	3.4	.4	—1.4	—1.1
1955	31.4	4.1	1.0	21.4	1.8	3.1	32.7	30.1	3.7	.5	—1.6	—1.3
1956	34.7	4.7	1.0	23.6	2.0	3.3	35.6	33.0	3.8	.5	—1.7	—.9
1957	38.2	5.2	1.0	25.5	2.3	4.2	39.5	36.6	4.2	.5	—1.8	—1.4
1958	41.6	5.6	1.0	27.0	2.5	5.6	44.0	40.6	4.6	.6	—1.8	—2.3
1959	46.0	6.3	1.2	28.9	2.7	6.8	46.8	43.3	4.8	.7	—2.0	—.8
1960	49.9	7.3	1.3	31.7	3.0	6.5	49.6	46.1	5.1	.7	—2.2	.2
1961	53.6	7.7	1.4	34.1	3.2	7.2	54.1	50.2	5.5	.8	—2.3	—.5
1962	58.6	8.7	1.4	36.9	3.5	8.0	57.6	53.7	5.7	.8	—2.6	.9
1963	63.4	9.4	1.7	39.4	3.8	9.1	62.2	58.2	6.0	.8	—2.8	1.2
1964	69.5	10.4	1.9	42.3	4.1	10.4	67.8	63.5	6.5	.7	—2.9	1.7
1965	75.5	11.8	2.1	45.9	4.5	11.1	74.5	70.1	6.9	.5	—3.0	1.0
1966	85.2	13.7	2.2	49.9	5.0	14.4	83.9	79.0	7.7	.3	—3.1	1.3
1967	93.5	15.5	2.4	54.1	5.7	15.8	95.1	89.4	8.7	.2	—3.2	—1.6
1968	107.1	18.3	3.2	60.6	6.4	18.7	107.5	100.8	10.0	.0	—3.4	—.3
1969	119.7	21.7	3.4	67.0	7.3	20.3	119.0	111.2	11.6	—.2	—3.5	.7

FIG. 14–9. State and local government budgeting.

1970	135.0	24.4	3.8	74.1	8.3	24.4	133.2	123.3	14.1	−.4	−3.8	1.8
1971	152.2	27.7	4.1	82.2	9.2	29.0	148.8	136.6	16.1	−.2	−4.1	3.4
1972	172.2	34.6	5.0	90.0	10.6	37.4	164.9	150.8	18.6	−.3	−4.4	12.3
1973	193.5	37.2	6.1	98.0	11.7	40.5	184.4	169.8	20.1	−.8	−4.7	9.2
1974	207.7	39.5	6.7	104.9	12.8	43.7	206.0	192.4	20.2	−1.6	−5.0	1.7
Seasonally Adjusted Annual Rates												
1972: I	166.1	32.7	4.6	87.0	10.1	31.7	159.5	145.5	17.9	−0.2	−4.2	6.7
II	176.2	33.9	4.8	89.2	10.4	37.8	161.7	147.9	18.4	−.3	−4.3	14.4
III	175.8	34.6	5.0	91.0	10.7	34.4	166.5	152.4	18.9	−.3	−4.4	9.2
IV	190.8	35.5	5.4	93.0	11.0	45.8	171.7	157.4	19.2	−.3	−4.5	19.1
1973: I	190.3	36.2	6.0	95.6	11.3	41.2	177.0	162.6	19.5	−.5	−4.6	13.2
II	192.0	36.9	6.2	97.2	11.6	40.1	181.7	167.1	19.9	−.7	−4.7	10.4
III	194.6	37.4	6.1	99.4	11.9	39.8	186.2	171.6	20.3	−.9	−4.8	8.4
IV	197.3	38.2	6.0	100.0	12.1	41.0	192.7	177.9	20.8	−1.2	−4.9	4.6
1974: I	200.6	37.8	6.3	101.2	12.4	42.9	197.4	184.8	19.1	−1.5	−4.9	3.2
II	205.3	38.8	6.7	104.0	12.7	43.2	203.3	190.1	19.8	−1.6	−5.0	2.0
III	210.9	40.3	7.3	107.0	13.0	43.3	208.8	195.1	20.4	−1.6	−5.0	2.1
IV	− − −	41.1	− −	107.6	13.3	45.5	214.4	199.6	21.4	−1.5	−5.0	− −

*Wage accruals less disbursements have been subtracted from total. These were (in billions of dollars at seasonally adjusted annual rates) −.6, −.1, .0 and .0 in the 4 quarters of 1972; .0, −.1, .0, −.1, .0, and .0 in the 4 quarters of 1973; and .0 in each of the 4 quarters of 1974.
†Deficit of $41 million.

Source: Department of Commerce, Bureau of Economic Analysis.

governmental level is closer to the individual, the social goods and services provided are more specific and "visible"; that is, a local government (county, city, school district), faced by a real and immediate population, must provide schools, roads, sewers, street lights, police and fire services, and all the daily necessities of modern life.

The consequences of providing these state and local government services for rapidly increasing local populations have been a proportionately rapid increase in both state and local spending and taxation—a 70 per cent rise in five years for state and local taxes! In order to provide for these mounting expenditures, state and local governments have turned to many sources of revenue. The traditional sales (state) and property (local) taxes have been hiked to the "taxpayer rebellion" stage, state lotteries have been adopted, and newer areas of city income taxes and personal property taxes have been added. Even such additions, however, have not sufficed to meet the rapid increase in state and local spending needs; the result has been an increased dependence upon federal government taxation and a continuing buildup of postponed state and local needs. It is no secret to any newspaper reader that our large urban areas are in desperate need of funds to meet problems of urban renewal, mass transit, pollution control, and welfare services, not to mention demands for increased government salaries and police protection on the streets.

Given all these state and local spending requirements and their largely unmet needs for social services (have you ever read Galbraith's *The Affluent Society?*), perhaps you can see the seriousness of the financial problem. The basic conflict is one of greatly increased need for resources (social goods) vs. limited resource supply (represented by budget limits)—a basic economic issue; hence the current demands for increased federal revenue sharing or welfare takeover or federal-city contracting—all schemes whereby federal tax revenues may be used to meet state and local spending needs. At this point the authors can see no alternative to the continued growth of such spending-taxation pressures and continuous and increasing forms of "shared" spending between federal, state, and governmental levels. You, the citizen, will have to understand and vote on the course of possible remedies and the appropriate representatives.

One further point, in order to bring all this discussion directly to your attention: As we asked before, what do you pay and what do you get in terms of taxes? That is, have you ever figured out just how much of a tax bill your family pays annually (review Figure 14-2) and what you receive for these taxes? If you haven't, try your hand at the exercise in Figure 14-10. First, figure out all of your typical family taxes. Second, attempt to compute the value of social services received, figuring the value by estimating what you'd pay to a private company for such services if not provided by government. How good is the "tax deal" you get? We realize this is a difficult question, but weighing public costs and benefits—even if you must "guess"—is required to evaluate the "worth" of taxes paid.

"How High Are Taxes?"

The following exercise is designed to illustrate types of taxes and arising issues associated with such at different governmental levels.

Tax

a. The personal income (gross pay before taxes) of this family is $12,000 per year. With three children, their federal income tax amounts to 18% of personal income (deductions included), and state income tax is 1%. Total income tax is: _____

b. This family spends 95% of their disposable income (personal income minus income tax). Figure a state sales tax of 6% on this amount of consumption spending. The sales tax is: _____

c. This family owns a home in Los Angeles with a market value of $35,000. If the assessed valuation ratio is 25% and the total tax rate is $11.15 per $100 assessed valuation, their local property tax is: _____

d. Assume other federal/state/local taxes (car license, fishing and hunting tags, business license, etc.) amount to: $150.00
   Total taxes amount to: $_____

e. Total taxes thus amount to_____% of total personal income for this "typical" family. How does this tax bill compare to that of your own family?

f. Suppose now a local government bond issue (might be for new building at a community college or city council building or county park development) is up for your vote. The proposal entails a 20¢ increase in the tax rate (refer to "c" above), so a "yes" vote would cost this family $_____   Do you see the "tax revolt" issue?

g. Classify the above taxes noted as progressive, regressive, or proportional.

h. How do the above taxes affect the "fundamental questions" the American economic system must answer—government role in economy?

i. Can you figure out what you are getting for the taxes you pay and thus whether you are "getting your money's worth" (*MU/P*)? To do so, you would have to "impute" the value of federal/state/local social goods that you receive (as community college education, city police services, county flood control, state highway patrol, federal road construction, etc.) Try it and see how you come out.

FIG. 14–10. Tax exercise.

TAX FUNCTIONS

We've talked a good deal so far about types, amounts, and impacts of taxes. Let us now analyze more explicitly what a tax does in our modern U.S. economy. Basically, the functions served by taxes today are (1) to *allocate social goods production,* (2) *to counterbalance economic disturbances* in the form of fiscal policy, and (3) to *equalize income distribution.*

Allocation of Social Goods

It's probably obvious that if governmental units (federal, state, local) are to purchase and distribute social goods and services, there must be some mechanism for financing allocation. (Do you see here additional components of the *what to produce* and *for whom to produce* questions?) The many types of taxes we've discussed provide this mechanism. Recall that the *production*

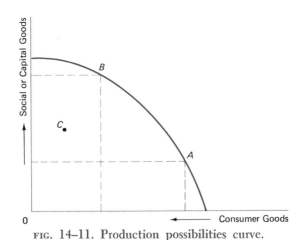

FIG. 14–11. Production possibilities curve.

possibility curve of Figure 14-11 illustrates society's ability to produce goods and services, whether they are intended directly for individual consumer consumption (*consumer goods*), for goods and services provided for the entire society and paid for collectively (*social goods*), or for such goods as machinery and factories necessary to produce other products (*capital goods*).

You may wonder what the production possibilities curve has to do with tax functions. How do taxes allocate social goods? Remember that the production possibilities curve illustrates that society must choose the mixture of consumer and social and capital goods it desires. Every society must decide how many of its limited resources will go for these types of goods. In our modern U.S. economy taxes are one mechanism by which resource allocation choices are made.

To see just how this choice process works, consider a "typical" issue of a tax override (vote to increase taxes) for local schools. The question is whether citizens will decide (vote yes or no) to approve higher taxes (property taxes at the local level) to finance new or improved school services. If the vote is no, citizens retain income to buy consumer goods, there is no increase in social goods output, and we stay at the same point on the production possibilities curve. However, if the vote is yes, taxes rise, citizens have less disposable income, and so they buy fewer consumer goods. There would then be more social goods produced, and this change in social choice would be indicated by a point further to the left on our production possibilities curve.

Do you see from the preceding example how *a tax serves to reallocate resources away from consumer goods output and into social goods production?* In a market economy, the use of resources is commanded by purchasing power (dollars!), and a tax shifts such purchasing power from the individual consumer to the governmental unit involved. Thus we have a move leftward (toward social goods) on our production possibility curve. The shift also represents an impact on equality of income distribution, depending on the types of taxes emphasized, the types of social goods provided, and the income groups affected. The allocation mechanism of taxes thus operates on both a macroeconomy level (what to produce; consumer vs. social goods) and a microeconomy level (for whom to produce; equality of income distribution).

There are two additional points to be noted on this tax function of reallocating resources. The first is that social goods are enjoyed and used by the individual consumer, just as are consumer goods, although the individual doesn't separately own or use up the social good. You may own your car (consumer good), but you also use social goods in the form of roads, bridges, fire and police protection, traffic courts, and so on. Although your use of (and payment for) social goods may differ from your neighbor's, the difference doesn't necessarily mean you're being cheated. Again, to evaluate your personal tax impact, you need to do a "cost-benefit" analysis like that of Figure 14-10. (Did you do it yet?)

The second point about tax reallocation of resources to social goods is that only on local government property taxes does the citizen vote directly. Although this type of tax is important, most taxes (sales tax of state governments and income tax of state and federal governments) are set, not by voters directly, but by legislators and federal congressmen (whom voters select) voting on the large issues of defense, pollution, poverty, education, energy, and so on. What this means is not that you as a citizen should just forget it. Rather, it means you'd better be sure you vote for a representative who votes as you'd wish, or get yourself another. On the one hand, this is "old hat," pushing for citizen involvement in representative government (yes, the authors do believe your vote counts!); on the other hand, there is obviously a need for economic understanding. How are you to choose representatives intelligently unless you understand the economic issues these representatives are to vote on and can evaluate the platforms espoused?

Countercyclical Fiscal Policy

The second large function of taxes today is that of counterbalancing economic disturbances. We introduced this function in Chapter 13, where we examined modern countercyclical fiscal policy, but let's review a few points here:

1. Fiscal policy seeks to avoid inflation or recession.

2. Inflation or recession often results from too much or too little total spending (termed *aggregate demand—AD*) in relation to total supply (termed *aggregate supply—AS*) at full employment.

3. Total spending may be influenced by the federal government's raising or lowering of either government spending levels (G) or taxation levels (T).

As we review the countercyclical tax function in Figure 14-12, let us suppose we have inflationary pressures generated by large amounts of spending relative to the goods and services available (*demand-pull inflation*). To offset this condition, the federal government would raise taxes. The result would be reduced consumer incomes, reduced consumer spending, and less spending pressure on prices. In a recessionary condition, where spending is too low to support full employment of resources, taxes might be lowered (as in 1975). This step leads to increased consumer incomes; increased consumer spending; and, consequently, to higher spending, output, and employment levels. (Recall the circular-flow economy model concept of Chapter 2? Run this tax logic through that model a bit.)

The preceding description of taxes as a fiscal policy device is only a review of the analysis in Chapter 13. There are many more complex issues if you want an advanced study. We have touched on the problems of inflationary and recessionary conditions, the types and amounts of taxes to change, and especially the "politics" involved in getting a majority (or one third plus one to override a veto) of the congressmen to agree on the direction and use of tax policies. The point is that tax policies are recognized today as having important effects on the functioning of our economy and that a tax is useful not only in the allocation of social goods. Remember that this countercyclical fiscal policy function exists mainly at the federal government level. State and local governments do not often attempt to offset inflationary and recessionary pressures.

FIG. 14–12. Countercyclical fiscal policy logic.

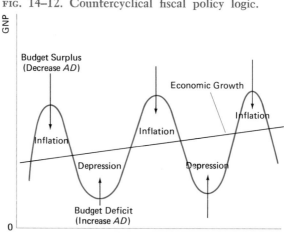

Families	1947	1950	1960	1966	1972
Lowest Fifth	5.1	4.5	4.8	5.8	5.4
Second Fifth	11.8	11.9	12.2	12.4	11.9
Third Fifth	16.7	17.4	17.8	17.8	17.5
Fourth Fifth	23.3	23.6	24.0	23.8	23.9
Highest Fifth	43.3	42.7	41.3	40.5	41.4
Top 5 Per Cent	17.5	17.3	15.9	15.6	15.9

Shares of Total Income (before Taxes) Received by Fifths of Families, Ranked by Income

Source: Department of Commerce, Bureau of the Census.

FIG. 14–13. Personal income distribution in the U.S.

Income Distribution Impacts

As you will realize from your own tax burden, taxes affect the amount of income received by any family. The greater the taxes paid (on an absolute or relative basis), the less disposable income is available to spend or save. Now the question is "How purposeful is this tax impact on income received?" Is there a particular level of income or trend toward equality of income aimed at in the design of a tax structure, or does this tax impact "just happen"? This is a basic question of tax reform to which we'll turn in the following section. At this point we assume that the income distribution impact of taxes is intentional, and thus we may speak of the *income redistribution function* of taxes.

FIG. 14–14. Lorenz curve of U.S. income distribution.

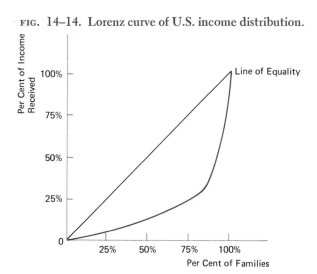

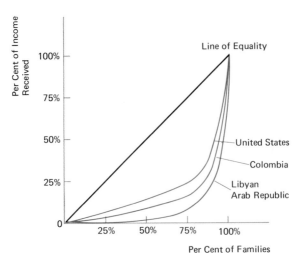

FIG. 14–15. Comparative income distribution.

Let us first make sure we're clear on the meaning of *income distribution* and relate our definition to Figure 14-13. By income distribution we mean the percentage of total income received by certain percentages and income classes of the population. So we may point to the 1 per cent of income that is received by the lowest-income 5 per cent of population as compared to the 16 per cent of income received by the highest-income 5 per cent of population. Where are you in this income distribution? Another way to view income distribution is to graph the statistics of Figure 14-13, resulting in a *Lorenz curve* like that in Figure 14-14.

Whether you consider Figure 14-13 or Figure 14-14, it is quite clear that income in the United States is not equally distributed. Although there appeared to be some gain in equality (a greater percentage to low income; a lower percentage to high income) through the 1950s and 1960s, this income equality trend appears to have stalled (perhaps even reversed?) in the 1970s. The relationship of these income distribution statistics to our tax analysis is that the overall U.S. tax structures (federal, state, local taxes combined) do not significantly affect the degree of equality in income distribution. Before we further criticize our tax system, you should realize the equality of U.S. income distribution is ahead of many developed nations, but behind some others, such as Sweden. Study Figure 14-15.

Now to the basic issue of tax impact on income distribution. Changes in our tax structure could produce greater equality of income distribution! Greater income equality could be achieved by emphasizing the collection of progressive income taxes, based on the ability-to-pay taxation principle. Fiscal policy could also concentrate tax expenditures on social goods and services for low-income groups. These policies surely contribute to greater income equality, especially if tax incidence is focused on upper income groups, if tax deduction provisions are reduced or eliminated, and if tax expenditures actually get to low-income groups instead of being soaked up in the bureaucratic maze of welfare administration.

Notice we've said changes in the tax structure *could* promote greater income equality. Given our complex political process and multitude of other economic goals, such tax reform is not an easy task! Let us examine the obstacles to it.

TAX REFORM

The last issue we'd like to explore—and perhaps the thorniest—is that of *tax reform*, perhaps more aptly titled "How to squeeze painlessly!" More seriously, tax reform refers to the many proposals that seek in some way to revise, modify, or replace our current U.S. tax structure. Such reform changes may be suggested at the federal, state, or local tax structure level and may consist of only minor patching or may represent an entirely new tax structure. The goals of tax reform may also be greater equality in income distribution or protection and promotion of some special industry (increased depreciation allowance for electric utilities to stimulate capacity expansion). Tax reform is not a simple objective, and perhaps little reform has occurred because different groups have different reform goals in mind.

One of the recurring issues in tax reform is that of *fairness*. Are the amounts and structure of a tax system fair to those paying taxes? Is it, for example, fair to have a condition existing in which the multimillionaire pays no taxes? Many of you might say this is unfair. But is it more fair to require greater taxes to be paid by those who exhibit incentive and effort to earn and retain higher incomes? Can you really define what, then, is fair? Should everyone pay the same or different rates (the progressive, proportional, regressive tax categories)? Should one pay taxes according to an ability to pay, or should he or she be taxed for benefits received? Which tax rate structure and which taxation principle are most equitable?

Don't feel confused if you're unable to answer these questions about what's fair, as there are few, if any, correct answers. Of course, many divergent opinions exist on the floor of Congress, in economic journals, and in college lecture halls. This text is not about to settle the question of a fair tax, and neither are most tax proposals. Let us, rather, bring out the issues involved in current tax reform proposals, centering on the issues of "income tax matchup" and "special-interest deductions."

A central issue of many tax reform proposals—and also a basic concern of tax fairness—is how much should be paid by various income groups. Note that this issue involves the ability-to-pay principle vs. benefits-received prin-

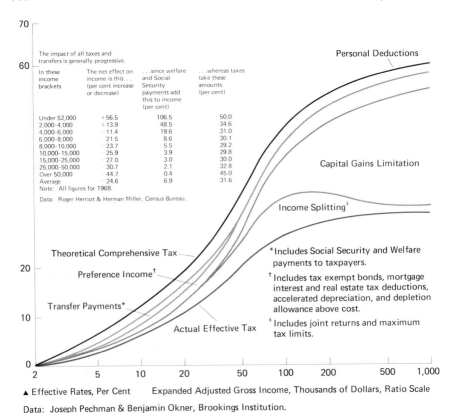

The impact of all taxes and transfers is generally progressive.

In these income brackets	The net effect on income is this... (per cent increase or decrease)	...since welfare and Social Security payments add this to income (per cent)	...whereas taxes take these amounts (per cent)
Under $2,000	+56.5	106.5	50.0
2,000–4,000	+13.9	48.5	34.6
4,000–6,000	-11.4	19.6	31.0
6,000–8,000	-21.5	8.6	30.1
8,000–10,000	-23.7	5.5	29.2
10,000–15,000	-25.9	3.9	29.8
15,000–25,000	-27.0	3.0	30.0
25,000–50,000	-30.7	2.1	32.8
Over 50,000	-44.7	0.4	45.0
Average	-24.6	6.9	31.6

Note: All figures for 1968.

Data: Roger Herriot & Herman Miller, Census Bureau.

Personal Deductions

Capital Gains Limitation

Income Splitting[‡]

Theoretical Comprehensive Tax

Preference Income[†]

Transfer Payments[*]

Actual Effective Tax

[*]Includes Social Security and Welfare payments to taxpayers.

[†]Includes tax exempt bonds, mortgage interest and real estate tax deductions, accelerated depreciation, and depletion allowance above cost.

[‡]Includes joint returns and maximum tax limits.

▲ Effective Rates, Per Cent   Expanded Adjusted Gross Income, Thousands of Dollars, Ratio Scale

Data: Joseph Pechman & Benjamin Okner, Brookings Institution.

Source: Internal Revenue Service

FIG. 14–16. U.S. income tax structure.

ciple, in that although high-income groups may pay large absolute amounts of taxes, they don't pay an exceptionally large percentage of their total income received. We have a conflict. Should we "soak the rich" by increasing the percentage of income tax they pay, even though this small group may already pay high total taxes? If we have higher taxes on the rich, would this reduce incentive to produce and succeed in our marketplace? Don't the lower-income groups use social goods even more than higher-income groups (for example, public vs. private schools)?

But some tax reform proponents will present evidence, as in Figure 14-16, showing that high-income groups may not really pay greater taxes and may even pay less. In fact, you've probably read of the millionaire who paid no taxes—the authors paid more taxes in 1971 than did former President Nixon! Did you?—or the multinational corporation paying a 1 per cent tax on gross earnings or the many legal opportunities to reduce tax liabilities (recall Chapter 10?) These exceptions and the tax deduction framework produce the dif-

Approximate Amounts of Taxes Lost to the Government because of Tax Preferences for Individuals and Corporations, in Year Ended June 30, 1973

For Individuals	Tax Loss to Government (Millions of Dollars)
Benefits from Personal Deductions	
State and local income, sales taxes	$5,300
Interest on home mortgages	$3,500
Charitable contributions	$3,375
Property taxes	$3,250
Medical expenses	$1,900
Interest on consumer credit	$1,100
Excess of standard over minimum deductions	$1,040
Parent's exemption for students aged 19 or over	$640
Child and dependent-care expense	$180
Casualty losses	$150
Benefits from Income Not Taxes	
Pension plans—company contributions plus annual earnings of plan investments	$4,200
Special benefits for the aged, blind and disabled	$3,735
Company insurance, other nonwage benefits	$3,260
Earnings on investment in life insurance	$1,200
Military benefits and allowances	$700
Unemployment insurance	$700
Veterans' benefits	$480
Workers' compensation	$375
Sick-pay exclusion	$225
Scholarship, fellowships	$125
Tax credit for political contributions	$100
Welfare payments	$65
Income earned abroad by U.S. citizens	$60
Benefits for Investors and Businessmen	
Special treatment for capital gains	$7,000
Exemptions of Interest on State, local bonds	$1,000
Special treatment of farmers' expenses, capital gain	$850
Investment-tax credit	$750
Dividend exclusion	$300
Excess depletion allowances	$300
Rapid write-off of rental houses	$250
Rapid write-off of buildings other than rental housing	$170
All others	$180
For Corporations	
Investment-tax credit	$3,050
Lower tax rate on first $25,000 or annual profits	$2,500
Exemption of interest on State, local bonds	$1,900
Excess depletion allowances	$1,400
Extra depreciation deductions	$850
Special treatment of corporations engaging in world trade	$590
Deduction of exploration and development costs	$580
Research and developmental expenses	$570
Treatment of capital gains (excluding farming and timber)	$400
Excess allowance for bad debt reserves for financial institutions	$400
Rapid write-off of rental housing	$350
Rapid write-off of buildings other than rental housing	$330
All other	$430

Source: U.S. Treasury Department.

FIG. 14–17. U.S. income tax deductions.

ference between *stated* and *effective* federal income tax rates. Given this dif-ference, it is not difficult to see why a supposedly progressive tax structure has produced little real change in equality of income distribution over the years!

This basic tax reform issue of tax rate and income level blends into the re-lated issue of *special-interest deductions.* By this we mean that our present tax structure (federal, state, and local) provides legal "tax breaks" for special reasons to various groups. These groups or individuals pay lower taxes for reasons including promotion, building new factories, developing mineral re-sources, aid to property owners, contributions to charity, losses on designedly unprofitable business enterprises, and so on. The types of deductions allowed amount to billions of dollars a year, as illustrated by Figure 14-17.

Again there are some very complex questions about such deductions, especially when viewpoints in Congress differ greatly as to the benefit of these deductions. Remember that a deduction is usually allowed in order to pro-mote some worthwhile activity, such as charitable contributions or construc-tion of new buildings and equipment. Although such deductions do mean lower taxes, they also represent societal benefits (charity funds or jobs cre-ated). Strict tax reform may raise the tax, but eliminate the social benefit. So where is the "trade-off" line between greater income equality (no deductions) and maximized social benefits from deductible expenses? How would you, as a congressman, vote on a tax proposal offering these two extremes (especially if your state has groups who benefit from the bill and support you in your election)? Is it best to attempt "patchwork" tax reform or begin anew with a wholly different approach?

The previous paragraphs may resemble a patchwork quilt of unanswered questions, but that's exactly what tax reform is. It's extremely difficult to an-swer one tax reform question without raising another, just as it's difficult to secure one social goal without depriving another. We wish to be fair, yet to provide incentive; to promote equality, yet to reward the ambitious. Such goals are difficult indeed to achieve, but remember that economics is the study of choice making!

It's one thing to discuss present U.S. taxes in terms of types of taxes, amounts of taxes, tax uses and functions, and issues of tax reform. It's quite another thing to say which tax structure is best. In fact, such a prescription is not the intent or prerogative of this text. The purpose of this chapter is to ad-vance your economic understanding so that you may better analyze and de-cide economic issues.

A *final issue.* Taxpayer: "What's the difference between *avoiding* taxes and *evading* taxes?" I.R.S. agent: "About ten years!"

TERMS

Ability-to-pay principle. A taxation philosophy under which those with higher incomes pay proportionately greater taxes.

Benefits-received principle. A taxation philosophy under which only those who receive social goods and services pay for them.

Incidence of tax. Determination of what group actually pays the tax.

Income distribution. The percentage of total income received by a certain segment of the population.

Lorenz curve. A graphic illustration of income distribution in which the actual percentage of income received by a percentage of the families is compared to perfect equality.

Progressive tax. A tax in which the tax rate increases at a faster rate than income rises.

Proportional tax. A tax in which the tax rate changes at the same rate as income changes.

Regressive tax. A tax (e.g., sales tax) in which the tax rate falls as income rises.

Revenue sharing. A collection of tax revenue by one government level (such as federal), to be expended by another government level (such as state and local).

Tax deduction. An allowance (reduction) against taxable income for some specific purpose (medical, charity, capital gains, interest paid, depletion, and so on).

Tax reform. Some proposal to change the tax structure for a specific goal (equitable income distribution, promotion of special interest, and so on).

QUESTIONS FOR STUDY

1. Precisely what is meant by a progressive tax? A regressive tax? A proportional tax?
2. What is the benefits-received theory of taxation? The ability-to-pay-taxes concept?
3. How do taxes allocate social goods?
4. Analyze a copy of the latest tax budget of your state or city. How does the cost of the direct services you receive compare with the taxes you pay?
5. Some people are objecting to paying taxes to support defense spending. Should people be able to pick and choose the taxes they want to pay?
6. How equitable is U.S. income distribution? How do taxes affect this distribution?
7. Secure a copy of *Your Federal Income Tax*, published by the Internal Revenue Service. What are some of the exemptions that are permitted to taxpayers?
8. How may taxes offset economic fluctuation?

9. Should the government adjust its expenditures and tax rates to keep the nation's economy stable, or should it base its decisions on how much it thinks is needed?

10. For what major purposes are taxes used in the United States (federal, state, and local levels)? What are the major tax sources?

11. Would there be any advantages in having the federal government collect all or most of the taxes and then redistribute the money to the states (recent revenue-sharing proposals)?

REFERENCES

Gordon, David M. *Theories of Poverty and Underemployment.* Lexington, Mass.: D. C. Heath and Company, 1972.

Kolko, Gabriel. *Wealth and Power in America.* New York: Praeger Publishers, 1962.

Pruger, Robert, and Leonard Miller. *Income Maintenance Programs.* New York: Modular Publications, 1974.

Sharkonsky, I. *The Politics of Taxing and Spending.* Indianapolis: Bobbs-Merrill, 1969.

Smith, Dan Throop, *Federal Tax Reform.* New York: McGraw-Hill Book Company, 1961.

Stern, P. H. *The Rape of the Taxpayer.* New York: Random House, 1973.

Tuckman, Howard P. *The Economics of the Rich.* New York: Random House, 1973.

Williamson, J. *Federal Taxation.* Glenview, Ill.: Scott, Foresman, 1971.

15

WHAT IS MONEY?

SHORT ANSWER. Money is a mechanism of exchange by which people trade goods and services, compare values, and store purchasing power. Its value depends on common acceptance and official recognition for use within a society.

YOUR USE OF MONEY

Have you ever wondered what money really is and what it does for you and other citizens? You walk into a store with a little green piece of paper and walk out with a useful and satisfying good. That doesn't sound too profound, does it? Consider, however, the significance of this transaction. The merchant exchanged a real and useful good or service for a green piece of paper (currency) or a little piece of metal (coin) or a piece of paper with your own name on it (check). You have an item that gives you satisfaction, and the merchant has the money. He can't eat, clothe himself, or derive any satisfaction from the money itself, so why did he accept your offer? Because he can, in turn, take the money to some other merchant and receive real goods and services that give him satisfaction.

Money Functions

The previous description of money use surely appears commonplace to you, for you exchange money every day for goods and services. But this simple

FIG. 15–1. Money in the U.S. economy.

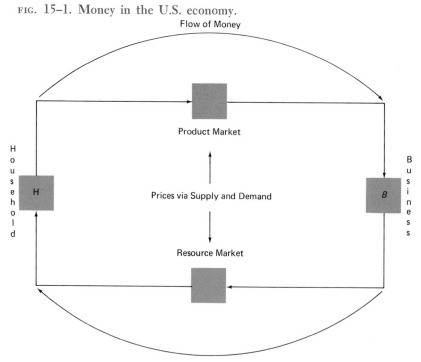

Flow of Money

Product Market

Household

Business

H

B

Prices via Supply and Demand

Resource Market

transaction perhaps illustrates one of the basic functions of money. Exchanges take place between individuals in a society easily because money functions as a *medium of exchange*. Because I will accept your money, we do not have to engage in direct exchange of products or labor (barter). Thus the use of money allows you to work at whatever career you choose, yet also shop at whatever location you choose because the money you earn is accepted at all stores. To the economist this money function allows *specialization of labor* (people work at only one task) to take place, thereby promoting rising productivity and economic growth. Did you ever hear about Adam Smith and the pin factory?

Let's consider another function of money that you also encounter daily—shopping. You are walking around a store and stop to consider whether you wish to purchase a record or a Kaywoodie pipe. How would you make a decision between these items without the familiar tags of, say, $4.98 and $6.50? Because these items are priced in terms of money, the common denominator (dollars in our society), you may compare values and make a decision to buy or not, based on the money you have and the estimated satisfaction you may derive from the items. (Remember the discussion on demand in Chapter 4?) This instance of shopping illustrates another function of money. Money provides a *standard of value* by which different items may be compared.

Consider the case when we choose not to spend our income today, but rather to save it in one or more of various ways—under the mattress, in a bank, in a stock, and so on—for future use. What we are doing here is holding purchasing power for future consumption. This third use of money illustrates a long-term function; money may be used to *store up purchasing power* for future uses, and your purchase decisions may be made on either a short-term or long-term basis. For the economist, such a choice between consumer spending and saving is very important. Not only are national output and income levels affected (recall Chapter 12?), but so is availability of credit, investment, and economic growth (more about these topics in following chapters).

We have illustrated three functions of money: *medium of exchange, standard of value,* and *store of value.* All of us rely on these various functions of money daily, as illustrated in Figure 15–2. We receive our income, pay bills, go shopping, and save. But to appreciate money impacts fully, let us continue our analysis of them in the following paragraphs.

MONEY IN THE U.S. ECONOMY

Historical Money

As Figure 15-3 illustrates, various forms (from furs to coins) of money have been used at different times in the United States. We have used both *commodity money* (cattle, furs, or other goods used for exchange purposes) and

Medium of Exchange

Standard of Value

U.S. Money Supply

Store of Value

FIG. 15–2. Functions of money.

fiat currency (government says a coin or piece of paper must be accepted for exchange purposes), with various coins and paper bills in between. Much of our colonial money was that of foreign nations (the British pound or Spanish *dólar*—see where dollar $ came from?). After the War of Independence (Revolution), our Continental Congress and early land banks added printed paper currency to the circulation ("not worth a Continental?"). Some of our U.S. monies have had strong backing in that the federal government would redeem currency for gold or silver at set rates. For the U.S. citizen, gold redemption ended in 1933, whereas silver redemption was discontinued in 1964. At present our U.S. money supply has no gold or silver redemption features. Actually, the history of U.S. monies is a study unto itself and worth your further inquiry. (See the references at the end of the chapter.)

All of these historical types were money because all were used to exchange

Commodities

Coins

Currency

FIG. 15–3. Forms of money.

goods, compare values, and store purchasing power. As you might guess, some
of these functions were not well done. Suppose the moths got to your furs;
what happened to your savings for next year? Also, suppose the item you
wished to purchase cost only half a cow; what did you do with the change?
The advantages of coins and paper currencies over commodity moneys are
readily appreciated. However, even crude commodity forms of money were
better than the alternative of no type of money at all. Ponder about what
would be required if no money were available. You'd barter. If you wanted
something another person possessed (ruling out warfare to acquire the item),
you'd have to trade something you owned and that the seller wished. Suppose,
however, he didn't want what you had to offer. Well, then you'd have to
trade someone else and then trade again with the first fellow. The use of furs
as money of a generally accepted value permitted exchanges; however, the
later development of paper currency and coins promoted comparison of values
and stored purchasing power.

U.S. Money Today

Let us now examine our present U.S. money supply (over $300 billion in 1976), as illustrated in Figure 15-4. Study first the components of M_1. (M_2 is a broader definition of money, used by economists to include assets quickly converted to money of the M_1 definition.) Notice that most of our money supply (M_1) is in the form of *demand deposits,* or checking account balances—about 80 per cent. Only 20 per cent of our money supply consists of the physical and more traditional *coins and paper bills.* The greater part of our money supply, therefore, consists of bank balances ("little, black accounting entries and sometimes red ones"), which are constantly on the move through the process of clearing checks and granting loans.

To anticipate some of your questions regarding the U.S. money supply, we now have a *fiat currency,* which is regulated by the *Federal Resrve System.* By a fiat currency, we mean that money is to be accepted because the government says so. There is no "backing" (gold or silver) to the money! In fact, in the United States no gold redemption has existed since 1933, whereas the exchange of silver for dollars was ended in 1964, when the greenback stopped calling itself a "Silver Certificate" and became a "Federal Reserve Note." Paper currency is printed (Washington, D.C.), and coins are minted (Philadelphia, San Francisco, Denver) by the U.S. Treasury Department, and both are put into circulation through the Federal Reserve banks.

At this point you may well ask, "But what determines the value of money?" We have seen that furs, coins, or slips of paper may serve as money in the functions of medium of exchange, standard of value, and store of value. To be blunt, anything could be money that people in a society agree to exchange among themselves. *Acceptability* is the basic determinant of whether something may serve as money. Perhaps you can best see this in looking back at the previous illustrations. If the merchant would not accept the money offered him, then it really wasn't money.

But now, another question: Why does anyone accept the money? Why, because he knows others will accept it when he offers it to them, just as you accept a check for a difficult forty-hour workweek because you know you can spend it. In short, if everyone believes everyone else will accept the item they offer for exchange, that item may serve as money. This may sound like circular reasoning, but it is quite true. In fact, let's add here an old axiom on "self-fulfilling prophecies": If everyone believes our money system is sound, we most likely will have few money problems. Thus *confidence* joins acceptability as a criterion for determining what is money.

There is a third qualification for anything to act as money: *sanction by some central authority.* In the United States the amount of money in circulation is controlled by our Federal Reserve System. Because people have confidence in the *Fed,* as it's quaintly termed, they confidently accept money.

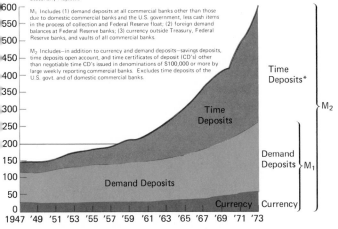

Money Supply and Its Components
Billions of Dollars
Average of Daily Figures
Seasonally Adjusted

M_1 Includes (1) demand deposits at all commercial banks other than those due to domestic commercial banks and the U.S. government, less cash items in the process of collection and Federal Reserve float; (2) foreign demand balances at Federal Reserve banks; (3) currency outside Treasury, Federal Reserve banks, and vaults of all commercial banks.

M_2 Includes—in addition to currency and demand deposits—savings deposits, time deposits open account, and time certificates of deposit (CD's) other than negotiable time CD's issued in denominations of $100,000 or more by large weekly reporting commercial banks. Excludes time deposits of the U.S. govt. and of domestic commercial banks.

Time Deposits*

Time Deposits

Demand Deposits

Currency

1947 '49 '51 '53 '55 '57 '59 '61 '63 '65 '67 '69 '71 '73

Time Deposits*

Demand Deposits M_1

Currency

M_2

The narrowly defined money supply (M_1)—demand deposits in commercial banks and currency held by the public —has been growing at a 3.3% average annual rate since 1947; in 1973 it reached an average level of $262 billion. When savings and time deposits (open account) in commercial banks and small certificates of deposit (under $100,000 are added to M_1, the aggregate is called "broadly defined" money supply (M_2). This has been growing at a 5.6% average annual rate over the same period and in 1973 it reached a level of $605 billion. If deposits held in savings banks and shares in savings and loan associations are also included, the third measure of money supply, M_3, the most widely defined, amounted to $1,000 billion in 1973.

*See M_2 for definition

FIG. 15–4. U.S. money supply.

SOURCE: Federal Reserve System.

However, we must add here that sanction of central authority alone will not guarantee worth. Society must have confidence in money supply control. Perhaps a good example is provided by the situation at the end of World War I, when the German mark became almost worthless. It was so worthless, in fact, that people were paid literally in buckets of cash, sometimes twice daily, and went shopping twice daily, for the purchasing power of the mark declined in worth through the day, every day. The German government said the mark was still of value, but destroyed confidence by a flood of newly printed marks. People did not believe the mark to be of value and instead used other currencies and retreated to barter for exchange of goods and services.

Perhaps we should add that for money to serve its three functions well, it must not only be acceptable, regarded with confidence, and controlled in supply, but also be

1. *Scarce.* This goes back to the confidence of people in the value of the money and to the control of issuance by a central authority.

2. *Easily divisible.* Money should be able to be "divided up" to make "change" in purchases. (Remember the example of half a cow?)

3. *Durable.* The money should "wear well" in usage, not only for immediate purchases, but for saving of purchasing power. (Suppose your fish rotted, your cows died, moths got your furs, or your gunpowder became wet.)

Just in case you're wondering if a *credit card* qualifies as money, the answer is no. True, you do use it to buy goods and services, but realize the "settlement" for the credit card use comes when the bill arrives, and you pay currency or by demand deposit (check). On the other hand, we should acknowledge the trend toward a "cashless" society, in which all transactions are conducted by card identification and automatic bank transfer of account balances. Imagine your "paycheck" automatically credited to your bank account, your monthly bills paid by account transfer, and any daily purchase debited directly to your account. (How does the likelihood of such developments strike you? Any "future shock" recorded?)

MONEY AND ECONOMIC ACTIVITY

Although we have described the functions and components of our U.S. money supply, we've said little about monetary impacts upon economic performance. Money, of course, promotes specialization of labor and by it increases efficiency and productivity. But there are also economic impacts that occur in direct relation to the *size and rate of the expansion* of our money supply. Note that money is not an economic resource, and thus it does not directly increase capacity or output.

Recall from Chapter 12 (national income theory) that levels of output, employment, income, and prices are determined by the volume of aggregate demand. For the practical force of aggregate demand, spending, to take place, there must be an adequate money supply to conduct economic transactions. The size and rate of the money supply expansion, therefore, compared to output capacity, can have important effects on inflation or recession. (M_1 has expanded some 3.5 per cent annually since 1947, with some increased rates in the 1970s.) If the money supply expands too rapidly (ΔM_1 exceeds output growth), prices may rise, whereas a lagging money supply (ΔM_1 falls short of output growth) may aggravate recession. Note that the amount of money available affects aggregate demand, not supply; the more money, the more aggregate demand—hence the greater the chance of inflationary price rises.

Actually, the exact role of the money supply in output-income determination is currently under much debate among economic theorists. Traditional *Keynesian* economists emphasize *AD* impacts with some monetary influences, whereas *monetarists* emphasize the impact of money on interest rates and price levels. The monetarist would claim that rates of change in the money supply *directly* determine economic activity, whereas the Keynesian would point to *indirect* monetary impacts. The monetarist argues that money supply is a prime economic factor in inflation and recession; the Keynesian, that it is a secondary or indirect one. Study Figure 15-5 for such impacts.

The authors see merit to both points of view, and perhaps you may judge the debate for yourself after we've analyzed bank operation and Federal Reserve Board monetary policy (Chapters 16 and 17). Money is unquestionably vital in our modern economy, and the *availability* (how easy to borrow) and *cost* (interest rate charged) of money definitely affect the rate of spending. The question (and focus of much econometric study) is the degree, mechanism, and timing of these monetary impacts. Before we move to discussion of these elements in monetary impact, however, let's clarify a few additional points about our money supply.

MONEY AND PRICES

As noted in the previous section, economists have long debated the role of the money supply in determining price levels. In fact, a common earlier economic theory held that the money supply directly determined general price

FIG. 15–5. Money impacts.

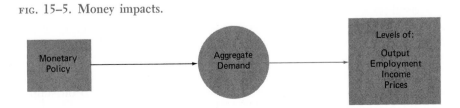

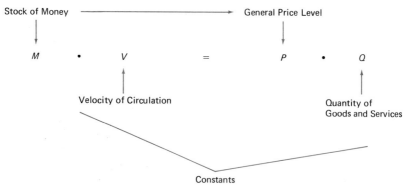

FIG. 15–6. Quantity theory of money.

levels. This classical economic theory, termed the *quantity theory of money* (see Figure 15-6), stated that the amount of money circulating (MV) would equal the spending on goods and services (PQ). The theory further stated that the *velocity of circulation* (V—number of times the money stock is used) and *output volume (Q)* were constants and did not influence M or P. The conclusion was that the money supply (M) directly determined the price level (P). Although present monetarist theory is much more complicated (V and Q are not constants), analysis of the quantity theory of money should help clarify the impact of money in the U.S. economy.

In case we lost you on the *velocity of circulation (V)*, V stands for the number of times the money supply is used (or "turns over") in a year. For example, the U.S. money supply in 1976 was about $300 billion, but total spending (GNP) was estimated at some $1.5 trillion. The velocity of circulation in 1976, therefore, was 5: Each dollar of money supply served in $5 worth of separate transactions. Actually, money works much harder than this, for remember that GNP does not include all spending (no resale items, no intermediate goods, no nonmarket purchases: see Chapter 12).

Another point to clarify is the "price of money" itself; *interest rates are charges for obtaining credit*. When you borrow money, you are really obtaining *credit*, so that the interest rate charge actually represents the cost of obtaining credit. As Figure 15-7 illustrates, there are many different types of interest rates, but they all represent a *cost of credit use* to some group. *Prime rates* are paid by large businesses; *discount rates* are paid by commercial banks to Federal Reserve banks; *Treasury Bill rates* are paid by the U.S. government; *mortgage rates* are paid by you and me. Interest rates are important, as they affect the degree to which various groups borrow money and, consequently, the level of total spending (recall Figure 15-5?).

Not only are *interest rates the price of credit*, but interest rates are themselves determined by market forces for credit (review Chapter 6 on supply-

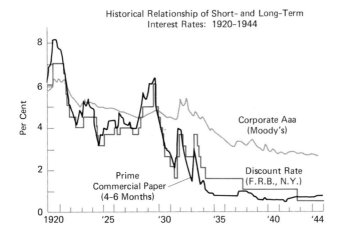

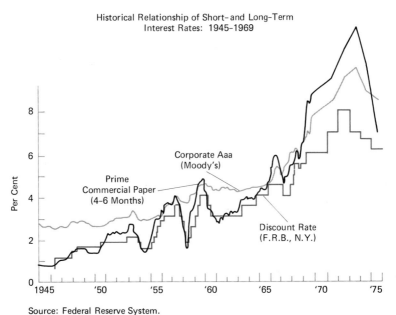

Source: Federal Reserve System.

FIG. 15–7. Types of interest rates.

demand theory). Figure 15-8 illustrates that the supply of loanable funds (consumer savings, bank loans, and so forth) and the demand for those funds (borrowing by consumer, business, government groups) determine interest rates in general, with specific interest rates determined by specific supply-demand conditions. (There are some government regulations involved here also, and we'll discuss Federal Reserve Board monetary policy in Chapter 17.)

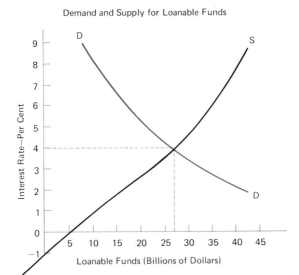

FIG. 15–8. Interest rate determination.

Money Versus Prices

Now that we have described U.S. money types and functions and have analyzed monetary impacts on economic activity, we must not fail to distinguish money and prices. *Money and a price are not the same thing.* Price is always stated in terms of the prevailing money. For example, a price of $5,400 for a Fiat sports car consists of two things, a *ratio of exchange* (number of items to number of monetary units) and the *monetary units* (dollars). Of course, money and price are always stated together, so perhaps this is a moot point to bring up and should not confuse anyone. But in barter the ratio of exchange is one or more cows for a horse or an apple for a peanut butter sandwich, and no money is involved. Thus a price exists whenever an exchange occurs (so many somethings for something else), although use of money surely simplifies the exchange and promotes economic activity

Another, more interesting point is how the value of money has declined in terms of *purchasing power*. This might also illustrate the difference between money and price. We have had the U.S. dollar since 1792, but it is not worth as much—its purchasing power has declined—compared to previous years. This problem, and indeed it is considered a problem by many in the United States at present, is properly termed *inflation*. Chapter 12 examined this shrinkage in value of the U.S. dollar over time. What this means is that it now requires more dollars to buy the same item than it did in 1939 or 1967.

True, the quality of items changes, but the decline in purchasing power is no less real if you are retired and are trying to live on past savings or a fixed pension. Your income is fixed, but prices continue to rise.

What causes inflation? We analyzed the aggregate demand explanation in Chapter 12 on the basis that inflation may generally be traced to demand-pull or cost-push (or a combination of both, as is common) forces in the economy. *Demand-pull inflation* means that because there is much money available and because people are trying to spend quickly and in great amounts, prices are pulled up. *Cost-push inflation* means that because costs of production increase, prices on final products rise to maintain profit margins for the producer and merchant. Note that although this explanation of inflation (especially the demand-pull type) emphasizes the aggregate demand approach, there is much room for monetary impacts as well. As we've discussed previously, the size and rate of expansion of the money supply may well slow or speed inflationary pressures.

How are such inflationary pressures to be controlled? Fiscal and monetary policy are necessary if inflation is to be limited from demand-pull pressures (fiscal policy to control government and consumer spending and monetary policy to control the volume of money issued). On the cost-push side, productivity (the amount produced per resource input) must increase as fast as, or faster than costs of production, and unionized or other demands for wage increases must be proportionate to such productivity.

TERMS

Commodity money. A noncurrency money consisting of physical items such as furs, cattle, gunpowder, or shells.

Currency. One portion (about 20 per cent) of the U.S. money supply, consisting of coins and paper bills.

Demand deposit. A checking account in a commercial bank allowing withdrawal at any time that composes 80 per cent of our U.S. money supply.

Federal Reserve System. The U.S. central banking agency, formed in 1913 to ensure an adequate supply of money and credit.

Fiat currency. A type of currency required by the government as acceptable in exchanges, but with no gold or silver backing.

Inflation. The increase of general price levels over time, which results in the loss of purchasing power for the currency used.

Monetarist. One who follows an economic theory that emphasizes the impact of changes in the supply of money on levels of economic activity.

Money. An item that is widely accepted by the public to serve the functions of medium of exchange, standard of value, and store of value.

Quantity theory of money ($MV = PQ$). A classical explanation of price level determination, in which the stock of money (M) directly determined the general price level (P). (Velocity of circulation [V] and output volume [Q] were assumed to be constant.)

Specialization of labor. A working condition in which a worker engages in a single, repetitive task, thereby increasing productivity.

Velocity of circulation (V). The number of times the stock of money is reused in the conduct of economic transactions.

QUESTIONS FOR STUDY

1. Name three functions that money provides.
2. How does commodity money differ from fiat currency?
3. Why are counterfeiters punished by law?
4. Suppose there were no money available in our society. How would your daily activities differ?
5. Is it true that currency is the largest component of the U.S. money supply, whereas demand deposits constitute only 20 per cent of our money?
6. Can a credit card be considered money?
7. What is the difference between a price and money?
8. Where does money come from? Who prints, coins, and issues it?
9. What currently "backs" the U.S. money supply? Why is the dollar accepted?
10. How does money affect economic activity? How do these impacts differ from those of changes in aggregate demand?
11. State the quantity theory of money, and define the four components. What does this theory explain?

REFERENCES

Chandler, Lester V. *The Economics of Money and Banking,* Sixth Edition. New York: Harper & Row, 1974.

Federal Reserve System. *Your Money Supply.* Washington, D.C.: Board of Governors, 1963.

Friedman, Milton. *Dollars and Deficits.* Englewood Cliffs, N.J.: Prentice-Hall, 1972.

Galbraith, John Kenneth. *Money: Whence It Came, Where It Went.* Boston: Houghton Mifflin, 1975.

Gill, Richard T. *Economics: A Text with Readings,* Second Edition. Pacific Palisades, Calif.: Goodyear Publishing Company, 1975. Chapter 11 and Great Debate 2.

Prager, J. *Monetary Economics*. New York: Random House, 1971.

Ritter, Lawrence S., and William L. Silber. *Money*. New York: Basic Books, 1970.

Rogers, A. J., III. *Goods and Not-So-Goods*. Hinsdale, Ill.: The Dryden Press, 1972.

16

WHY DO WE NEED BANKS?

SHORT ANSWER. Our banking system clears checks, channels consumer savings to loans and investments, and exercises control over the money supply.

YOU AND BANKS

How important is a bank to you? How many times have you been in a bank? Do you have a checking account or savings account at a bank? Have you ever received a loan from a bank? Have you ever received a check from someone else and cashed it at a bank? Do you have installment purchases financed by a bank? Do you know anyone working in a bank? Your answer to these questions will reveal how much contact you have with our banking system, and the questions themselves illustrate bank functions. Now, how important do you feel a bank is?

Banks existed long before there was a United States. Our modern banking system has evolved over a long process to perform many important functions in our present-day economy. These functions are important not only to your own daily economic activity, but also in our entire economy's operation. Banks promote your daily transactions (check clearing), provide credit (loans) for your purchases and for business investment, and represent the mechanism (monetary policy) controlling the money supply. Commercial bank structure and operation form an important institution, the economic understanding of which is well worth your study.

Let's begin by looking at what a *single* bank does directly for you. To start, let's think of services a local bank might provide. A local bank is a business and must compete with other banks for customers and profit. The services of most banks include checking accounts, saving accounts, and loans.

Banks and Savings

Perhaps your parents opened a *savings account* (termed a *time deposit*) for you at a local bank in your early years, and you know you're paid interest

FIG. 16–1. Banks channel savings to investment.

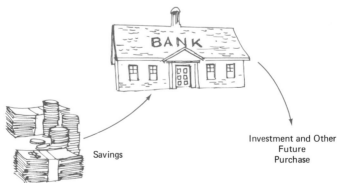

Savings

Investment and Other
Future
Purchase

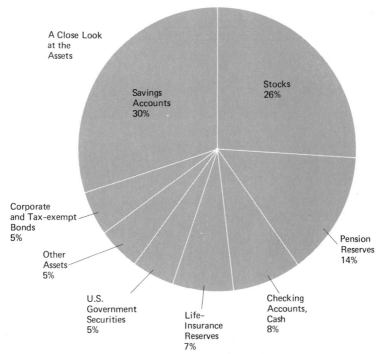

A Close Look
at the
Assets

Savings
Accounts
30%

Stocks
26%

Corporate
and Tax-exempt
Bonds
5%

Other
Assets
5%

U.S.
Government
Securities
5%

Life–
Insurance
Reserves
7%

Checking
Accounts,
Cash
8%

Pension
Reserves
14%

FIG. 16–2. Savings composition.

by the bank on money in your account. Many people have savings accounts in banks, and such accounts are important in sustaining the possibility of future spending as well as earning interest income for savers. Economists are most interested in these savings amounts, for they represent stored purchasing power capable of greatly increasing aggregate demand at consumer discretion. Figure 16-2 gives some comparison between consumer savings held at commercial banks and those held in other savings institutions. Figure 16–2 also indicates that commercial banks are not identical with other *financial intermediaries* (other financial institutions such as savings and loan associations, credit unions, and so on).

As a part of the entire economy, your savings account is important because it represents loanable funds that can be borrowed by other consumers or businesses. Such borrowing generates additional aggregate demand, thus affecting levels of output, employment, income, and prices. (Recall Chapter 12?) As your savings earn interest for you and provide a "nest egg," they also may enable another consumer to buy a new car or a business to build a new factory. Even small savings accounts are very important in keeping the economy moving and in helping to provide jobs for others. Can you place banks within the circular-flow process of spending within our economy? (See Figure

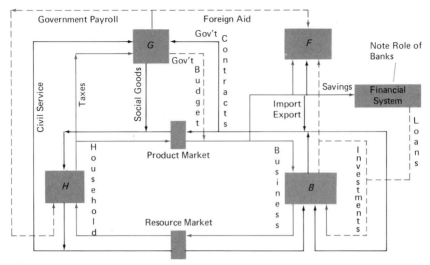

FIG. 16–3. Banks in the circular flow.

16-3.) Note that banks are the middle person or intermediary in getting your savings back into the spending flow as consumption or investment.

To pursue the importance of saving in our national economic operation, let's consider what is known as the *paradox of thrift*. We've said that consumer saving is important to the individual's financial security and supplies a basis for bank loans to consumers and businesses. That's true, but saving can go "too far." By this we mean that if the rate of savings exceeds the rate of investment so that savings cannot return to the spending flow (as in Figure 16-3), then aggregate demand will begin to decrease: Increased saving means decreased consumption. As AD falls, so will output, employment, and income. But if consumer incomes are lower, consumers can't save as much (recall APS and MPS from Chapter 4?). Do you now see the paradox of thrift? Economy-wide attempts to increase saving may actually lead to decreased saving.

The *paradox of thrift* is not presented here to discourage saving. Saving is necessary for an expanding economy, especially for capital stock formation (business investment). But there must be a "balance" of saving and investment, or economic problems of recession or inflation develop.

Banks and Checks

In addition to your savings account, you may well have a checking account—*demand deposit*, as it's termed by bankers—at your local bank. The differences between a checking and savings account are usually

1. *Withdrawal limits.* A checking account may be reduced (by writing a check) at any time. But withdrawal of funds from a savings

account may require some "waiting period" or a minimum deposit time in order to earn interest.

2. *Interest.* A savings account earns interest for you, whereas a checking account usually does not. Checking accounts, in fact, often charge a fee for each check written and serviced or require the maintenance of some minimum balance in the account that allows the bank to regard a portion of the account as savings, that is, as a sum the bank may loan or invest.

Function. The most frequent use of a checking account is the regular payment of bills; a savings account is assumed to be a deposit made for some period during which there will be few withdrawals.

In general, most consumers come into contact with checks daily in paying their bills and in receiving their income. As we stated in Chapter 15, the U.S. money supply of over $300 billion consists mainly of demand deposits. This large part of our money supply consists not of coins or paper currency, but rather of accounting records at banks, represented by all the checks floating around. A good way to verify this ratio is to add up during one month your or your family's purchases made by check and those made by coin and currency payments. Which sum is larger, and by how much? In what form do you receive your income? Does it make any difference to you or your creditors whether the payment is by check or in cash?

The total of check transactions in 1973 was over 27 billion checks written in the United States, representing some $30 billion changing hands! These checks were drawn on some 94 million demand deposit accounts and cost commercial banks about $5.4 billion (about twenty cents per check to process). That's a lot of checks! As these checks are in the process of clearing (prior to being charged to an account), a great deal of *float, or free credit,* is created; that is, between the time you write a check for some item and the time your bank honors the check by deducting the amount from your demand deposit (perhaps three to ten days, depending on deposit circumstances), you, in effect, have a loan of that money without charge. Of course, your bank also receives the use of your demand deposit without having to pay you interest on it.

From your own point of view, your contact with a check begins when you write it and give or send it to someone; the cycle ends later in the month when the check is returned to you "canceled" from your bank. (Ever look at the stamps on the back of the check to see where it's been?) Actually, a great deal of activity goes on between your writing a check and receiving it canceled; what goes on is generally known as the *clearing process*. Briefly, the clearing process includes the following:

1. You write the check and give or mail it to someone.

2. Someone, the payee, receives your check and deposits it in his or

her checking account in his or her bank (probably a different bank from yours).

3. The payee's account is increased by the amount of the check, and the payee's bank then sends the check to a Federal Reserve Bank. (More on this in Chapter 17.)

4. The Federal Reserve bank increases the account (yes, commercial banks have accounts just as you do) of the bank sending in the check and reduces the account of your bank by the check amount. The check is then sent as "cleared" to your bank.

5. Your bank receives the check and reduces your account. At month's end, a statement is sent you of amounts received and spent and balance ending, along with the canceled checks (many of which people keep as receipts of bills paid).

If this sounds like a complicated process, perhaps Figure 16-4 makes things clearer; check the preceding listing against this "picture process."

You'll note in the "clearing" example of Figure 16-4 that your bank was involved with other commercial banks, as well as with Federal Reserve Banks. The entire operation is known as our *Federal Reserve System*, of which your bank is probably (but not necessarily) a member. It should be noted that in Figure 16-4 the clearing process is often shortened by use of a *local clearinghouse* operation. *Clearinghouse* means that banks in one area exchange checks directly with each other, then send reports of such completed exchanges to the Federal Reserve Bank.

Thus far we've described the check clearing process from an individual point of view, that is, from its impact on you and other demand deposit holders. But there is another much more important impact of this clearing process on the economy as a whole—the ability of commercial banks to make loans. Checks are cleared at the Federal Reserve Banks by drawing down (the bank on which check is written) and adding to (the bank to which check is deposited) reserve accounts of commercial banks. These reserve accounts provide both the mechanism to clear checks and a limit to bank loan expansion. Only a fraction (the *required reserve ratio* is now about 15 per cent) of your demand deposit must be held in reserve by commercial banks in their accounts at Federal Reserve Banks. The remainder may be used by the commercial bank to make loans or to purchase other income-earning assets. As checks are cleared against these reserve accounts, the ability of commercial banks to make loans will change. And as loans vary, so does spending (aggregate demand) and, proportionately, the levels of output, employment, income, and prices. Although we'll explain this process more fully in the following section, do you see the importance of those 27 billion checks "floating" around?

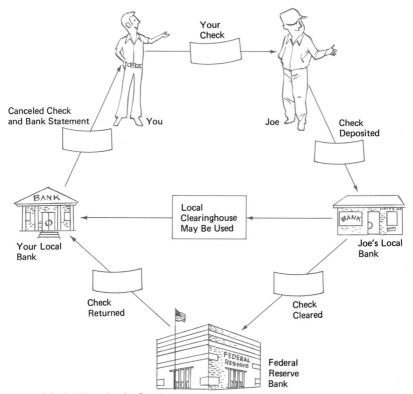

Your Check

You

Joe

Check Deposited

Canceled Check and Bank Statement

Local Clearinghouse May Be Used

BANK

Your Local Bank

Joe's Local Bank

Check Returned

Check Cleared

FEDERAL RESERVE

Federal Reserve Bank

FIG. 16–4. The check clearing process.

Although all the behind-the-scenes aspects of check procedure may sound a bit hazy to you, we've described it to make you aware that you probably take a lot for granted when you assume that your check will be properly cashed, credited, and returned to you in statement form, which, indeed, usually occurs. If you wish much more in-depth description of banking practices, read Chapters 6 and 7 of *The Bankers* by Martin Mayer (see the reference at chapter end).

BANKERS AND LOANS

There's one more very typical and very important banking service you may well have experienced, *bank loans*. From your own personal point of view, the significance of a bank loan (direct or installment loan) may have been the car or home or appliance you thereby purchased. From a total-economy viewpoint, the importance of bank loans is their effect on aggregate demand, which, in turn, determines output, employment, income, and so on, in our circular-flow process. (Recall this from Chapter 12?) Bank loans and the resulting supply of credit for spending are thus important to both you and our entire economy.

Types of Loans

When we say "bank loan," we mean that you, the consumer or business or government agency, are borrowing money from a bank. This may be a *direct bank loan* (you borrow directly from the bank, as on a promissory note), or it may be through an *installment loan* (you buy from some retailer, who "sells" your loan to a bank). These types of bank "loans" (more properly termed *credit*) may look quite different, but they have the same effect of allowing you, the consumer, to purchase now and pay later. One consumer economics caution here is to watch that *buy now, pay later* philosophy, or you may end up, like many, in bankruptcy. You should also do a bit of "shopping around" when you borrow because interest rates differ. A direct bank loan is usually at a lower interest charge than an installment loan rate, and a credit union loan charge may be lower than both.

Although all forms of bank loans may increase consumer spending, how each affects spending is a unique process. If it's a direct bank loan (promissory note), you go no further than the bank; and, if the loan is approved, the amount is usually added to your checking account. (Do you see that money—new demand deposits—has been *created* by the loan?) From then on, you write checks, and they clear by the process described previously in this chapter. Note that you'll have to pay back the loan plus interest in a lump sum in the future or through an established number of repayments of a specified amount spread over a given time.

On the other hand, you may receive a *credit card*, often issued by banks themselves—BankAmericard or Master Charge card—or by individual businesses with bank finance backup, and make purchases with businesses accepting these cards. You receive monthly statements and are charged interest on the balance not repaid at the time of the first billing. Note that recent federal legislation requires a full statement of finance charges and that these interest charges may run as high as 18 per cent annually. Use credit cards for convenience but attempt to pay off your balance at billing time to avoid delayed repayment interest charges!

A third way to receive a bank loan and one in which you don't contact the bank directly is by *installment contract*. In this case you buy an item on contract from a business, and the business sells this contract (purchase amount plus interest less bank finance fee) to a bank. This process allows the business to be paid immediately, and the borrower usually receives a coupon book of installment loan forms from the bank. Again notice how bank credit promotes retail sales, output, employment, and incomes, especially for "big-ticket" (autos, appliances, and so on) items. Although the initiation of installment loans dates back to the "Morris Plan banks" of 1910, the practice has since greatly increased in size and frequency, totaling some $75 billion in outstanding consumer installment debt in 1976.

In all these varieties of consumer credit, recall again the important impact of you, the consumer, receiving credit to purchase goods and services. If you multiply yourself by the total number of other consumers receiving credit, you'll get an idea of the very important effect credit has in our economy. (The total of all consumer installment credit was over $160 billion in 1976.)

Bank loans also go to government agencies (financing of bond sales by school districts, for example) and to businesses (stocks and bonds, accounts receivable, prime rate loans, and so on). These loans, too, add to aggregate demand through increases in government spending for social goods and business spending for capital goods. Without this credit extension by commercial banks ($174 billion in 1976), such social provision and economic expansion would be greatly limited. Indeed, bank loans have a significant impact on our national economy. And remember that credit expansion promotes not only the purchases made through the loans, but the output, employment, income, and multiplied spending results of the initial spending. Study Figure 16-5.

Loan Mechanics

As we've emphasized the importance of credit expansion by commercial banks, we should more thoroughly analyze its impacts on economic activity; that is, exactly what happens when a loan is made? Although we've hinted previously at the process, let's draw it together here, using a simple *T-Account* as in Figure 16-6.

Figure 16-6 illustrates a very simple *balance sheet* approach to analyzing

FIG. 16–5. Credit expansion promotes economic growth.

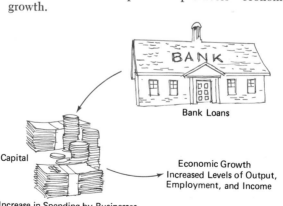

BANK

Bank Loans

Capital

Economic Growth
Increased Levels of Output,
Employment, and Income

Increase in Spending by Businesses,
Consumers, and Government Agencies

Banking System Worksheet

Basic Concepts to Remember:

$$RR = DD \cdot RRR$$
$$ER = AR \cdot RR$$

CB Loan Limit $= ER$
FRS Loan Limit $= ER \cdot M_B$

$$M_B = \frac{1}{RRR}$$

Basic T-Account Structure: $(RRR = 20\%)$

CB_1			CB_2			FRB	
A	L + C		A	L + C		A	L + C
$AR - 25$	$DD - 100$		$AR - 20$	$DD - 100$		$L - 200$	$AR_1 - 25$
$L - 50$	$C - 50$		$L - 50$			$B - 100$	$AR_2 - 20$
$B - 50$			$B - 25$	$C - 20$		$GC - 100$	$AR_N - 100$
$E - 25$			$E - 25$			$E - 20$	$G - 100$
							$C - 175$

Effect on T-Accounts: Make a Loan and Clear Checks (See Changes? Change in ER?)

CB_1 (Loan of \$5)			CB_2			FRB	
A	L + C		A	L + C		A	L + C
$AR - 20$	$DD - 100$		$AR - 25$	$DD - 105$		$L - 200$	$AR_1 - 20$
$L - 55$	$C - 50$		$L - 50$			$B - 100$	$AR_2 - 25$
$B - 50$			$B - 25$	$C - 20$		$GC - 100$	$AR_N - 100$
$E - 25$			$E - 25$			$E - 20$	$G - 100$
							$C - 175$

FIG. 16–6. Effects of bank credit expansion.

effects of credit expansion. We show two commercial banks $(CB_1$ and $CB_2)$ and a Federal Reserve Bank (FRB) both before and after a loan is made. Study the definition of terms in Figure 16-6, and then follow the loan process below:

1. CB_1 has the ability to make a \$5 loan, whereas CB_2 cannot make a loan initially. CB_1 has \$5 of excess reserves; CB_2 has no excess reserves.

   a. A commercial bank must hold a certain *required reserve ratio* (RRR—set by the Federal Reserve Board) of *demand deposits* (DD) on deposit at the Federal Reserve Bank (*actual reserves— AR*).

   b. CB_1 must have \$20 in *required reserves* (RRR of 20 per cent times DD of \$100 = \$20). Because CB_1 has AR of \$25, it has *excess reserves* $(ER = AR - RR)$ of \$5 and can loan this amount.

   c. CB_2 must also have \$20 in RR (RRR of 20 per cent times DD of \$100 = \$20). But because CB_2 has only \$20 in AR, it *has no ER and cannot make a loan.* If CB_2 attempted to make a loan, its actual reserves would be insufficient to service the checks drawn and cleared on the loans.

2. When CB_1 makes a loan, the money supply expands. Also, when the checks clear, other banks (like CB_2) can make further loans.

    a. When CB_1 loans $5, its DD expands by $5 and loans (L) expand by $5.

    b. As checks are written on CB_1 demand deposits, they will be deposited in CB_2, thus increasing CB_2 demand deposits to $105.

    c. When CB_2 sends the checks to FRB for clearing, the reserve account of CB_2 (AR_2) will increase by $5, whereas the reserve account of CB_1 (AR_1) will decrease by $5.

    d. The FRB then returns the checks to CB_1, which reduces DD by $5.

    e. Notice that CB_1 cannot now make further loans (AR of $20 equals RR of $20), but CB_2 has gained ER of $4 (RRR of 20 per cent times DD of $105 = $21 of RR; AR of $25 minus RR of $21 = $4 of ER) and can now loan $4.

The preceding enumerated example of credit expansion may appear tedious, but it warrants your careful study. By it you see in operation not only the "creation" of money (increased DD of $5 meant the money supply expanded by $5), but also the beginnings of the *multiple credit expansion process;* that is, notice how the initial loan by CB_1 allowed CB_2 to make a loan in turn (CB_2 gained excess reserves). If we continued this process (CB_2 loans would lead to other loans, and so on), we'd find that the total credit extended could reach a multiple of the original loan!

We will continue examination of this "loan multiplier" process in Chapter 17, and there we will further analyze the application of monetary policy by the Federal Reserve Board in affecting economic activity. The important issue at this point is that you understand exactly how a commercial bank *creates money when it extends credit* (makes a loan) and how such credit expansion moves through the bank system. Do you understand this process? (Review Figure 16-6.) Run through a loan by CB_1 to see what might happen if a bank attempted to lend more than its excess reserves. (It may end up "short" on covering RR, and thus the loan limit of a single commercial bank is its ER amount!)

HISTORY OF AMERICAN BANKING

After our previous discussion of multiple credit expansion, you probably realize that there's more to our banking system than your one bank servicing your accounts. In fact, there are over 15,000 commercial banks in the United States today, and about 7,000 are members of the Federal Reserve System. We'll discuss the Fed, as it's popularly termed, in detail in Chapter 17, but you should have noticed its coordinating role when we described the check-clearing procedure. Your bank, other commercial banks, and Federal Reserve

Banks are all involved in each check-clearing process, as well as in all savings and lending functions.

However, our present Federal Reserve System is of rather recent origin (Federal Reserve legislation was signed into law in December 1913 by President Wilson) and represents the culmination of a long, evolutionary banking history. In order to appreciate our present system fully, let's briefly review some of its history to see the origins of our present banking system.

Banking Prior to American History

The origins of banking may be traced as early as the seventh century B.C., when the Assyrians used commercial instruments recorded on clay tablets. In ancient Greece, funds were accepted for safekeeping, loans were made, and foreign and local coins were exchanged by money changers. In Rome, banking practices included money changing, receipt and loan of deposits, and the transfer of funds. Deposit slips were transferred fairly readily from hand to hand, serving as a substitute for money. Although the collapse of Rome reduced the need for banking facilities, moneylending activities were revived in the Middle Ages by the Jews and Moslems, because Christians believed they were forbidden to lend money at interest. ("Usury" was indeed frowned upon!)

The earliest Italian banks accepted deposits, but did not engage in lending. The Bank of Venice was established in 1171 by the Republic of Venice as a device for borrowing funds from the public from time to time. A similar institution, the Bank of Genoa, was founded about 1320. Not until the fourteenth century, when trade began to flourish in the cities of northern Italy, was money lending firmly established as a business. The real founders of banking for profit were the private banking houses established by families like the Medici, Peruzzi, and Bardi. In fact, the business insignia of the Medici firm, a cluster of three golden balls, is still used by pawnbrokers today. The private banks engaged in a wide variety of financial and investment activities, including the acceptance of deposits, lending of money, discounting of promissory notes and bills of exchange, and the transfer of funds. Checks came into gradual use for making local payments and were an important aid to the growth of trade, as the banking houses were able to *expand credit* by them.

As the *Commercial Revolution* spread to France, Germany, and the Low Countries, banking developed with it. The leading private banking house in the north was that of the Fuggers in Augsburg, Germany. This firm lent money to kings and bishops as well as to businesses and also aided in the international trading of the time. The private banks sometimes created credit without an adequate backing, and some failed. As a result, Venice established a *public bank* in 1587. This bank could take deposits, but could not lend or invest. Depositors could transfer funds by transfer of deposit slips or by addressing a written order to the bank. The Bank of Amsterdam, established in

1609, operated in a similar fashion. One of the most important functions of the public banks was to handle local and foreign coins because there were many different types of coins in circulation. The public banks accepted the coins and gave depositors credit on their books according to the metallic content, deducting a service charge.

In England, banking functions were performed by money changers and other merchants, such as goldsmiths in the 1600s. When the merchants kept their funds with goldsmiths, the latter quickly discovered that they could lend out deposits at a profit and began to offer interest to attract deposits. Payments were made by transfer of deposit slips and, later, by check. Promissory notes were regularly discounted (sale by a lender of a loan for less than the loan's maturity value in order to receive immediate repayment). During the seventeenth century a number of governments established banks to serve their own financial needs. These banks later developed into true *central banks* and survive today. The first of these institutions was the Bank of Sweden (1656). In 1694 the British Crown borrowed 1.2 million pounds sterling from individuals at 8.5 per cent interest and, as a further inducement, gave the lenders the privilege of operating a banking business known as the Bank of England. This bank was authorized to issue notes, thus furnishing for the first time a true bank note circulation. In the early nineteenth century, Napoleon Bonaparte established the Bank of France to permit a more efficient control over fiscal affairs.

From such banking history, one can see that a bank foundation of experience has been developed for American use and expansion. Notice especially the innovation of credit expansion, holding deposits, loans for interest, public banking, and a central bank system.

Colonial Banking

Although the American colonists desired to increase their trade and to improve their standard of living, they were handicapped by the lack of money. As a result, they began their long experiment with money and banking, which lasted for a century and a half between 1620 and the early 1780s. (Chapter 15 described some of the "commodity money" types.)

The most obvious way to get credit in sufficient quantity was to organize banks. In the Old World, accumulation of gold and silver had preceded the establishment of banks. In early America, however, banks faced great difficulties in building up adequate capital and specie reserves as a basis for their operations. Thus early banks were not always soundly organized by traditional standards. Nevertheless, banks did spring up and were able, through issuance of bank notes, to provide the money and credit needed to develop the country's resources and establish and operate farms and businesses.

And in this developmental process it is interesting to note that American banking developed as a part of our competitive private enterprise system (private businesses owned and managed by their stockholders and operated for profit), but was also an industry subject, then as now, to a high degree of governmental regulation. The government was particularly concerned with banks because they were custodians of public funds and suppliers of credit. Thus controls were imposed on banks to assure a safe, continuous, adequate, and efficient banking system. A large part of the story of American banking is concerned with efforts to achieve a satisfactory balance between the forces of private enterprise on the one hand, and an adequate degree of governmental supervision on the other.

Colonial banks were not banks at all as we know them today. They did not receive deposits from the public and did not regularly make loans. Their main purpose was to issue *paper money*. The shortage of money led to the organization of a variety of note-issue banks, some privately owned and some publicly owned. Most of these banks were organized by associations of landlords and were called *land banks*. The money (or notes) printed by these banks was backed by land. In addition, *specie banks* were organized between 1733 and 1739. These banks issued notes redeemable in silver in fifteen years.

These early colonial bank forms experienced problems because money was often issued beyond the needs of trade, and it began to decline in value. The colonists lacked both experience in controlling money and the means (a central banking system) to do so. Farmers generally favored liberal issuance of paper currency because they thought that a large supply of money would ensure high prices for their produce and help them avoid economic difficulties. Colonial and British merchants and other creditors, however, favored sound money because they feared that inflation would reduce the value of their outstanding loans. New England merchants appealed to Britain for protection against excessive issuance of paper money in Rhode Island. In 1741, Parliament enacted legislation forcing the Massachusetts land and specie banks to close shop. Ten years later, Parliament prohibited the New England colonies from establishing new land banks and from making bills of credit legal tender for debts. In 1764 these prohibitions were extended to all the colonies. Also in 1764, Benjamin Franklin, then agent for Pennsylvania, suggested to the British government that it establish a bank in the colonies and authorize the bank to issue paper currency, but the proposal was rejected.

At the start of the Revolution, the Continental Congress was in desperate need of money and had little authority. It could borrow money and spend it, but lacked the power to tax. Funds were urgently needed to pay the cost of military operations, and once again the only source available was the printing press. Congress had already asked the states to contribute money to its treasury, but they refused. Taxes probably wouldn't have provided all the revenue needed anyway, because trade among the states was suppressed, farmers could not sell their produce, and tax collections were poor. Between 1775 and 1780, the Continental Congress issued $242 million in paper money, which depreciated rapidly in value. Although the Bank of North America was important for the services in the Revolutionary War effort, it was also an important step forward in the development of our money and banking system because idle money could be deposited and borrowers could obtain funds from the bank on their promissory notes. In 1787 the bank received a charter from the state of Pennsylvania because of doubts over Congress's authority to grant bank charters.

In 1784 the Massachusetts Bank and the Bank of New York were organized. The first money ever borrowed by the U.S. government—$200,000— came from the Bank of New York through a series of promissory notes, then called *warrants*, signed by Secretary of the Treasury Alexander Hamilton in 1789–1790. By the turn of the century additional state banks had been established, most of them in New England. In 1802 the Kentucky Insurance Company was authorized to conduct banking operations west of the Alleghenies. The country's first three banks have withstood the pressures of history, and the Bank of New York still operates today under the same name. The Bank of North America is now known as the First Pennsylvania Banking and Trust Company, and the Massachusetts Bank is now the First National Bank of Boston.

Central Bank Beginnings

The history of American banking from the end of the Revolution to 1836 revolves around the efforts of the federal government to exert greater influence on banking through establishment of the First Bank of the United States and the Second Bank of the United States. When the new government was established in 1789, financial problems were predominant concerns; especially important was the need for a soundly based currency. The Constitution authorized the federal government to "coin" money, but it did not say anything about issuing paper money or establishing a bank. However, Secretary of the Treasury Hamilton forwarded a proposal to Congress for the establishment of a federally chartered bank. (One of the liveliest legal debates in American history!) A *national bank*, Hamilton argued, would provide a much-needed paper currency, would benefit government and business by providing sound credit, and would act as the government's fiscal agent and provide a facility for the safekeeping of government funds.

Congress approved Hamilton's proposal, and in 1791 the *First Bank of the United States* was chartered for a term of twenty years. The First Bank of the United States was essentially a private bank operating under federal charter, with the government a part owner (sounds like Amtrak today?). In evaluation, this first U.S. bank operated very successfully. Loans were made to businesses, federal government bonds were issued by the Treasury, and a start was made on a sound and stable currency. However, the First Bank of the United States had its opponents from the start, including state banks and others who felt that control over banking should be in the hands of state governments. When the proposal to renew the bank's charter was advanced in 1811, it was defeated. The bank was liquidated, and its assets were sold to Stephen Girard of Philadelphia (the Girard Bank), whose enterprise later merged with other institutions to form what is today the Philadelphia National Bank.

In 1816 a *Second Bank of the United States* was established. Again, opposition forces were strong, especially from President Andrew Jackson. The end of the Second Bank of the United States was thus certain even before its charter expired in 1836. The end of the Second Bank of the United States brought to an end for a long period of time the policy of regulating bank credit and the nation's currency through a federal bank. Until the Civil War it was left to the state banks to meet the country's needs for paper money. Federal control over commercial bank credit was not to reappear as a concept of national policy until the establishment of the *Federal Reserve System* in 1913. However, the first era of the United States banks did not end as a total loss. After it, principles of sound currency and good banking were understood more clearly and, in the older sections of the country, were embodied in general practice.

When the restrictions imposed on state banks by the First Bank of the United States and the Second Bank of the United States ceased to exist, the way was open again for an unbridled expansion of the state banks. The push westward and the great need for capital and credit to develop the country fostered their growth, and many local banks were hastily organized by profit minded promoters. Some limit to this growth occurred in July 1836, when the government announced that thereafter its land agents would take in payment for government lands only specie (gold or silver) or the notes of specie-paying banks. This restriction, in additon to crop failures and other developments, caused many banks to fail. Following these collapses, the *Independent Treasury System* was established. Under this system, money of the federal government was stored in Treasury vaults in Washington and at subtreasuries throughout the country, so that federal government and banking were completely separated.

The panic of 1837, a recession induced by monetary restriction, was but a temporary growing pain. The number of banks continued to mushroom. In 1820 there had been 300. By 1840 the number was 1,000, and by 1860 there were nearly 2,000 banks. The reason for the establishment of banks was the pressing need for credit to develop the new country, and these banks supplied credit in the form of both loans and investments. The need for currency was another growth factor, as after 1836 the only paper currency in circulation was that issued by the state banks. The state banks were operated soundly or unsoundly, depending on the ability and character of their owners and the effectiveness of governmental supervision. In spite of the many weaknesses of the pre-Civil War banking system, many banks within it maintained sound banking practices that later furnished the basis for the establishment of an effective commercial banking system. State banks furnished the bulk of the nation's money supply and were the chief institutional sources of credit and capital. Without them rapid economic development could not have taken place.

Civil War Banking

By the mid-1850s the country had felt the impact of the industrial revolution. The population had grown tremendously and industry had developed considerably. Transportation had also improved, with advances including steamboats, canals and turnpikes, and railroad lines. Banking in the early 1860s reflected the state of the country's overall development, with some large banks in the East and many small banks scattered throughout the country. The customers of banks in the 1850s and 1860s were businessmen, farmers, and governments. Banks did not extend personal loans as they do today; consumer credit was handled by storekeepers, who, in turn, borrowed from banks. Banks in the 1850s, particularly those in large cities, were becoming active in the acceptance of demand deposits, and checks were at that time in common use by shopkeepers and merchants. The *New York Clearing House* was established in 1853, and by 1855 checks had surpassed bank note currency as a means of payment for the nation as a whole. Savings by individuals at commercial banks were small, but a start was made in organizing savings banks. By 1860 there were 278 savings banks with 694,000 depositors and $149 million in savings deposits.

Although state regulation in some sections had eliminated many abuses, the country still had no strong, stable banking system. In periods of prosperity, banks frequently overextended credit, which fostered speculation and led to overissuance of paper currency. Booms sometimes got out of hand and were followed by collapses and financial panics. There was no central banking system, such as we have today under the Federal Reserve Act, to help banks in an emergency by providing them with additional cash reserves. Furthermore, the nation's currency was in a chaotic condition because the only paper currency consisted of bank notes issued by individual banks. (There were some 7,000 different issues in circulation in 1861!) Therefore, at the start of the Civil War the federal government found it necessary to direct its attention to the improvement of the nation's banking and monetary system.

At the outbreak of the Civil War, the federal government and state banks suspended gold payment on paper currency and silver coins presented for redemption. Soon thereafter, Treasury Secretary Chase sought to finance the war, in part, by printing paper money ("greenbacks"). The new currency enabled the government to finance some of its needs, but there was much discontent over its quality. There was similar concern over the continued value deterioration of the notes issued by state banks. Chase took this opportunity to reform the country's confusion of note issues and to provide a means for marketing government securities. He proposed a *system of federally chartered banks* authorized to issue notes backed by United States government bonds. The proposal was made law, and on February 25, 1863, President Lincoln signed the *National Bank Act.*

Under the 1863 National Bank Act and its subsequent amendments, nationally chartered banks were allowed to issue national bank notes up to 90 per cent (later, 100 per cent) of the amount of government bonds they held.

The notes were uniform in design and were engraved under federal government regulation. Each national bank was required to maintain redemption centers in large cities and to redeem its own notes. The new legislation was successful in providing a currency that gained the confidence of the public. Because the national bank notes were backed by government bonds, there could be no question of their soundness. In 1865, Congress enacted a law placing a 10 per cent federal tax on all state bank notes, which had the effect of driving them out of circulation. Thus, the nation came to have a *uniform national currency* for the first time in its history.

The first state bank to apply for a *national charter* was the New Haven Bank, now the First New Haven National Bank, in Connecticut. However, this bank received Charter No. 2; Charter No. 1 went to the First National Bank of Philadelphia. The number of nationally chartered banks increased slowly at first. Subsequent amendments to the National Bank Act encouraged growth, and by mid-1866 there were 1,600 chartered banks. Many banks, however, preferred to continue operating under *state charters* and did not come into the national system. It was thought in 1865 that the federal tax on state bank notes would drive the state banks out of business. However, the state banks were only slightly affected by the tax. State banks increased from 335 in 1870 to 12,000 in 1910, and to over 14,000 in 1913, when the Federal Reserve Act was passed. In 1913 there were 7,500 national banks. The system of national and state-chartered banks, which started in 1863, has endured to this day. Our banking system is thus called a *dual banking system* because we have both national and state banks operating side by side.

It was not long after the Civil War that flaws were detected in the new national banking system. The financial panics of 1873, 1884, 1893, 1903, and 1907 were attributed by many to the malfunctioning of the banking system. Difficulties included the system of *redeposited reserves* (national banks could keep part of their legally required reserves in the form of deposits with other national banks in larger cities), the inflexibility of bank credit, an inadequate currency system, and the complexities of an inefficient system of clearing and collecting checks. Although the National Bank Act was a decided step forward, it did not give as good a banking system as the country needed. It greatly improved the general quality of American banking, provided safety for our currency, and established the principle of federal responsibility for the issuance and quality of the currency. But additional changes were required to provide the strength and flexibility necessary in a banking system that would accommodate the demands of the growing economy without periodic setbacks.

The Federal Reserve System

Given the continued need for banking system reform after the National Banking Act, Congress appointed the *National Monetary Commission* in 1907. The commission's purpose was to devise a banking system to remedy the aforementioned deficiencies of the National Bank System. The commission did indeed formulate a proposal, and, in December 1913 President Wilson signed the Federal Reserve Act.

The *Federal Reserve Act* created our present Federal Reserve System, whereby we have a "compromise" of central monetary control through private enterprise bank concerns. Chapter 17 will deal with the Fed in greater detail, especially with regard to monetary policy, but it should be emphasized here that the system resulted only from the long U.S. banking history earlier in this chapter. Its particular structure and functions are a direct result of historical forces.

The functions of the Fed were specified in the act as requiring the Federal Reserve Banks and the Board of Governors to perform various *central banking functions:*

1. To supervise the member banks. Supervisory functions include issuance and enforcement of regulations, disciplinary action to remove bank officers and directors for unsafe or unsound banking practices, permission to holding companies to acquire stock in banks and to vote stock in member banks, and permission to member banks to engage in banking in foreign countries. Examinations of state member banks are conducted by the Federal Reserve; examinations of national banks are conducted by the comptroller of the currency.

2. To handle the clearing and collection of checks for both member and nonmember banks. This function is now performed much more efficiently than it was before 1913, and funds can be transferred from one part of the country to another with great speed.

3. To act as fiscal agents for the government, holding its deposits and assisting it in other ways.

4. To hold responsibility for issuing the great bulk of the nation's paper currency. Over the years, national bank notes have been gradually withdrawn from circulation. (National banks have not issued notes since 1935.) Starting in 1913, each Federal Reserve Bank has issued notes called *Federal Reserve notes*. These, together with coins issued by the Treasury, make up the nation's circulating currency (M_1). Federal Reserve notes represent direct obligations of the U.S. government.

5. To serve as reserve depositories for the member banks (recall the

actual reserves in Figure 16-6?). Each member bank is required by law to maintain specified percentages of cash reserves (required reserves) against its demand and time deposits. These reserves must be kept on deposit with district Federal Reserve Banks, except for any amounts (perhaps 2 per cent) that the member bank may choose to keep in the form of currency in its vaults.

6. To make loans (called rediscounts or advances) to member banks when the latter need additional cash reserves. Thus, if a bank is faced with unexpected deposit withdrawals or unusually heavy loan demands, it can turn to its district Reserve Bank for help (a discount rate is the interest charge). As we have seen, one of the weaknesses of our banking system before 1913 was the absence of any central reservoir of funds that banks could tap in emergencies.

Summary

After such a long historical survey, perhaps it's best to recap a bit. Our survey has revealed the initial great variety of bank types, the resulting monetary problems, and the slow recognition of need for a central banking system with strong regulatory powers. Again, realize our present Fed system is only some sixty years old, compared to a bank history in the United States of 350 years.

We've stressed in this chapter that banks affect both yourself and our entire national economy. In their functions as savings depositories, check clearers, and lenders and creators of credit, commercial banks indeed affect the economy levels of aggregate demand, output, employment, income, and prices. We'll get into the nature of these impacts, especially from a policy viewpoint, in Chapter 17.

TERMS

Actual reserves (AR). The amount of money held on deposit at Federal Reserve banks by commercial banks.

Clearinghouse. An establishment that charges a check to its bank of origin and credits the bank that received the check.

Demand deposit. An account balance in a bank that may be withdrawn without advance notice, for example, a checking account.

Excess reserves (ER = AR − RR). The deposits that are held by commercial banks over and above those required by reserve ratio, and that constitute the loan ability of the bank holding them.

Federal Reserve System. The U.S. central bank agency, created in 1913.

Financial intermediaries. Institutions that receive and dispense money and credit other than commercial banks.

Float. A credit without charge created by the time period during which a check is cleared.

Land banks. Colonial banks that issued paper money backed by property ownership.

Multiple credit expansion process. The spreading effect of an initial loan on total loan capacity throughout the entire bank system.

Paradox of thrift. The contradiction in economy-wide attempts to increase saving that lead to an actual decrease in saving.

Required reserve ratio (RRR). The percentage of demand deposits that member commercial banks must keep on deposit, as required by the Federal Reserve Board.

Required reserves (RR = DD · RRR). The minimum deposit that member banks must hold against their demand deposits.

Specie banks. Colonial banks that issued paper money redeemable in silver or gold.

T-Account. A simplified manner of showing assets, liabilities, and capital of a business operation.

Time deposit. A deposit that is not subject to withdrawal by check and on which the bank may require a specified period of notice of intention of withdrawal. Such deposits usually earn interest.

QUESTIONS FOR STUDY

1. What are the basic functions of commercial banks? How do commercial banks differ from other financial institutions?

2. What is credit? What types exist?

3. How do banks "create money"?

4. Can a commercial bank loan any amount of money it wishes to?

5. In a college community local merchants extend credit to new faculty members who merely state that they are employed by the college. Merchants are also liberal in extending credit to college students. Why?

6. Distinguish excess reserves from required reserves and actual reserves.

7. If a commercial bank has $200,000 in demand deposits, the required reserve ratio is 15 per cent, and actual reserves are $40,000:

    a. Required reserves are $_____.

    b. Excess reserves are $_____.

    c. This bank could loan a maximum of $_____.

8. What kinds of services do you receive from your local commercial bank? What is the charge for such services?

9. What is meant by "clearing and collecting checks"? How does this process occur?

10. Describe the process by which greater federal government control over our banking system was established in the United States.

REFERENCES

American Bankers Association. *The Story of American Banking.* New York: American Bankers Association, 1963.

Campbell, Colin. *Introduction to Money and Banking*, Second Edition. Hinsdale, Ill.: The Dryden Press, 1975.

Chandler, Lester V. *The Economics of Money and Banking*, Sixth Edition. New York: Harper & Row, Publishers, Incorporated, 1974.

Faulkner, Harold Underwood. *American Economic History*, Eighth Edition. New York: Harper & Row, Publishers, Incorporated, 1960.

Federal Reserve System. *The Federal Reserve System: Purposes and Functions*, Fifth Edition. Washington, D.C.: Board of Governors, 1963, particularly Chapters 1 and 4.

———. *The Story of Checks.* Washington, D.C.: Board of Governors, 1966.

Mayer, Martin. *The Bankers.* New York: Weybright and Talley, 1974.

O'Brannon, Helen B., et al. *Money and Banking: Theory, Policy, and Institutions.* New York: Harper & Row, Publishers, Incorporated, 1975.

Smith, Harlan. *The Essentials of Money and Banking.* New York: Random House, 1972.

Studenski, Paul, and Herman E. Kross. *Financial History of the United States.* New York: McGraw-Hill Book Company, 1963.

17

WHAT IS THE FEDERAL RESERVE SYSTEM?

SHORT ANSWER. The Federal Reserve System (usually called simply the Fed) is the U.S. central banking system. It formulates and implements monetary policy to affect the nation's money supply, which, in turn, affects the volume and availability of loans and commercial bank rates of interest.

YOU AND THE FED

As an individual, you probably have little direct contact with the entire Federal Reserve System (*Fed* for short). By the "entire" Federal Reserve System, we refer to the components illustrated in Figure 17-2. Although you may have frequent financial dealings with your local commercial bank, which may or may not be a member of the Fed (have you looked for a "member of Federal Reserve System" sign at your bank?), you as an individual do not bank at a Federal Reserve Bank and may seldom have heard of monetary policy decisions by the Fed's Board of Governors. You may ask, then, why is the Fed so important?"

The Fed is important to our economy because most of us are affected by its policies and operation. The activities of the Fed make possible the efficient operation of your own commercial bank, and the Fed's conduct of monetary policy determines to a great extent the performance of our economy. An examination of Figure 17-1 may give some indication of the Fed's impact on our economy, and the remainder of this chapter will analyze this economic impact in its various forms. Perhaps a more specific answer to your question is that Fed monetary policies determine whether you can obtain bank loans, what interest rates you pay, and even whether you are employed!

The most important Fed function is that of conducting *monetary policy* to modify levels of national output, employment, income, and prices. Figure 17-3 should indicate this function's impact. Monetary policy restricts or expands commercial banks' ability to loan, thereby contracting or enlarging spending components of aggregate demand and hence levels of output, employment, income, and prices. Does this sound important enough to warrant your pursuit of an economic understanding?

The Fed also supervises and makes possible the process of *check clearing*. Notice in Figure 17-4 that commercial banks and Federal Reserve Banks are an integral part of making this process work. By providing for a fast, efficient, nationwide check-clearing mechanism, the Fed facilitates your personal buying and the operation of our economy as a whole. As you may recall from Chapter 16 (review Figure 16-6), this check-clearing process also involves credit expansion and the issuance and control of our money supply. Commercial banks may loan only to a limit of their excess reserves. If they attempted to loan greater amounts, they would fall short of the Fed's required reserve amount as checks cleared.

Other important functions of the Fed that indirectly affect you include the Fed's service as fiscal agent for the U.S. government. Did you receive an income tax refund this year or a G.I. benefit, or Social Security check? Look at it closely to see where the account is held. The Fed also affects the entire

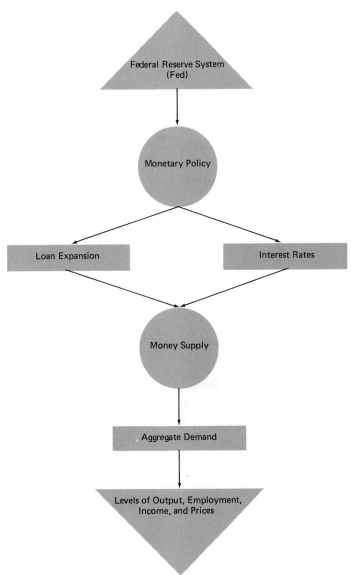

FIG. 17–1. Monetary policy by Fed affects the economy.

structure of commercial bank interest rates by varying its own discount rate (interest charged on loans to commercial banks). As the Fed raises or lowers the discount rate that commercial banks must pay to borrow, the commercial banks will, in turn, raise or lower the interest rates charged their customers. The Fed also serves as a depository for some of our nation's gold supply and handles flows of foreign exchange used in international trade.

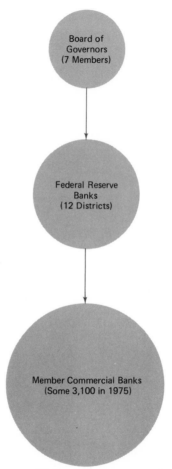

FIG. 17–2. Overall view of
the Federal Reserve System.

All of these functions are essential to our entire economy! Let us, therefore,
analyze Fed structure and operation to see how these diverse functions are
performed.

THE HISTORY AND STRUCTURE OF THE FED

Figure 17-2 outlined the overall Fed structure, Figure 17-5 laid out its parts in
detail, and Figure 17-6 shows how Fed services are spread over the United
States. In studying these illustrations, you should be impressed by the fact
that the Fed is a pretty big operation, involving many parts and subparts, individual banks, and regions of the country. Your own commercial bank may
be an important, even though small, component of this total Federal Reserve
System.

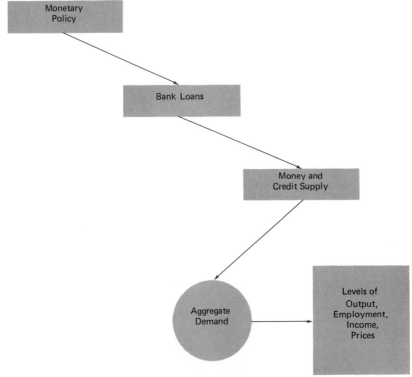

FIG. 17–3. Monetary policy impacts on the economy.

The importance of these components of the Fed is that all are necessary to achieve the Fed's overall functions. The parts and their relations to functions are as follows:

1. *Board of Governors.* The Board of Governors is a seven-man group, now chaired by Dr. Arthur Burns. It is the policy-making "brains" of the Fed. The board determines overall monetary policy and relays policy directives to Federal Reserve Banks, which carry them out. It should be emphasized that the board is an autonomous body independent of Congress, although, of course, goals of each body may be similar, and advice is frequently exchanged between them. True, the Fed must function within the guidelines of the Federal Reserve Act (1913) promulgated by Congress, but Congress does not determine monetary policy.

2. *Federal Advisory Council.* The Federal Advisory Council is a twelve-man group. One representative from each Federal Reserve district (Figure 17-6) meets with the Board of Governors to offer advice on the conduct of monetary policy.

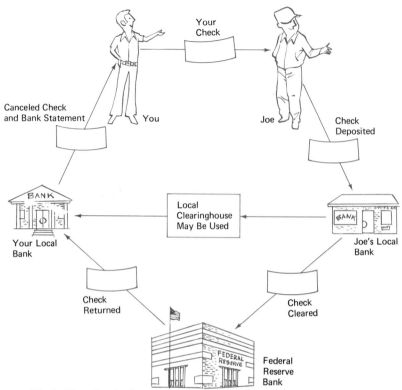

FIG. 17–4. The check clearing process.

3. *Federal Open-Market Committee.* The Federal Open-Market Committee is a twelve-man group. Acting on overall policy directives from the Board of Governors, it conducts open-market operations. U.S. government securities (issued by the U.S. Treasury, such as savings bonds or short-term bills) are bought and sold, according to Open-Market Committee recommendations, in market trading to limit commercial banks' ability to make loans.

4. *Federal Reserve Banks.* The twelve Fed banks, together with the twenty-four Fed branch banks (see Figure 17-6 for locations), carry out Fed functions. It is these banks that clear checks, lend to commercial banks, issue currency, regulate the credit expansion process, and conduct other Fed functions. These banks are often called "banker's banks," for they hold accounts and perform services for commercial banks just as your own commercial bank aids you.

5. *Member Banks.* Here we have some 6,700 member commercial

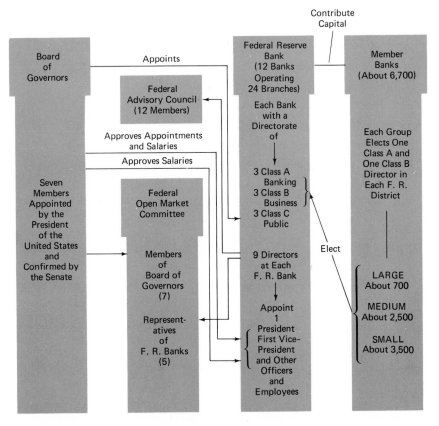

Source: *Federal Reserve Bulletin,* Board of Governors of the Federal Reserve System, Washington, D.C.

FIG. 17–5. Components of the Federal Reserve System.

banks. It should be noted that only about 45 per cent of all commercial banks belong to the Fed (there are over 15,000 commercial banks in the United States today), but member banks handle over 80 per cent of all bank deposits. Recall from Chapter 16 that commercial banks have existed since the Colonial period in the United States, whereas the Fed began only in 1913. Thus many *state banks* (which received their charter to operate from state banking commissions) choose not to become Fed members. However, *national banks* (which receive their charter to operate from the comptroller of the currency in the U.S. Treasury Department) must be members of the Fed. Although there are restrictions resulting from Fed membership (audit, reserve controls, loan limits, and so on), there are also many advantages. Member commercial banks may borrow from Federal Reserve Banks, clear checks with-

Legend

—— Boundaries of Federal Reserve Districts   ▲ Federal Reserve Bank Cities
—— Boundaries of Federal Reserve Branch Territories   • Federal Reserve Branch Cities
■ Board of Governors of the Federal Reserve System

FIG. 17–6. Districts of the Federal Reserve System.

out charge, buy and sell government securities to Federal Reserve
Banks, and receive emergency financial assistance. One point perhaps not widely known is that these member banks actually own
the Federal Reserve Bank in their district and receive a maximum
6 per cent dividend on their investment in Fed annually ($40
million was paid in dividends during 1974).

Notice in the previous description and also in Figure 17-5 that the *Federal
Deposit Insurance Corporation (FDIC)* and other *financial intermediaries*
(savings and loan associations, credit unions, finance companies, and others)
are not components of the Federal Reserve System. Although FDIC is perhaps of the most immediate importance to you (it now insures your demand
deposit to $40,000 in losses), it was not established until 1934 and was not

included in initial Fed operations. The FDIC operates under the direction of the U.S. Treasury Department. The other financial intermediaries may affect credit availability and aggregate demand, but do not fall under monetary policy control by the Fed.

Although the preceding listing details each part of the Fed as a separate component, remember that the groups together compose the total Federal Reserve System and that each group is involved in conducting our banking activities. It should also be noted that the Fed is far from a true central banking system; that is, although the Board of Governors does make general monetary policy, such policy is carried out in varying degrees in the twelve Federal Reserve districts, and commercial banks respond to such policy in varying degrees. Our banking system is really a compromise (recall the long struggle over central bank development in Chapter 16?) between public interests, represented by the Board of Governors and Federal Reserve Banks (nonprofit), and private interests (loan for profits), represented by commercial banks. Our Fed is a long way from the "monopoly bank" approach of many nations, where a single state bank may exist with hundreds or thousands of subsidiaries and control all elements affecting credit and financial activity. Let's now take a closer look at just how all the groups of the Fed work together.

FED CONTROL OF MONEY

You should recall from Chapter 16 that a major function of commercial banks is credit extension (making loans). As illustrated in Figure 16-5, such loans allow consumers, businesses, and government agencies to spend. As commercial banks extend credit, new aggregate demand is created, thus stimulating output, employment, income, and further spending. One feature of credit expansion is that it affects our entire economy. A further feature is that the volume of such credit may be expanded or contracted by the Fed, which, a point once removed, thus affects levels of output, employment, income, and prices. In short, by managing credit expansion (monetary policy), the Fed contributes to attempts at achieving the economic goals of full employment, price stability, and economic growth.

To understand monetary policy fully, however, we first need to review some of the mechanics of the banking system. Perhaps the simplest step is to return to your own commercial bank making a loan. Is there any limit to what a bank may loan or to the money supply that is being created by that loan? An excellent question, for money is created by credit extension, and large problems (inflation, loss of confidence in money) might result without controls. A loan is usually made simply by a bookkeeping addition to your checking account, but money has been created in the process. To answer the question, yes, there is a limit to each commercial bank's credit extension: the amount of its *excess reserves* (ER). The amount of excess reserves (and hence the amount of credit extension possible) is, in part, determined by the monetary policy of the Fed.

A representative balance sheet of a typical commercial bank (Figure 17-7) shows how the loan limit for a commercial bank comes about. A bank's *assets* (items owned and producing revenue) must equal a bank's *liabilities* and

FIG. 17–7. Commercial bank relationships to Fed.

Banking System Worksheet

Basic Concepts to Remember:

$RR = DD \cdot RRR$ CB Loan Limit = ER $M_B = \dfrac{1}{RRR}$

$ER = AR = RR$ FRS Loan Limit = $ER \cdot M_B$

Basic T-Account Structure: ($RRR = 20\%$)

CB_1			CB_2			FRB	
A	$L+C$		A	$L+C$		A	$L+C$
$AR-25$	$DD-100$		$AR-20$	$DD-100$		$L-200$	AR_1-25
$L-50$	$C-50$		$L-50$			$B-100$	AR_2-20
$B-50$			$B-25$	$C-20$		$GC-100$	AR_N-100
$E-25$			$E-25$			$E-20$	$G-100$
							$C-175$

Effect on T-Accounts: Make a Loan and Clear Checks (See Changes? Change in ER?)

CB_1 (Loan of $5)			CB_2			FRB	
A	$L+C$		A	$L+C$		A	$L+C$
$AR-20$	$DD-100$		$AR-25$	$DD-105$		$L-200$	AR_1-20
$L-55$	$C-50$		$L-50$			$B-100$	AR_2-25
$B-50$			$B-25$	$C-20$		$GC-100$	AR_N-100
$E-25$			$E-25$			$E-20$	$G-100$
							$C-175$

Effect on T-Accounts: Raise Required Reserve Ratio (See Changes? Change in ER?)

CB_1 ($RRR = 25\%$)			CB_2			FRB	
A	$L+C$		A	$L+C$		A	$L+C$
$AR-25$	$DD-100$		$AR-20$	$DD-100$		$L-200$	AR_1-25
$L-50$	$C-50$		$L-50$	$C-20$		$B-100$	AR_2-20
$B-50$			$B-25$			$GC-100$	AR_N-100
$E-25$			$E-25$			$E-20$	$G-100$
							$C-175$

Effect on T-Accounts: *CB* Borrow from *FRB* (See Changes? Change in *ER*?) (or Sell Bonds?)

CB_1			CB_2 (Borrow $5)			FRB	
A	$L+C$		A	$L+C$		A	$L+C$
$AR-25$	$DD-100$		$AR-25$	$DD-100$		$L-205$	AR_1-25
$L-50$	$C-50$		$L-50$	$C-20$		$B-100$	AR_2-25
$B-50$			$B-25$	$L-5$		$GC-100$	AR_N-100
$E-25$			$E-25$			$E-20$	$G-100$
							$C-175$

capital (debts to others and net worth). So much should be obvious. The same relationship is true of any other business and is a basic accounting concept. Notice that one, usually the major, liability of a commercial bank is *demand deposits* (checking accounts). Notice also that one of the commercial bank assets is a *reserve account* (actual reserve) at the Federal Reserve Bank.

This relationship between the demand deposits and the reserve account is significant, for this relationship bascially determines the loan limits. To be more specific, as a member of the Fed, the commercial bank must maintain on deposit with the Federal Reserve Bank a sum equal to a certain percentage (the *required reserve ratio*, an average 15 per cent) of its total demand deposit liabilities. Put another way, the commercial bank can do what it likes (within Fed restrictions) with about 85 per cent of anything you deposit until you withdraw funds, but it must hold the other approximately 15 per cent on reserve. A commercial bank, therefore, may extend credit only to the extent that its actual reserves (AR) on deposit at Federal Reserve Banks exceed the required reserves (RR); that is, its *excess reserves (ER)* constitute the loan limit of a single commercial bank.

1. Loan Limit of $CB = ER$
2. $ER = AR - RR$
3. $RR = DD \cdot RRR$

The *required reserve ratio* (RRR) therefore establishes a loan limit for each commercial bank. As an example of how this reserve requirement works, suppose a new demand deposit is made of $100,000. If the required ratio were 16 per cent, then $16,000 must be held back for required reserves, leaving $84,000 as the excess reserves and loan limit, as illustrated in Figure 17–8.

If you study Figures 17-7 and 17-8, perhaps another important Fed concept may appear—the *bank multiplier*. When a commercial bank initiates an extension of credit, other commercial banks gain demand deposits, increased reserves, and, thus, increased loan capacity. (Clearing the $5,000 check in Figure 17-7 gave CB_2 $4,000 of new excess reserves.) But as these "second round" commercial banks lend from such added reserves, other banks gain reserves and loan ability, and so on, as in Figure 17-9.

The total credit extended—the loan capacity of the entire commercial banking system—is thus a *multiple of the initial excess reserves*, even though no single commercial bank may loan more than its excess reserves. (Is the whole greater than the sum of its parts?) The extent of this multiple is limited only by the required reserve ratio: The higher the RRR, the fewer are the excess reserves available for relending, and the lower is the bank multiplier (M_B).

1. Loan Limit for Bank System = $ER \cdot M_B$
2. $M_B = 1 \div RRR$

The importance of the bank multiplier is that it gives leverage to Fed

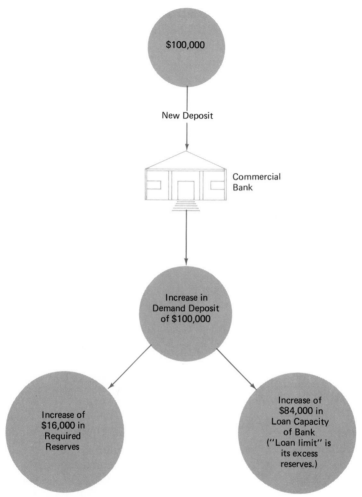

FIG. 17–8. Bank loan creation and limitation.

monetary policy. An initial small change in excess reserves leads to a large total impact on credit extension, affecting aggregate demand to a degree considerably greater than the direct influence of the original change and (are you ready?) causing changes in the levels of output, employment, income, and prices (study Figure 17-3).

Does this credit extension procedure make sense to you? Do you see how it works? Review the preceding paragraphs again, and study Figures 17-7, 17-8, and 17-9 to see the same explanation in "picture perspective." Just as an intellectual exercise, consider what would happen, if the reserve requirement were raised to 20 per cent or lowered to 12 per cent, in terms of the effect on the loan limit? With the same $100,000 initial deposit, a 20 per cent *RRR* would allow total system loans of $400,000 (initial excess reserves of $80,000

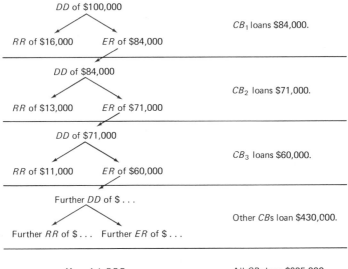

$$M_b = 1 \div RRR$$

All *CBs* loan $625,000.

FIG. 17-9. **Bank multiplier process.**

times a bank multiplier of 5; $M_B = 1 \div RRR = 1 \div 20\% = 5$), thus reducing credit expansion by $225,000. The former limit with a 16 per cent RRR was $625,000 in Figure 17-9. But if the RRR is reduced to 12 per cent, the same $100,000 initial deposit leads to total system loans of $730,400 (initial excess reserves of $88,000 times a bank multiplier of 8.3; $M_B = 1 \div RRR = 1 \div 12\% = 8.3$), thus increasing credit expansion by $105,400.

If you relate the principles of the preceding examples to all commercial banks, perhaps you will appreciate the credit extension process on demand deposits. Similarly, there's a reserve ratio requirement on time deposits, although the required percentage is more like 6 per cent. As demand deposits occur, new excess reserves may be used to make loans and to purchase government securities. By charging interest on loans and also earning interest on securities purchased, the commercial bank makes its profit.

The commercial bank's reserve account that restricts credit extension is the same reserve account used to clear checks drawn upon this bank and received from other banks. (See Figure 16-4.) The reserve account is important, therefore, not only in setting loan limits, but also in clearing checks.

Fed Impacts on Commercial Banks

Now let's go further into Fed relationships and suppose that a commercial bank is all loaned up; that is, suppose the actual reserve account balance exactly equals required reserves; for example, $1.6 million in the reserve account against $10 million demand deposit, given a 16 per cent reserve requirement. Such a bank has no excess reserves ($ER = AR - RR$) and cannot grant further credit; it has reached its loan limit. At this point the commercial bank has the option of either selling securities to the Federal Reserve Bank or borrowing from the Federal Reserve Bank. These options introduce two additional monetary policy instruments, termed respectively, *open-market operations* and *discount rate policy*.

Notice in Figure 17-10 that one of the commercial bank's assets is bonds, especially those of U.S. government issue. (Fed regulations limit the types and amounts of securities a commercial bank may purchase.) Now if the Federal Reserve Bank wishes to buy these U.S. government securities from the commercial bank or other sellers, the commercial bank can use the funds obtained from the bank's sale or from new deposits to make further loans to

FIG. 17–10. Fed impacts on commercial banks.

Banking System Worksheet

Basic Concepts to Remember:

$$RR = DD \cdot RRR$$
$$ER = AR - RR$$

CB Loan Limit $= ER$
FRS Loan Limit $= ER \cdot M_B$

$$M_B = \frac{1}{RRR}$$

Basic T-Account Structure: $(RRR = 20\%)$

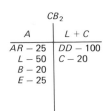

CB_1	
A	L + C
$AR - 25$	$DD - 100$
$L - 50$	$C - 50$
$B - 50$	
$E - 25$	

CB_2	
A	L + C
$AR - 20$	$DD - 100$
$L - 50$	
$B - 25$	$C - 20$
$E - 25$	

FRB	
A	L + C
$L - 200$	$AR_1 - 25$
$B - 100$	$AR_2 - 20$
$GC - 100$	$AR_N - 100$
$E - 200$	$G - 100$
	$C - 175$

Fed buys securities from commercial bank.

CB_2	
A	L + C
$AR - 25$	$DD - 100$
$L - 50$	$C - 20$
$B - 20$	
$E - 25$	

FRB	
A	L + C
$L - 200$	$AR_1 - 25$
$B - 105$	$AR_2 - 25$
$GC - 100$	$AR_N - 100$
$E - 20$	$G - 100$
	$C - 175$

Fed makes loan to commercial bank.

CB_2 (Borrow \$5)	
A	L + C
$AR - 25$	$DD - 100$
$L - 50$	$C - 20$
$B - 25$	$L - 5$
$E - 25$	

FRB	
A	L + C
$L - 205$	$AR_1 - 25$
$B - 100$	$AR_2 - 25$
$GC - 100$	$AR_N - 100$
$E - 20$	$G - 100$
	$C - 175$

bank customers. The Federal Reserve Bank simply receives the securities (bonds) from the commercial bank and increases the commercial bank's reserve account by the amount of the securities sale. (See left column of Figure 17-10.) The commercial bank can then loan this entire added amount, for no demand deposit reserve account requirement is involved. Does this make sense? The commercial bank could also loan a portion of new deposits from other bond purchases. Try the same procedure in reverse: the Federal Reserve Bank sells U.S. government securities to the commercial bank (excess reserves are reduced, and credit expansion is limited) or to other buyers. Although the Fed may not force commercial banks to buy or sell government bonds, the Fed encourages transactions by offering attractive prices or bargains to push selling or buying by commercial banks. Such open-market operations are undoubtedly the most frequently used and most important aspects of present monetary policy.

Return again to our commercial bank all loaned up, and, this time, let's suppose the open-market-operation option is not made available by Federal Reserve Bank policies. The commercial bank may still grant further customer loans if that commercial bank is able to borrow from the Federal Reserve Bank. (Remember we earlier termed Federal Reserve Banks as *banker's banks?*) Just as you may obtain a loan and get an increased demand deposit, the commercial bank may secure a loan at the Federal Reserve Bank as an addition to its reserve account there (see the right-hand column of Figure 17-10). And just as the commercial bank charges you interest on its loan to you, the Federal Reserve Bank charges the commercial bank an interest rate, termed the *discount rate*. As you might guess, the level of the discount rate charged the commercial bank by the Federal Reserve Bank will greatly influence the interest rate charged by the commercial bank to its public customers. For example, the *prime rate* is the interest rate charged the most credit-worthy customers (like major corporations), and it is usually 1 per cent above the discount rate. Less credit-worthy companies or individuals (like the authors) are charged even higher rates.

Well, that's a pretty convoluted slice of Fed relationships and internal mechanics. There's lots more, of course. If you want some more study, read *The Federal Reserve System* by—you guessed it—the Fed. We hope the relationships we have analyzed summarize the basic and most important central banking mechanics. Understanding of these mechanics sets the stage for an analysis of monetary policy.

MONETARY POLICY

It will first, perhaps, be a good idea to define what *monetary policy* is. The Fed, specifically the Board of Governors, tries to counteract the volume of total spending (aggregate demand, or AD) by changes in the *reserve ratio*, the *discount rate,* and *open-market operations*. The manipulation of money supply to repress or stimulate aggregate demand is monetary policy. When the three instruments of monetary policy are employed, a change occurs in commercial banks' ability to loan (review the preceding section); and as loans vary, so does total spending. And, of course, as total spending (AD) changes, so do the inevitable levels of output (O), employment (E), income (Y), and prices (P). That may sound a bit difficult all at once, but let's chew it.

To put monetary policy operation in perspective, consider the somewhat detailed summary of Figure 17-11. Monetary policy seeks to achieve the goals of full employment, stable prices, economic growth, and so on. These goals are the same as those of fiscal policy (review Chapter 13) and appear in newspapers and news broadcasts daily.

Recall from Chaper 11 and from our discussion of the circular flow of our economy that levels of output, employment, income, and prices depend on the level of total spending or aggregate demand (AD). If you wish to modify

FIG. 17–11. The mechanics of monetary policy.

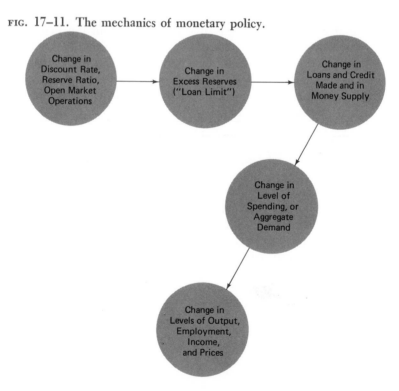

Goals of Monetary Policy: Stable prices, full employment, economic growth

Countercyclical Monetary Policy:
1. Inflation: Raise discount rate. Raise reserve ratio. Sell on open market.
2. Recession: Lower discount rate. Lower reserve ratio. Buy on open market.

these levels, you must change the level of aggregate demand. In fiscal policy, change is brought about by altering the levels of government spending (G) and taxation (T). But under monetary policy this change is effected by varying the required reserve ratio (RRR), discount rates (DR), and open-market operations (OMO).

To see just how this change occurs, consider again some points made in the preceding section on commercial banks:

1. Consumer, business, and government agency spending (all part of AD) varies in proportion to credit made available.

2. Banks extend credit (make loans) and expand the money supply (M_1) on the basis of excess reserves (ER). The excess reserve is the loan limit of a commercial bank. For the entire bank system the loan limit equals the excess reserves times the bank multiplier (Loans = $ER \cdot M_B$). The bank multiplier equals 1 divided by the required reserve ratio ($M_B = 1 \div RRR$).

3. This excess reserve, or loan limit, is influenced by changes in the required reserve ratio, the discount rate, and open-market operations.

To see monetary policy in action, let's suppose *inflationary* pressures prompt the Board of Governors to pursue a *contractionary monetary policy;* that is, they wish to lower total spending by reducing the commercial banks' ability to make loans. This could be achieved by

1. *Raising the required reserve ratio.* If a higher percentage of reserves is required, then less is "left over" (fewer excess reserves) to make loans. A greater required reserve ratio would also result in a lower bank multiplier. This method is infrequently used because it's almost too powerful in its effect.

2. *Raising the discount rate.* By charging commercial banks more interest for borrowing from Federal Reserve Banks, the board discourages bank borrowing for credit extension and also makes it more expensive for customers to borrow (banks usually "pass on" higher charges). This is a frequently used policy, especially in recent years, ranging from 8 per cent in 1974 to 6.25 per cent in 1976. Individuals usually see the effects of discount rate changes in the rates charged for home mortgages.

3. *Selling U.S. government securities in open-market operation.* If commercial banks use their excess reserves to buy securities, then such purchases replace loans that might have been to customers. Commercial banks are verbally encouraged to buy (Fed bulletins) and induced by low prices (resulting in higher interest return) on

the securities. If you recall Figure 17-5, the operation is conducted largely by the Open-Market Committee through Federal Reserve Banks.

This process appears clear to you now, we hope, and some of the little notes and arrows in Figure 17-11 should make more sense. If not, run through this whole process a few more times. For practice, consider what the Board of Governors would prescribe during *depressionary* periods to secure an *expansionary monetary policy*. A hint: Just run the preceding three points through in reverse, and study Figure 17-12.

Well, after all this theory about monetary policy operation, you may well wonder if the policy is really practiced as such and if it has any really big effect on our economy. The answer to both questions is yes. Monetary policy has been practiced for some time in our economy and has had significant economic effects on the levels of aggregate demand, output, employment, income, and, especially, prices. If you read some of the current reports from the St. Louis Federal Reserve Bank or some of Dr. Milton Friedman's statistical studies on monetary effects, you will question whether the impact of monetary

FIG. 17–12. Countercyclical monetary policy.

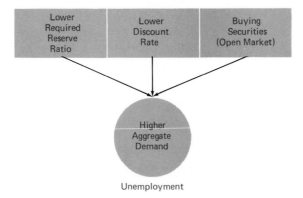

policy has contributed to inflationary pressures. These readings are pretty heavy going, even for a professional economist, and are indicative of controversy among economists over the extent, timing, and mechanics of fiscal policy and monetary policy impacts. Without sorting out all the arguments at this point, let's just conclude that both policy approaches affect our economy.

However, because monetary policy has a definite effect on our economy, it doesn't follow that there are no economic problems. For one thing, the effect of the policies may not be the one desired. As Dr. Friedman has cautioned for years, the Fed may overreact at times by coming down too forcefully with policy actions. At other times, there may be a lack of policy effect at crucial periods. The authors require more analysis on such debate themselves and can only summarize as follows:

1. The theory describing monetary policy impact is far from perfect, especially in regard to extent and timing of effect (when and to what degree economic results occur after policies are implemented). Although statistical models are improving, their defects limit policy measure analysis and evaluation.

2. Given any "perfect" monetary theory, policy making still rests on value judgments of people (Board of Governors). There will be disagreement about, and compromise on, the policy measures to take because "trade-off decisions" must be made on priorities assigned policy goals (more employment or less inflation?).

Monetary Policy and Fiscal Policy

Having said all we have in this chapter regarding monetary policy, let us conclude by comparing briefly fiscal policy (discussed in depth in Chapter 13) and monetary policy, because, for greatest impact, both policy approaches should work in harmony.

Study Figure 17-13 on fiscal policy and monetary policy, comparing the goals and mechanics of each. Notice that purposes are similar and that both policies affect levels of output, employment, income, and prices through changes in aggregate demand. However, the change in aggregate demand is brought about by quite different methods (spending and taxation vs. required reserve ratio, discount rate, and open-market operations) and may thus lead to different degrees of economic effect in different time periods. Notice also the differences in advantages and disadvantages between the two policy approaches.

Perhaps the best way to summarize the differing effects of fiscal and monetary policies is to emphasize that the two policies should work together for maximum effect. To obtain the advantages of each, a coordinated effort must occur, in lieu of an expansionary fiscal policy versus a contractionary monetary policy (as was somewhat true in 1976). There has been cooperation to an extent, though the results are far from perfect. The theories describing impact

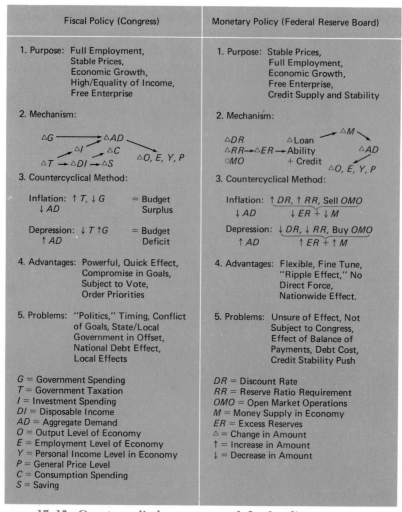

Fiscal Policy (Congress)	Monetary Policy (Federal Reserve Board)
1. Purpose: Full Employment, Stable Prices, Economic Growth, High/Equality of Income, Free Enterprise	1. Purpose: Stable Prices, Full Employment, Economic Growth, Free Enterprise, Credit Supply and Stability
2. Mechanism:	2. Mechanism:
3. Countercyclical Method:	3. Countercyclical Method:
Inflation: ↑ T, ↓ G = Budget ↓ AD Surplus	Inflation: ↑ DR, ↑ RR, Sell OMO ↓ AD ↓ ER ┼ ↓ M
Depression: ↓ T ↑ G = Budget ↑ AD Deficit	Depression: ↓ DR, ↓ RR, Buy OMO ↑ AD ↑ ER ┼ ↑ M
4. Advantages: Powerful, Quick Effect, Compromise in Goals, Subject to Vote, Order Priorities	4. Advantages: Flexible, Fine Tune, "Ripple Effect," No Direct Force, Nationwide Effect.
5. Problems: "Politics," Timing, Conflict of Goals, State/Local Government in Offset, National Debt Effect, Local Effects	5. Problems: Unsure of Effect, Not Subject to Congress, Effect of Balance of Payments, Debt Cost, Credit Stability Push
G = Government Spending T = Government Taxation I = Investment Spending DI = Disposable Income AD = Aggregate Demand O = Output Level of Economy E = Employment Level of Economy Y = Personal Income Level in Economy P = General Price Level C = Consumption Spending S = Saving	DR = Discount Rate RR = Reserve Ratio Requirement OMO = Open Market Operations M = Money Supply in Economy ER = Excess Reserves $\triangle$ = Change in Amount ↑ = Increase in Amount ↓ = Decrease in Amount

FIG. 17–13. Countercyclical monetary and fiscal policy.

are imperfect enough to render the precision of projections questionable. Consequently, decision makers involved may well disagree on what goal to pursue or to what degree of emphasis there should be.

We close by urging you to do homework on monetary and fiscal policies by reading your newspaper and listening to appropriate broadcasts; that is, apply economic understanding (the goal of this course and textbook) to these policies by reading about their design and impact on your own daily economic activities. See if the newspaper analysis makes more sense to you now, and really listen to that political speech to see if the oracle knows what he or she is talking about!

TERMS

Bank multiplier. The total extension of credit throughout the bank system, equal to 1 divided by the required reserve ratio ($M_B = 1 \div RRR$).

Discount rate. The interest charge to commercial banks borrowing from Federal Reserve Banks.

Excess reserves. The amount of reserve over the commercial bank's required reserves; excess reserves constitute the commercial bank's ability to loan.

Federal Reserve System (Fed). Composed of the Board of Governors, the Federal Advisory Council, the Federal Open-Market Committee, the twelve Federal Reserve Banks and their twenty-four branches, and the member commercial banks.

Monetary policy (required reserve ratio, discount rate, and open-market operations). The central banking practice of influencing loan ability, thus spending, and so output, employment, income, and prices.

Open-market operations. The buying and selling of government securities by the Federal Open-Market Committee.

Required reserves. The amounts commercial banks must hold (required by the Fed) to back up demand deposits. They equal demand deposits times the required reserve ratio ($RR = DD \cdot RRR$).

QUESTIONS FOR STUDY

1. What does the Fed consist of? Does Congress make monetary policy? Do all commercial banks belong to the Fed?
2. What limits the ability of commercial banks to grant loans? What limits the entire bank system's ability to loan?
3. Suppose you are a member of the Board of Governors of the Federal Reserve System. The economy is experiencing a sharp and prolonged inflationary trend. What changes in (a) the required reserve ratio, (b) the discount rate, and (c) open-market operations would you recommend? Explain in each case how the changes you advocate would affect commercial bank loan ability and influence the money supply.
4. If the required reserve ratio is 15 per cent, the bank multiplier equals _____.
5. Suppose a commercial bank has $500,000 in demand deposits:
   a. If the reserve requirement is 16 per cent, the required reserves are $_____.
   b. If this bank has $100,000 in its reserve account, its ability to

loan (excess reserves) is $————. The bank system may loan
$————.

   c. Suppose the reserve requirement is reduced to 10 per cent. Required reserves are now $————, and the ability to loan of
the commercial bank is now $————. The entire bank sys-
tem could loan $————.

REFERENCES

Board of Governors of the Federal Reserve System. *The Federal Reserve
System: Purpose and Functions*, Fifth Edition. Washington, D.C.:
Board of Governors, 1963.

Chandler, Lester Vernon. *The Economics of Money and Banking*, Sixth
Edition. New York: Harper & Row, Publishers, Incorporated, 1974.

Mayer, Martin. *The Bankers*. New York: Weybright and Talley, 1974.

O'Brannon, Helen B., et al. *Money and Banking: Theory, Policy, and
Institutions*. New York: Harper & Row, Publishers, Incorporated, 1975.

Publications. Note: All of the Federal Reserve Banks have educational
materials available for distribution. These publications cover a wide range
of monetary and economic subjects. It is suggested that inquiries be directed to the closest Federal Reserve Bank. Available from the New
York Federal Reserve Bank are the following:

Essays in Domestic and International Finance (1969), 86 pages. A collection of nine articles dealing with a few important past episodes in
United States central banking, several facets of the relationship between financial variables and business activity, and various aspects of
domestic and international financial markets.

Essays in Money and Credit (1964), 76 pages. A collection of eleven
articles on selected subjects in banking, the money market, and technical problems affecting monetary policy.

Federal Reserve Bulletin. Published monthly by each of the twelve Federal Reserve Banks. The New York and St. Louis bulletins are especially
interesting.

Money: Master or Servant? (1966) by Thomas O. Waage, 48 pages. A
comprehensive discussion of the roles of money, commercial banks,
and the Federal Reserve in our economy.

The New York Foreign Exchange Market (1965) by Alan R. Holmes
and Francis H. Schott, 64 pages. A detailed description of the organization and instruments of the foreign exchange market, the techniques
of exchange trading, and the relationship between spot and forward
rates.

Open Market Operations (1969) by Paul Meek, 48 pages. A basic explanation of how the Federal Reserve uses purchases and sales of
government securities to influence the cost and availability of money
and credit.

Perspective. Published each January, 9 pages. A brief, nontechnical review of the economy's performance and the economic outlook.

The Velocity of Money (1960) by George Garvy and Martin R. Blyn, 116 pages. A thorough discussion of the demand for money and measurement of, influences on, and implications of changes in the velocity of money.

18

WHO NEEDS ECONOMIC GROWTH?

SHORT ANSWER. Economic growth offers a nation greater employment opportunities and a higher level of living, but all too frequently at a high cost of pollution, resource depletion, and social disruption.

YOU AND ECONOMIC GROWTH

"So who needs more economic growth, especially if it means more pollution? What I'd really like is better quality and a simpler way of life!" Is this point of view yours or that of your friends? Do you wonder why economists are

FIG. 18–1. Benefits of economic growth.

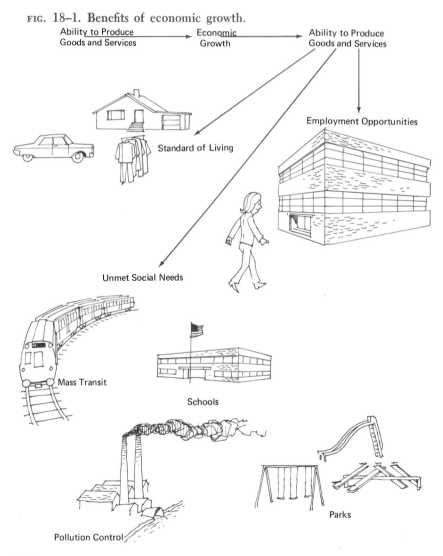

Ability to Produce Goods and Services → Economic Growth → Ability to Produce Goods and Services

Standard of Living

Employment Opportunities

Unmet Social Needs

Mass Transit

Schools

Pollution Control

Parks

often concerned with economic growth? There are many debatable issues associated with economic growth that we'll examine in this chapter.

Let's look at some of the benefits of U.S. economic growth that affect you before we examine the costs. Economic growth basically means that our economy continually increases production of goods and services, providing U.S. citizens thereby with a successively higher living standard (two 300-horsepower cars, suburban home, electric toothbrushes and can openers, three TVs, colored toilet paper, and so on, and so on). In addition, producing more entails more employment opportunities (recall our circular-flow model of Chapter 2?) and higher incomes. And because our U.S. economic growth has entailed greater productivity and increased use of capital, leisure time to enjoy yourself has also increased. (Can you see why?)

Although all of the mentioned growth benefits represent personal consumer gains, there are also a number of possible social benefits from economic growth; that is, an increased productive capacity may also provide mass transit systems; rebuild urban slums; construct more schools and parks; or improve provision for the poor, elderly, and ill in our society. Notice that we're again at a choice here (what to produce?), as we discuss allocating resources for more consumer goods or more social goods. Furthermore, the U.S. economy might also share its increased output with the poorer nations of the world.

The benefits of economic growth should impress you that growth issues are worth your economic understanding and have a daily effect on your economic life. Now let us get into economic growth analysis via a definition of the growth process and an evaluation of its costs and benefits.

ECONOMIC GROWTH THEORY

Growth Measures

We must define economic growth, and, for a start, you might review Chapter 12. *Real GNP per capita* is our basic measure of economic growth in both the U.S. and world economies. Recall that GNP (gross national product) is a measure of final output produced and purchased, and an increase in real GNP per capita defines economic growth. Further, recall that real GNP corrects for price changes so that any inflationary or recessionary impacts are removed. (Recall from Chapter 12 that Real GNP = Money GNP $\times$ 100 $\div$ Price Index.) The per capita concept means that you divide real GNP by the number of the population in order to arrive at the average output available to each citizen. Thus, this real GNP per capita measure is an indication of the level of living provided each citizen. Notice in Figure 18-2 that real GNP per capita in the U.S. economy has expanded rather steadily for some time, thus

Population (Millions)	Year	GNP	Real GNP (1958 dollars)	NNP	PI	DI	Real DI (1958 dollars)
160.2	1953	$2,276	$2,577	$2,115	$1,799	$1,583	$1,726
163.0	1954	2,238	2,497	2,065	1,780	1,585	1,714
165.9	1955	2,399	2,640	2,209	1,874	1,666	1,795
168.9	1956	2,482	2,641	2,281	1,972	1,743	1,839
172.0	1957	2,565	2,631	2,349	2,041	1,801	1,844
174.9	1958	2,558	2,558	2,335	2,065	1,831	1,831
177.8	1959	2,720	2,677	2,488	2,157	1,905	1,881
180.7	1960	2,788	2,699	2,547	2,219	1,937	1,883
183.7	1961	2,831	2,707	2,585	2,264	1,984	1,909
186.5	1962	3,004	2,841	2,737	2,373	2,065	1,969
189.2	1963	3,121	2,912	2,843	2,460	2,138	2,015
191.9	1964	3,295	3,028	3,003	2,592	2,283	2,126
194.3	1965	3,525	3,180	3,217	2,774	2,436	2,239
196.6	1966	3,814	3,347	3,489	2,987	2,604	2,335
198.7	1967	3,995	3,398	3,649	3,167	2,749	2,403
200.7	1968	4,306	3,521	3,935	3,432	2,945	2,486
202.7	1969	4,590	3,580	4,187	3,704	3,130	2,534
204.9	1970	4,769	3,526	4,343	3,945	3,376	2,610
207.1	1971	5,097	3,599	4,643	4,169	3,603	2,680
208.8	1972	5,533	3,787	5,042	4,498	3,816	2,767
210.4	1973	6,123	3,980	5,602	4,922	4,195	2,890

Source: *Economic Report of the President*, 1974.

FIG. 18–2. Economic growth impacts (all dollar figures on a per capita basis).

providing the average U.S. citizen with one of the highest living standards in the world.

Real GNP per capita provides not only a measure of U.S. economic growth, but also provides a comparative standard for other economies; that is, you may gain a rough idea of differing living standards in various economies by their real GNPs per capita, as in Figure 18-3. Realize, however, that there are problems and distortions in such comparisons related to accuracy of available statistics of output, foreign exchange rate conversions, costs of living, and different value standards. Even allowing for such differences, Figure 18-3 should indicate the tremendous range of world living standards.

Before we become awed by our real GNP per capita growth measure, let us also state that there are numerous problems with this indicator. Recall from Chapter 12 that GNP does not measure many outputs that may well contribute to your living standard; that is, GNP does not include resale items (your "new" used auto or textbook does not count in GNP!), intermediate goods (inputs to other products), or nonmarket output (weekend gardening and homemaker services are not included). Although such omissions may result in a slight understatement of your own living standard, the discrepancy becomes significant in economies that are more self-sufficient, less interdependent, and less urban than ours.

A further problem—and one more serious in the authors' view—is that real GNP per capita does not distinguish between quantity and quality or provide any cost-benefit comparison; that is, GNP measures only "things" produced and purchased, but does not provide any indication as to the relative satisfaction provided from such output. True, it may be most difficult to arrive at such a "quality" measure (discussed in Chapter 12), but there is surely a difference in impact on living standards between producing missile systems and mass transit lines or between basic food and a better deodorant. The authors cannot provide an acceptable measure of quality here (value judgments differ on what is a "quality of life" or a "quantity of life" increment), but urge some caution in analysis of GNP data.

Another problem of real GNP per capita measures that bears on economic growth debates is that this standard does not incorporate costs of economic growth. (*Diseconomies* is a term we've used previously.) For example, the output of automobiles is counted in GNP, but not the concomitant exhaust pollution or transport congestion. The reduction of such diseconomies through further output (such as catalytic converters, new highways, or factory air and noise filters) would increase GNP, although with doubtful increase in long-term life "quality."

One last problem with real GNP per capita is that it provides no information as to income distribution (the *for whom* question). A real GNP per capita figure of some $5,400 in 1976 or a mean family income of $16,400 does not mean that all citizens were equally well off. These growth measures should be accompanied by personal income distribution statistics (Figure 14–13) or a Lorenz curve (Figure 14-14) to see how such output is divided among the population. In fact, it may well be that certain income groups become less well off, even though economic growth for the entire economy proceeds, as illustrated by Figure 18-4.

After noting these various problems in the use of real GNP per capita as an economic growth measure, you may question why it is so widely used. Well, it's a case of "the best thing going." Despite all its shortcomings, real GNP per capita is still perhaps the most adequate measure and certainly the most accessible. Other measures of productivity, such as direct output, education, or health levels are available (see Figure 18-5), but are cumbersome to use and entail even more problems than real GNP per capita. Suffice it to say we'll go with what's available until a new measure turns up! In the meantime, we now turn to analysis of just what determines real GNP per capita.

Growth Factors

Although our examination of real GNP per capita laid the groundwork for the measurement of economic growth, we've not yet analyzed the causes of economic growth. We must investigate what determines an economy's ability to produce and why output capacity changes over time. With understanding of economic growth theory, you should be able to evaluate policies to promote or curb growth, whether in a developed economy like that of the United

Country	1970 GNP per Capita (U.S. Dollars)	1960–70 Growth Rate (Per Cent)
United States	4,760	3.2
Sweden	4,040	3.8
Canada	3,700	3.6
Switzerland	3,320	2.5
Denmark	3,190	3.7
France	3,100	4.6
Germany, Fed. Rep. of	2,930	3.5
Norway	2,860	4.1
Australia	2,820	3.1
Belgium	2,720	4.0
New Zealand	2,700	2.1
Germany (East)†	2,490	4.2
Netherlands	2,430	3.9
Finland	2,390	3.9
United Kingdom	2,270	2.2
Czechoslovakia†	2,230	3.8
Austria	2,010	3.9
Israel	1,960	4.7
Japan	1,920	9.6
U.S.S.R.†	1,790	5.8
Libya, Arab Rep. of	1,770	20.4
Italy	1,760	4.6
Puerto Rico	1,650	5.8
Hungary†	1,600	5.4
Poland†	1,400	5.2
Ireland	1,360	3.6
Argentina	1,160	2.5
Greece	1,090	6.6
Spain	1,020	6.1
Venezuela	980	2.3
Hong Kong	970	8.4
Romania†	930	7.7
Singapore	920	5.2

Country	1970 GNP per Capita (U.S. Dollars)	1960–70 Growth Rate (Per Cent)
Mexico	670	3.7
Portugal	660	5.3
Yugoslavia	650	4.3
Albania†	600	4.8
Lebanon	590	0.5
Costa Rica	560	3.2
Cuba†	530	−0.6
Mongolia†	460	0.0
Peru	450	1.4
Saudi Arabia	440	8.0
Nicaragua	430	2.8
Brazil	420	2.4
Zambia	400	7.1
China, Rep. of	390	7.1
Iran	380	5.4
Malaysia	380	3.1
Guatemala	360	2.0
Dominican Republic	350	0.5
Colombia	340	1.7
Korea (North)†	330	5.1
Iraq	320	2.5
Turkey	310	3.9
Ivory Coast	310	4.5
Ghana	310	−0.4
Angola	300	3.2
El Salvador	300	1.7
Algeria§	300	1.7
Papua New Guinea	300	4.5
Syria, Arab Rep. of	290	3.4
Ecuador	290	1.7
Honduras	280	1.8
Rhodesia	280	0.4
Paraguay	260	1.3

Country	1970 GNP per Capita (U.S. Dollars)	1960–70 Growth Rate (Per Cent)
Philippines	210	2.9
Egypt, Arab Rep. of	210	1.7
Viet-nam, Rep. of	200	1.0
Thailand	200	4.9
Sierra Leone	190	4.7
Cameroon	180	3.8
Bolivia	180	2.5
China (Mainland)†	160	2.1
Kenya	150	3.6
Central AFrican Rep.	140	0.2
Mauritania*	140	4.5
Togo	140	1.2
Malagasy Rep.	130	1.2
Khmer Rep.	130	0.1
Uganda	130	2.4
Nigeria	120	0.1
Laos*	120	1.9
Sudan	120	1.0
Guinea*	120	2.7
Yemen, People's Dem. Rep. of	120	−5.0
Sri Lanka	110	1.5
India	110	1.2
Haiti	110	−0.9
Tanzania||	100	3.6
Viet-nam (North)†	100	3.2
Pakistan and Bangladesh	100	2.4
Niger*	90	−2.0
Dahomey*	90	0.1
Zaire*	90	2.7
Chad*	80	0.4
Nepal*	80	0.5
Burma*	80	0.6
Yemen, Arab Rep. of*	80	2.0

Country	GNP per capita (US $)	Growth rate (%)	Country	GNP per capita (US $)	Growth rate (%)	Country	GNP per capita (US $)	Growth rate (%)
Trinidad and Tobago	860	1.9	Tunisia	250	0.5	Indonesia*	80	1.0
Uruguay	820	−0.4	Korea, Rep. of	250	6.8	Ethiopia*	80	2.8
Bulgaria†	760	7.4	Jordan*	250	2.9	Afghanistan*	80	0.5
South Africa‡	760	3.0	Liberia	240	0.9	Malawi*	80	2.1
Panama	730	4.2	Mozambique	240	3.4	Somalia*	70	−1.1
Chile	720	1.6	Morocco	230	1.0	Mali*	70	4.4
Jamaica	670	3.5	Senegal	230	0.0	Upper Volta*	60	−0.6
						Surundi*	60	0.8
						Rwanda*	60	−1.5

Note: In view of the usual errors inherent in this type of data and to avoid a misleading impression of accuracy, the figures for GNP per capita have been rounded to the nearest $10.

The gross national product estimates on which the per-capita figures are based are calculated at *market prices*. Thus they include indirect taxes net of subsidies.

* Estimates of GNP per capita and its growth rate are tentative. In some instances GNP per capita estimates of under 100 dollars are based on data that have a large margin of error and are thus likely to be less reliable than estimates of over 100 dollars.

† Estimates of GNP per capita and its growth rate have a wide margin of error mainly because of the problems in deriving the GNP at market prices from net material product and in converting the GNP estimate into U.S. dollars.

‡ Including Namibia.

§ Growth rate relates to the period 1963–1970.

‖ Mainland Tanzania.

FIG. 18–3. GNP comparisons in the world.

SOURCE: *World Bank Review*, 1973.

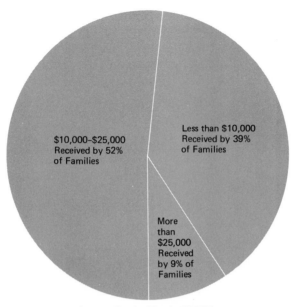

Incomes Received by the 57 Million
American Families in 1973

FIG. 18–4. Economic growth impacts.

States or in an underdeveloped economy like that of India. You must, of course, consider that growth theory applied to an underdeveloped economy without experience in detail of that economy's life-style and physical properties may produce inaccurate conclusions.

To begin our analysis of economic growth causation, let's again use our *production possibilities curve* (PPC) of Figure 18-6. Recall from Chapter 2 that the PPC indicates the maximum possible output combinations of consumer goods or social and capital goods. Although the society may choose various combinations of output (the what to produce question), the PPC sets an upward limit, or *potential* of the economy at any particular time.

The location of any economy's PPC depends on the quantity and capacity (productivity) of its economic resources; *human resources, natural resources, capital stock,* and *technology-management.* That is, any economy's ability to produce goods and services will depend on the amounts and efficiency of its economic resources necessary to produce that output. At any point in time, an economy's amounts and productivity levels of labor, land (another term for natural resources), capital stock (machinery and equipment), and knowledge (technological level and managerial skills) permit only certain output combinations, thus defining that economy's PPC. Study this concept in Figure 18-7, and also note the forces influencing these *growth factors.*

Realize that if any or all of these four growth factors change, either in quantity or quality, there occurs a change in the economy's PPC, as in Figure 18-8. If the growth factors increase (more or better trained workers, new mineral exploration, more or better machinery, technological breakthroughs), the PPC will expand, indicating an *increase in the potential* of the economy to produce. But the growth factors could also decrease (fewer or less healthy workers, minerals depleted, machinery destroyed, technology forgotten), resulting in a contraction of the PPC and indicating a *decrease in the potential* of output capacity.

There can also occur a gap (indicating unemployment) between the potential of an economy to produce (the PPC) and what the economy actually achieves. As illustrated in Figure 18-9, an economy may operate far below its output capacity while experiencing high unemployment and depression conditions. With a 7 per cent unemployment rate in 1976 and previous business cycle dips (25 per cent unemployed in the 1930s depression), such a gap between potential and achievement can obviously occur.

The gap between potential and actual output levels is crucial to any economy; it is the actual output that constitutes GNP; that is, a large potential to produce is desirable for any economy, but citizens receive benefits only from output actually produced: Standard of living is an achievement, not a potential. The gap between potential and actual output (see Figure 18-10 for U.S. economy estimates) represents "lost" goods and services, lack of employment opportunities, and a lower than desirable level of living. Reduction of such a gap (some $100 billion in 1976) is, of course, a major goal of fiscal and monetary policy.

If our discussion of national income theory (Chapter 12) and fiscal and monetary policies (Chapters 13 and 17) has promoted your economic understanding, you should have a pretty fair idea of what causes the difference between achievement and potential output. Aggregate demand is the growth factor that determines what the actual output level of an economy will be. Recall that a full-employment equilibrium (aggregate demand equals the full-employment, or maximum PPC, aggregate supply) is not thereby assured. If *AD* is less than *AS* at full employment, actual output will fall below potential (review Figures 18-9 and 18-10). Or if *AD* is sufficient to equal *AS* at full employment, the actual and potential output levels will be identical, and the economy will operate along the PPC. Should *AD* exceed *AS* at full employment, inflationary pressures will develop as the economy tries to operate beyond the PPC. (Note that spending is not confined by the PPC.) Study Figure 18-11 to compare these three conditions of aggregate demand.

Given our previous analysis of fiscal and monetary policies, you should realize that the rate of economic growth (change in real GNP per capita actually achieved) is affected by manipulations of aggregate demand. But there is also another growth factor that determines the actual output level: *allocative efficiency* (AE), which is the degree to which resources are used to full capacity, thus maximizing output from a given resource base. Although the

	U.S.A.	U.S.S.R.
Gross National Product—Per Capita		
Value of total goods and services produced per person (1970)	$4,756	$2,000
Population/Area		
Population (1969)	203,213,000	240,567,000
Area (square miles)	3,615,123	8,649,489
Labor Force, Energy, Manufacturing (1969)		
Economically active population	82,272,000	115,493,000
Production of electric energy (millions of KWH)	1,552,298	689,050
Consumption of sources of energy (coal equivalent):		
Total (1,000 short tons)	2,413,431	1,113,543
Per capita (pounds)	23,752	9,257
Manufacturing establishments	311,140	40,709
Manufacturing persons engaged	19,095,000	26,659,000
Imports ($1,000s)	$35,863,000	$10,327,000
Exports ($1,000s)	$37,462,000	$11,655,000
Foodstuff Production (1969)		
Wheat (1,000 short tons)	43,766	88,093
Rice	4,565	1,220
Corn	128,178	13,177
Potatoes	15,601	101,168
Meat	18,052	11,684
Sugar	5,480	11,110
Cotton	2,403	2,149
Industrial Materials (1969)		
Coal (1,000 short tons)	595,960	469,354
Crude petroleum (1,000 barrels)	3,371,748	2,458,255
Cement	73,443	98,920
Iron ore, iron content (1,000 short tons)	57,885	111,316
Sulfuric acid (1,000 short tons)	28,727	11,754
Steel (1,000 short tons)	141,261	121,615
Steel consumption: Total (1,000 short tons)	152,900	115,654
Steel consumption: Per capita (pounds)	1,504	961
Communications		
Telephone in use	115,222,000	12,000,000
Telegrams sent, domestic	61,874,000	357,000,000
Pieces of mail sent, domestic (1,000s)	79,968,000	7,584,000
Daily newspapers	1,758	628
Daily newspaper circulation	62,060,000	26,911,000
Daily newspaper circulation per 1,000 population	305	320
Radios	285,000,000	90,100,000
Televisions	81,000,000	30,744,000
Milk, Beer, Cigarettes, Fish, and Yarn (1969)		
Milk (short tons)	58,099,000	89,882,000
Beer (1,000 gallons)	3,801,963	1,048,921
Cigarettes and cigarillos (millions)	573,002	307,602
Fish catches (short tons)	2,751	761
Cotton yarn (short tons)	1,805	1,585
Wool yarn (short tons)	194	355
Rayon and acetate yarn (short tons)	387	240

FIG. 18–5. Economic growth comparisons.

	U.S.A.	U.S.S.R.
Transportation		
Shipping		
Merchant shipping fleets (gross tons) (1970)	18,463,000	14,832,000
Vessels entered (1969)	177,860	N.R.
Freight, loaded (1,000 short tons)	199,813	115,706
Freight, unloaded (1,000 short tons)	310,020	12,238
Rail Traffic (1969)		
Passenger-miles (millions)	12,160	162,361
Short ton-miles (millions)	767,793	1,621,213
Civil aviation miles flown (1,000)	2,384,933	N.R.
Motor vehicles in use	103,865,000	N.R.
Housing and Health		
Housing		
Dwellings per 1,000 population (1960)	261	211
Average number of rooms per dwelling (1963)	4.7	3.3
Average number of persons per room (1963)	0.7	1.5
Health		
Number of hospitals	7,137	26,429
Number of hospital beds	1,663,000	2,567,000
Number of physicians	305,453	555,400
Persons per physician	700	400
Dentists	98,670	87,100
Education and Book Production		
Primary Schools (1968)		
Teachers	1,244,000	1,782,000
Students enrolled	32,018,000	40,310,000
Secondary Schools (1968)		
Teachers	955,000	N.R.
Students enrolled	19,053,000	8,702,000
Public Expenditures for Education (1967)		
Total ($1,000s)	$45,300,000	$17,962,000
% of national income so spent	5.6%	7.2%
Book Titles Produced (1969)	62,083	74,611

N.R.—Not Released by U.S.S.R.

Comparative Standard of Living July 1, 1970:

Approximate Worktime Required to Buy Selected Commodities at State-fixed Prices in Moscow and at Retail Stores in New York City.

Commodity	New York City	Moscow
White bread (1 pound)	5 minutes	17 minutes
Potatoes (1 pound)	2 minutes	4 minutes
Beef, rib roast (1 pound)	41 minutes	137 minutes
Butter, salted (1 pound)	16 minutes	140 minutes
Sugar (1 pound)	3 minutes	45 minutes
Milk, fresh (1 quart)	6 minutes	24 minutes
Eggs, 2nd grade (1 dozen)	12 minutes	93 minutes
Men's shirt, cotton	1.7 hours	11.4 hours
Men's suit, wool, single-breasted, medium price range	26.3 hours	157.0 hours
Men's shoes, leather oxfords (pair)	6.0 hours	35.0 hours
Women's dress, street, man-made fibers	5.6 hours	42.0 hours
Women's shoes, leather oxfords, medium price range	5.3 hours	33.0 hours
Woman's stockings, nylon (pair)	17.5 minutes	2.9 hours
Soap, toilet (3½ ounce cake)	2.0 minutes	16.3 minutes
Cigarettes, nonfilter, regular size, package of 20	8.5 minutes	15.1 minutes
Vodka (fifth)	1.2 hours	4.4 hours

FIG. 18–5. Continued.

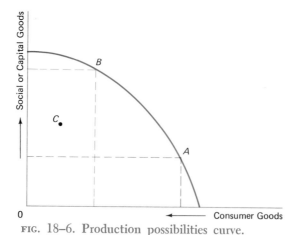

FIG. 18–6. Production possibilities curve.

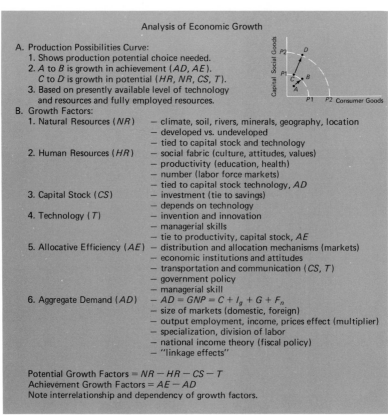

FIG. 18–7. Growth factors in economic growth.

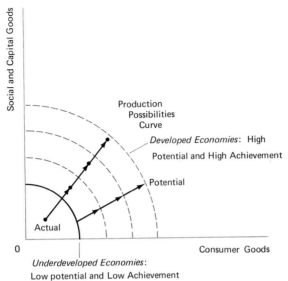

FIG. 18–8. Changes in production possibilities curve.

AD level determines the extent of unemployed resources, a high level of AE in the economy ensures against underemployment (the resource is employed, but at less than capacity: an engineer sweeps floors). To achieve PPC, economic resources must be used to capacity, and such use is set by the AE level.

FIG. 18–9. Actual vs. potential GNP on PPC.

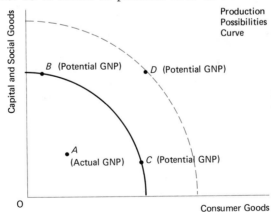

A   Unemployed Resources
B   Full Employment; Emphasis on Capital Goods
C   Full Employment; Emphasis on Consumer Goods
D   Expansion of Production Capacity (Economic Growth)

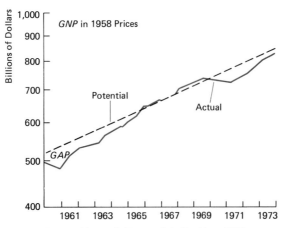

Source: *Economic Report of the President*, 1974.

FIG. 18–10. Actual vs. potential GNP.

Allocative efficiency is usually influenced by business management skills, government regulation, market incentives, and any barriers that prevent operation at full capacity. Note that fiscal and monetary policies affect *AE* as well as *AD*, and such policies have a powerful effect on economic growth levels.

We hope your economic understanding of economic growth theory has greatly expanded to this point. Let us now apply that theory to a historical review of U.S. economic growth and an evaluation of the resulting growth costs and benefits.

U.S. ECONOMIC GROWTH RECORD

As Figure 18-2 indicates, the U.S. economy has enjoyed a fair measure of economic growth for a long time. Although some other nations have experienced more rapid rates of economic growth than the United States (see Figure 18-12), these rates have existed over relatively short periods and on a small GNP base. (A 15 per cent growth on a $200 billion GNP base for Japan is only one-half the amount of a 4 per cent growth on a $1.5 trillion GNP base of the United States.) Although the U.S. growth rate has varied a good deal, the long-term average has been about a 4 per cent annual increase in real GNP, and some 2 per cent increase annually in real GNP per capita (our long-term population growth is 2 per cent annually). If you feel this is a rather small percentage, remember that they compound economic growth over very long periods to demonstrate that the United States has the world's most productive economy!

Why has the U.S. economy produced this large and sustained record of

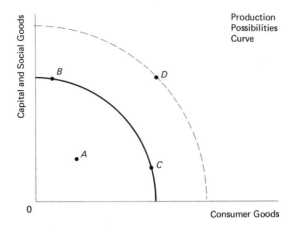

A   Unemployed Resources—Aggregate demand is less
      than aggregate supply at full employment.
B   Full Employment; Emphasis on Capital Goods—
      Aggregate demand is equal to aggregate supply at full
      employment.
C   Full Employment; Emphasis on Consumer Goods
D   Expansion of Production Capacity (Economic
      Growth) in Future, but Inflation at Present—
      Aggregate demand exceeds aggregate supply at full
      employment.

FIG. 18–11. Aggregate demand determines actual GNP.

economic growth? To answer this question let's review our previous growth factor analysis and apply the theory developed from it to explaining U.S. economic growth. We can say, overall, that the U.S. economy has steadily increased its potential to produce (PPC expanded outward) and that it has usually achieved a high degree of that potential (actual GNP close to potential GNP of Figure 18-10). But an explanation of U.S. economic growth must include an understanding of the growth factors affecting potential and actual output levels.

On the potential side, the U.S. economy has long experienced an increase in both amount and productivity of potential growth factors. Our human resource base had a "cultural fabric" base (materialistic, hardworking, little consumption, "Protestant ethic" approach) conducive to growth, immigration waves (especially in the 1860s, 1880s, and early twentieth century) enlarged our farm and factory labor force, and steady gains in education and health levels have continually spurred productivity. Our initial natural resource base was both plentiful and easily available to early technology (forests, soil, streams, fishing) and increased by continual new mineral discoveries and expanded uses over the years.

Capital stock increases and technological gains have proceeded hand in hand to increase U.S. potential for economic growth. Our technological break-

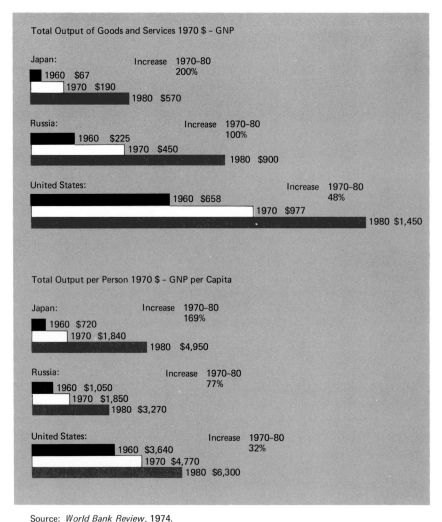

Source: *World Bank Review*, 1974.
FIG. 18–12. Economic growth comparisons.

throughs (backed by public "faith," the government patent system, and business investment in research and development) have always appeared to respond to growing consumer product demand and have been eagerly accepted by consumer and business groups. This "spirit of technological advance" in our society has spurred capital stock formation, not only from the simple gains by invention, but also from the continuous emphasis on machinery use and automation. (On the average, each U.S. industrial worker is supported by $40,000 of capital stock, and the average farmer is backed by $100,000 of capital.) Furthermore, capital stock formation has long been promoted by an adequate money and banking system (allowing transfer of savings to investment) and by a public faith that encourages saving, investment, and the profit motive.

Given these growth factors that appear to have worked hand in hand to enlarge U.S. growth potential continuously, we've also had growth factors working to achieve that enlarged potential. Aggregate demand has continually expanded (with some drops in depressionary eras), based initially on exports. Tobacco and cotton exports allowed Southern colonies and states to purchase Northern colonies' and states' production, thus spurring domestic output and spending. As the "industrial North" expanded, it allowed a specialization of commercial farming in the West to develop, with growing markets and demands in North and West. The increase in population, accompanied by growing disposable incomes, added to consumer spending, and business investment soared on the plowing back of earnings into new plant and equipment. Did you ever think of the "Robber Barons" as economic growth forces?

Achievement growth levels have also been aided by a sustained high degree of allocative efficiency in the U.S. economy. Increased allocative efficiency was promoted by market operation and incentives, increased business management skills, availability of public transportation and communication support (sometimes termed *overhead capital*), and a financial system to balance saving and investment. In addition, there has long existed a favorable public disposition toward flexibility and change, thus supporting and encouraging invention and innovation.

Although the previous paragraphs perhaps provide only a very brief review of U.S. economic history, they should indicate that U.S. economic growth has been both substantial and somewhat unique. Growth factors have long promoted gains in potential and actual output and have also interacted and reinforced each other. Whether underdeveloped economies of today could "do it as the U.S. did" in economic growth is thus a difficult question, but the answer is probably no. (We'll examine this issue in Chapter 19.) In any case, your growth factor theory should allow you to analyze causes, problems, and policies of economic growth (U.S. or underdeveloped economies). Let us now apply more of the analysis to examining various "costs" of economic growth.

COSTS OF ECONOMIC GROWTH

Perhaps Figure 18-13 is a bit dramatic, but it does make that point that the benefits previously noted from economic growth involve certain costs. Although the U.S. economy has experienced much economic growth (review Figure 18-2) leading to a high material standard of living, it has also created problems of pollution (air, water, noise), congestion, inequality, and depletion of natural resources. All of these problems are to some extent caused or aggravated by our industrialized way of life, and their alleviation may involve

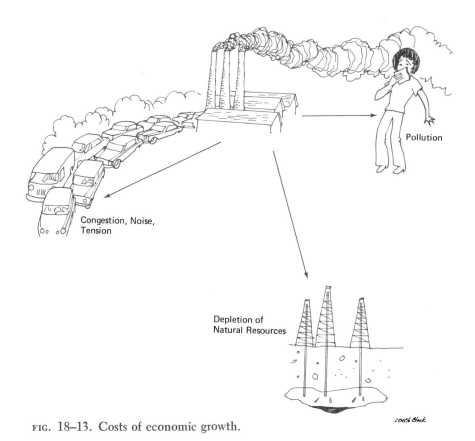

Pollution

Congestion, Noise,
Tension

Depletion of
Natural Resources

100% Black

FIG. 18–13. Costs of economic growth.

some limiting of economic growth. Thus we are again faced by the fundamental issue of economics: choice making. Let us examine three possible approaches to the problem, as illustrated by Figure 18-14.

"No Growth" Position

One approach to the growth-pollution trade-off is to maintain an absolute
limit on future economic growth; that is, the economy may continue to produce at current output levels, but must avoid expansion. This position emphasizes recycling of resources (a "spaceship earth" concept, to use Kenneth
Boulding's terms); an emphasis on reduction of pollutive processes; and
usually some movement to smaller, rural, self-contained communities.

Although such a position may appeal to the ardent ecologists, the authors
doubt that such a societal choice is feasible or realistic. (Whether the choice
is desirable, we leave for your value judgment.) A "no growth" position would
entail vast changes in personal life-styles and perhaps greatly increased gov-

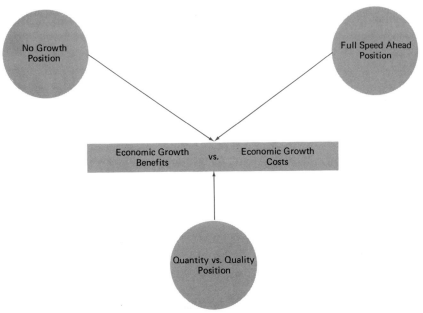

FIG. 18–14. Approaches to controlling economic growth.

ernment control. Though it is not an impossibility, the authors doubt such a position would be acceptable politically or socially to most Americans.

"Full-Speed-Ahead" Position

Another extreme approach to the growth-pollution trade-off is simply to ignore the pollution and other costs of economic growth. Under this thesis, one must assume that growth benefits so outweigh the costs that an emphasis on rapid economic growth is desirable above all things. If one used this approach, high levels of output and employment would be of top priority for fiscal and monetary policy, with minimum attention paid to pollution standards or output restrictions. This view would almost inevitably emphasize a maximum of market operation (little government restriction on production) and would assume a high degree of market substitution and technological advance to counteract possible shortages of natural resources.

Although such a position does have much political and public appeal, especially to the unemployed and poverty level groups, the authors consider this approach an equally unrealistic one for any long-term period. The "full-speed-ahead" position ignores the steadily mounting dangers of pollution (*smog can kill,* and it is quite uncomfortable long before that point!), as well as the quickly decreasing levels of fossil fuel and other energy resources. To assume that technological advance will easily eliminate pollution and produce cheap energy sources is, in the authors' view, a shortsighted, unrealistic, and naive view for the citizen or public policy maker.

"Quantity vs. Quality" Position

As you may have guessed, the authors (and many other economists and citizens) would prefer a compromise approach to the growth-pollution trade-off. This approach would encourage further economic growth, but would seek to divert increased productive capacity toward output that increases the "quality" of life for the average citizen. An example of such resource allocation (review the PPC of Figure 18-6) is an emphasis on mass transit systems over personal auto output, an increase of public health and education facilities over fast food service chains, and increased provisions for low-income, school-age, and elderly citizens.

This position would also emphasize pollution controls (air, water, noise) on a cost-benefit analysis basis; that is, any pollution program (or public program in general) should be carried to the point at which the *marginal social benefit* (MSB—additional gains to society) equals the *marginal social cost* (MSC—additional disadvantages to society). Such a calculation, as illustrated in Figure 18-15, recognizes that costs and benefits change at quite different rates and also admits that these costs and benefits are quite difficult to calculate. Yet the *MSB* = *MSC* approach also promises a more realistic and efficient tool to be used in trade-offs between economic growth and pollution control proposals.

The "quantity vs. quality" position would also accord high priority to resource substitution, alternative energy source development, and technological

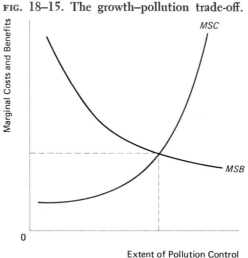

FIG. 18–15. The growth–pollution trade-off.

advance. In the authors' view, these priorities (in addition to the previous priorities) are most effectively achieved by emphasis on market incentive within governmental guidelines and encouragement (a mixture of tax incentive, direct subsidy, and control standard policies seems desirable). True, this approach involves some increased governmental intervention, but, given that intervention on a $MSB = MSC$ basis, it appears possible to gain the advantages of market incentives and efficiencies, as well as resource allocation, to achieve social priorities of a nonprofit nature.

At this point, the authors would ask you for your own position in this growth-pollution trade-off issue. Do any of these three positions appear to you as desirable and realistic? Do you have an alternative proposal? Whatever your response may be, the growth-pollution issue is of major social relevance, and we hope this chapter has increased your economic understanding of such choices.

TERMS

Actual output. The existing level of production in an economy, as measured by real GNP.

Allocative efficiency (AE). The achievement growth factor relating to whether resources are used to full capacity.

Economic growth. An increase in real GNP per capita from year to year.

Growth factors. Those forces spurring economic growth, including human resources, natural resources, capital stock, technology-management, aggregate demand, and allocative efficiency.

Marginal social benefit (MSB). The additional gains to society resulting from some economic policy.

Marginal social cost (MSC). The additional disadvantages to society resulting from some economic policy.

Potential output. The maximum ability of an economy to produce, as represented by a production possibilities curve.

Real GNP per capita. The basic measure of economic growth, obtained by adding all components of final spending, correcting for price changes, and dividing by total population.

QUESTIONS FOR STUDY

1. How does economic growth affect your own economic activity?
2. How is economic growth defined and measured?

3. Can you distinguish "quantity" from "quality" in your own standard of living?

4. What causes economic growth to occur? State and define the six growth factors.

5. Distinguish an economy's potential to produce from its actual output level. Why may these output levels diverge?

6. What conflicts do you see between the goals of rapid economic growth and reduction in pollution? What position do you prefer in approaching this trade-off issue?

REFERENCES

Dorfman, Robert, and Nancy S. Dorfman. *Economics of the Environment.* New York: W. W. Norton & Company, Inc., 1972.

Edel, Matthew. *Economics and the Environment.* Englewood Cliffs, N.J.: Prentice-Hall, Inc., 1973.

Enthoven, Alain C., and A. Myrick Freeman III. *Pollution Resources, and the Environment.* New York: W. W. Norton & Company, Inc., 1973.

Garvey, Gerald. *Energy, Ecology, Economy.* New York: W. W. Norton & Company, Inc., 1972.

Gill, Richard T. *Economics: A Text with Readings,* Second Edition. Pacific Palisades, Calif.: Goodyear Publishing Company, Inc., 1975, Chapter 30 and Great Debate 5.

Goldman, Marshall I. *Ecology and Economics: Controlling Pollution in the 70s.* Englewood Cliffs, N.J.: Prentice-Hall, Inc., 1972.

Hinrichs, Harley H., and Graeme M. Taylor. *Program Budgeting and Benefit-Cost Analysis.* Pacific Palisades, Calif.: Goodyear Publishing Co., Inc., 1969.

North, Douglas C. *The Economic Growth of the United States 1790–1860.* New York: W. W. Norton & Company, Inc., 1966.

Olson, Mancur, and Hans H. Landsberg, eds. *The No-Growth Society.* New York: W. W. Norton & Company, Inc., 1973.

Savage, Donald T., et al. *The Economics of Environmental Improvement.* Boston: Houghton Mifflin Company, 1974.

19

WHY IS THE UNITED STATES INTERESTED IN UNDERDEVELOPED NATIONS?

SHORT ANSWER. No nation's economy can function in isolation today. Underdeveloped nations are suppliers of raw materials essential to U.S. manufacture and are also potential markets for the products of that manufacture. Their inability to provide minimum standards of living for their populations is a threat to world peace.

YOU AND THE "GREAT ASCENT"

As an introduction to the problems of underdeveloped economies, consider a typical citizen who is provided few of the social and private goods you may take for granted in the United States. Around this citizen you see no TV antennas, hospitals, automobiles, buses, electric appliances, sewage treatment plants, newspapers, or swimming pools. Rather, you see the citizen of the underdeveloped economy on the brink of starvation, diseased, and illiterate. The tragedy of underdeveloped economies is that they are unable to use their human or other resources effectively to reduce this poverty. In fact, you may quickly realize just how high and unique your American standard of living is compared to that in an underdeveloped economy if you study further Figure 19-2.

You may, of course, be asking, "But what does this have to do with me in the U.S.A.? I can have compassion for the peoples of underdeveloped economies, but how does their plight affect me? After all, we have poverty in the United States that also needs our attention. And what is this *great ascent* term, anyway?" These are some very rational, sound questions; we'll try answering them in this chapter and expanding your own economic understanding.

Last things first, the term *great ascent* comes from Robert Heilbroner (he wrote a fascinating paperback with that title) and is used to describe the possible developmental process of the presently underdeveloped economies. In this book, Heilbroner describes problems confronting the economic growth

FIG. 19–1. Underdeveloped economies' impacts on the U.S. economy.

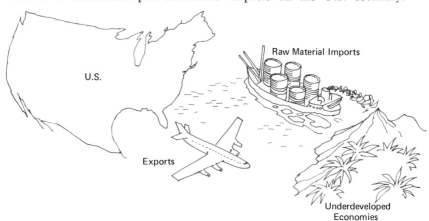

Sixty Americans in a Boiled Down World
By Alan Cranston
State Controller
(California—1970)

President Johnson has driven home the fact that poverty exists in the midst of affluent America. Abrupt, unimaginable poverty afflicts the human race and—unresolved—threatens peace.

Let's pretend, for a moment, that the world's three billion people are compressed into one town of 1,000 inhabitants. In that town—the world reduced in exact proportions—there would be 60 Americans.

The 60 Americans would receive half the income of the entire town, whereas the other 940 people would divide the remaining half.

More than half of the families of the town would live on incomes of less than $80 year.

The Americans would produce 16 per cent of the town's rotal food supply. Eating more than humans need and producting more food than they could eat, the Americans would store their surplus food—at enormous cost. The Americans would pay themselves not to grow food—although 666 of the other people of the community suffered from malnutrition.

The 60 Americans would have an average life expectancy of 70 years; the others, a life expectancy of less than 40 years.

The 60 Americans would have 15 times as many personal possessions as all the rest of the people. They would enjoy an incredibly disproportionate share of the electric power, coal, fuel, steel, and general equipment.

The lowest income group among the Americans would be much better off than the average of the rest of the town. Less than 200 of the other 940 would be relatively well off—representing Western Europe, South Africa, Australia, and a few wealthy Japanese.

An overwhelming majority of the 940 would be not only poor and hungry , but wholly uneducated and chronically ill.

There would be 303 so-called white people and 697 nonwhite. The treatment of the six nonwhite Americans by all too many of the other 54 Americans would not go unnoticed in the rest of the town.

Half of the 1,000 people would never have heard of Jesus Christ or what He taught. More than half would have heard of Karl Marx, Stalin, Khrushchev, and Mao. Eighty of the townspeople would be Communists. Three hundred and seventy-nine would be under Communist domination.

The American families would be spending vast sums—73 per cent of their overall public funds—for military purposes. They would be feverishly preparing to land a man on the moon—at incalculable cost—though they would be forbidden to set foot in certain parts of the town.

FIG. 19–2. U.S. abundance in a world of scarcity.

of poor nations and discusses whether these nations will ever attain higher standards of living.

But back to the main question of whether you should be interested or may be affected by the "great ascent." Aside from obvious humanitarian reasons, you and the U.S. economy may achieve *economic* gains if the "great ascent" succeeds! Now that you're probably listening (the profit motive at work!), review Figure 19-1 and consider the comments made in Chapter 20 regarding the economic growth impact of foreign trade. Remember that export sales (including those to underdeveloped economies) add to U.S. aggregate demand, and it is the level of aggregate demand that determines our present levels of output, employment, income, and prices. Our present level of exports to underdeveloped economies is quite small (approximately 30 per cent of all U.S. exports) because these poor nations cannot afford many U.S. products. However, if these underdeveloped economies enjoyed steady economic growth, they could then purchase more of our exports, and the U.S. economy might, in turn, experience further economic growth. ("You can't get rich off a poor neighbor?")

Remember from Chapter 18 that natural resources are a growth factor in potential output capacity. Whereas the U.S. economy possesses many important natural resource reserves, many of our domestic resources are dwindling. The United States is more and more dependent on foreign nations for raw materials to produce many of your consumer goods. We've previously analyzed the large impact of oil imports on the U.S. economy in Chapter 6, but be aware that these economy-wide impacts occurred from an imported raw material constituting 50 per cent of our domestic oil consumption. As Figure 19-3 points out, the U.S. economy is much more dependent (more than 75 per cent of domestic consumption in the case of some resources) on imported raw materials in many categories other than oil. Many of these resources lie within underdeveloped areas. Imagine the impact on the U.S. economy if these underdeveloped economies were to embargo or greatly increase prices on their natural resource exports to us. The point we're making is that the economic growth of these areas, with an accompanying desire to improve their living standards, may make these resources more accessible to the United States and, consequently, benefit your own consumption patterns.

We have pointed out possible reasons for your interest in the "great ascent," even putting aside humanitarian motives. Access to needed raw materials and increased domestic employment are indeed significant starting points. There are, of course, other self-interest motives for concern with the "great ascent," which centers more on cold war tensions and self-protection. Put bluntly, if the economic gap between the haves and have-nots of the world were reduced, there might be a greater chance for democracy, as we know it, and world peace and stability. In general, the wealthier a country becomes and the more it has to lose, the less likely it may charge quickly into wars and the less it may envy its wealthy neighbors. All world problems may not be solved by increased economic growth, but some minimum economic standard of living may be necessary before issues of political ideology may be debated. Do you suppose starving people really care which "ism" fills their bowls until the bowls are filled?

UNDERDEVELOPED ECONOMIES

Defining Underdevelopment

Although underdeveloped economies often include widespread poverty, this quality alone does not define them. There are many characteristics and causes of underdevelopment that we'll analyze shortly, but let us first review a few

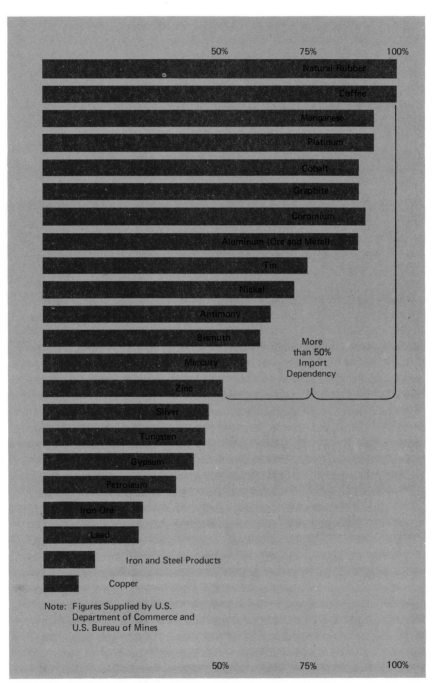

FIG. 19–3. U.S. dependency on imported resources.

points of economic growth theory from Chapter 18. Recall that economic growth (or lack of such) involves the ability to increase production of goods and services measured by real GNP per capita. The usual definition of under-developed countries is also stated in terms of a minimum *real gross national product (real GNP) per capita.* This measure accounts for price changes (real), for total output in the country (GNP), and on an individual basis (per capita). Real GNP per capita thus indicates a standard-of-living meas-ure (the amount of real output available to each person) and is the basic international measure used to describe levels of underdevelopment.

So we now have the measure, but how low must a real GNP per capita level be to classify an economy as underdeveloped? There are, indeed, argu-ments on this cutoff point, just as there are in describing poverty in the United States. But the "generally accepted" level for defining an underde-veloped economy is $300 real GNP per capita and below. Actually, there are often three levels and terms used in economic growth theory:

1. *Underdeveloped* economies: $300 or less real GNP per capita (the very poor areas of Africa and Asia). About 50 per cent of the world's population. It is with this group this chapter is most con-cerned.

2. *Developing* economies: between $300 and $1,200 real GNP per capita (much of Latin America, some of southern Europe, many Communist-bloc countries). About 35 per cent of the world's population.

3. *Developed economies:* Over $1,200 real GNP per capita (Western Europe, Sweden, Australia, United States, U.S.S.R., Japan, and Canada).

There may be some disagreement on these classification levels, depending on your reference, but they're generally accepted, and this threefold division is often used to apply the categories to some of the world's economies. (See Figure 19-4.)

In applying the real GNP per capita levels to arrive at a classification of underdevelopment in Figue 19-4, you'll notice there are general areas of pov-erty in the world. There are virtually "belts of underdevelopment," with many of the underdeveloped and developing economies in the region of the equator (Asia, Africa, and Latin America). The developed areas, on the other hand, form pockets in the Northern Hemisphere (Canada-United States, Western Europe, Japan, and parts of the Southern Hemisphere such as Australia and New Zealand). You should also notice that the great ma-jority of the world's population lives in dire poverty, with only a small per-centage experiencing absolute or relatively high living standards. Reread Fig-ure 19-2, and consider your own unique position in the world's income dis-tribution pattern! Also notice that Figure 19-4 indicates the growth rate of world economies (their annual increase in real GNP per capita). Not only do most of the world's economies have low real GNP, but their growth rates are quite low. A negative growth rate means that the real GNP actually declined from the previous year.

We should at this point post a warning against overreliance on this real GNP measure as a guide of underdevelopment. Price levels and living standards differ in underdeveloped economies, often extraordinarily. Statistical gathering procedures may be quite poor in underdeveloped areas, and certain oddities may influence the measure. An example of the latter is provided by Kuwait, the "richest" country in the world (some $12,500 real GNP per capita in 1976). In case you aren't familiar with Kuwait, it's a small (8,000 square miles; 300,000 in population) Middle Eastern country lying on the Persian Gulf and bordered by Iraq and Saudi Arabia. By any other characteristic of underdevelopment (capital stock, productivity, output, and so on), Kuwait is underdeveloped, except for huge oil royalty incomes paid by foreign oil firms. So if you divide large royalty checks among a few people, the real GNP statistic is quite high.

Another failing in the use of real GNP per capita is that it provides no information regarding income distribution; it is only an "average" measurement. As Figure 19-5 illustrates, another typical characteristic of underdeveloped economies is a high degree of income inequality. Such inequality may result in an even lower standard of living than indicated by the real GNP measure and makes comparisons of relative poverty extremely difficult. Again, we urge caution on use of the real GNP statistic and any other unless it is determined in detail how the statistic was derived and how it's used.

Another approach to defining an underdeveloped country is to look for characteristics of underdevelopment. Any underdeveloped economy exhibits visible aspects (such as poor housing; massive illiteracy; and lack of adequate food, sanitation, and health care) that classify that country as underdeveloped. Especially visible and serious are those characteristics resulting from rapid population growth; lack of capital stock; and little investment in transportation, health, and education. There is another aspect to such characteristics of underdevelopment. The characteristics may define an underdeveloped economy, but they also tend to explain causes of underdevelopment. Thus the preceding "visible problems" are both definitions and explanations of underdevelopment. Think through this comment, and we'll analyze the logic.

Causes of Underdevelopment

We've said underdeveloped countries concern the United States and have defined and located them. However, an important question remains in explaining why a country is underdeveloped.

What causes economic underdevelopment? Standard economic growth theory as described in Chapter 18 gives us an answer. Whether you are ex-

FIG. 19-4. Real GNP per capita in the world.

Country	1970 GNP per Capita (U.S. Dollars)	1960-70 Growth Rate (Per Cent)
United States	4,760	3.2
Sweden	4,040	3.8
Canada	3,700	3.6
Switzerland	3,320	2.5
Denmark	3,190	3.7
France	3,100	4.6
Germany, Fed. Rep. of	2,930	3.5
Norway	2,860	4.1
Australia	2,820	3.1
Belgium	2,720	4.0
New Zealand	2,700	2.1
Germany (East)†	2,490	4.2
Netherlands	2,430	3.9
Finland	2,390	3.9
United Kingdom	2,270	2.2
Czechoslovakia†	2,230	3.8
Austria	2,010	3.9
Israel	1,960	4.7
Japan	1,920	9.6
U.S.S.R.†	1,790	5.8
Libya, Arab Rep. of	1,770	20.4
Italy	1,760	4.6
Puerto Rico	1,650	5.8
Hungary†	1,600	5.4
Poland†	1,400	5.2
Ireland	1,360	3.6
Argentina	1,160	2.5
Greece	1,090	6.6
Spain	1,020	6.1
Venezuela	980	2.3
Hong Kong	970	8.4
Romania†	930	7.7
Singapore	920	5.2
Mexico	670	3.7
Portugal	660	5.3
Yugoslavia	650	4.3
Albania†	600	4.8
Lebanon	590	0.5
Costa Rica	560	3.2
Cuba†	530	-0.6
Mongolia†	460	0.0
Peru	450	1.4
Saudi Arabia	440	8.0
Nicaragua	430	2.8
Brazil	420	2.4
Zambia	400	7.1
China, Rep. of	390	7.1
Iran	380	5.4
Malaysia	380	3.1
Guatemala	360	2.0
Dominican Republic	350	0.5
Colombia	340	1.7
Korea (North)†	330	5.1
Iraq	320	2.5
Turkey	310	3.9
Ivory Coast	310	4.5
Ghana	310	-0.4
Angola	300	3.2
El Salvador	300	1.7
Algeria§	300	1.7
Papua New Guinea	300	4.5
Syria, Arab Rep. of	290	3.4
Ecuador	290	1.7
Honduras	280	1.8
Rhodesia	280	0.4
Paraguay	260	1.3
Philippines	210	2.9
Egypt, Arab Rep. of	210	1.7
Viet-nam, Rep. of	200	1.0
Thailand	200	4.9
Sierra Leone	190	4.7
Cameroon	180	3.8
Bolivia	180	2.5
China (Mainland)†	160	2.1
Kenya	150	3.6
Central AFrican Rep.	140	0.2
Mauritania*	140	4.5
Togo	140	1.2
Malagasy Rep.	130	1.2
Khmer Rep.	130	0.1
Uganda	130	2.4
Nigeria	120	0.1
Laos*	120	1.9
Sudan	120	1.0
Guinea*	120	2.7
Yemen, People's Dem. Rep. of	120	-5.0
Sri Lanka	110	1.5
India	110	1.2
Haiti	110	-0.9
Tanzania‖	100	3.6
Viet-nam (North)†	100	3.2
Pakistan and Bangladesh	100	2.4
Niger*	90	-2.0
Dahomey*	90	0.1
Zaire*	90	2.7
Chad*	80	0.4
Nepal*	80	0.5
Burma*	80	0.6
Yemen, Arab Rep. of*	80	2.0

Trinidad and Tobago	860	1.9	Tunisia	250	0.5	Indonesia*	80	1.0
Uruguay	820	-0.4	Korea, Rep. of	250	6.8	Ethiopia*	80	2.8
Bulgaria†	760	7.4	Jordan*	250	2.9	Afghanistan*	80	0.5
South Africa‡	760	3.0	Liberia	240	0.9	Malawi*	80	2.1
Panama	730	4.2	Mozambique	240	3.4	Somalia*	70	-1.1
Chile	720	1.6	Morocco	230	1.0	Mali*	70	4.4
Jamaica	670	3.5	Senegal	230	0.0	Upper Volta*	60	-0.6
						Surundi*	60	0.8
						Rwanda*	60	-1.5

Note: In view of the usual errors inherent in this type of data and to avoid a misleading impression of accuracy, the figures for GNP per capita have been rounded to the nearest $10.

The gross national product estimates on which the per-capita figures are based are calculated at *market prices*. Thus they include indirect taxes net of subsidies.

* Estimates of GNP per capita and its growth rate are tentative. In some instances GNP per capita estimates of under 100 dollars are based on data that have a large margin of error and are thus likely to be less reliable than estimates of over 100 dollars.

† Estimates of GNP per capita and its growth rate have a wide margin of error mainly because of the problems in deriving the GNP at market prices from net material product and in converting the GNP estimate into U.S. dollars.

‡ Including Namibia.

§ Growth rate relates to the period 1963-1970.

|| Mainland Tanzania.

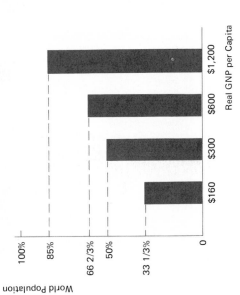

Real GNP per Capita

World Population

	Poorest 0-20%	Low Middle,* 21-39%	Middle, 40-60%	Upper Middle, 61-79%	Highest 20%	Highest 5%
Argentina	7.00	10.30	13.10	17.60	52.00	29.40
Bolivia	4.00	13.70	8.90	14.30	59.10	35.70
Brazil	3.50	9.00	10.20	15.80	61.50	38.40
Burma	10.00	13.00	13.00	15.50	48.50	28.21
Ceylon (Sri Lanka)	4.45	9.21	13.81	20.22	52.31	18.38
Chad	12.00	11.00	12.00	22.00	43.00	23.00
Chile	5.40	9.50	12.00	20.70	52.30	22.60
Colombia	2.21	4.70	8.97	16.06	68.06	40.36
Costa Rica	6.00	7.30	12.10	14.60	60.00	35.00
Dahomey	8.00	10.00	12.00	20.00	50.00	32.00
Ecuador	6.30	16.00	13.40	22.60	41.80	21.50
El Salvador	5.50	6.80	11.30	15.00	61.40	33.00
Gabon	2.00	6.00	7.00	14.00	71.00	47.00
Greece	9.00	12.80	12.30	16.40	49.50	23.00
India	8.00	12.00	16.00	12.00	42.00	20.00
Iraq	2.00	6.00	8.00	16.00	68.00	34.00
Israel	6.80	13.40	18.60	21.80	39.40	11.20
Ivory Coast	8.00	10.00	12.00	15.00	55.00	29.00
Jamaica	2.20	6.00	10.80	19.50	61.50	31.20
Japan	4.70	10.60	15.80	22.90	46.00	14.80
Kenya	7.00	7.00	7.00	15.00	64.00	22.20
Lebanon	3.00	4.20	15.80	16.00	61.00	34.00
Libyan Arab Republic	0.11	0.39	1.28	8.72	89.50	46.40
Malagasy Republic	7.00	7.00	9.00	18.00	59.00	37.00
Mexico	3.66	6.84	11.25	20.21	58.04	28.52
Morocco	7.10	7.40	7.70	12.40	65.40	20.60
Niger	12.00	11.00	12.00	23.00	42.00	23.00
Nigeria	7.00	7.00	9.00	16.10	60.90	38.38
Pakistan	6.50	11.00	15.50	22.00	45.00	20.00
Panama	4.90	9.40	13.80	15.20	56.70	34.50
Peru	4.04	4.76	8.30	15.30	67.60	48.30
Phillipines	4.30	8.40	12.00	19.50	55.80	27.50
Rhodesia	4.00	8.00	8.00	15.00	65.00	60.00
Senegal	3.00	7.00	10.00	16.00	64.00	36.00
Sierra Leone	3.80	6.30	9.10	16.70	64.10	33.80
South Africa	1.94	4.17	10.16	26.37	57.36	39.38
Sudan	5.60	9.40	14.30	22.60	48.10	17.10
Surinam	10.70	11.56	14.74	20.60	42.40	15.40
Taiwan	4.50	9.70	14.80	19.00	52.00	24.10
Tanzania	9.75	9.65	9.85	9.75	61.00	42.90
Trinidad and Tobago	3.60	5.76	9.16	24.48	57.00	26.60
Tunisia	4.97	5.65	9.95	14.43	65.00	22.44
Venezuela	4.40	7.00	16.60	24.90	47.10	23.20
Zambia	6.27	9.58	11.10	15.95	57.10	37.50
Averages	5.6	8.40	12.00	17.71	56.00	30.00
U. S.	5.4	11.9	17.5	23.9	41.4	15.9

*Computed from original table.

Source: I. Adelman and C. T. Morris, "An Anatomy of Income Distribution Patterns in Developing Countries,"—*Development Digest*, October, 1971. Department of Commerce, Bureau of the Census.

FIG. 19–5. Distribution of income in the world.

plaining why growth has occurred (as in the United States as described in Chapter 18) or why it is absent (underdeveloped economies), you use the same logic and growth concepts. You also use the same growth theory whether analyzing a large geographical area, an entire nation, or one small region of one country. What we're saying is that the economic growth theory about to be presented can be applied in a great many ways and is thus another item in your toolbox of economic understanding.

First, let's review (Figure 19-6) the *production possibilities curve*. We've used this very basic concept on a number of occasions, and it's at the heart of the economic growth theory to be applied here. Recall (Chapters 2 and 18) that a production possibilities curve indicates a country's potential to produce goods and services. This potential, or maximum, output level is based on present resource amounts and quality: *labor, natural resources, capital stock, technology-management*. Furthermore, the PPC level indicates full employment of this fixed resource base at whatever level of technology already exists.

Looking at Figure 19-6, you see the potential and achieved PPC levels compared between a developed and underdeveloped economy. Notice that the actual output level in an economy may fall below the potential PPC level. The present PPC level depends on the present fixed resources and fixed technology and assumes full employment of resources to give the present potential output levels. The underdeveloped economy has a much lower PPC potential than the developed economy and also achieves a lower degree of that potential. This potential could, of course, grow over time (outward expansion), given any increase in the size or quality of the resource base or the technological level at which the resources are used. If a country is to have increasingly higher standards of living, it must have this expanding potential to allow

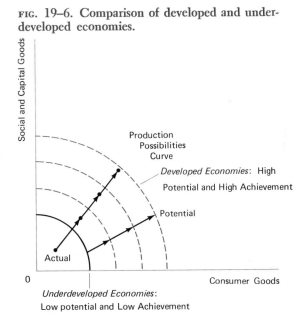

FIG. 19–6. Comparison of developed and under-developed economies.

maximum resource allocation and output of consumer or social and capital stock goods. As an aside, a war could reduce this potential when resources are destroyed.

However, remember that a country (or person) may not reach its full potential, as is indicated in Figure 19-6. The actual economic growth achievement level is usually less than the potential level of output. This failure occurs for a variety of reasons, but the most basic include a shortage of aggregate demand and/or a low level of allocative efficiency in using the limited resource base. The aggregate-demand cause was examined in depth in Chapter 12 (circular flow, employment theory, derived demand, and multiplier concepts), and modern fiscal policy (Chapter 13) attempts to maneuver aggregate demand toward full employment. A low allocative efficiency in the use of resources may arise because of limited or undeveloped markets, little or unstable currency, the impact of an unstable or unwise government on the economy, or a host of factors resulting in available resources not being used as effectively as possible. If a country's standard of living, therefore, is to be as high as possible at whatever the level of present development, there must also be an expanding achievement level in reaching the economy's full potential.

To consolidate these preceding paragraphs, we "summarize" as follows: An underdeveloped country's lack of economic growth occurs because (1) it has a *low potential to produce* and (2) it has a *low achievement* level in reaching such potential. In order to secure economic development, therefore, that

FIG. 19–7. Growth prospects of an underdeveloped economy.

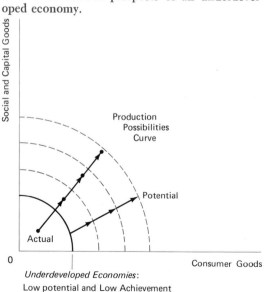

Underdeveloped Economies:
Low potential and Low Achievement

country must expand its potential and also expand its achievement level of that potential. Do you see this from Figure 19-7? To see just how such development can occur and what limits development, let's analyze causes of underdevelopment as they relate to this theory of economic growth. We will ascertain what prevents these growth factors from reaching their full potential and achievement levels.

Limits on Growth Factors

Recall again that economic growth and development basically are defined as the production of more output, thus implying both an increase in a country's potential to produce and its rate of achieving that potential. The growth factors—natural resources, human resources, capital stock, technology, allocative efficiency, aggregate demand—discussed previously determine the existing level of output and achievement. If a country is not developed and is experiencing many economic growth limitations, the economist analyzes what growth factors are blocked or limited and to what degree. To put it another way, if development is determined by growth factors, then any condition within a country that seriously limits the growth factors' operation may be said to be a cause of economic underdevelopment.

Limiting conditions include overpopulation, low spending and saving, untrained workers, social and political instability or upheavals, and many others as listed in Figure 19-8. Although not all of these problems may simultaneously face all underdeveloped countries (and others may have extra problems not on the list), these are typical problems. The problems often limit a specific growth factor, although a single problem—like rapid population growth—may hinder several growth factors. Realize also that these problems and growth factors are interdependent and that the separation is only for example. To illustrate, the underdeveloped condition of natural resources may be related to the low amount of capital stock and the lack of a skilled labor force.

Although all the preceding growth factor limits are important and must be remedied if economic development is to occur, there are specific problems that loom even larger, and we'll review these here. One of the most important problems facing most underdeveloped countries is rapid population growth. (A few areas do perhaps require more people to settle new land, such as the interior of Brazil and the "outback" of Australia.) We've previously stated that most of the world's population lives in underdeveloped economies. But in addition to the large populations already existing, the underdeveloped countries are plagued by a very high birth rate, as indicated in Figure 19-9.

You may wonder why population growth is such a problem if human resources are one of the growth factors. Well, one reason is that more people does not necessarily mean a larger labor force, the entity that really produces the country's output. The United States has 215 million people, whereas

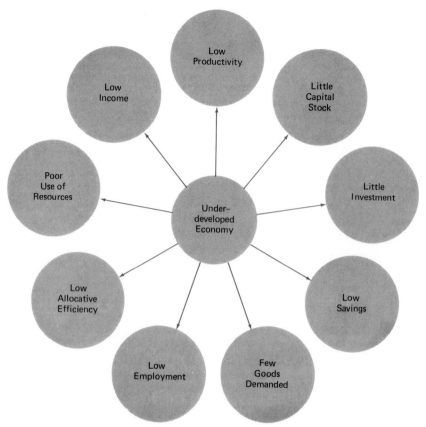

FIG. 19–8. Problems of underdeveloped economies.

China has over 800 million, but the U.S. real GNP per capita far exceeds that of China. More people may mean only more mouths to feed, especially the old, the sick, and the very young, and may add an even greater strain on a country's already low ability to produce. Furthermore, resources in the face of rapid population growth must be used mainly for consumption output, allowing little growth of capital stock. A major question raised is whether the underdeveloped countries can even continue to feed their rapidly expanding populations unless there is foreign aid, some effective limit on population growth, and/or technology gains in food production.

True, there are present attempts to limit rapid population gains, but a country's birth rate is the result of basic biological drives coupled with complex and persistent social forces (a large family constitutes "social security" for the parents). Whereas Western medical technology may reduce the death rate, a reduction in the birth rate may have to await the far-off arrival of a developed, progressive society. In the meantime, the population soars, and people starve daily. Some of you may challenge the implicit assumption of limiting population growth by the authors.

Remember, however, that there are two approaches to population control —*increasing the death rate*, or *reducing the birth rate*. In all too many places, the former control dominates through disease, famine, war, inadequate medical care, and poor education and personal hygiene. Although religious, social, and cultural differences often limit the effectiveness of birth control, its rapid but still inadequate use seems to transcend ideological bounds. Both Communist China and highly capitalistic Singapore, for example, have focused significantly on this problem, and both seem to be making enviable headway in limiting population growth. The Chinese use centralized political propaganda to delay marriages and thereby limit reproduction, and the Singaporeans use "free market disincentives" to achieve the same goals. In Singapore, the first two children born to each couple are "on the house," as the government pays for delivery and pre- and postnatal care. After that, the couple must pay out of their own pocket for this care and are, in addition, put at the bottom of the waiting list for housing in a nation that has a major housing shortage.

Of course, you, the individual, must make your own decision as to your own practice. However, the underdeveloped countries may not be able to afford such considerations if the choice comes down to starving or limiting population growth. For many of the underdeveloped areas, the starvation point has arrived or is fast approaching (India). As a whole, the underdeveloped economies' food output growth is lagging well behind population growth. Starvation may be a very real long-run result. Thomas Malthus may be proved right in his eighteenth-century prediction that population growth would eventually exceed food production.

Associated to some extent with population growth is the serious growth factor limit of *deficient capital stock*. Because the underdeveloped economy typically has few factories and machinery, the output of food and other products is very low. Low productivity prohibits surplus output so that some resources may be invested in new capital stock construction. In addition—and to illustrate further the interrelatedness of the growth factors—unskilled human resources limit capital stock use; rapid population growth allows few resources to be diverted to capital goods output; the low level of domestic aggregate demand creates little need for mechanized factories. The farmer cannot afford, say, a modern tractor; he couldn't run or service one anyway. He may have a superstition that prevents him from using one; his acreage may be too small to permit its use; he may live too close to starvation or be too backward to risk an untried food production method. For example, one of the authors witnessed the introduction of a relatively modern agricultural method in a central African state in the early 1960s. A wooden plow was

Country	1970 Population (Thousands)	1960-70 Growth Rate (Per Cent)	Country	1970 Population (Thousands)	1960-70 Growth Rate (Per Cent)	Country	1970 Population (Thousands)	1960-70 Growth Rate (Per Cent)
China (*Mainland*)	836,000	2.0	Sri Lanka	12,514	2.4	Chad	3,640	1.8
India	538,129	2.3	Kenya	11,250	3.1	Rwanda	3,596	3.0
U.S.S.R.	242,768	1.2	Nepal	11,060	1.8	Burundi	3,544	2.0
United States	204,800	1.2	Malaysia	10,945	3.1	El Salvador	3,534	3.7
Pakistan and Bangladesh	130,166	2.7	Venezuela	10,399	3.5	Laos	2,962	2.4
Indonesia	115,567	2.0	Hungary	10,331	0.3	Ireland	2,944	0.4
Japan	103,390	1.0	Uganda	9,814	2.7	Israel	2,910	3.2
Brazil	92,764	2.9	Chile	9,780	2.3	Uruguay	2,886	1.3
Germany, Federal Rep. of	61,560	1.0	Belgium	9,683	0.6	Puerto Rico	2,842	1.8
United Kingdom	55,730	0.6	Iraq	9,678	3.5	Somalia	2,828	2.4
Nigeria	55,070	2.9	Portugal	9,635	0.9	New Zealand	2,816	1.7
Italy	53,667	0.8	Greece	8,892	0.7	Lebanon	2,726	2.5
France	50,775	1.0	Ghana	8,640	2.6	Dahomey	2,708	2.9
Mexico	50,670	3.5	Bulgaria	8,490	0.8	Sierra Leone	2,555	1.4
Philippines	36,850	3.0	Cuba	8,390	2.1	Honduras	2,520	3.3
Thailand	36,218	3.1	Sweden	8,040	0.7	Papua New Guinea	2,420	2.3
Turkey	35,230	2.5	Mozambique	7,729	1.9	Paraguay	2,379	3.1
Spain	33,645	1.1	Khmer Rep.	7,485	3.2	Jordan	2,317	3.5
Egypt, Arab Rep. of	33,329	2.5	Austria	7,390	0.5	Albania	2,170	2.9
Poland	32,807	1.0	Saudi Arabia	7,360	1.7	Singapore	2,075	2.4
Korea, Rep. of	31,793	2.6	Malagasy Republic	7,310	2.6	Nicaragua	1,984	3.5
Iran	28,662	2.9	Switzerland	6,281	1.5	Togo	1,956	2.7
Burma	27,584	2.1	Syria, Arab Rep. of	6,098	2.9	Libya, Arab Rep. of	1,940	3.7
			Ecuador	6,093	3.4	Jamaica	1,888	1.6
			Cameroon	5,836	2.1	Costa Rica	1,727	3.3

FIG. 19–9. Problems of population growth in underdeveloped economies.

Country	Population	Rate		Country	Population	Rate		Country	Population	Rate
Ethiopia	24,625	2.2		Yemen, Arab Rep. of	5,730	2.2		Central African Republic	1,552	2.6
Argentina	23,212	1.5		Angola	5,501	1.3		Liberia	1,520	3.0
				Upper Volta	5,384	2.1		Panama	1,464	3.3
South Africa*	22,160	3.0		Rhodesia	5,310	3.3		Mongolia	1,280	3.0
Colombia	21,632	3.2		Guatemala	5,190	3.1		Yemen, People's Dem. Rep. of	1,255	2.3
Canada	21,406	1.8								
Viet-nam (North)	21,150	2.8		Tunisia	5,075	3.0		Mauritania	1,170	1.9
Yugoslavia	20,540	1.1		Mali	5,018	2.1		Trinidad and Tobago	1,027	2.1
				Ivory Coast	4,941	3.0				
Romania	20,253	0.9		Bolivia	4,931	2.6				
Zaire	18,800	2.8		Denmark	4,921	0.7				
Viet-nam, Rep. of	18,332	2.6								
Germany (East)	17,250	0.0		Haiti	4,867	2.0				
Sudan	15,695	2.9		Finland	4,695	0.6				
				Malawi	4,440	2.6				
Morocco	15,495	2.9		Zambia	4,136	2.5				
Czechoslovakia	14,467	0.6		Dominican Republic	4,068	3.0				
Algeria	14,330	3.1								
Afghanistan	14,300	2.0		Niger	4,020	2.9				
China, Rep. of (Taiwan)	14,035	2.9		Guinea	3,980	2.6				
				Hong Kong	3,960	2.5				
Korea (North)	13,890	2.7		Norway	3,879	0.8				
Peru	13,586	3.1		Senegal	3,870	2.1				
Tanzania†	13,270	2.5								
Netherlands	13,019	1.3								
Australia	12,552	2.0								

*Including Namibia.
†Mainland Tanzania.

hitched to a bullock instead of being pushed by the farmer's wife. Grain production in that particular area soon had a threefold increase in grain output.

Don't jump to the conclusion from the preceding discussion that underdeveloped economies are doing nothing about increasing capital stock. Many underdeveloped and developing economies have shifted resources in an ambitious growth plan to speed output of capital stock. (The Soviet Union, India, Brazil, Mexico, Taiwan, and Greece are all examples.) Often, however, these plans have fallen short of objectives because output was used ineffectively or capital stock output caused serious deficiencies elsewhere in the economy or other problems arose. Capital stock limitation is, indeed, a pressing problem and is frequently of central concern in development plans, foreign aid discussions, and economic "growth models" used to predict future development of an economy under varying development plans.

THE "GREAT ASCENT"

Economic Planning

One could, of course, go on and on describing specifically each of the many growth problems facing underdeveloped economies, although the previous section may have discouraged your view of the growth potential for them. Economic growth that occurs in underdeveloped economies (review Figure 19-4) faces large obstacles indeed. The limits on growth factors in underdeveloped economies are numerous and substantial, but in a few hopeful instances there are possible internal and external economic growth remedies.

To focus on internal economic growth remedies, there are many underdeveloped economies adopting some type of *economic planning;* that is, a high degree of coordination is followed (usually through central government command) in allocating economic resources to maximize the gains in potential and actual output. The essence of such plans is their attempt to reduce limitations on growth factors and to emphasize the interdependence of growth factor limitations. To promote one growth factor, the plan provides improvement in another, but that requires growth in a third factor, and so on. This is easily understandable if you realize that a country's ability to produce is the result of many complex interrelationships of resources, and it requires complex forethought in making development plans. In planning just where you might allocate your limited resources to achieve maximum output, you must pick out key elements in these interrelated growth factors that will, in turn, cause further growth effect. Thus, you attempt to maximize the *linkage effect* (term by Hirschmann in *The Strategy of Development*) by improving those growth factors that themselves aid in improving other growth factors.

An example of this key-element and linkage-effect planning is government construction of schools and roads (new social capital stock). The schools should improve the quality of the human resources, thus aiding output (especially if education stresses vocational skills), adoption of advanced technology, and possible future birth control and consumer savings gains. The newly built roads may open natural resources for extraction, may allow ideas and new customs to expand and unify the country, and may spur aggregate demand by making available new markets to business people. Note that the government may be "priming the development pump" by selecting those capital stock investment priorities that will lead most effectively to further economic growth.

The economic plans of some underdeveloped economies also often emphasize various approaches to limiting population growth and encouragement to domestic and foreign businessmen by providing low-interest loans to construct new capital stock for one approach and promotion of an adequate supply of money and credit for another. In addition, export sales are often emphasized, with the resulting export earnings channeled into specific investment categories designed to speed economic growth. In all of these various efforts to reduce limitations on growth factors, economic planners must apply economic growth theory and make difficult economic choices as to what social needs are to take priority. Of course, internal economic planning does not guarantee success of the great ascent theory, and most underdeveloped economies seem to be doomed to a perpetual cycle of poverty and its attendant evils.

Foreign Aid

In an attack on the serious problems in an underdeveloped economy, an alternative (or, better yet, a coordinated attack on growth limitations) to internal economic planning is the external use of foreign aid. An underdeveloped economy may accept capital stock (factory, tools, tractor, school, and so on) from a foreign nation and thereby avoiding diverting its own meager resources from consumer to capital goods. In addition, with foreign aid, the capital stock can be obtained immediately rather than by waiting until the country itself could produce the item. The underdeveloped economy may, therefore, greatly speed up the developmental process (on either an industrial or agricultural front) through the use of foreign aid. Notice that we use foreign aid here as either the use of investment funds or the provision of actual equipment, and such capital stock may be obtained from either foreign governments or private business firms.

Foreign aid benefits may also affect growth factors by other means than addition to growth of capital stock. For example, technology may come from foreign sources (government or private business) in the form of improved production techniques, hybrid seed grains, education programs, medical knowledge, or trained workers. However, the underdeveloped economy must typically modify and adapt this advanced foreign technology to meet its own limited abilities and backward cultural patterns. A further "foreign aid" benefit might include reduced trade barriers by the country conferring the benefit (tariffs or quotas) on the exports of the underdeveloped economy. Such reduction allows underdeveloped economies greater export earnings, increased aggregate demand, and greater domestic investment. The point we're making is that foreign aid should be viewed in the broad sense of any favorable foreign impact on growth factors in the underdeveloped economy.

We should point out that there are also some disadvantages to an underdeveloped economy in using foreign aid. Such unfavorable aspects from the recipient's viewpoint include possible foreign intervention in the economy, mortgaging the country's earnings to meet debt repayments, and possible economic and political corruption accompanying the foreign aid. The factor that often causes the most tension is the first one cited. The nationalistic drive of many underdeveloped economies may demand that the foreign influence "get out." Such feelings may culminate in the take-overs of private foreign business concerns, destruction of foreign buildings or offices, and cessation of foreign government contact. Perhaps the lesson of recent decades is that foreign aid does not necessarily win friends or influence people or even increase the recipient's living standard.

An evaluation question that is perhaps proper here is "How much has foreign aid helped underdeveloped economies, and what has been the U.S. role in it?" An overall answer to such a question would have to be that most programs have had mixed success in general and that the direct U.S. aid role was and is important, but it is rapidly declining. Figure 19-10 indicates U.S. foreign aid amounts and distribution since World War II. Although large in total, this aid has averaged "only" some $5 billion annually (less than 1 per cent of U.S. GNP), and much of that aid has not gone to underdeveloped economies. Success stories of countries "making good" through some degree of foreign aid vary from Iran to Taiwan, from Brazil to Israel; outstanding successes include Western Europe (Marshall Plan aid of post-World War II) and Japan. The very rapid Japanese economic growth has been of special note.

Although the United States is not the only country supplying foreign aid and technology to underdeveloped countries (other donors include the Soviet Union bloc, Western Europe, China, Canada, Israel, Japan, and some Arab states), the U.S. commitment has been of major importance and significance. We can examine this continuing aid program by studying Figure 19-10. Notice that the post-World War II average is approximately $5 billion annually, concentrated at first in Western Europe, but now largely in the Southeast Asian and Latin American economies. These foreign aid moneys are administered by varying agencies, usually the Agency for International Development (AID), and include funds for strictly economic development purposes and

Europe	$49,343	India*	$9,127	Africa	$5,355
Britain	$9,694	Turkey	$5,974	Morocco	$ 846
France	$9,603	Pakistan*	$4,021	Tunisia	$ 743
Italy	$6,442	Greece	$3,994	Zaire	$ 476
West Germany	$5,089	Iran	$2,746	Ethiopia	$ 440
Yugoslavia	$2,927	Israel*	$1,345	Nigeria	$ 389
Netherlands	$2,549	United Arab Republic	$ 912	Ghana	$ 303
Spain	$2,456	Jordan*	$ 671	Liberia	$ 288
Belgium	$2,021	Afghanistan	$ 419	Libya	$ 232
Austria	$1,334	Ceylon	$ 183	Algeria	$ 194
Norway	$1,310	Nepal*	$ 164	South Africa	$ 151
Denmark	$ 921	Iraq	$ 104	Guinea	$ 121
Poland	$ 580	Lebanon	$ 102	Sudan	$ 105
Portugal	$ 528	Saudi Arabia*	$ 94	Ivory Coast	$ 94
Sweden	$ 207	Syrian Arab Republic	$ 61	Kenya	$ 92
Ireland	$ 193	Kuwait	$ 50	Somali Republic	$ 80
Czechoslovakia	$ 193	Yemen	$ 45	Tanzania	$ 75
Russia	$ 186	Cyprus	$ 23	Sierra Leone	$ 50
Finland	$ 184	Region aid, not		Zambia	$ 45
West Berlin	$ 132	allocated by		Senegal	$ 42
Iceland	$ 91	country	$1,949	Uganda	$ 42
Switzerland	$ 47	Western Hemisphere	$17,101	Comeroon	$ 35
Hungary	$ 33			Mali Republic	$ 28
Albania	$ 20	Brazil	$4,153	Malawi	$ 26
Malta	$ 9	Chile	$1,691	Botswana	$ 20
Romania	$ 8	Colombia	$1,441	Niger	$ 18
East Germany	$ 1	Mexico	$1,220	Togo	$ 18
Regional aid, not		Argentina	$ 959	Upper Volta	$ 18
allocated by		Peru	$ 793	Malagasy Republic	$ 14
country	$2,585	Bolivia	$ 562	Dahomey	$ 13
		Venezuela	$ 532	Lesotho	$ 12
Far East	$34,610	Dominican Republic	$ 503	Chad	$ 10
		Guatemala	$ 380	Burundi	$ 8
Korea	$8,554	Ecuador	$ 368	Gabon	$ 8
Vietnam*	$6,872	Panama	$ 273	Rwanda	$ 8
Taiwan	$5,425	Costa Rica	$ 218	Southern Rhodesia	$ 7
Japan	$4,356	Nicaragua	$ 197	Central African Republic	$ 6
Philippines	$2,240	Uruguay	$ 186	Marutitius	$ 5
Indo-China†	$1,535	Paraguay	$ 158	Mauritania	$ 5
Indonesia	$1,525	El Salvador	$ 155	Congo (Brazzaville)	$ 4
Thailand	$1,238	Canada	$ 136	Gambia	$ 4
Laos*	$ 742	Honduras	$ 134	Swaziland	$ 4
Cambodia	$ 598	Haiti	$ 127	Regional aid, not	
Ryukyu Islands	$ 412	Jamaica	$ 110	allocated by	
Burma	$ 108	Trinidad and Tobago	$ 65	country	$ 276
Malaysia	$ 106	Guyana	$ 64	Oceania	$1,558
Hong Kong	$ 44	Cuba	$ 52		
Singapore	$ 43	Bahamas	$ 39	Australia	$1,079
Brunei	$ 14	Surinam	$ 10	New Zealand	$ 129
Western Samoa	$ 2	British Honduras	$ 6	Regional aid, not	
Regional aid, not		Barbados	$ 1	allocated by	
allocated by		Regional aid, not		country	$ 380
country	$ 796	allocated by		Aid not allocated	
		country	$2,568	by regions	$9,604
Near East and				Grand Total	
South Asia	$31,984			U. S. Foreign Aid	$149,585

* Excluding military aid.
† Aid to Indo-China area before it was split into North and South Vietnam, Cambodia, and Laos.

Source: Agency for International Development.

FIG. 19–10. U.S. foreign aid total.

417

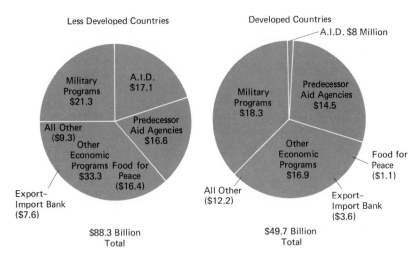

Source: Agency for International Development.

FIG. 19–11. U.S. foreign aid analysis.

for military aid and support (see Figure 19-11). The trend to be observed is that the Agency for International Development (AID) has in its assistance expenditures attempted (1) to shift more funds to development purposes, (2) to concentrate aid on a few key countries (as in Southeast Asia and Latin America), and (3) to stress self-help and reform by the underdeveloped countries affected.

How successful has this U.S. foreign aid program been? It's a "mixed" picture, as stated! Western Europe and Japan are showcases of success in terms of U.S. foreign aid. Some Latin American and Southeast Asian economies have had improved economic development (Brazil, Venezuela, Taiwan, Thailand). Yet there are many countries where U.S. aid has produced few examples of positive development (India) or where internal problems and nationalistic drives have adversely affected the United States and the recipient economies (Chile).

If one evaluates U.S. foreign aid programs purely on an economic basis, the score is fairly good. Our aid programs have spurred development projects in many underdeveloped economies; have been models or other economies; and have increased exports and output, employment, and income. Although such increased exports to the underdeveloped economies may themselves be considered a form of repayment, repayment of the loan aspect of foreign aid also occurs. Such repayments may at present fall short of the total advanced, but remember these are long-term loans, with varying repayment arrangements. It would be quite difficult to calculate a rate of return on foreign aid by adding up interest payments on loans, private U.S. business profits, and increases in exports to those receiving aid.

However, a favorable appraisal of U.S. foreign aid may not apply if viewed from a political or diplomatic viewpoint. The United States has not become a friend in the minds of all concerned because of its foreign aid expenditures. Brickbats tossed at the foreign aid program include exploitation, imperialism, "giveaway" of public funds, and aid to the "enemy." Although the authors are incapable of reconciling these varying viewpoints, it should be noted that a political judgment standard for foreign aid may be quite unfair. If the purpose of aid is economic growth, there's no necessary "friendship" required or expected, and an evaluation on that basis would thus be unwarranted. Foreign aid, however, is still a political football in the U.S. Congress!

By the way—and added only to avoid possible confusion—remember we've emphasized here *foreign aid*, not *foreign investment*. Foreign aid is conducted by the U.S. government, whereas foreign investment is made by a private firm for profit. Although both may benefit the underdeveloped economy, their motives differ. Chapter 20 will further analyze foreign investment.

CURRENT ISSUES AND PROBLEMS

Although there are a great many issues regarding underdeveloped countries deserving consideration (foreign trade policies, growth strategies, diplomatic relations, and so on), there appear to be two vital areas. The first involves U.S. expectations of the developmental process; the second centers on future quantity and quality growth projections.

On the first issue, it may well be that economic growth in the underdeveloped countries may not occur as the United States expects or achieve the preferred results and impacts. Consider yourself as a U.S. senator about to vote on a foreign appropriation bill and presented such conclusions as the following: the aid will result in dictatorship, revolution, possible failure, and social upheaval (outcomes postulated in *The Great Ascent* by Robert Heilbroner and echoed by many other growth theorists). These conclusions may very well shake you up a bit, especially if you're debating whether to contribute U.S. resources to the process. You may be aiding the start of a very chaotic, revolutionary change, leading to a dictatorship that may eventually fail in its attempts at economic development. How do you vote now? Although these conclusions may seem unappealing, they are realistic prospects in underdeveloped countries. One must remember that the U.S. economic growth experience has been exceptional and may not be easily duplicated somewhere.

The second issue is much more complex, involving economic choice, resource supplies, and comparative living standards. Let's approach it by considering what would happen if all the world were to rise at once to present U.S. living standards. After all, the goal of economic development is usually put as increased output (measured by greater real GNP per capita), presumably to raise low standards of living. However, the United States now consumes some 40 per cent of the world's resources for its 6 per cent of the world's population to live at its high standard of living. (We also produce a disproportionate amount of goods, such as agricultural exports.) If the rest of the world rose, therefore, to such living standard levels without commensurate increases in productivity, the world's resources would be entirely consumed by 15 per cent of the world's population, leaving 85 per cent (some 3.6 billion people) with no resources! Does that appear possible to you?

The point we're getting at, of course, is that future economic development (in the U.S. and world economies in general) may have to consider a deemphasis of material goods production (resource use). Of course, technological advance may provide some measure of greater productivity from resource supplies, but an infinite expansion of output and resources does not appear either reasonable or possible. Somewhere along the line there must occur a revolution in resource use, particularly by those economies consuming most of the resources. Of course, those at the bottom rung of the living standard are not about to consider such an issue until their living standards increase to some minimum level. How does one go about persuading wealthy economies to consume less or underdeveloped economies not to emulate the present values of developed economies?

Another aspect to this very difficult issue is that present economic growth projections show that this *living standard gap* between have and have-not nations will increase over time. Such projection does not promote consideration of quality over quantity in economic growth choices of allocating resources. Although there is evidence in the United States of concern for the environment, a ground swell of support to reduce the output of material goods can hardly be said to exist. The authors urge greater public awareness of, and regard for, the "costs" of economic growth: the type of economic growth, as well as amount, must be given greater consideration.

TERMS

Economic planning. Some degree of central direction in use of economic resources within an economy.

Growth factors. The forces that determine an economy's potential output (work force, natural resources, capital, technology) and actual output levels (aggregate demand, allocative efficiency).

Underdeveloped economy. A economy in which real GNP per capita is less than $300. See Figure 19-4.

QUESTIONS FOR STUDY

1. How does one define an underdeveloped economy? Is Japan an underdeveloped economy? Is India?
2. What are the major characteristics of an underdeveloped nation?

3. Have you ever traveled to an underdeveloped economy? What growth problems did you see? Was economic planning in operation?

4. How does rapid population growth affect the production possibilities curve of an underdeveloped economy?

5. What prevents an underdeveloped economy from attaining rapid economic growth?

6. State and explain the major avenues of economic development available to an underdeveloped economy.

7. Using the production possibilities concept, describe how American foreign aid might help the "great ascent" of underdeveloped economies.

REFERENCES

Agency for International Development. *Foreign Aid in Perspective.* Washington, D.C.: Agency for International Development, 1968.

Heilbroner, Robert L. *The Great Ascent.* New York: Harper & Row, Publishers, 1963.

Hirschmann, A. O. *The Strategy of Development.* New Haven, Conn.: Yale University Press, 1958.

Lewis, W. Arthur. *Development Economics: An Outline.* New York: General Learning Corporation, 1974.

McCormack, Arthur. *The Population Problem.* New York: Thomas Y. Crowell, 1970.

Sahlins, M. *Stone Age Economics.* Chicago: Aldine Publishing Company, 1972.

Swamy, S. *Economic Growth in China and India.* Chicago: University of Chicago Press, 1973.

20

WHY IS FOREIGN TRADE IMPORTANT?

SHORT ANSWER. Foreign trade provides essential products, both finished and raw materials, for U.S. consumption. In addition, foreign trade may open markets abroad and thus increase employment for American workers. Furthermore, trade can promote international cooperation through mutually beneficial commercial relationships.

YOU AND FOREIGN TRADE

"How important is foreign trade to me? Why should I spend time studying this issue?" You may well ask these questions, for it appears that U.S. citizens underestimate the impact of foreign trade on their individual activities and on our entire economy. The United States is the world's largest foreign trader ($300 billion in exports and imports in 1976). Export-import flows greatly affect our economy's levels of output, employment, income, and prices. Foreign trade should concern you, therefore, because it is very significant to the U.S. economy. We will attempt in this chapter to clarify this point, and in this process we hope to promote your understanding of the basic economics of foreign trade.

Perhaps the most direct and visible area in which you may be affected by foreign trade is your purchase of a foreign product (an *import* to the United States; an *export* from the foreign country). The list of foreign products is varied, indeed, as illustrated in Figure 20-2. Do you drive a VW (filled with Shell gasoline), wear a Swiss watch, listen to a Japanese-made radio or TV,

FIG. 20–1. Foreign trade importance.

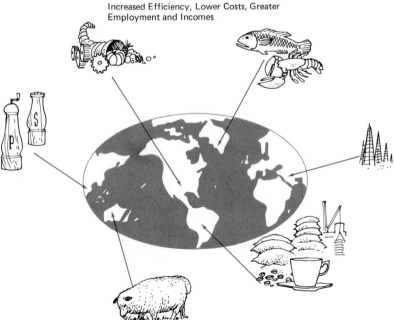

Comparative Advantage

Increased Efficiency, Lower Costs, Greater Employment and Incomes

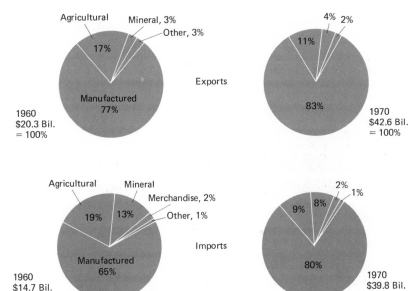

Source: President's Economic Report, 1975, p. 352.

FIG. 20–2. U.S. foreign trade composition.

wear Italian shoes, or wash with a British soap (Lever Brothers)? Many Americans consume a variety of foreign products for reasons of price, quality, desired features, and availability and, by following the dictum of consumer sovereignty, "getting your money's worth." In so doing, they may also spark response from American manufacturers and trade unions. Consumer purchase of foreign compact cars has generated a variety of new American products: Falcon, Valiant, Corvair, to start; then Pinto, Colt, and Vega, with Pacer and Chevette as recent editions. Some of these models are now out of production, and new lines are doubtless in preparation. Foreign competition has spurred the American automobile manufacturer, as well as many other industries. How would you classify a Colt, which is made in Japan by a Chrysler-owned plant?

Even if you don't purchase a foreign product directly, foreign trade may affect your purchase of domestic products by American manufacturers' use of raw materials from abroad. Many of our everyday domestic products depend on imported raw materials (see Figure 20-3), such as iron ore (Brazil), oil (Kuwait and Venezuela), copper (Zaire), and rubber (Liberia). Were we to rely exclusively on our own natural resource base, some domestic products could not exist, and the manufacture of others would necessarily be curtailed. The experiences of the oil embargo in 1973 on the U.S. economy (review Chapter 6) should leave us little need to emphasize the importance of im-

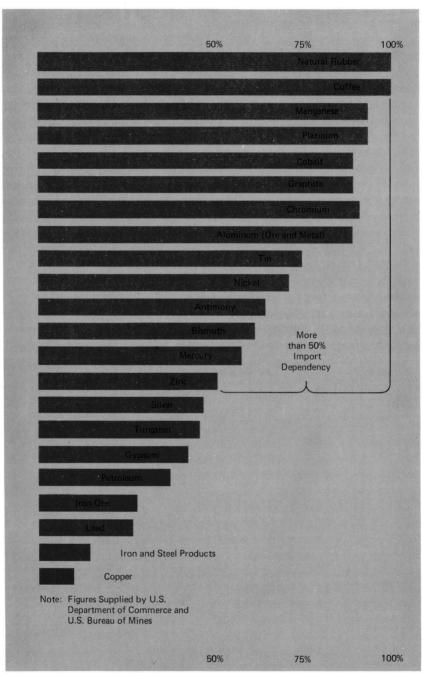

FIG. 20–3. Foreign imports in U.S. consumption.

ported raw materials on our domestic output levels. And recall from Chapter 19 (see Figure 20-3) that the United States is much more dependent on imported raw materials other than oil.

There are some disadvantages of foreign trade in that the dependence of the United States on foreign suppliers makes our economy vulnerable to foreign political pressures and threats of nationalism. Another disadvantage is the often hurled charge by underdeveloped economies of exploitation, because U.S. multinational businesses extract and export natural resources from these countries for allegedly inadequate royalty payments. In fact, an often quoted statistic regarding antipollution and economic growth issues is that the United States, with some 6 per cent of the world's population, uses about 40 per cent of available world resources.

On the one hand, we have the issues (review Chapter 19) of U.S. diplomatic and economic relationships with underdeveloped economies or, more bluntly put, the "haves vs. have-nots." In another regard, there is the question of proper and prudent consumption rates of resources as discussed in Chapter 18. Although there are ecology vs. growth conflicts, the United States must still depend on foreign trade as a source of many raw materials, whereas underdeveloped economies depend on the aggregate demand of export earnings.

To return to the concern of the individual in foreign trade, consider the role in *generating income* played by our exports to other nations. Your own job may be a direct result of foreign demand (U.S. exports) for the product you help produce. Income earned by others from foreign sales may furnish product demand supporting your job. Foreign demand stimulates domestic output, employment, and income (really, the circular-flow theory of Chapter 12 again), and it raises some associated issues. Notice in Figure 20-4 that the income necessary to foreign nations who wish to buy U.S. products may well come from our purchases of those nation's products. Thus, U.S. imports that generate foreign incomes may well lead to U.S. exports through the spending

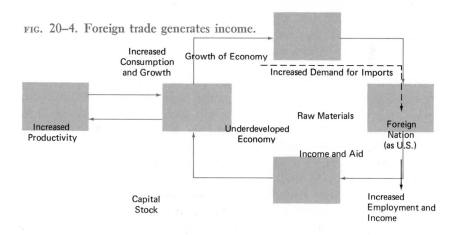

FIG. 20–4. Foreign trade generates income.

Increased Consumption and Growth

Growth of Economy

Increased Demand for Imports

Increased Productivity

Underdeveloped Economy

Raw Materials

Foreign Nation (as U.S.)

Income and Aid

Capital Stock

Increased Employment and Income

of the foreign incomes earned. Perhaps you can see, then, that if we attempt to reduce our imports (tariffs reduce foreign sales), we may well also reduce our exports (less foreign income generates fewer U.S. sales). On the other hand, two-way foreign trade may produce increased sales for both parties.

Although it represents a small percentage of GNP compared to the foreign trade of other nations (some 4 per cent in United States, but 30 per cent in Denmark), foreign trade affects the U.S. economy through products we consume, raw materials provided, and income produced. The small percentage is misleading (recall that the U.S. is the world's largest foreign trader) because only net (exports minus imports) foreign trade is computed as a percentage of the very large GNP of the U.S. economy. In addition—and as we'll further discuss in this chapter—there are many related aspects of foreign trade, such as balance of payments, gold flows, U.S. dollar role in foreign exchange, foreign aid in underdeveloped economies, and our political and diplomatic relations with other nations.

FOREIGN TRADE HISTORY

Before we analyze issues of modern foreign trade, let us briefly survey the historical development of this important economic activity. Foreign trade has been and is today an economic force that has spurred commerce, promoted technology and growth, spread cultural patterns, stimulated exploration and colonization, and frequently fanned the flames of war. To appreciate this modern economic force fully, we must examine its historic roots.

Beginning of Trade

The history of foreign trade has gone hand in hand with the development of civilizations. From very ancient times foreign trade brought about the exchange of products and raw materials between one land or nation and another. Although such trade was often conducted in barter form and was of small volume by today's standard, this interchange of products was important in economic and historical development.

Foreign trade from its earliest beginnings was necessary, and not just because it provided one society with products such as spices from the Orient available only from other areas. Foreign trade also formed the basis for cultural interchanges, thus trading not only products, but also life-styles, customs, and technology. (The value of trade in spreading technological progress is a fascinating story by itself!) In addition, foreign trade prompted the development of monetary systems, of record keeping and accounting, and of an entire vocation of commerce. In fact, foreign trade aided in making the businessman respectable and reduced public displeasure toward usury. One can state that the economic and political development of the entire Western world was spurred and enhanced by foreign trade.

Another distinct contribution of foreign trade was the strong promotion given the field of exploration, map making, and ship construction technology. Early trade routes ranged over vast expanses, thus requiring advances in transportation to make possible further search for new products and markets. Let us not forget, of course, that such desire for new trade routes, products, and markets was the driving force that launched explorations leading to discovery of the New World. Columbus set out, as you recall, not to settle a new nation, but to discover a new trade route to the Orient. The interest upon his return to Europe centered not on his accounts of forests and soil, but on the new products available, such as tobacco, corn, and so on.

As foreign trade progressed and technology developed, these explorations were to turn up another area of foreign trade, still important today. This was the import of raw materials by a nation and the re-export of finished and manufactured products. As a result, not only were living standards advanced, but national incomes were also increased.

Mercantilism to Now

The importing of raw materials and the exporting of finished products for an income (gold accumulated) formed a very decisive step in the economic and political development of, particularly, European powers. The process led not only to technological progress and the industrial revolution, but also to expanded political and diplomatic relations between nations. Countries discovered that they need not necessarily have abundant domestic raw materials to advance economically if advantages of foreign trade were exploited. Prime examples of such development through trade have included Italy (Venice was a commercial center in the 1400s), Portugal, Spain, the Scandinavian countries, and Great Britain. Our own northern colonies demonstrated such trade dependence, and Japan today is an excellent example of a highly industrially developed nation growing rapidly while depending heavily on foreign trade.

From your reading of history books, you are undoubtedly aware of the premises upon which our nation was founded. Great Britain financed the initial settlement and colonization of our thirteen colonies because of the promise of potential raw materials (lumber, wheat, rice, and so on, to start) and the prospect of a "captured" market for finished goods. Such a purposeful manipulation (attempted, anyway) of foreign trade flows was called *mercantilism*, and colonial settlement was seen from the British point of view as essentially of economic benefit to Britain herself. Various laws (Iron Act, Hat Act) were passed in an attempt to prevent the development of finished goods in the colonies, and at the same time revenue measures (Stamp Act) were legislated. The result, of course (you did read those history books, didn't you?), was not exactly as planned in the British view; these policies, among other things, led to our nation's independence. Colonial governments themselves were concerned with trade provisions, references were made in the Constitution to foreign trade regulation by Congress, and tariffs were among the earliest pieces of legislation our new Congress enacted.

Beyond the importance of foreign trade in our nation's founding, trade patterns have continuously spurred our economic growth and westward expansion. (Review Chapter 18.) Early foreign purchase of cotton exports from Southern U.S. states generated Southern income, thereby enabling purchase of Northern U.S. manufactured goods. Foreign demand for Northern U.S. shipping services provided a market base for Western U.S. farm products. Furthermore, U.S. manufactured products exported abroad have continuously provided stimulus for domestic employment and income, and foreign investment (an export) aided us from the start in our development. By the way, if this seems to resemble the conditions found in underdeveloped economies today, you are on the right track. Just as foreign trade was vital in our own growth, so is trade of utmost concern to the "have-nots" in the world today. (Perhaps you should recall this in your next debate on tariffs or foreign aid.)

The point has been made, we hope, that foreign trade has long been significant in the economic and political development of nations. In our own case, trade was central not only to our initial settlement, but to our continued expansion. The importance of foreign trade remains today, albeit with a few new issues, as we'll note.

LIMITATIONS ON FOREIGN TRADE

We've described the importance of foreign trade to you and our economy on both a present and historical basis. You might think that foreign trade is "free" and without problems or limitations. Such is not the case, however, as foreign trade restrictions have as long a history as trade itself. Foreign trade appears to have always existed under some degree of limitations, be it in Egypt, Venice, Spain, or the American colonies (recall mercantilism).

These limitations on the conduct of foreign trade trouble the economist, as the result is generally a misallocation of resources, less than efficient production, reduced output, and a lower standard of living. These glum results are predictable from the *principle of comparative advantage*, an economic theory stating in essence that by specialization of labor and exchange of output, the consumption standards of both producers making the exchange may increase. Although we've previously noted this principle in Chapter 2, let us analyze it in detail here.

The logic of comparative advantage was first stated by David Ricardo (1771–1823), a British economist who investigated the amount of resources an economy required to produce a given amount of output under various methods of production. Ricardo was not interested in measuring whether an economy merely produced a greater amount than another economy (*absolute advantage*), but in comparing the *relative costs* of output between the two economies (*comparative advantage*). Such a comparison is really an application of the opportunity cost concept and determines in what output area an economy is most efficient (has the lowest relative cost or the greatest comparative advantage). If each economy were to *specialize* in those outputs of greatest efficiency and then *exchange* (foreign trade role) surplus output, both economies would gain in terms of increased efficiency of resource allocation and greater output and consumption.

If this explanation of Ricardo's sounds a bit complicated, let's examine two examples to clarify the principle. First, consider the business manager who hires a typist. Suppose the business manager is a better typist and a better decision maker than the typist; the business manager has an absolute advantage in each field. But further suppose that the business manager is twice as productive at typing and five times more productive in decision making than the typist. The business manager has a comparative advantage in decision making, whereas the typist has a comparative advantage in typing. If both specialize in these respective fields, both will benefit (and our economy also gains). "A simpleminded example" you may reply, but it does illustrate the principle of comparative advantage, and people do tend to choose those careers in which they are relatively more productive.

If the career choice example did not fully clarify the principle of comparative advantage, let's analyze Figure 20-5 in step-by-step fashion:

1. Initially and for the sake of example only, the United States and Japan each produce autos and chemicals (using one-half of their available resources in each output), with total output and consumption of five autos and six chemicals.
   a. The relative costs (amount of foregone output) of U.S. production are one-half auto for one chemical (give up two autos for

FIG. 20–5. Principle of comparative advantage.

	Autos	Chemicals	
U. S.	2	4	Before
Japan	3	2	Specialization
Total Output	5	6	

	Autos	Chemicals	
U. S.	0	8	After
Japan	6	0	Specialization
Total Output	6	8	

	Autos	Chemicals	
U. S.	3	4	After Foreign
Japan	3	4	Trade
Total Output	6	8	

four chemicals) and two chemicals for one auto (give up four chemicals for two autos).

  b. The relative costs of Japanese production are one and a half autos for one chemical (give up three autos for two chemicals) and two thirds of a chemical for one auto (give up two chemicals for three autos).

  c. The United States has a comparative advantage in chemical output, for her relative cost (one half auto per chemical) is lower than that of Japan (one and one half autos per chemical).

  d. Japan has a comparative advantage in auto output, as her relative cost (two thirds of a chemical per auto) is lower than that of the United States (two chemicals per auto).

2. If both economies now specialize in the output area of their comparative advantage, total world output will rise owing to increased efficiency and decreased relative costs (six autos and eight chemicals vs. five autos and six chemicals before specialization).

3. If these economies now trade their surplus output (as three autos from Japan for four chemicals from the United States), both economies may enjoy higher consumption levels than before specialization and trade.

  a. Japan now has three autos and four chemicals, compared to initial consumption of three autos and two chemicals. And her relative cost of obtaining chemicals is now lower (three fourths of an auto per chemical—gave up three autos for four chemicals) than previously (one and one half autos per chemical).

  b. The United States now has three autos and four chemicals, compared to initial consumption of two autos and four chemicals. And her relative cost of obtaining autos is now lower (one and one third chemicals per auto—gave up four chemicals for three autos) than previously (two chemicals per auto).

Although the previous enumeration is somewhat long, you ought to follow each point for economic understanding. Notice especially that each economy is to specialize in the output of comparative advantage (lowest relative cost) and that both nations gain (greater consumption and reduced relative cost) through specialization and foreign trade. You may also notice that the exact extent of gain to each economy depends on the *terms of trade* (the ratio of exports a nation gives up for imports, as three autos for four chemicals by Japan in Figure 20-5) in foreign trade.

The basic point is that since the days of Ricardo (and long before) foreign trade has prompted efficiency of production and increased consumption. But note that for these benefits to be realized, there must be *free foreign trade*, that is, no restrictions on the extent of specialization and exchange. If there is to be total benefit from world foreign trade, economies must be able to specialize and exchange in a broad variety of outputs and with a large range of trading partners. Realize that our two-economy, two-output example of Figure 20-5 is simple compared to daily foreign trade flows. Trading arrangements become more complex with more nations and products, with different currencies, and with varying motives of nationalism or economic development. Still, there are benefits resulting from unimpeded foreign trade.

However, although there may be many good reasons for free foreign trade, foreign trade today is not an unlimited bridge of commerce and culture between all nations. Neither is foreign trade exempted from serious problems of different currencies, balance-of-payments problems and gold flows, and politics. All of these problems tend to limit foreign trade in various degrees, although tariffs may limit efficiency gains more than other factors. Let us examine the arguments stated for this trade-off of economic efficiency against other objectives.

Tariffs

Although there are advantages of free foreign trade (availability of goods, raw materials source, income generation, increased productivity by specialization, mutual diplomatic interests), it should be realized that present foreign trade is not free. There are really a number of barriers to present foreign trade, but the most immediate and direct is that of *tariffs*.

Tariffs have been around a long time and are essentially taxes on imported goods. Their effect on the consumer is higher prices for foreign goods purchased, and their typical effect on the foreign producer is reduced sales (the law of demand, from Chapter 4). Of course, the very idea of a *protective tariff* (a *revenue tariff* is to generate income) is precisely to achieve such reduction of foreign import sales and encourage the consumer to substitute domestically produced products. Applying some of your economic understanding (concepts of demand elasticity, economic growth, circular-flow theory), perhaps you see problems in such an attempt. The consumer may not buy at all if the price is then too high, and reduced foreign imports in one product line may lead to reduced U.S. exports of another product. (Would Japan buy our chemicals if we didn't buy their autos?)

This concept of protecting U.S. industry (the same principle is applied in other nations as well) from foreign competition is the basic tariff argument and comes in several forms; that is, labor may wish protection against low-cost labor in other nations, saying higher U.S. wages must be guarded by tariffs. As a rebuttal, recall that the cost of production involves other resource costs besides labor (capital stock, raw materials, management) and that you must match productivity against wages to determine cost of production. Other types of argument for tariff include protecting an essential industry (need technical skills in national emergency), protecting an infant industry (need higher prices because of high initial costs, to be reduced later), or guaranteeing national security (regulate trade with certain nations in specific trade items). One or all of these arguments have been used in U.S. economic history from colonial times through today.

Quotas are another means of restricting foreign trade. A *tariff places a tax on imports* (thus raising prices); *a quota places a restriction on actual numbers sold.* Although the mechanisms differ (a quota is more sure and direct), the end result of both tariffs and quotas is protection for U.S. industry by reduced import sales. As our congressmen debate, apply your own economic understanding to this protection issue, and see where you stand. Then quiz the next political candidate you see on his opinion, and vote accordingly.

We should note here that although tariffs exist to limit foreign trade, there have been steps to reduce trade barriers; tariffs and quotas have been reduced. Trade agreemnts on an international basis have been consistently pursued since World War II, and fruitful agreements have been made to increase trade flow and reduce tariffs. Perhaps the most impressive of these trade agreements is the *European Economic Community (EEC)*, better known as the *Common Market.* The EEC represents an economic union of nations (see Figure 20-6) who have set aside certain economic conflicts in order to free trade among the member nations. The result is as theory would predict: greater productivity, increased trade flow, lower prices, and increased economic growth.

One may, of course, regard the EEC as a competitor to the United States and thus oppose its development. The EEC represents increased foreign trade competition (with the United States and other world markets) and does have common tariff agreements against U.S. products. On the other hand, improved economic conditions in the EEC countries enable them to purchase more U.S. products. Another measure of EEC success is that new members wish to enter (Great Britain and Denmark received full membership in 1973), and other economic unions are beginning to form now in Latin America and West Africa. Did you realize that the United States is, in fact, the world's largest "common market" in terms of GNP (fifty states, one currency, no internal tariffs, virtually free labor and investment movement, and one governmental and legal system)?

U.S. FOREIGN TRADE TODAY

Although we've discussed the benefits and background of foreign trade, we have not yet analyzed specific issues of U.S. foreign trade flows. Indeed, U.S. foreign trade in the 1970s has produced a number of varied and complex trends.

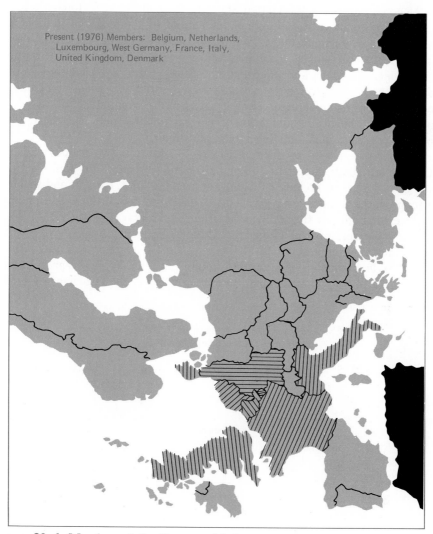

Present (1976) Members: Belgium, Netherlands,
Luxembourg, West Germany, France, Italy,
United Kingdom, Denmark

FIG. 20–6. Members of the Common Market.

Composition of U.S. Foreign Trade

As noted previously, the United States is the world's largest foreign trader, conducting exchange with hundreds of nations in thousands of items. Our $300 billion of foreign trade in 1976 touched many parts of the world, affecting both underdeveloped economies and our own domestic levels of output employment, income, and prices. Notice from Figure 20-7 that the United States *exports* (sells to foreign nations) a great variety of products, including both finished manufactured items (planes, arms, computers, trucks, drill presses, and chemicals) and farm or natural resource output (wheat, soybeans, corn, rice, fruits and vegetables, and lumber).

The list of exported products in Figure 20-7 hints at two major trends in U.S. exports, both important to emphasize and evaluate. One trend is that the United States is no longer the only, or even the most, efficient and sought-after producer of industrial goods. This enviable position of the U.S. economy really existed only for the two decades after World War II. Since World War II, many nations, especially Japan and those of Western Europe, have rebuilt vast industrial complexes to rival those of the U.S. economy. Thus, rather than the lone supplier of industrial goods (as after World War II), the United States is now one competitor among many in the fast-changing tech-

FIG. 20–7. U.S. foreign trade composition.

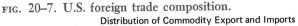

Distribution of Commodity Export and Imports

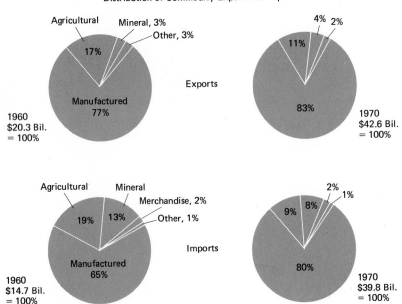

Source: President's Economic Report, 1975, p. 352.

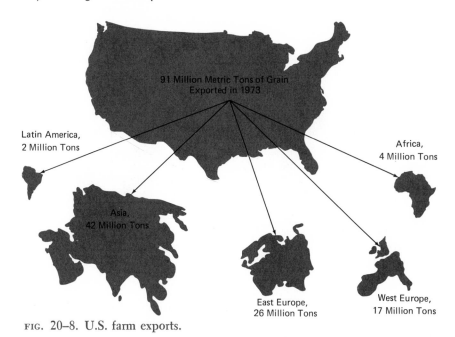

91 Million Metric Tons of Grain Exported in 1973

Latin America, 2 Million Tons

Africa, 4 Million Tons

Asia, 42 Million Tons

East Europe, 26 Million Tons

West Europe, 17 Million Tons

FIG. 20–8. U.S. farm exports.

nology of electronics, autos, chemicals, and machine tools. This trend is noted, not as a criticism of the U.S. economy, but rather as a point of fact on which to base foreign trade analysis. In fact, many of the present U.S. trade competitors (Japan, Germany) were rebuilt with U.S. foreign aid and technology.

Another foreign trade trend to be noted in Figure 20–7, which is emphasized by Figure 20-8, is the large *U.S. role as a world "breadbasket"*; that is, U.S. export of food items has greatly increased in the 1970s, and all predictions point to further growth. Our large food exports are due partly to high U.S. farm productivity allowing surplus gains for trade and partly to rising foreign demand for foodstuffs. Not only do increased populations (recall Chapter 19?) and expanded diets of other nations prompt rising food demand, but some foreign food supplies have also been hard hit by drought and plant disease. As just one example, the Soviet Union purchased 19 million metric tons of grain from the United States in 1972 and imported another 10 million metric tons in 1975. Such purchases prompt some serious questions, which each person will have to answer for himself or herself.

1. If we assume that foreign exports of grains increase grain prices in the United States (as happened with the Soviet grain deal of 1972), should farm exports be limited?

2. If grain surpluses in the United States are reduced by export sales, is there any danger to adequate food supply for U.S. citizens?

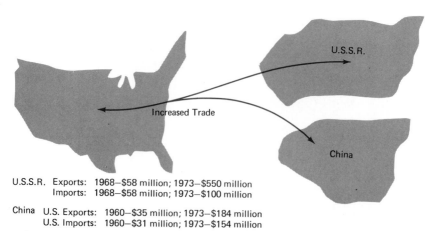

U.S.S.R. Exports: 1968—$58 million; 1973—$550 million
       Imports: 1968—$58 million; 1973—$100 million

China U.S. Exports: 1960—$35 million; 1973—$184 million
      U.S. Imports: 1960—$31 million; 1973—$154 million

Source: U.S. Department of Commerce, Federal Reserve Bank of San Francisco, author estimates.

FIG. 20–9. U.S.–Communist bloc foreign trade.

3. If there may be a conflict between providing food to U.S. citizens and feeding starving peoples of underdeveloped economies, how should the U.S. government respond?

Some large, nasty questions are posed above, but they may demand immediate answers if present trends continue! There is also a more favorable trend (this may be a value judgment as well?) in the previous problem issues. The 1970s have experienced a *much-expanded foreign trade between the United States and Communist-block economies.* As Figure 20–9 illustrates, U.S. trade with the Soviet Union and the People's Republic of China has especially increased, and all projections point to further growth. These expanded foreign trade flows are the result of growing world willingness to compromise on differences of political ideology, of increased economic necessity for trade output, and of increased necessity for an establishment of diplomatic détente between the Soviet and U.S. governments. Whether such trends are "real," stable, and promise future growth is currently debated by many citizens. The authors would only comment that increased foreign trade and interdependence of world economies appears to be one method to reduce possibilities of armed conflict!

Balance-of-Payments Accounting

To explain the financial trends of U.S. foreign trade, we must now analyze the standard accounting procedure (used by the United States and other nations) of *balance of payments* (BOP for short). BOP is important because it records the impact of foreign trade activity and thus provides further analysis of trends and problem areas. In addition, BOP indicates any surplus or deficit

Balance of Payments

I. Trade Account
   A. Includes physical trade flows plus "invisibles" of services and tourism.
   B. U. S. record strong, but surplus lost in 1971.

II. Capital Account
   A. Includes private domestic investment abroad plus government foreign aid and expenditures.
   B. U. S. record is of large outflow and deficits.

III. Adjustment Account
   A. Includes gold flows, holding of domestic currency by foreigners, and short-term debt.
   B. U. S. has had large gold outflows to 1971.
   C. Provides overall balance to any deficit or surplus in trade and capital accounts.

FIG. **20–10. Balance-of-payments account.**

trends, which then affect gold flows and foreign exchange conditions (our next section).

Let us first examine the structure of BOP accounts, as illustrated by Figure 20-10. Notice that this overall account is composed of these separate accounts: *balance of trade, balance on capital account,* and *adjustment account balance.* Notice also that in an overall sense, the entire BOP is always "in balance" (no surplus or deficit). The "popular" reference to a BOP deficit or surplus is technically incorrect, as any imbalance between the trade and capital accounts is compensated in the adjustment account. Let us specifically define each account.

1. *Balance of Trade (BOT).* The balance of trade is the most typical flow of foreign trade, recording physical flow of imports and exports, as well as payments for shipping services, tourist expenditures abroad, and other miscellaneous spending (termed the "invisibles"). The BOT would record the Soviet grain purchases as a U.S. export (Soviet import) and your purchase of a Toyota as a U.S. import (Japanese export).

2. *Balance on Capital Account (BCA).* The balance on capital account records money and investment flows between nations, on both a governmental and private business basis. Thus, U.S. foreign aid to India is recorded as a U.S. import (Indian export), whereas a Saudi Arabian purchase of U.S. government securities would be a U.S. export (Saudi Arabian import). On the private business side, the construction of a factory in Chile by International Telephone and Telegraph would be a U.S. import (Chilean export), whereas Japanese businessmen purchasing an American hotel would produce a U.S. export (Japanese import). If you question export-import rules, remember that a *U.S. export occurs when*

income flows into the United States, whereas a *U.S. import means
that income flows out of the United States.*

3. *Adjustment Account (AA).* The adjustment account consists of
   gold movements (rare, especially since 1971), short-term capital
   flows (business and government debts and the International Mon-
   tary Fund's obligations termed *special drawing rights*—SDRs) and
   buildup of domestic currency in foreign holdings. Basically, this
   AA acts as a "balancing mechanism" to correct for any surplus or
   deficit in the first two accounts. Thus, if a "BOP deficit" (popular
   term in newspapers, really meaning that the BOT and BCA together show a negative result) occurs, compensating balancing in
   the AA might include gold outflow, U.S. government drawing of
   SDRs (more on this in the following section), or buildup of U.S.
   business debts to foreign companies.

The preceding enumeration should aid you in sorting out the often confused references to BOP accounting in local newspapers. For example, it is
quite typical (often occurred in the 1950s and 1960s) to experience simultaneously (1) a BOT surplus, (2) a BCA deficit, (3) a deficit for BOT and
BCA together (perhaps termed a "BOP deficit" in newspapers), and (4) an
overall balance in BOP because of compensating adjustments in the AA. To
exemplify and examine further these BOP results, notice that Figure 20-11
records surpluses or deficits between the BOT and BCA components, although the BOP is in overall balance at all times.

You may discover in Figure 20-11 an alarming trend toward growing deficits between the BOT and BCA components. Such deficits are not too surprising when one examines foreign trade trends since World War II, though
these trade flows have caused considerable confusion and adjustment in foreign exchange markets. Basically, these trends are a large and continuing deficit in the BCA (government foreign aid and private business investment
abroad) and a declining surplus becoming a deficit in 1971 for the BOT (foreign competition, inflation, U.S. dollar as foreign exchange standard).

The significant depreciation of the U.S. dollar since 1971 has caused our
BOT to vary, but move in the direction of reestablishing a positive balance
trend. And our BCA has improved, thanks mostly to large inflows of Arab oil
moneys ("petrocurrency") seeking investment outlets in the U.S. economy.
Whether these favorable BOP trends will continue remains to be seen, but
do not become alarmed by deficits noted in Figure 20-11. True, these deficits
force adjustments in foreign exchange mechanisms (see the following section), but realize the BOP entries generally result from profitable business
operation; that is, an export or import results from consumer purchase, business agreement, and government accounting: The U.S. government is not "in
debt" (especially since 1971, when the gold-for-dollars promise was dropped).
We note this distinction because there are sometimes radical "solutions" sug-

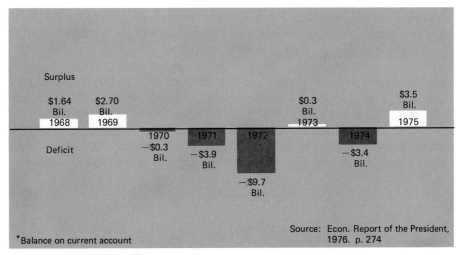

Source: U.S. Department of Commerce.

FIG. 20–11. Balance-of-payments record for U.S.

gested to correct BOP imbalances. Such solutions may produce detrimental impacts in our economy.

Can we correct these BOP problems without resort to "radical" solutions, you may well ask? The answer is not an easy yes, especially in view of the U.S. "world leadership" position. Consider the alternatives:

1. *Increase goods and services exports.* A greater BOT surplus would help, but currently we are plagued by our relatively high inflation rate, which makes our products less competitively priced. And, of course, we could increase tariffs. But higher tariffs can decrease exports as well as imports and do not support our efforts (especially to underdeveloped economies) to promote world trade. Perhaps the best we can do is increase productivity, reduce inflation at home, and press to reduce tariffs worldwide.

2. *Decrease capital flows.* A reduced BCA deficit would help, but presents large problems. Restricting private investment flows is not in the interests (efficiency, profits) of most economies because these investments are of profit to domestic businesses and underdeveloped economies. As for reducing U.S. government loans and aid, there are strong political and diplomatic pressures (cold war, underdeveloped economies, world leadership role) that urge continued public capital outflow. Perhaps the best hope here is for continued growth of private capital profit returns and an increased "sharing" of other governments in foreign aid burdens.

Neither of these approaches would appear to reduce significantly the U.S. BOP problems. One bright spot may be the previously noted increase in East-West trade. U.S. foreign trade, as well as that of other nations, with both the Soviet Union and the People's Republic of China has grown steadily, and recent diplomatic contact should prompt further trade increases. Although some may shout, "Trading with the enemy!" another view is that increased trade may lead to improved BOT results for the United States and reduced political tensions for all. The prospect of mutual economic gain may lead to some reduction of cold war pressures! Again, this is an issue you will have to decide through your own economic analysis and value judgment.

FOREIGN EXCHANGE MARKETS

There is one additional important aspect of foreign trade we must analyze— the *foreign exchange markets* presently in existence. The importance of foreign exchange is best realized if you think back to the last time you purchased a foreign product (Dutch cheese, Yamaha, Swiss watch, and so on). You paid for this product with your own currency, the U.S. dollar. However, you must realize that eventually the foreign manufacturer must be paid for that same product in his country's currency (mark, yen, krona, and so on). Therefore, for foreign trade to take place there must be some mechanism whereby the currency of one country is converted into the currency of another country. This conversion process is what the foreign exchange market is all about. The foreign exchange markets determine the *ratio of exchange* between different currencies, thus permitting export and import flows of foreign trade to be exchanged in different currency standards. This ratio of exchange between currencies is termed the *foreign exchange rate*, illustrated in Figure 20-12.

The comparative monetary values (foreign exchange rates) resulting from foreign exchange market operation show, for example, how many U.S. dollars are required to purchase one unit of a foreign country's currency. Approximately $0.95 equals one Canadian dollar, $0.45 equals one West German mark, $0.003 equals one Japanese yen, and so on. A little math exercise extra for you: If $0.45 equals one West German mark, how many marks equal one U.S. dollar? (The answer is that 2.2 marks equal $1.) By doing this problem, you'll see what foreign exchange quotations look like from a foreign viewpoint. Given one foreign exchange rate (FER), you find the reciprocal FER from dividing one by the initial FER; that is, whereas U.S. citizens would view the FER as so many U.S. dollars for one unit of a foreign currency, foreign citizens would look at the reciprocal of that same FER as so many units of their currency for one U.S. dollar.

There is also some variation in the foreign exchange rates of Figure 20-12 from one date to another. Such variation should tip you off as to how such foreign exchange rates are determined, and Figure 20-13 illustrates the process

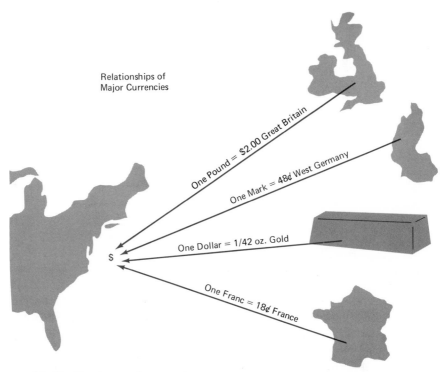

Relationships of
Major Currencies

One Pound = $2.00 Great Britain

One Mark = 48¢ West Germany

One Dollar = 1/42 oz. Gold

$

One Franc = 18¢ France

FIG. 20–12. Foreign exchange rates.

more clearly. A foreign exchange rate is, in fact, a price of one currency in terms of another currency. Like most prices, supply-demand forces in the marketplace determine the existing FER. (Recall Chapters 3 to 6?)

A few extra features should be pointed out in the price determination of foreign exchange rates. One is that demand for foreign currency arises from the desire for imported products, and supply comes from export to that country. German marks are demanded by the United States in order to purchase VWs, and German marks are earned by U.S. companies selling chemicals to German firms. Therefore, the FER is really determined by foreign trade flows, and shifts of trade volume create differences in FER rates. For example, an increased U.S. demand for Japanese products (more U.S. imports from Japan) increases the dollar price of yen and decreases the yen price of the dollar.

In addition to the effect of trade flows, the market forces of supply and demand of foreign currencies are also affected by *speculation* between different currencies. For example, if different governments, corporations, and citizens feel the U.S. dollar is losing its value, they may wish to hold marks instead of dollars. On the foreign exchange markets this fear of the dollar produces an increased demand for marks and an increased supply of dollars. The result is

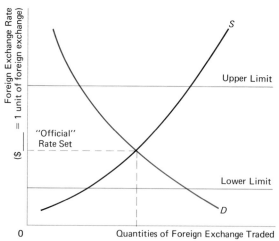

FIG. 20–13. Determination of foreign exchange rate.

an increase in the dollar price of marks (as from 30 cents to 45 cents = 1 mark), and a decrease in the mark price of the dollar (as from 3.3 marks to 2.2 marks = $1).

Another point to be noticed in Figure 20-13 is that there may not be a "free" market for foreign exchange rates. The upper and lower FER limits in Figure 20-13 represent the "boundaries" beyond which a country may not wish its currency to vary in terms of the currencies of other countries. These limits may be enforced by central banks stepping in to buy or sell the domestic currency to maintain the "official" foreign exchange rate. If a currency is falling in its foreign exchange rate, the central bank buys (pushing up FER via increase in demand); the central bank sells if the rate rises above the limits (pushing down FER through increase in supply).

Notice we've said in the previous paragraph that the market limits on FER determination "may" exist and be enforced by central banks. The question of practice arises because of the "off-on" experience of the 1970s in FER determination. Prior to 1971 such FER limits were fairly rigid and enforced both by central banks and by International Monetary Fund (IMF) agreements. Even after the U.S. dollar "closed the gold window" (more on this later) in 1971, many nations attempted to maintain some degree of *fixed exchange ratio* (no or little variance in FER). However, market pressures were too great (Japan and German central banks purchased some $20 billion in a futile attempt to fix their FERs against the dollar), and a *floating exchange rate system* became widespread by 1973 (Figure 20-13 wih no limits).

The experience of "floating" (no limits on FER) exchange rates from 1973 to 1975 has drawn both criticism and support, and you may again experience some degree of fixed FER (back to Figure 20-13) in the coming years. Those supporting a floating FER point to the advantages of flexibility, efficiency in resource allocation, and decreased production and trade distortions between economies. But those criticizing a floating FER to do so on the grounds that it contributes to uncertainty in foreign trade flows, increased inflationary pressures between nations, and avoidance of responsible fiscal and monetary policies by the economies involved. Many of these critical nations wish to see a fixed FER system reestablished, though the U.S. government is currently resisting such pressures. Whether such argument will reestablish a controlled FER market is a moot question, but the authors draw an analogy to similar issues in our domestic economy. We've previously discussed many examples of direct governmental intervention in U.S. markets with varying results. (The authors are dubious of such efforts.) Are there any similarities or differences that you see in FER markets?

FOREIGN EXCHANGE HISTORY

Although we've described the current mechanism (floating markets) for determining foreign exchange rates, we should also review a bit of historical evolution in such determination. For, as previously noted, there currently exists dissatisfaction with a floating FER mechanism, and proposals for change frequently rely on historical examples. If you are to understand and evaluate such proposals, you should be familiar with historical methods of FER determination: the *gold standard* and the *dollar standard*.

Prior to 1933, the *gold standard* (see Figure 20-14) foreign exchange mechanism provided fixed exchange rates. Because everyone accepted gold as the medium of exchange (no logical reason, except for custom and tradition) and because all nations said that so much of their currency equaled one ounce of gold, *foreign exchange rates were fixed;* that is, as long as all nations kept their currency-gold rate, there was no variation in currency value. If $32 and 160 francs both equaled 1 ounce of gold, then $32 equaled 160 F, and $0.20 equaled 1 F. However, dwindling gold supplies, a worldwide depression, and desire for more independent domestic monetary policies forced abandonment of the gold standard during the 1930s.

In place of the gold standard, a mixture often termed the *gold exchange standard* (or *dollar standard*) was set up through a series of international meetings following World War II, especially at the Bretton Woods Conference of 1945. Remember that gold was still the only internationally accepted medium of exchange and that the United States at that time was the only nation with adequate gold stocks to promise currency redemption. Therefore, the United States alone "pegged" the U.S. dollar in terms of gold ($35 equals 1 ounce of gold), whereas the other nations attempted to maintain past exchange rates with the dollar through limits placed on supply-de-

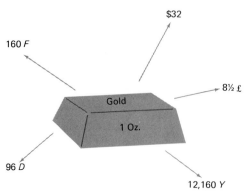

FIG. 20–14. Gold standard (prior to 1933).

mand FER determination. What you have, then, is the U.S. dollar as the "world's currency," with other countries basically dependent on this dollar foundation and market forces for FER determination of currencies. Perhaps you see from this historical evolution the key role the U.S. dollar has played in foreign exchange determination and why loss of confidence in the dollar actually threatens the entire foreign exchange system.

We return to the problems previously noted; the gold exchange standard became increasingly shaky because the United States steadily lost its gold base, as illustrated in Figure 20-16. Persistent BOP deficits led to U.S. gold outflow. Because the U.S. gold stock was so low (about $11.6 billion in 1971) compared to dollar claims existing (about $55 billion), the dollar foundation was quite weak. This weakness was spotlighted in August 1971, when President Nixon ordered a stop to the exchange of dollars for gold. The halt resulted in both a *depreciation* (the dollar buys less of foreign currency) and a *devaluation* (the dollar buys less of gold) of the U.S. dollar. Thirty-five dollars equaled one ounce of gold in 1970, but the dollar was devaluated so that $38 equaled one ounce of gold in 1971, and further devalued so that $42 equaled one ounce of gold in 1973.

Reaction to the United States "closing its gold window" was both alarmist and worldwide, as there was then no effective world monetary standard. Gold was not plentiful enough (or possessed by sufficient nations) to reestablish the gold standard, and the dollar no longer commanded the confidence or gold backing to serve as a substitute. For some two years an attempt was made by various countries to support currencies at fixed FER levels (review Figure 20-13), but the floating FER mechanism described previously became widespread in 1973. There is some large degree of dissatisfaction with this floating FER determination, but no widely accepted solutions are yet available.

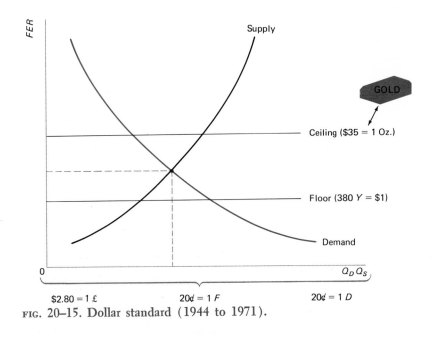

FIG. 20–15. Dollar standard (1944 to 1971).

Proposals to reform or revise the present floating FER mechanism include reverting to either the gold standard or the dollar standard or else adopting a *new international currency system*. Readoption of either the gold standard or dollar standard faces many obstacles, including the deficiency of an adequate gold stock by many economies and the heavy burden on the U.S. economy of redeeming outstanding dollars. A more radical proposal centers on the idea of some *international currency* accepted by all nations (the "Triffin Plan" coined the name *international monetary unit*, or IMU) to replace both gold and the U.S. dollar as a basic medium of exchange. The theory is that this international currency would be accepted by all nations to service foreign trade, and then domestic currencies would be convertible to the international currency and thus to each other, as in Figure 20-17.

Although the international currency proposal sounds promising, the world is at present some distance from achieving such a goal. Faced by cold war tension, international economic rivalries, and hesitancy to change from present systems, international agreements on this basic issue have been slow in coming. True, some short-range agreements have been worked out (as *special drawing rights*—SDRs), but arrival at a true international currency unit still appears to lie some time in the future. The SDR concept was initiated in 1972 by the *International Monetary Fund* (IMF—a group of 70 nations formed in 1944 to promote world trade flows; now 128 members) and represents an attempt to bolster temporarily those economies in need of foreign

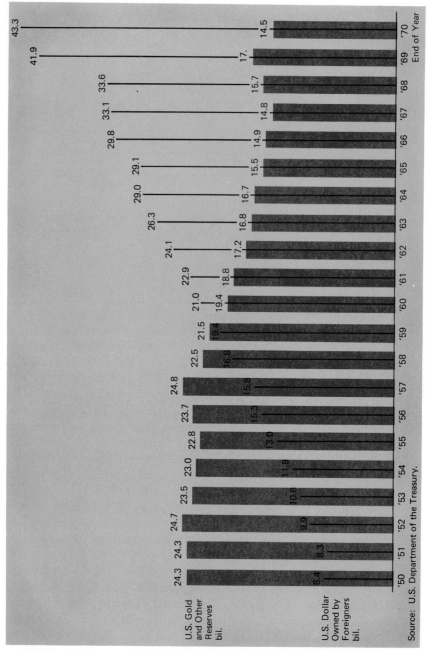

FIG. 20–16. Decline in U.S. gold reserves.

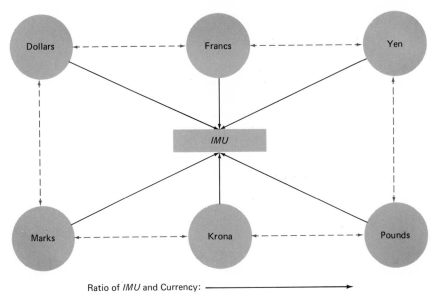

FIG. 20–17. The International Monetary Unit (proposal).

currencies by "loans" of these foreign currencies. Implementing this concept, each member nation subscribes a certain pledge of its currency to the SDR fund and, in turn, receives the ability to borrow other currencies from that fund at a set conversion factor. (The conversion factor determines the rate at which each currency exchanges against an SDR and is composed of a weighted average of some twenty-five currencies; it was $1.25 = one SDR in 1975.) Again, the SDR mechanism has increased foreign exchange liquidity and provided temporary aid to ailing currencies, but its adoption as an international currency foundation has much opposition.

CURRENT ISSUES AND FUTURE CONCERNS

We've described many complex issues in the area of foreign trade and foreign exchange: comparative advantage, protective tariffs, floating FER determination, and FER reform proposals. If you feel these issues are all interwoven and continuously in a process of change, you're quite correct! The areas of foreign trade and foreign exchange have changed tremendously in the 1970s, and the authors can only predict further changes in these fields. We wish at this point to examine three more issues that promise to be of continuing concern and constant change: *currency depreciation, Eurodollar markets,* and *recycling of petrocurrencies.*

1. *FER*: $0.25 = 1 *D*
   — *VW* worth 8,000*D* costs $2,000,
   — Ford worth $3,000 costs 12,000*D*.

2. *FER*: $0.50 = 1 *D*
   — VW worth 8,000*D* costs $4,000.
   — Ford worth $3,000 costs 6,000*D*.

3. $ has depreciated; *D* has appreciated.
   A. U. S. exports tend to rise.   ⎰ B. O. P.*
        U. S. imports tend to fall.   ⎱ improves.
   B. German exports tend to fall.   ⎰ B. O. P.*
        German imports tend to rise.   ⎱ worsens.

*Balance of Payments

FIG. 20–18. Foreign trade impacts of currency depreciation.

The *currency depreciation* issue is a constant concern and has a large impact on foreign trade flows. By currency depreciation, we mean that one currency decreases in value relative to another currency. An example would be the U.S. dollar declining in value in 1971 relative to other currencies, as described in Figure 20-18. Notice that as the dollar price of the mark increases (equivalent to the mark price of the dollar declining), U.S. exports become relatively cheaper in Germany (fewer marks required), but German exports become relatively more expensive in the U.S. (more dollars required). The effect of such currency depreciation, therefore, would be to aid the U.S. BOP position (increase in exports and decrease in imports), but hinder the German BOP position (decrease in exports and increase in imports).

Although many economists would point to such changes in BOP positions resulting from currency depreciation as the expected consequences of free-market operation, such FER movements cause much concern. When, in particular, there are very large and rapid depreciations, as in the 1970s, concern is expressed over the stability of foreign trade flows and international business firms' ability to establish long-term contracts. Although Milton Friedman may point to the currency *futures market* (buy or sell foreign exchange at a future delivery date) as a method to decrease currency risk, the possibility exists that such fluctuation may discourage foreign trade flows. We are thus back to the proposals to replace the current floating FER mechanism and the obstacles facing such proposals. Do you see how the whole complex of issues intertwines?

Another issue of current international concern (pros and cons here also!) is the development of the *Eurodollar market*. Simply stated, the term refers to the use (loans and currency swaps) of U.S. dollars that have been accumulated in foreign nations (especially Europe; $50 billion by 1975) by foreign or U.S. businesses. On the one hand, this large availability of dollars represents a potential loan source for foreign or U.S. firms and thus may promote investment and capital stock expansion. But large shifts of such funds may also lead to currency depreciations as we have already described or to the subverting of domestic monetary policies. Suppose the Fed is pursuing a "tight money policy" (review Chapter 17) in the United States but U.S. companies avoid credit stringencies by borrowing in the Eurodollar market. Or suppose a "dumping" of dollars against the mark causes currency depreciation of the dollar. Again, there are complex pros and cons as to the impact of the Eurodollar market on foreign trade and exchange stability, and such issues will be of continuing importance.

The last issue we'll examine is, indeed, of large impact on foreign trade and exchange stability: the recycling of petrocurrencies. By *petrocurrencies*, we refer to the huge ($60 billion in 1975) buildup of foreign exchange in Middle Eastern treasuries, received as revenue from the sale of oil at greatly increased prices. Since 1973, the quadrupled price of petroleum has drained huge sums from the United States, Japan, and European nations that must import oil for their industrialized economies to function. The real problem is *recycling* these petrocurrencies back into world trade and exchange markets; that is, can—and will—the Arab oil economies place these revenues back into international money markets so as to avoid a worldwide depression?

The possibility of a worldwide depression results from the decrease in aggregate demand (recall Chapter 12?) in other economies as a result of money shortages caused by imported oil purchases at higher prices. If domestic aggregate demand does decline and if the Middle Eastern nations do not recycle the revenue via increased foreign imports and investments, the result may be a large drop in world aggregate demand, reduced output, rising unemployment, and declining incomes. To date (1976) there has been some increase in Arab purchases of foreign goods, including both industrial plants to build their economies and arms sales to conduct war efforts. (The United States totaled a record $9 billion in arms exports in fiscal 1975!) In addition, Arab investments have increased in both underdeveloped economies (Arab foreign aid totaled some $3 billion in 1974) and developed economies. (The United States experienced $2 billion of Arab investments in 1974, including the sale of U.S. securities and the purchase of corporate ownership.) In fact, some economists have concern that the petrocurrency inflow may act as a "takeover" of domestic businesses!

Although many of the concerns as to the inadequacy of world monetary markets to absorb and recycle these petrocurrencies have been somewhat allayed since 1973, there still exist many questions as to future trends. The petrocurrency revenues are predicted to increase (perhaps $100 billion annually by 1980), as many economies (that of the United States included) find it difficult to reduce demands for oil imports or develop alternative energy sources. And there is some indication that OPEC (Organization of Petroleum Exporting Countries) may increase oil prices still further.

This last issue of recycling petrocurrencies is perhaps a fitting summary to our analysis of economic choice making in this text. For this issue not only affects future international trade and foreign exchange stability, but also portends large impacts on all domestic economies. Review many of our previous discussions (especially Chapters 6 and 8) regarding market operation, government intervention, business decision making, and growth-ecology issues, and you will realize that imports of foreign energy sources have an intertwined impact in all of these areas. Indeed, we end with an issue of increasing future concern and of highly likely impact on your own daily life-style! The authors cannot predict with accuracy exactly what the future trends and impacts may be, but we would surely maintain that such economic issues will be of primary social and political importance.

TERMS

Adjustment account (AA). The BOP account that compensates for any surplus or deficit in the other BOP accounts by change in gold ownership, short-term liabilities, or currency holdings by other economies.

Balance of payments (BOP). The accounting mechanism used to record economic relations between nations, composed of the balance of trade (BOT), balance on capital account (BCA), and the adjustment account (AA).

Balance of trade (BOT). The BOP account that records the exporting and importing of products and services.

Balance on capital account (BCA). The BOP account that records the export and import of money flows from government and private business sectors.

Comparative advantage. The ability of one nation to produce at a lower relative cost than another nation, thus encouraging specialization and foreign trade.

Depreciation. The decrease in the price (FER) of one country's currency relative to another country's currency.

Devaluation. The decrease in a country's currency relative to gold, as evidenced by an increase in the gold price in terms of that country's currency.

Dollar standard (gold exchange standard). The previous (1945 to 1971) foreign exchange mechanism whereby the U.S. dollar was exchanged directly against gold, with other currencies then based on the dollar.

Eurodollar market. The existence of dollar balances in European economies, available for loans or currency swaps.

European Economic Community (EEC—also termed the "Common Market"). The current nine European nations who have formed an economic union to reduce trade barriers and promote internal economic development.

Export. The inward flow of income to an economy, resulting from the sale of products or services to foreign nations or from capital flows to that economy.

Foreign exchange rate (FER). The price at which currency of one country is exchanged for the currency of another country.

Gold standard. A foreign exchange mechanism in effect prior to 1933 whereby all nations agreed to exchange their currencies against a fixed amount of gold, thereby establishing a fixed foreign exchange rate.

Import. The outward flow of income from an economy, resulting from the purchase of products or services from foreign nations or from capital flows from that economy.

Mercantilism. The foreign trade philosophy of eighteenth-century England, whereby foreign trade flows were controlled so as to promote the British balance of payments.

Petrocurrency. The revenues of Middle Eastern economies resulting from the export of oil to foreign nations.

Recycling. The importing and investing of petrocurrencies by OPEC economies in world trade markets and other world economies.

Special drawing rights (SDR). A line of credit, which may consist of foreign or domestic currency, granted by the International Monetary Fund, generally for use in supporting a nation's currency.

Tariff. A tax on imported products, designed to reduce imports (protective tariff) or increase government income (revenue tariff).

Terms of trade. The ratio of prices (direct or relative production costs) between what a nation pays for imports and receives from exports.

QUESTIONS FOR STUDY

1. Cite illustrations of items that you use that come entirely or in part from other nations. Which of these cannot be produced economically in the United States?

2. Define the comparative advantage concept, and set up an example to show its operation.

3. If free foreign trade may benefit all nations, why do many world economies impose tariffs?

4. Evaluate the use of artificial trade barriers such as tariffs and import quotas as a means of achieving and maintaining full employment.

5. State the purpose of balance of payments accounting. What are the three components of BOP?

6. Define and compare (a) the balance of payments and the balance of trade and (b) a balance-of-trade deficit and a balance-of-payments deficit.

7. Define a foreign exchange rate. How is it currently determined?

8. If the current FER, from the U.S. viewpoint, is $0.0035 = 1 yen, what is the FER from the Japanese viewpoint?

9. Compare the operations of the gold standard, the dollar standard, and the floating FER standard. Why were the gold standard and dollar standard replaced?

10. How do currency depreciations affect trade flows?

11. What is an SDR? How does it operate? What role might SDRs play in an international currency mechanism?

12. Describe and evaluate the challenge of "recycling petrocurrencies" to the U.S. economy.

REFERENCES

Adelman, M. A. *The World Petroleum Market*. Baltimore: Johns Hopkins University Press, 1973.

Barnet, Richard J., and Ronald E. Miller, *Global Reach*. New York: Simon and Schuster, 1974.

Caves, R. E., and R. W. Jones. *World Trade and Payments*. Boston: Little, Brown, 1973.

Clarke, William M., and George Pulay. *The World's Money: How It Works*, Second Edition. New York: Praeger Publishers, 1972.

Committee on Finance, United States Senate. *U.S. Balance of Trade and Balance of Payments*. Washington, D.C.: U.S. Government Printing Office, 1974.

Economic Outlook (periodical). Washington, D.C.: OECO Publications Center, published early July and December.

Erdman, Paul E. *The Billion Dollar Sure Thing*. New York: Pocket Books, 1974.

Ingram, James C. *International Economic Problems*. New York: John Wiley & Sons, 1966.

Jensen, Finn B., and Ingo Walter. *The Common Market: Economic Integration in Europe*. Philadelphia: J. B. Lippincott, 1965.

Krueger, Robert B. *The United States and International Oil*. New York: Praeger Publishers, 1975.

Ozga, S. A. *The Rate of Exchange and the Terms of Trade*. Chicago: Aldine Publishing Company, 1967.

Pen, Jan. *A Primer on International Trade*. New York: Vintage Books, 1967.

Roosa, Robert. *The Dollar and World Liquidity*. New York: Random House, 1972.

Solomon, Ezra. *The Anxious Economy*. San Francisco: W. H. Freeman and Company, 1975, Chapters 3 and 6.

Index*

* Italicized page numbers refer to text figures.